D1349494

Treason in Tudor England

Politics and Paranoia

Treason in Tudor England

Politics and Paranoia

Lacey Baldwin Smith

JONATHAN CAPE
THIRTY-TWO BEDFORD SQUARE LONDON

First published 1986
Copyright © 1986 by Lacey Baldwin Smith

Jonathan Cape Ltd, 32 Bedford Square, London WC1B 3EL

British Library Cataloguing in Publication Data

Smith, Lacey Baldwin
Treason in Tudor England : politics and paranoia.
1. Treason——England——History——16th century
I. Title
364.1'31   DA315

ISBN 0-224-02805-7

Printed in Great Britain by Ebenezer Baylis & Son Ltd
The Trinity Press, Worcester

To Jean
Without whose devotion, critical sense
and manifold skills,
this book would neither have been
conceived nor completed

CONTENTS

I	'Treason Doth Never Prosper'	1
II	'The Black Poison of Suspect'	36
III	'The Agreement of Its Minds'	72
IV	Tudor Cosmology and Commonality	118
V	'The World is Queasy'	143
VI	A 'Wonder to Behold'	178
VII	'Win the Queen'	192
VIII	'If You Have Any Enemies'	218
IX	'Give Losers Leave to Talk'	239
	Notes	277
	Bibliography	317
	Index	334

IN THANKS

Scholarship, almost by definition, is a collective enterprise: the product of ideas gleaned from a host of unlikely sources, tested upon a myriad of long-suffering friends, and nurtured in a very special environment. I am grateful to my colleagues in the History Department who individually and collectively have supplied — sometimes knowingly, sometimes inadvertently — that intellectual atmosphere and challenge which are the indispensable conditions for scholarship. And I am indebted to Northwestern's College of Arts and Sciences and the National Endowment for the Humanities for their generous support.

June 1985   L.B.S.

I

'TREASON DOTH NEVER PROSPER'

Treason doth never prosper, what's the reason?
For if it prosper, none dare call it treason.
Sir John Harington, Epigrams

Sir John Harington's terse lines not only contain a grim-fisted truth — success writes its own history and imposes upon sedition a self-fulfilling dynamism whereby treason, by definition, is branded failure — but the rhyme also goes to the core of the Tudor political mentality and poses a question that has baffled historians over the centuries. Why did traitors indulge in a variety of sedition so unbelievably bungling and self-defeating in character that it is difficult to believe they were totally sane or that their treason, as perceived by the government, actually existed at all? If sedition had been nothing more than an occasional aberration upon the normal graph of Tudor political activity, the question might not be worth the asking. The century, however, was a veritable graveyard of unsuccessful intrigues, machinations, complots, and conspiracies. The grisly skulls decorating London Bridge and the mutilated corpses displayed throughout the kingdom were evidence enough that men risked their lives for reasons noble and ignoble, and that they knew the unpleasant consequences of failure. 'To confess the truth', sighed one observer in 1541, 'it is now no novelty among us to see men slain, hanged, quartered or beheaded... Some for one thing and some for another.'[1] Seventeen years later, Étienne Perlin, whose French distaste for all things English is transparent, reported in his journal the existence of a macabre jest: in order to achieve gentle status, an English family had to have at least one head impaled upon

London Bridge.[2] So why then did traitors by their conduct play into society's hands and get caught, and conversely why did society see in such performances motives and actions dangerous to all established order, both human and divine?

Tudor England had a straightforward answer at least to the first half of the question: traitors reckoned with God as well as man. Their treachery could not long remain hidden, for 'God will have that most detestable vice both opened and punished'.[3] It was clearly and logically written: 'The spirit of the Lord fills the world, and that which embraces all things knows all that is said... A jealous ear hears everything... So beware of useless grumbling.'[4] Every Englishman knew the words of Ecclesiastes reiterated in endless official admonitions concerning rebellion: 'Wish the king no evil in thy thought, nor speak no hurt of him in thy privy chamber; for the bird of the air shall betray thy voice, and with her feathers shall bewray thy words.'[5] It is little wonder that society believed God loved and protected the prince and detested and destroyed the traitor, for the malcontents of the century entered into sedition with such abandon, naivety and babbling indifference to the most elementary principles of secrecy, and seemed to believe that almost any scheme was possible simply by willing it into existence, that even the humblest sparrow was quite capable of frustrating their evil designs.

Our own age is less willing to accept the deity either as a detective agency or as an instrument of vengeance, and it suspects that God more often than not leaves men to arrange for their own destruction and punishment. Even the sixteenth century acknowledged that the 'bird of the air' had considerable help from the fear of judicial interrogation with benefit of rack and dungeon and from the terror of the traitor's agonizing and humiliating end — hanging, castration, and disembowelment. Erasmus, as was his wont, hedged his bets and warned in words memorized by schoolboys all over Europe that 'kings have many ears and many eyes... They have ears that listen a hundred miles from them; they have eyes that espy out more things than men would think. Wherefore, it is wisdom for subjects not only to keep their princes' laws and ordinances in the face of the world but also privily... for conscience sake.'[6] Sir Walter

Raleigh was considerably more secular and forthright in his approach to treason. He also did not doubt that 'the evil affection of men may be oftentimes discovered' by inquisition and punishment, but he added a third factor to the formula for discovery: the possibility that the inner logic of treason itself, what he called 'destiny', and not some interfering and righteous deity, determined failure.[7] Tudor conspirators were defeated by a logic that was written indelibly upon the tablets of time: traitors were born incompetent. Caught by an inescapable destiny, they were driven to desperation because they could not make the political system work for them, but the same stupidity, egotism, and greed that led them into sedition in the first place guaranteed their failure, and they sacrificed themselves upon the altar of their own infantile dreams. The intelligent, the lucky, and the ruthless seldom had need for treason; only the inept, the ill-starred, and the weak travelled the inevitable road to Tyburn and Traitors' Gate. Desperation might drive a man to rebellion, and the 'artificial nourishing and entertaining of hopes' were advised as 'the best antidotes against the poison of discontentments', but it was invariably assumed that traitors were basically unthrifty types who 'having consumed their own, seek by violence to possess themselves of other men's goods'.[8] Disloyal subjects without fail, said William Cecil, fell into three categories: those who were unable 'to live at home but in beggary', those who were 'discontented for lack of preferments', and those who were 'bankrupt merchants'.[9]

Cecil's cynical limiting of the causes of treason to personal greed and simple-minded political and economic ineptitude made no allowance for ideology or governmental policies that could drive a man to sedition. And he totally ignored both the frequency and style of the endless efforts to overthrow the existing order. Tudor treason was protean, but whatever face it assumed — feudal, religious, political, economic, or personal — it tended to be not only unbelievably maladroit but also 'more wildly fantastic than any fiction'.[10] Embedded in this current of deviant malcontent was a self-destructiveness and hysteria that far exceeded mere artless mismanagement and bordered upon the neurotic.

Much of the treachery of the century appears so absurd and so juvenile that some scholars have suggested that many of the plots were, in fact, fictitious. They never existed at all but 'were more or less bogus' figments in which 'agents-provocateurs were sacrificed to the exigencies of party politics'.[11] Historian after historian has echoed those words in one form or other, and has questioned such conspiracies as the Ridolfi plot in 1570 to unseat Elizabeth and replace her on the throne with a partnership of Mary Queen of Scots and the Duke of Norfolk, and Thomas Stafford's 'hare brained and provocative' invasion of England in 1557 with a tiny army of no more than a hundred followers.[12] Certainly contemporaries, especially Catholics under Elizabeth, had their doubts, and although Jesuit special pleading is obvious, their point that, after thirty years of listening to Tudor propaganda, the world was growing 'over well acquainted with these tales of Queen-killing' is well taken.[13] If care is maintained in selecting the evidence, it is quite possible to argue that such plots as the Lopez, Moody, Squire, and Stanley schemes to assassinate Elizabeth by a variety of unlikely means, including deadly perfumes, balls of fatal incense, poisoned potions, and silver bullets, were carefully orchestrated trumperies in which relatively innocent, albeit not overly bright, political small-fries fell victim either to deliberate government efforts to demonstrate the existence of treason or to the political machinations of court factions. Nevertheless, to dismiss such performances as calculated fabrications is to misunderstand the pressures under which traitors themselves operated, the hysterical response their treason generated, and the mentality that could translate real or imagined sedition into a fundamental threat to all good order on earth and throughout the universe.

The evidence dealing with treason is mountainous, and the Tudor archives are filled with information relating to behaviour which the authorities regarded as deviant at best and downright seditious at worst. But three examples of sedition — Gregory Botolf's scheme to betray the port of Calais in 1540, Dr William Parry's so-called plot to assassinate Elizabeth in 1585, and Sir Thomas Seymour's efforts to overthrow his brother, the Lord Protector, in the winter of 1548–49 — will be sufficient to introduce the social and psychological complexities embedded in so much of Tudor treason.

Sweet-Lips Gregory

The Botolf conspiracy was the figment of the facile imagination of a gentleman by the name of Gregory Botolf, better known to his contemporaries as 'Gregory Sweet-Lips'.[14] Sweet-Lips belonged to the most socially restless, economically unstable, and demographically prolific element within Tudor society — the lesser gentry.[15] Born a younger son, he suffered the double affliction of his kind: over-education and under-endowment. Translated into human terms, this meant that Gregory was fated, like the hundreds of other hangers-on at court and in the houses of the great, to a life of boredom and relative poverty. He and his two privy associates in treason, Clement Philpot and Edward Corbett, were grist for the moralists' mill — 'beware of idleness' — and evidence for those educators who warned against too much education. Destined to scrape along on expectations never realized, hopes constantly deferred, and rewards that were always too small, they lounged about the ante-rooms of the mighty, ran messages and did favours for those in command, bowed and scraped before their betters, and took out their frustrations in violence, drink, and bad temper.[16]

Botolf first made his appearance in history in mid-April of 1538 as Sir Gregory Buttoliff, chaplain to my Lord Lisle, the Deputy of Calais who, as a pleasant, if rather ineffectual, scion of fifteenth-century royal fecundity, was Henry VIII's 'illegitimate' uncle. Arthur Plantagenet Lord Lisle and his wife Honor seem, even in the teeth of overwhelming evidence, to have been taken in by the Latinate tongue, gracious manners, and expensive tastes of the convincing Mr Botolf, for Lord Lisle enthusiastically endorsed his chaplain as a man 'of sufficient literature', 'good discretion', and 'honest behaviour'. Except for the 'sufficient literature', the good lord totally misjudged Sweet-Lips who, according to one of his clerical colleagues, was 'the most mischievous knave that ever was born' and thoroughly deserved to be hanged. Constantly in debt, a consummate liar, and a confessed thief of ecclesiastical property, Botolf's fertile mind and golden tongue concocted a plot that ended at least one of his friends at Tyburn, but for which nimble Sir Gregory appears to have got off almost scot-free.

Gregory Botolf was of the papal persuasion, yet there is not a scrap of evidence to indicate that he was a religious fanatic. He obviously delighted in theological debate and dreamed heroic dreams of striking a blow — appropriately rewarded by money and honour — for God and the Pope, but he was equally at home at the dicing table and was a master of the tavern-room yarn. Moreover, Botolf's decision to decamp to Rome may have had more to do with worldly matters than with any concern for his immortal soul, for evil reports of Sir Gregory's past were being spread about Lord Lisle's household, and he feared that if he 'tarried a day longer' he would be charged with felony. Nor were his two closest associates religious extremists. Clement Philpot was 'a proper young man' who is described as 'the third and wisest' of the sons of Sir Peter Philpot, a Hampshire gentleman and family friend of the Lisles, who had sufficient means and status to consider Lord Lisle's stepdaughter as an appropriate match for his youngest offspring. And it was partly for reasons of matchmaking that he placed his son in April of 1538 in the Deputy's Calais household. Clement was an impressionable youth of 'gentle conversation' who stood to inherit an income of 500 marks a year, an amount which, along with his innocence, may explain why Gregory Sweet-Lips cherished him as his friend and bedfellow. Edward Corbett, genealogically speaking, is a far more shadowy figure. He was a close friend of Clement and was equally well educated. What made Corbett so useful to his colleagues was that he acted as a messenger-cum-secretary for His Lordship and was willing to trick Lord Lisle into signing almost any document, especially those essential passports that permitted the seventy or so members of the Deputy's household to travel and live abroad. Like Philpot, he held an ambiguous position — part retainer, part personal servant on 'petty wages', and part preferment seeker waiting for a vacancy in the Calais Spears, those prestigious and politically determined officers of the Retinue. As a collaborator in and witness to the events that followed, Corbett, one of his interrogators remarked, was 'a man of sense', and his statements, unlike most of the others, have the ring of verisimilitude about them.

Botolf's plan was predicated upon the role of Philpot and, to a lesser extent, of Corbett as Trojan horses inside England's last toe-hold on the Continent, the Calais pale. The port city with its 120 square miles of surrounding marches was a religious-political weather vane exposed to all the doctrinal and diplomatic winds of the Reformation. Caught between two worlds, a decaying Catholic and medieval past when England had been a great European power and a future that was not yet Protestant and insular, Calais was a sink of spying, railing, and informing. Each side, Protestant reformers and Catholic conservatives, struggled in the hot-house environment of a beleaguered military bastion and panicked every time Henry's government sent over inspectors to observe and report on the condition of the defences, the state of religion, and the loyalty of His Majesty's officials. As Catholic Europe in 1538–39 talked more and more loudly of joining together in a crusade to punish schismatic England, the denizens of Calais lived in a constant state of agitation, made more frantic by the knowledge that religious informing for profit and political preferment had become a way of life. John Foxe's description of the city in the spring of 1540 is laden with Protestant exaggeration but it is probably an accurate picture of the atmosphere in which Sweet-Lips and his friends lived and out of which the Botolf conspiracy emerged: 'Such fear and distrust assaulted all men, that neighbour distrusted neighbour, the master the servant, the servant the master, the husband the wife, the wife the husband, and almost every one the other...'[17]

What triggered Botolf's decision to go over to Rome is not known; possibly it had something to do with his ill-advised and alcoholic confession to his 'friend' and fellow chaplain, Sir Oliver Brown, that a number of years before he had 'liberated' church plate belonging to the Chantry House of St Gregory in Canterbury. Sir Oliver proved to be of Sir Gregory's own ilk, for he immediately used this damning information as a weapon in the ceaseless domestic rivalry and backstairs warfare that beset most lordly establishments, and by February of 1540 Sweet-Lips felt that he had too 'many foes' for his own good. By the 5th of the month he had found the necessary funds for a whirlwind trip to Rome, where, as he later boasted, he, His Holiness and Cardinal Pole met

'no more but we three together in the Pope's chamber' and worked
out plans to betray Calais to French and papal forces. Rewarded
with 200 crowns and the advice to leave Calais as soon as he could
arrange to get Lord Lisle's licence to go as a student to the University of Louvain, Botolf returned on March 17th. He remained in
town scarcely forty-eight hours — just long enough to settle his
affairs and indulge in a violent row with Sir Oliver and others over
seating precedence in the great hall — and took himself to Bourbourg, immediately over the Flemish border. Safe in imperial territory, he wrote to Corbett asking him to do a series of favours
and to arrange for Lord Lisle to sign his licence for travel to Louvain.

At Bourbourg on Good Friday, March 26th, 1540, Clement
Philpot met Sir Gregory and was introduced to his grand design.
The two friends had missed each other in Calais, for Clement had
been away in England, and their reunion at Bourbourg was fervent: 'My most joy of the world, welcome as my own heart!' cried
Botolf, 'for you are he that I do put most trust and confidence in...
And there is none on earth that I dare trust so well as you... I
dare no less disclose the secrets of my heart to you as to God.' It
was a fatal disclosure, and never was friendship bought at a greater
price. 'Gold', Sweet-Lips assured Clement, 'ye shall have plenty.
And whereas we now be inferiors, we shall be superiors. The world
shall be ours.' Having whetted the appetite and excited the imagination, Sir Gregory then proceeded to details. He had, he explained,
already been given 200 crowns; shortly he expected to travel to the
imperial court at Ghent where the papal ambassador was residing,
and there he would receive still more money. The betrayal would
be planned for 'the herring time' when, between September 29th
and November 30th, Calais was crowded with herring buyers and
sellers, and when, as a consequence, the guard on the Lantern Gate,
located just off the market square, would be greatly reduced. Philpot
'with a dozen well appointed' followers would seize the gate in
the dark of the night, and defend it from within while Botolf scaled
the outer walls of the city with 500 to 600 men.

When Philpot questioned whether he could possibly capture the
gate or whether 600 men could take and hold the entire port, Botolf
countered with two other pieces of information. First, he explained

that 'we shall have aid, both by sea and by land within a short space'. 'Put no distrust,' he assured Philpot, 'all shall be handled after the best' and most politic fashion 'that is possible to be devised by man's wit'. Second, money would shortly be made available for Philpot to purchase, 'even if it cost a thousand marks or more', the Captaincy of Rysbank, an office that would make it possible for him to seize the Lantern Gate. In the meantime Philpot was to be 'sad and discreet [so] that there may appear such towardness in you that it may be thought that ye are a man meet for such a room'. Finally, in proper conspiratorial tradition, Botolf informed Philpot that he had given Edward Corbett ten gold pieces and he wanted them melted down into three rings, one for each of them, as tokens of their undying friendship, with each ring containing '3 letters — a P for Philpot, a C for Corbett, and a B for Botolf!' Oddly enough the manufacturing of these rings was probably the only sensible suggestion in the entire caper, for the coins were papal crowns and Botolf wisely sensed that it would not do for the conspirators to be found with enemy currency in their possession.

Such was Sweet-Lips's plot. How much was based on truth, how much upon wild imagination is impossible to say. How 600 mercenaries were to be hired and brought unbeknown to the walls of Calais; how an inexperienced Philpot expected to purchase the Rysbank Captaincy and where the money was coming from; or how 'aid both by sea and by land' could be organized without alerting the English authorities were trifles that were never explained. If this constituted the best 'that is possible to be devised by man's wit', then the comment of the editor of the *Lisle Letters* that the conspirators seem to have been afflicted with 'almost unbelievable light-headedness'[18] is the understatement of a story that ground to its tragic and ironic conclusion with surprising speed. The moment Botolf took off for Ghent, Clement Philpot proved the truth of Sir Walter Raleigh's observation 'that dangerous enterprises, the more they be thought upon, the less hope they give of good success; for which reason conspiracies not suddenly executed are for the most part revealed or abandoned'.[19] Philpot fell prey to attacks of bad conscience, hysterical alarm, and growing panic, but unfortunately he kept his mouth shut just long enough to make it impossible for him to play convincingly the role of loyal informer.

If Philpot's conscience proved his downfall, Botolf's wagging tongue and indiscretions contributed to the final fiasco. Accompanied by Edward Corbett's servant, John Browne, Sir Gregory set off for Ghent, but on the way he had the misfortune of encountering Frances, one of the government couriers, in company with Sir John Mason who was travelling on diplomatic business to Ghent. Both men proved to be exceedingly curious about a chaplain of Lord Lisle travelling with someone else's servant, purportedly to the University of Louvain. When Botolf arrived at Ghent, he sent Philpot a letter by 'Frances the Post' and a Mr Gresham; both of whom were returning to England via Calais. The stupidity of this act seems to have dawned upon Sweet-Lips too late, for he tried unsuccessfully to retrieve the letter for fear that it would be opened by the English Ambassador at Ghent, as indeed it appears to have been. In growing alarm, Botolf sent Browne back to Calais with a second letter to Philpot, alerting him to be on the watch for his first letter in the diplomatic pouch. Browne arrived in Calais after a terrible trip, but because the dates are unclear we do not know how long before the official post Browne arrived or whether Philpot had already turned king's evidence and confessed all. Certainly by April 8th Philpot, Corbett, and a handful of others had been imprisoned and closely interrogated.

Once treason was out, no one could say enough, and by the 17th the government in London knew the complete story and had taken steps to apprehend the elusive Mr Botolf. The Privy Council ordered a shield of absolute secrecy and instructed Philpot to write a carefully penned letter to his erstwhile friend to lure him back to Calais. If Sir Gregory ever received this letter, he did not take the bait, for he settled down at Louvain 'under the colour of a student' until his past and the long arm of the English government caught up with him. The Council wanted Botolf badly — especially if Lord and Lady Lisle could possibly have been involved in his treason — and it sent a courier to inform the Mayor of Louvain and the University scholars that Sir Gregory was a thief, having stolen church property, and should be imprisoned and extradited. The English government was not completely successful. Botolf was jailed but apparently papal influence saved him from trial and, worse, extradition, for he disappears from the records, presumably a free, if not wiser, man. Clement Philpot, however, paid sorely for his idiocy in as painful and degrading a way as Tudor vengeance could devise. On August 4th, 1540, he and four other named traitors were 'drawn from the Tower of London to Tyburn . . . and with six persons more, were there hanged, drawn and quartered'. As an added touch, his father, four days before his son's execution, wrote him out of his will. As for Edward Corbett and his servant John Browne, we know nothing. It would be comforting to think that they were not included in those 'six persons more'.

'The wicked and intended treason' of Dr William Parry

Botolf and his brothers in treason were small fry, petty villains operating in a sensitive outpost of English authority but nevertheless far from the centre of real power, and they were tracked down and punished as much for reasons of example as for revenge. The case of Dr William Parry was different: his treason was directed against the person of the Queen herself, and the government was determined to extract from it every possible ounce of propaganda value. The official account of the William Parry conspiracy as recorded by John Stow is a marvellous piece of melodrama replete with suspense, fiendish plotting, two-timing, and an arch scoundrel — Dr William Parry, 'a man of very mean and base parentage, but of a most proud and insolent spirit'.[20] Tudor villains were usually cast as malcontents eaten up with pride and envy who were unwilling to accept that station in life for which God had destined them. Parry played the part perfectly. 'This vile and traitorous wretch', according to Stow, was one of the sons of a common alehouse keeper, a Welshman named Harry ap David, and of a mother who 'was the reputed daughter of a priest'. He was put out to service with 'a poor man' who 'professed to have some small skill and understanding in the law', and who kindly permitted young William 'to go to grammar school where he got some little understanding in the Latin tongue'. The ungrateful lad, however, being of a 'villainous and dangerous nature and disposition', attempted on numerous occasions to run away from his master and, for his disobedience, was 'chained, locked and clogged to stay his running away'. Imprisonment was in vain, for he eventually escaped to seek his fortune in London.

In the capital William moved 'from service to service and from one master to another', aspiring to 'the name and title of a great gentleman' and forgetting 'his old home, his birth, his education, his parents, his own name and what he was'. Eventually the impudent fellow changed his name to Parry and asserted kinship to families of 'great worship and behaviour'. Parry lived a 'wasteful and dissolute life', for he was constantly in debt and survived only by living off unsuspecting women who fell victim to his hypocritical tongue and false manners. Using the 'wealth and livelihood' of a silly wife, who was old enough to be his mother, to maintain himself as 'a man of very good behaviour and degree', he wormed his way into the respect and confidence of the great and mighty, and in 1570 was actually 'sworn her Majesty's servant'. During the next decade he went through the inheritance of two wives, deflowered his stepdaughter, attempted to murder one of his many creditors, was committed to Newgate prison and was tried and condemned to hang. Justice, however, was staid by the inestimable clemency of the Queen who pardoned Parry. Whereupon he 'left his natural country' and, because he mistrusted 'his advancement in England' and feared debtors' prison, fled to Europe, there to continue his nefarious career by plotting with exiled English Catholics to assassinate his sovereign. His proposal to kill the English Jezebel was 'commended and warranted' by the Pope himself, who absolved him of all sin and assured the hero a hearty welcome in heaven.

In late December of 1583 Parry returned home determined to rid the kingdom of its usurping and excommunicated Queen and to time her death with a proposed invasion by a Scottish army, twenty to thirty thousand strong. Partly to shore up his flagging courage, partly to arrange for Mary of Scotland's safety once Elizabeth was dead, Parry posed as a loyal-hearted informer. He cleverly revealed to the Queen that he had been sent over by Catholic malcontents to murder her and went so far as to prove his story by displaying a letter from Cardinal Como, the papal Secretary of State, assuring him of the Pope's blessings. During this period Parry was presumedly deeply troubled by his conscience. More than once he had taken the Oath of Supremacy, and his perjured soul cried out in anguish at the thought of murder and regicide, so much so that once, when he actually had the opportunity to strike the Queen down with a dagger, he became wonderfully 'appalled and perplexed', for he saw 'in her the very likeness and image of King Henry the Seventh', and he broke into tears at the thought of what he contemplated.[21]

Despite the treason that lay hidden in his heart, the rogue had the audacity to demand the mastership of St Catherine's Hospital as payment for his information, but much to his chagrin he was refused. 'Utterly rejected, discontented' and careless of life, he left the court in July and returned to London where he contacted his eventual betrayer, his 'cousin' Sir Edward Neville who, according to Parry, 'came often to mine house, put his finger in my dish, his hand in my purse and the night wherein he accused me, was wrapped in my gown'. For six months the two friends discussed the moral imperative of regicide, and dreamt up ways and means to rescue Mary Queen of Scots, raise the Northern shires in her favour, and seize Queenborough Castle on the Kentish side of the Thames Estuary, as a base of operations for rebellion. Then, taking an 'oath upon a Bible to conceal and constantly to pursue the enterprise for the advancement of religion', they fell to discussing methods of dispatching Elizabeth. Their proposals were more detailed and more realistic than Botolf's plans to betray Calais because their task was easier — Gloriana was notoriously negligent about her safety. Nevertheless, the same optimistic aimlessness, ineptitude, lack of attention to details, and disregard for planning prevailed. Parry seems to have favoured striking the Queen while she walked 'very privately' in the gardens of Whitehall Palace, the conspirators making their escape by barge to carry them 'with speed down river where we will have a ship ready to transport us if it be needful', but, he added, 'upon my head, we shall never be followed so far'. Another possibility was to attack the Queen in her carriage as she drove to St James's Palace. 'Let us furnish ourselves in the mean time with men and horses fit for the purpose. Nay, each of us [can] keep eight or ten men without suspicion... I shall find good fellows that will follow me without suspecting mine intent.' Parry was certain that not even an escort of 100 guards could save Gloriana if Neville 'on the one side and I on the other' discharge 'our dags [pistols] upon her', and 'if we should both miss her...I shall bestir me well with a sword ere she escape me'. Such a 'villainous and damnable enterprise' was too much for loyal Sir Edward, who on February 9th, 1585 went to court and 'laid open' his friend's 'most traitorous and abominable intention against her Majesty'.

Parry was immediately apprehended and a delicate cat and mouse game ensued. Elizabeth, still merciful and believing in Parry's loyalty, ordered that he be told that a conspiracy had come to light against her life and asked whether he knew anything about it or whether he could have inadvertently done anything to associate his name with it. Parry 'with great and vehement protestations denied it utterly'. He was then informed that a man of quality 'better than himself and rather his friend than enemy' had in fact accused him. Parry still denied that he was ever 'party or privy to any such motion, enterprise or intent'. The following morning, however, he had second thoughts and 'declared that he had called to remembrance' that he had indeed spoken to Neville about the theory of regicide but nothing else. Finally, when confronted with Sir Edward, he voluntarily confessed in a written statement his 'wicked and intended treason', which he repeated first in a letter to the Queen and then in an appeal for mercy addressed to Lord Burghley and the Earl of Leicester. It was, he admitted, 'the dangerous fruits of a discontented mind' for 'a natural subject solemnly to vow the death of his natural Queen'.

Retribution was swift and dramatic. Parry was arraigned on February 25th, 1585 and willingly pleaded guilty to the charges. This, however, did not suit the purposes of the Crown which wanted to extract full propaganda value from Parry's confession and requested that judgment be deferred until his statement to Burghley and Leicester and the letter from Cardinal Como had been read and submitted as evidence. The government also wanted it recorded that the culprit had 'freely and willingly' confessed 'without any constraint'. Parry was extremely co-operative, even offering to read his confession out loud.

Up to this point the Crown's case proceeded according to plan, but then Parry 'prayed leave to speak', and suddenly the carefully orchestrated trial fell apart, for the traitor now categorically announced that he had never intended to harm the Queen. 'This is absurd,' shouted Christopher Hatton, who was presenting the government's case. 'Thou hast not only confessed generally that thou were guilty...but thou also saidest particularly that thou were guilty... Sayest thou now that thou never meantest it?' Parry countered that fear of torture had made him confess. Hatton assured the court this was a lie; 'no torture or threatening words' had been 'offered him'. In considerable irritation the Lord Chief Justice lectured Parry for using 'such dark speeches', and finally delivered the awful sentence. 'Thou shalt be had from hence to the place whence thou didest come, and so drawn through the open city of London upon a hurdle to the place of execution, and there to be hanged and let down alive, and thy privy parts cut off, and thy entrails taken out and burnt in thy sight, then thy head to be cut off, and thy body to be divided in four parts, and to be disposed at her Majesty's pleasure; and God have mercy on thy soul.' Execution followed within the week. On March 2nd Dr William Parry was drawn from the Tower to the courtyard at Westminster Palace where he died 'most maliciously and imprudently', still claiming that his only offence had been to enter into 'conference with his kinsman and friend (as he took him) Mr Neville, and in concealing what passed between them'. He died, he said, 'a true servant of Queen Elizabeth; for any evil thought that ever I had to harm her, it never came into my mind... I know her to be the anointed of God; and therefore not lawful for any man to lay violent hands on her.'[22]

At best, the line between historical fact and governmental fiction is cloudy; in cases of treason it tends to vanish entirely. The case for the Crown is not inaccurate: most of what the authorities said appears to have been true. It is what Christopher Hatton and the others failed to mention that is so disturbing; and although the expurgated material does not put Parry's actions in any better light or make any better sense of them, it does cast doubt upon his guilt.

On closer inspection Dr William Parry turns out not to have been a base-born rogue; he was instead a gentleman-born rogue. His father was of excellent Catholic gentry stock and his mother was the daughter of a highly respectable archdeacon and rector of Northop, Wales. William was, he later maintained, one of thirty children (by two wives) of a father who died in 1566 at the age of 108, but Parry's love of hyperbole and delight in fabrication make these statistics somewhat suspect.[23] He had a solid grammar school education and actually received a degree in law from the University of Paris in 1583.[24] Moreover, there is little doubt that he was socially well connected, for he found employment in the household of William Herbert, first Earl of Pembroke, and had influential friends at court. The Crown's scandalous tales, however, of womanizing, con-artistry, and would-be murder and theft are substantially correct. Parry went through the fortunes of two wives; there is independent evidence that he 'abused' the daughter of his second wife;[25] he was certainly in debt and would have been hanged for attempted murder in 1580 except for the Queen's pardon; and he did in fact leave the country in July of 1582, but not solely, as the government suggested, to escape his creditors. He had been in Europe earlier and was without doubt in the employ of both Lord Burghley and Sir Francis Walsingham as a government agent paid to send back information about conditions on the Continent in general and to spy upon the exiled English Catholic community in particular.[26] Parry seems to have been a Gregory Sweet-Lips writ large — a gentleman hanger-on at court with no visible salary or exact duties who, like so many others, went bankrupt in order to maintain the costly role of courtier. Ten thousand marks,[27] he later confessed, he had wasted. The money had purchased him friends and given him access to the Queen, whose favour he retained to the very end, but it had failed to gain him one of those advowsons, monopolies, deaneries, annuities, or reversions so necessary to a courtier's financial well-being. All that the money had won him was a host of creditors, in particular Mr Hugh Hare, 'a cunning and shameless usurer', to whom he owed the sum of £600 and whom he attempted to rob and murder.[28]

While in Paris and later at Lyons, Parry played the perfect spy. He possessed all the healthy paranoia of his kind, complete with appeals not to believe the 'malicious reports of his enemies', letters ending 'read and burn', and warnings to Burghley to 'be careful of me' and to Walsingham that intercepted letters 'may cost me my life'. Before long he was reporting that 'my credit amongst the malcontents is such as it should be' and that he 'doubted not in [a] few months to be well able to discover their deepest prac- tices', especially if Burghley would send him money for a few 'trifling gifts and friendly entertainment'.[29] What can never be answered is whether Parry was playing a double game; whether his recon- ciliation to the Roman Church, after not having gone to mass for twenty years, and his offer to assassinate Elizabeth were part of an elaborate confidence game and cover to win his way into Catholic circles both in England and abroad; or whether they were evidence that a man in mid-life, whose career as a courtier was in ruins and who was hounded by creditors, experienced a religious conversion and became the willing instrument of militant Catholicism.

Whatever the truth, Parry returned home 'with some matter of importance' that he insisted upon delivering to the Queen in person. He was 'welcomed with fine speeches', granted a 'liberal pension', and sent in November 1584 to Parliament as a member for Queenborough, Kent.[30] A month later, he outraged a hysterically anti-Jesuit House of Commons by speaking out against a bill ordering all Jesuits and seminary priests to depart the kingdom within forty days on pain of high treason and making any attempt to harbour or abet them a felony. 'In very violent terms', he denounced the proposed law as 'full of blood, danger, despair and terror' to all subjects of the realm, and he hoped it would be vetoed by the Queen, to whom, he said, 'he would reserve his reasons of his negative voice against the bill'.[31] Such words were guaranteed to produce an explosion, for the kingdom was still reeling from the shock of the Throckmorton plot of 1583 to invade England and replace Elizabeth with Mary of Scotland, and from the assassina-

tion in July 1584 of the leader of the Protestant forces in the
Lowlands, William of Orange. With scarcely a dissenting voice,
the Commons voted to place Dr Parry in the custody of the Sergeant
of the House. Again, however, the long protective arm of the Queen
intervened, and Elizabeth begged her loyal Commons to forgo
punishment since Parry had reserved his explanations to herself and,
now that her Council had heard them, she thought the House,
after receiving his humble submission, could pardon him. With
some reluctance the Commons obliged, only to receive two months
later the news of Sir Edward Neville's awful revelation of Parry's
intended treason. Unseating such a devil as Parry was not sufficient, and the House asked Elizabeth's permission to devise a death
even more excruciatingly painful and humiliating than that prescribed
by law. The Queen refused, and Dr William Parry died a 'normal'
traitor's death.

Parry's treason, however, was far from normal; he himself
described it as 'rare and strange'.[32] One school of historical
thought tends to see his execution either as a monstrous cover-up
job — the destruction of 'the spy who knew so much and who
could no longer be trusted' — or as a cold-blooded plot on the part
of Burghley and Walsingham 'to keep the Queen and the realm
under the impression that they were threatened by a great religious
conspiracy'.[33] Other scholars favour the thesis that Parry's extraordinary parliamentary outburst and devious conversations with Neville
were part of his elaborate 'cover' to maintain credibility in extreme
Catholic circles. The unfortunate man, however, became so completely entangled in his own espionage that he began to confuse
reality with illusion, and in the midst of national hysteria not even
Elizabeth dared save him.[34] Finally, there is the argument that
Parry had in fact turned double agent and was contemplating treason
in thought, if not necessarily in deed.[35]

In the midst of such confusion, one point is certain: Sir Edward
Neville was the Judas of the piece. Parry was unimaginably idiotic
to have trusted his 'familiar friend' and 'cousin', as he called Neville,
for the two men were, with one important exception, like two peas
in a pod. Sir Edward was a well-born but impecunious ne'er-do-
well who claimed to be the rightful heir to his late great uncle,

Henry Neville, fourth and last Lord Latimer, and who also aspired
to the 'land and dignity' of the earldom of Westmorland. He lived
most of his life in Europe where, like Parry, he operated in that
never-never-land of the double agent whose true loyalties were questioned by both sides. Parry and Neville obviously knew one another,
but who approached whom first is unclear; not surprisingly their
confessions disagree on this point. Both men purported to be devout
Catholics; both claimed to have grievances against the Queen —
Parry because he had been refused the mastership of St Catherine's
and Neville because he was unable to get a hearing for his claims
to the barony of Latimer — and neither was particularly truthful.
What, however, set Neville apart was the excellent reason he had
for betraying his friend and kinsman. As the sole male heir to the
Latimer estates, he was a serious threat to the claims of his cousin
Dorothy, daughter and co-heiress of the last Lord Latimer and Lord
Burghley's daughter-in-law.[36] The Lord Treasurer obviously had
reason to keep close watch on the potentially dangerous Mr Neville
who, knowing himself to be under surveillance, had excellent cause
either to ingratiate himself with Burghley by revealing the existence
of a dangerous plot or to embarrass His Lordship and weaken his
position at court by proving that one of the Lord Treasurer's most
trusted spies was a traitor. Either way it was to his advantage to
betray his associate whose idle and boasting tongue and fertile
imagination had placed him at Sir Edward's mercy. Given the circumstances, it is understandable that the behaviour of Dr Parry,
indeed his entire career, has puzzled modern historians,[37] and persuaded contemporaries that only divine interference saved the
Queen's life — 'it was the Lord that revealed it in time'.

'So great a flame' — the Case of Sir Thomas Seymour

Botolf and Philpot had operated as minor malcontents outside the
gilded focus of power about the sovereign; Dr Parry, whatever the
truth of his undertaking — inept and fatal counter-espionage or
religiously inspired fanaticism — was a predictable hazard in an era
of ideological hypertension. In contrast, Sir Thomas Seymour's abor-

tive palace revolution during December and January of 1548–49
to unseat his brother Edward, the Lord Protector, struck at the
aristocratic core of political authority, placing in doubt the entire
educational and cultural systems upon which Tudor society
rested.[38]

Thomas Seymour ricocheted from relative obscurity into political
prominence when he found himself in late January 1547 the uncle
of a reigning king, 9-year-old Edward VI, and the younger brother
of a ruling Lord Protector who had succeeded in monopolizing most
of the titles and honours of the new reign. There but for the accident of primogeniture might have ruled Thomas, not his brother
Edward, who styled himself: 'Edward by the grace of God, duke
of Somerset, earl of Hertford, viscount Beauchamp, lord Seymour,
uncle to the most noble prince Edward... governour of his highness'
person and protector of all his realm, dominions [and] subjects, lieutenant general of all his Majesty's arms both by land and sea... and
Knight of the Most Noble Order of the Garter.'[39] In contrast,
Thomas received the important, but far lesser, office of Lord Admiral,
the title of Baron Seymour of Sudley, and the dignity of Knight
of the Garter. But what irked him most was that he never succeeded
in gaining entrée into the ruling élite about the new Lord Protector.

Both the speed with which Thomas displayed his envy of his
ducal brother and the intensity of the rivalry between them caught
history unaware, for there is no evidence of sibling competition
while the old King lived. Under Henry VIII, Edward Seymour,
partly on the basis of his friendship with his sovereign, more on
the grounds that his sister was Queen, was elevated to the peerage
first as Viscount Beauchamp and then, six days after the prince's
birth in October of 1537, as Earl of Hertford. Thomas also gained
from his sister's royal marriage; he was knighted and benefited
immensely from the dissolution of the monasteries; but, unlike his
brother, he continued to operate on the periphery of power in a
number of lesser military and diplomatic positions.

The circumstances of the new reign were alarming at best;
authority which had once been wielded by a senile, suspicious but
regal old monarch, who called upon God as his ally and upon
everyone else as his subjects, was now held by the young King's

maternal uncle, a man who had no other qualifications for authority
except that he was 'of fit age' and relatively popular with his fellow
councillors. No Tudor blood coursed through the Duke's veins,
no divinity hedged his office, and no charisma earned him the hearts
of his fellow Englishmen, who, once the magnetic personality of
King Hal was removed, became increasingly restless and disrespect-
ful. The most troublesome of them all was the new Lord Admiral,
who proceeded to outrage almost everyone by marrying his old
flame, Catherine Parr, the Dowager Queen. It was a dangerous and
calculated act, designed to affront the Lord Protector and the Council
and to move Thomas further up the political ladder. If the Lord
Admiral could not reach the top of the greasy pole on his brother's
coat-tails, he was quite prepared to capitalize on his highly developed masculine charms and make it on his wife's apron-strings.
When that failed, he turned to treason.

Tudor England had difficulty in handling sedition in high places;
it did not fit the accepted formula of personal greed and prodigality
that engender political and economic desperation. Seymour was
called many names by his contemporaries — a godless man, a prof-
ligate man, an ambitious man, 'a horribly covetous man', and he
was accused of 'slouthfulness to serve' and 'greediness to get',[40]
but none of these stock sins seemed adequate to turn brother against
brother and rend asunder the basic unit of Tudor society — the family.
There had to be some outside and satanic agent, an Iago figure,
to divide and inflame the jealousy, pride, and fear that could lead
one brother to treason and the other to fratricide. Historians have
postulated a number of possible villains, John Dudley Earl of Warwick being the favourite candidate,[41] but the chauvinistically
masculine sixteenth century preferred a *femme fatale*, the acerbic
Anne Stanhope, Duchess of Somerset and wife of the Lord Protector. The Duchess loathed her new sister-in-law and challenged her
right as Dowager Queen to take precedence over the wife of a Lord
Protector. 'Difference...about precedency', so the argument went,
'breedeth many quarrels among women, who can better endure
almost any kind of injury than to have such as are of meaner degree
than themselves to take place before them.' They therefore 'commonly draw their husbands to maintain factions, to discontent their

best friends, and to wrap themselves in diverse inconveniences. This feminine quarrel was the first occasion of the breach between the Protector and the Admiral... This little spark, alighting upon such combustible matter as the heart of an ambitious and ireful woman, did in short time kindle so great a flame as could [in] no way be extinguished but by the blood of them both.'[42]

The falling out, however, between the brothers had as much to do with Thomas's mercurial personality as with his sister-in-law's pride, for Seymour flaunted his wife's rank at court and was deeply insulted when his brother went off to fight in Scotland and failed to appoint him Vice-Chamberlain of the King's household. His touchiness over seating arrangements was on a par with Gregory Sweet-Lips's when the new Lord Admiral objected that he had not been given, along with his brother, a special seat in Parliament as one of the King's uncles.[43] There was nothing the Duke of Somerset could do that did not appear to Thomas as a deliberate slight either to himself or to his wife. When the new government in the name of clemency and toleration repealed much of the Henrician treason legislation making it high treason to speak against the King's title and marriage, Seymour knew 'what was meant by this matter' — the true purpose was to expose his wife, the Dowager Queen, to slander.[44] 'The acid of Seymour's paranoia' was contagious and soon consumed his wife as well because the Lord Protector was withholding the jewellery Henry VIII had given her on the grounds that it was the property of the Crown.[45] To make matters more acrimonious Thomas and Catherine were convinced that the Duke's real reason for keeping the jewels had little to do with issues of state and everything to do with personal malice over their clandestine marriage and with the influence of 'that hell' his Duchess who was nagging him on.[46]

After Catherine's death on September 6th, 1548, Thomas carried on the fight for her inheritance, but by that time the level of his paranoia had reached a point where he knew full well that the Duke and Duchess were not only conspiring to keep his wife's jewels but also trying to steal from him the guardianship and right of marriage-bestowal of Henry VIII's grand-niece, Lady Jane Grey, and out of sheer spite were thwarting his moves to marry the Princess

Elizabeth. Since the Lord Admiral had persuaded himself 'that none
of the council would say anything not of the Lord Protector's lik-
ing', the unanimous decision on the part of that organization to
stop him, or anyone else, from marrying a potential heir to the
throne was viewed by Seymour as nothing more than a cover for
his brother's wicked designs against him.[47] In the end Somerset
could not even propose setting up a new mint at Durham Place
without arousing his brother's suspicions, nor could he increase
the size of his personal guard without the Lord Admiral boasting
that his brother was 'in fear of his own estate, and had him in a
great jealousy'.[48]

Fear, suspicion, and obsessive sensitivity became so much a part
of the Lord Admiral's world that the final months of his life were
wrapped in an atmosphere of black distrust and melancholy.
Everyone suspected the Lord Admiral who in turn suspected everyone
else, and he assured the young Earl of Rutland that his mistrust
was so great that he would act as 'no man alive should accuse
him'.[49] Unfortunately, Thomas failed to practise his own excellent
advice, for he proceeded to violate the cardinal rule of all successful
politics, seditious or otherwise — secrecy and discretion. Every word
he spoke, every act he made was guaranteed to alert the opposition
and to breed fear and suspicion on the part of the Lord Protector
and the entire Council. Precisely what the Lord Admiral was plotting was clear to nobody; that he was up to no good was apparent
to everybody.

What was confusing to contemporaries remains even more baffling to historians, but in retrospect it seems reasonably certain that
Thomas Seymour was developing, with no particular timetable in
mind, a three-pronged vendetta against his brother. First, he attempted by parliamentary means to limit the power of the protectorship; second, he tried to undermine the Duke's influence over young
Edward, turning the prince against his older uncle; and third he
sought to build up a political faction in the countryside as a counter-
poise to his brother's entrenched position as legal head of state.
All three designs were befuddled and intensified by Thomas's per-
sistence in playing boudoir politics. Not content with upsetting
the delicate balance of power at the start of the new reign by his

unauthorized marriage to the old King's 'relic', he further rattled
the political structure after Catherine's death first by blandly asser-
ting that it would be better for the King's half sisters — Mary and
Elizabeth — 'to be married within the realm than in a foreign place',
and then by outrageously suggesting: 'Why might not I, or another,
made of the king their father, marry one of them?'[50]

Whatever purpose the Lord Admiral may have had in sending
dynastic shivers up and down the Council's spine at the thought
of joining Tudor and Seymour blood, Thomas's efforts to embarrass his brother in Parliament are perfectly clear. He denied that
Henry VIII had wanted the offices of Lord Protector and Governor
of the King's person united in a single man, and, he argued, it
was more appropriate that the positions be divided between the
two uncles. He also pointed out that his brother had in fact violated
the old King's will by establishing a protectorate in the first place
and then seizing the office for himself. Try as he could, the Lord
Admiral was unable to have his brother's authority revoked, and
even his one successful shot — a law changing the office of Lord
Protector from one tied to the duration of the young prince's
minority to one based on the King's pleasure — suffered what was
tantamount to a pocket veto: it never received the great seal.[51]

Making the Duke's authority dependent upon a young boy's
pleasure would have suited Seymour's purposes perfectly, for he
had already set about undermining his brother's control over the
King. The ability to shape the royal mind, to stuff it with carefully
edited information, sly flatteries, and subtly coloured opinions
designed to favour one's own affairs and defeat the purpose of one's
enemies was central to the successful operation of monarchical politics. When the royal mind was young, malleable, and innocent,
it was essential to control entrée not only to the King's apartment
but also to the educators, servants, and friends who influenced his
opinions and moulded his sentiments. The Vice-Chamberlain of
the prince's chamber and the Deputy-Keeper of the King's person
held the keys to Edward's household and consequently to his mind,
and they were offices deeply coveted by Thomas Seymour. Unfortunately, the first was held by Sir Richard Page, whom Thomas
regarded as a 'drunken fool', and the second by Sir Michael Stanhope,

the brother-in-law of the Lord Protector.[52] If the front entrance were too well guarded, there was always the back door, and Seymour, almost the moment the reign began, started a campaign to reach the prince through the gentlemen and grooms of his chamber, especially the agreeable and obliging John Fowler, to whom the Lord Admiral presented large sums of money both for his own use and as presents to the other intimates of the privy chamber. The restricted circumstances of Edward's household and the universal acceptance of gratuities to assure special favours made the Lord Admiral's generosity welcome to those who served the prince, for in the name of economy the Duke not only kept his nephew short of spending money but also constantly changed his mind as to the proper size of the young King's establishment.[53] Consequently, it was not difficult for Seymour to spot those who prized his favour.

In the growing rift between the brothers and especially in the heated controversy over the Queen's jewels, it was useful for the Lord Admiral to have someone such as Fowler in a position to put his side of the argument to the King and to pass on messages between the royal nephew and his uncle, for young Edward lived in a gilded prison, his every move watched by zealous servants who reported directly to the Lord Protector. Seymour wanted to know whether the King asked after him; who about His Highness might profitably be offered gifts; at what time did the prince rise each morning; and most important of all, would Fowler ask Edward whether he needed pocket money and would the King write him 'some little recommendation with his own hand?' It was difficult for Edward to comply, but eventually he bade Fowler to 'go into the little house within where he dined, and to take the writing that lay underneath the carpet in the window there', and send it 'to my Lord Admiral'. The writing was only two lines long: 'My Lord, I recommend [me] unto you and the Queen, thanking you always for your remembrance.'[54] In response Seymour sent the King £40 as spending money. Seymour took every advantage of his back door to the King and spent nearly £200 greasing the receptive palms of grooms, educators, and musicians, and supplying funds to the King.[55] He was also able on a number of occasions to arrange private interviews with his nephew who later reported that his uncle had told him that the Duke of Somerset was old and would not live long (he was, in fact, only three years Thomas's senior), that Edward was 'a very beggarly king' with nothing 'for play or to give to his servants', that the King 'was too bashful' in demanding his rights, and finally that 'if anything was said against' his younger uncle, the prince 'should not believe it'.[56]

The power to possess the child-monarch's mind and to influence it against the Lord Protector was serious enough; the possibility of possessing his body as well smelled of treason. Despite the danger involved, however, there is overwhelming evidence that Thomas Seymour actually toyed with the idea of abducting the King. He wished he could 'have the King in his custody as Sir Richard Page had', and he actually tried to persuade Edward to sign a statement saying that he preferred his uncle to Sir Michael Stanhope as Deputy-Keeper of his person. He further admitted that he had spoken to Fowler about the ease with which 'a man might bring' the King 'through the gallery to his chamber and so to' the Lord Admiral's 'house'.[57]

Kidnapping a king, even a willing king, requires some sort of military and political presence, and during the months before his arrest, the Lord Admiral was busy befriending every dissident element at court, lecturing his friends on how to build up their influence in the shires, and violating the kingdom's laws against the possession of armed retainers and the establishment of private armies. He loaned the Marquis of Dorset £2,000 without bond in return for the guardianship of the Marquis's daughter, Lady Jane Grey, and promised to arrange the lady's marriage to the King if he could 'once get the King at liberty'.[58] He assured the young Earl of Rutland that he was his friend and would support him in his efforts to sit in the House of Lords while still a ward of the Crown.[59] He explained to almost anyone who would listen why it was important to 'keep a good house' and be generous with 'a flaggon or two of wine and a pasty of venison' in order to 'make much of the head yeomen and franklins of the country, especially those that be the ring-leaders, for they be men that be best able to persuade the multitude'.[60] This, he told his good friend Sir William Sharington, was what he himself was doing on his own estates surrounding Sudley Castle in Gloucestershire. There, he boasted, he could 'if he should be commanded to serve' muster 'ten thousand men'.[61] Nor was his influence limited to the countryside; he had, he informed Sharington, 'as great [a] number of gentlemen that love him as any nobleman in England...[and] he thought that he had more gentlemen that loved him than my Lord Protector had'.[62]

Political 'love' and the potential of putting 10,000 retainers in the field cost money. Wealthy as he was, the Lord Admiral could not stockpile the necessary wheat, powder, and shot unless he had other sources of income.[63] Fortunately, he had two profitable but illegal channels of ready cash: piracy and blackmail. Clearly even by sixteenth-century standards, which had difficulty distinguishing between piracy, privateering, and war-time plundering, the Lord Admiral was indulging in criminal piratical activities. He used his office to protect pirates on the high seas, to siphon off a percentage of the loot into his own pocket, to imprison those who brought charges of piracy in the Admiralty Courts, and to seize and plunder the goods of shipwrecked vessels. Such abuse of his office was all extremely unsavoury and caused the Protector and his government considerable embarrassment, but it was also highly lucrative.[64] It was not, however, as rewarding as Thomas's understanding with Sir William Sharington, the Vice-Treasurer of the royal mint at Bristol. Sir William came to Seymour in great alarm in December of 1548 to ask his help in an elaborate cover-up of the Treasurer's systematic and extensive embezzlement of government funds. Sharington's weakness was a passion for Renaissance architecture and he had sunk every penny he possessed, plus a great deal more, into the lavish rebuilding of Lacock Abbey as his country home. By the time he was caught with his hand in the mint, he was in debt to the staggering amount of £9,300, of which £4,000 had been generated by issuing clipped and debased currency and then falsifying the records to conceal the theft. The price of Seymour's aid 'in any trouble that might befall him' was an advance from the mint of £4,000 and the promise to coin another £10,000 worth of bullion, for both men had agreed that it would take at least that sum to maintain 10,000 men in the field for a month.[65]

The Vice-Treasurer was an ingenious and obliging friend, but how either of the conspirators expected that he would be able to continue his illegal activities without detection is one of the most incomprehensible aspects of this mystifying caper. Even the lax and negligent government of the Lord Protector must have grown uneasy when Sir William in 1548 purchased lands costing £2,808 4s.0d., presumably out of his salary as a government functionary.[66] Eventually the inevitable occurred: the government got word of the Vice-Treasurer's activities, from which a great many people were recklessly profiting. Early in January Dr William was called to task, and worse, his house at Lacock Abbey was searched. Oblivious to even the most rudimentary efforts to conceal his actions, the careless man had left at Lacock evidence of his association with the Lord Admiral. It took several weeks and a series of ever more revealing confessions, but once Sir William realized that he was enmeshed in treason, he sang as sweetly and loudly as Sir Edward Neville about Dr William Parry, and with the same results.

As the Council began its probe, the Lord Admiral's house of dreams came tumbling down. At first the Lord Protector tried to keep the scandal within the family and ordered his brother to appear before him privately. This Thomas refused to do, and a war of nerves ensued. Seymour knew full well that the Council was meeting in secret emergency session, but 'he could not learn the effect thereof'. He suspected 'they went about to see if they could get out any thing of Sharington against him...but for that he cared not, for he was able to answer to all things that should be laid to his charge'.[67] The Lord Admiral's confidence, however, was badly shaken when he learned that his friend the Earl of Rutland was planning to betray his trust and had spoken to the Council. He learned of the betrayal from his servant Pigot, whose brother, waiting upon the Earl, had overheard his master dictating a statement against the Lord Admiral. The observant fellow had spotted a 'little piece of paper of four or five lines as a beginning of a matter', and had delivered it to his brother, who in turn had brought it to Seymour's attention.[68] At first the Lord Admiral was defiant, and when on January 18th the Council required his appearance, his initial response was to demand a hostage 'for his free return'. But the bubble of his optimism soon vanished and he took a barge to Westminster, growling: 'I am sure I can have no hurt, if they do me right; they cannot kill me, except they do me wrong... If they take my life from me, I have a master that will [at] once revenge it.'[69]

The story of Thomas Seymour's treason grew with the telling, and by the time it reached François Van der Delft, the Imperial Ambassador, it was confidently reported that 200,000 crowns had been found at Sudley Castle; the Lord Admiral had 'induced 400 young lords to join him' in his conspiracy to overthrow his brother; he was in the pay of the French King; he had planned to emulate Richard III and murder his nephew, eliminate the Princess Mary, and elope with Elizabeth; and finally that he had been caught in the act of abducting the King, for he had been 'found within the palace late at night with a large suite of his own people, and the dog that keeps watch before the King's door' had been found dead.[70] Van der Delft was a notoriously unreliable source because he spoke no English and was willing to believe anything the government fed him, but the story of the plot to kidnap Edward was all over Europe before the Ambassador arrived in England. Moreover, the Imperial Ambassador in Paris was convinced the French were somehow involved in the plot, and the Lord Admiral himself admitted that he possessed a key to the King's apartment and that he thought Sir Michael Stanhope had placed extra guards at the door at night to prevent him from gaining access to the prince.[71]

Thomas Seymour, like William Parry, denied treasonous intent. He had, he said, not planned to kidnap, let alone harm, his nephew, and his statements about Edward bearing 'rule as other kings' did were meant only in terms of the future, three or four years hence. As for the Duke, Seymour never aimed at taking 'the King from my Lord my brother by force; I never meant, nor thought it'. And he challenged the Lord Protector: 'If I meant either hurt or displeasure to your grace, in this or any other thing that I have done, then punish me by extremity.'[72] In the end this is exactly what happened; early in March of 1549 a bill of attainder passed through Parliament; on March 17th the Council, including the Duke, signed the death warrant; and on the 20th Thomas died by sixteenth-century standards 'very dangerously, irksomely, horribly'.[73]

The Lord Admiral was difficult to the last, for he refused to confess his sins before God and man as a dutiful and repentant subject of the Crown was expected to do. Instead, his final words simply cast further confusion upon the motives and actions of a most unusual man whose treason was as self-defeating and self-destructive as any in English history. Seconds before the axe fell, he turned to a servant of the Lieutenant of the Tower and said: 'Bid my servant speed the thing that he wots [knows] of.' These words, as Seymour must have realized, were overheard, and under interrogation the Lord Admiral's servant admitted that his master had written two letters to the royal princesses urging 'that they should conspire against my Lord Protector's grace'. The messages had been written in the Tower and 'sown between the soles'[74] of the Lord Admiral's velvet shoes.

To the bloody end paranoia prevailed. The Lord Admiral's obsessions brought him to the scaffold but his fears and suspicions were contagious. It was, as the Princess Elizabeth later reminded her sister Mary, 'the persuasions' made to the Lord Protector 'that he could not live safely if the Admiral lived . . . that made him give consent to his [brother's] death'.[75]

The Signature of the Age

Gregory Sweet-Lips, Clement Philpot, Dr William Parry, and Thomas Seymour, a more unlikely and incompetent gaggle of traitors is difficult to imagine, but they are not isolated cases. Throughout the century, treason not only failed to prosper, but the higher the social and political rank of the miscreant, the more hysterical and self-destructive his actions became: Edward Stafford third Duke of Buckingham, executed 1521; Henry Pole Lord Montague and Henry Courtney Marquis of Exeter, liquidated 1538; Henry Howard Earl of Surrey, beheaded 1546; John Dudley Duke of Northumberland, decapitated 1553; Thomas Howard fourth Duke of Norfolk, executed 1571; Robert Devereux second Earl of Essex, put to death 1601. The list is far from complete,[76] but no matter the difference in name, rank, or circumstances, Tudor traitors, great and small, performed so clumsily that their sedition reads more like a series of bad historical novels than real history. Almost without exception they behaved in an unimaginably irrational and infantile fashion as if they were asking to be destroyed; and understandably the verdict of history has been 'of unsound mind'. Buckingham, it is said, 'drew disaster upon himself with reckless thoroughness' and 'in a sense... destroyed himself'.[77] The 'manifest incompetence' of the Courtney-Pole plotters, according to G.R. Elton, only 'adds to one's pity of them'.[78] Muriel St Clare Byrne regards Clement Philpot as 'typical of the average Tudor conspirator who appears as a rule quite incapable of taking action at the right moment'.[79] The Earl of Surrey has been dismissed by one historian as a 'gifted juvenile delinquent' and by another as a young man of 'almost insane indiscretion' who was completely out of touch with facts.[80] Seymour and Parry have both been called certifiable. W.K. Jordan states that Seymour's 'plotting was feckless, scarcely concealed, and bizarre' and concludes that the Lord Admiral 'was more than a little mad'.[81] The same judgment has been passed on Dr Parry; everyone is agreed he was 'unstable in his mind', 'a little mad', and 'not quite sane'.[82] Northumberland, although more rational, 'was handicapped by chronic ill-health, self-righteousness, and despair'.[83] As for the fourth Duke of Norfolk, he 'threw all caution to the wind and behaved as one possessed'.[84] Finally, the Earl of Essex, according to his biographer, spent the last three months of his life in 'a confused jumble of fears, rages, sly plotting and crude irrational outbursts of emotions culminating in the tragic and dismal fiasco of the 8 February rebellion'.[85]

How is such persistent idiocy and failure to be explained? It can, of course, be argued that the Crown was extraordinarily adept at digging out sedition and at translating any kind of stupidity into a sinister plot. Trained interrogators could manufacture conspiracies out of whole cloth, and even without the aid of thumb-screw and rack they could tie their victims up in so many verbal knots that they were guilty by their own confessions. But anyone with even the most rudimentary knowledge of the 'new monarchies' of the sixteenth century knows that the gap between the bureaucratic will to rule and the actual ability to enforce law was dangerously large.

The early modern nation-state possessed a soft feudal underbelly, and neither statutes written in blood nor the doctrine of absolute obedience to an authority ordained by God and propounded from every pulpit and schoolroom could entirely dispel the fear on the part of royal magistrates and administrators that public duty to the Crown might be corrupted, even replaced, by private loyalty to rank, birth, and religion. The government's obsessive fear of treason is evidence enough of its inability to root it out. Possibly Tudor England was incredibly lucky and Murphy's law operated with a deadly vengeance; if anything could go wrong for the traitor it did. Or finally, it is possible that the historians are correct: the behaviour of Sweet-Lips, Seymour, Norfolk, and the rest surpasses rational understanding. The one common denominator possessed by them all was unbelievable stupidity; as W.K. Jordan has noted, the treason of Seymour does recall 'the inexplicable action of two other Tudor peers, Surrey and Essex'.[86]

The operating word is 'inexplicable', and when Seymour and Parry are called 'not a little mad' or 'not quite sane', it is assumed that the cause of their apparent irresponsibility and preposterous activities is concealed in some locked but malfunctioning compartment of their minds. No one can refute such a proposition, for history is immune to psychoanalysis. But the cause of irrationality need not lie exclusively in the tortured chambers of the mind; it can be external, and the self-destructive traitor can be a symptom of his society as well as a victim of his own private insanity. Sedition is an integral part of any political system which possesses the means and the will to defend itself. The Tudor traitor could not function outside or independent of the political world that spawned him, for he fell prey as much to his own perception of treason — its heinousness, its risks, and its rewards — as he did to society's rejection of his mad-dog behaviour. The links of the chain that fettered his mind with misconceptions, hysteria, fears, and suspicions and that made him 'incapable of taking action at the right moment' were forged in the crucible of a society that itself defined the terms of both treasonable and acceptable political behaviour and that transformed his actions into conspiracy, sedition, and treachery. Traitors, great and small, were performers upon a political and psychological stage. Each was confronted with a particular historical predicament, but each was destroyed not so much by the deviousness or intelligence of his enemies as by the script which birth, chance, and cultural conditioning had placed in his hands. The chains that held these traitors were not theirs alone, but belonged to the century in which they were born and bred. Their actions were made in response to the same rhythm that set the pulse of all Tudor politics, and their strange behaviour and failure were, as often as not, little more than normal politics that had developed an exaggerated but fatal twist.

Ask why Tudor traitors were so inexplicably inept; ask why government officials could see only sinister and profoundly dangerous plots in such lunacy; and ask why society insisted on divorcing the deeper economic and social causes that stood behind treason from the immediate and muddle-headed motives of the traitor, and in effect one has asked what makes sixteenth-century English politics unique. In a sense, the traitor becomes a spectroscope which breaks up and separates the distinctive characteristics of Tudor politics: its cosmic view, its modes of perceiving and experiencing human relationships, and its assumptions about human nature and society which were shared by all members of the ruling élite. Ultimately any explanation of sedition, both its maladroit style and society's response to those who risked it, must be tied to the psychological, social, and human links of the chain that entangled and hampered the loyal and the disloyal alike. The proper study of treason, therefore, is the study of the entire sink and puddle of sixteenth-century politics.

If Tudor plotting appears 'feckless, scarcely concealed, and bizarre', the infantilism must be judged and explained in terms of the larger political world whence it sprang and which manifested the same childishness, absurdity, suspiciousness and apparent irrationality. Isolating and labelling the dominant social traits of a society is a dangerous pastime, for at best historical generalizations lull the reader into a false sense of security and at worst they hopelessly distort and oversimplify reality, but over the years scholars have been impressed and astonished not solely by the high incidence of wantonness and violence in sixteenth-century treason but also by the irrational bloodshed and bad temper of all subjects. 'At a distance', it has been said, 'the age presents the spectacle of a series of disasters and fulminations. Certainly this vividness of existence, these contrasts of daily life, sudden joy and sorrow, hope and despair, friendship and hatred, are part of the general temper of the times, which was indeed a time of enduring conflicts, fierce duels, *impossible conspiracies,* and sudden killings in the heat of passion.'[87] The records are littered with evidence that violence was in fact 'a characteristic of greatness', and Elizabethans, at least in their own estimation, appear like so many Tamburlaines, spreading their 'fame through hell and up to heaven', and holding 'the fates bound fast in iron chains'.[88] An Englishman always felt obliged to 'carve himself a satisfaction', and malice was 'so mad that it will not spare [a] friend to wreak vengeance on foes'.[89] A man was 'ready to kill and slay, if one break wind in his company'. The insult — calling your opponent 'a Spanish codpisse [piece]' — was a carefully cultivated art. 'Of all the disordered passions wherewith men's minds are vexed', there was none 'that troubleth and disquieteth them more than ambition and desire of honour',[90] and in revenge, especially of a dishonour, it was 'allowable to use any advantage or subtlety'.[91] Tudor England was, as Sir Thomas Smith noted, 'prodigal of life and blood',[92] and Lawrence Stone in *The Crisis of the Aristocracy* concluded that 'the behaviour of all classes was characterized by ferocity, childishness and lack of self control. To quarrel was a moral duty. This absence of restraint was all the more serious since men in the sixteenth century were so exceedingly irritable. Their nerves seem to have been perpetually on edge, possibly because they were nearly always ill...'[93]

Tudor England was 'nearly always ill'. Few historians doubt it; but of what? Was it simply the usual assortment of toothaches, kidney stones, black bile, skin diseases, malnutrition, and medical neglect that beset the human species until the mid-nineteenth century,[94] or does there lurk behind this 'lack of self control' some variety of mental illness common, if not to everyone in society, to enough men and women to warrant calling it an endemic disease? Even the most humanistically inclined social scientist maintains that 'every age develops its own peculiar forms of pathology, which express in exaggerated form its underlying character structure',[95]

and the sociologist Kai Erikson is, in all likelihood, correct when
he asserts that 'each historical age has its own particular problems
and poses its own particular strains on the human nervous system,
and each historical age, as a result, can be said to produce its own
special brand of neurosis'. The neuroses that are characteristic of
any given period are 'a part of its signature, because they reflect
the dilemmas and ambiguities to which people had to respond'.[96]

What then is the signature of Tudor England that set the pace
of treason to which Dr Parry, Philpot, Seymour, Essex, and the
rest danced their way to the block? That neurosis was paranoia,
what contemporaries called a 'Saturnian' disposition,[97] and the
playwright Jonson termed the 'plague' of all mankind:

> A new disease? I know not, new or old,
> But it may well be call'd poor mortals' plague:
> For, like a pestilence, it doth infect
> The houses of the brain...
> . . .
> Till not a thought, or motion, in the mind,
> Be free from the *black poison of suspect*.[98]

II

'THE BLACK POISON OF SUSPECT'

The World is all the richer for having a devil in
it, so long as we keep our foot upon his neck.
William James, *Varieties of Religious Experience*

To burden a century with a medical term which is at best imprecise
even in its clinical usage, to impose a disease of the individual upon
the collective mentality of a kingdom, and to describe Tudor England
as paranoid is to risk the legitimate wrath of both historian and
psychiatrist. Humpty Dumpty, however, was correct: not only do
words mean exactly what their users want them to, especially when
hauled out of disciplinary context, but they must also be properly
garbed in expensive definitional dress. Obviously, the sixteenth century was not clinically paranoid; it was neither incapable of handling reality nor schizophrenic, delusional, or unduly oppressed by
a persecution complex. On the other hand, it did manifest many
of the symptoms of what Richard Hofstadter has described as 'the
paranoid style' of thought and David Shapiro the paranoid 'mode
of cognition'.[1]

The central feature of the paranoid cognitive response to life is
not simply suspicion, 'the black poison of suspect'; it is the conviction that things are never as they appear to be — a greater and
generally more sinister reality exists behind the scenes — and the
corollary that what is standing hidden in the wings, prompting,
manipulating, but always avoiding exposure to the footlights, is
the presence of evil. Evil is for such a view of man and his universe
a palpable, measurable force. Its cosmic shape is Satan, the mastermind who is for ever conspiring to destroy God's order and man's

welfare; and its human form is the omnipresent enemy who wishes you ill and is actively working against you. The paranoid man, therefore, is ever vigilant and on his guard. He is extremely touchy and at all times on the alert and mobilized so that neither he nor society can be overthrown by the outside threat. Everything becomes a clue, for he assumes that nothing, not even the most trifling occurrence, can be an accident or a matter of chance. The pattern, the design, the conspiracy must exist; it is simply a matter of interpreting and integrating the evidence in the right fashion in order to reveal the hidden reality and menace that lurks just out of sight but never out of mind. No cognitive process is so rigidly logical and rational as the paranoid approach to political affairs and human relationships. The paranoid mind does not make up the evidence. There are real enemies in life; seducers, hypocrites, and traitors are not figments of the imagination. Political conspiracies do subvert the existing order of things, and the desire to do wrong for wrong's sake is, alas, a documented attribute of human nature. But the selectivity, intensity, rigidity, and above all the logic with which the paranoid mentality records, tabulates, catalogues, and evaluates the data sets it off from what, for lack of a better term, is called the normal response to the problems of daily life.

Paranoia appears under the most unlikely circumstances. An Ethiopian graduate student at Cambridge University doing a doctoral thesis on the modernization of the imperial dynasty was convinced that Haile Selassie's government was attempting to prevent him from completing his dissertation. He lived in a boarding house and every morning got up at five to meet the milkman lest his bottle be poisoned while it stood unprotected on the doorstep. He would never discuss his subject except while standing in the centre of his college quad for fear the Emperor's spies might hear him, and, when he travelled up to London to do research at the British Library, he carried all of his notes with him in three trunks because he knew they would be stolen if he left them behind. It all sounds ridiculous, but a week after he left Cambridge his boarding house caught fire and burned to the ground. The paranoid response, based on verifiable fact, is obvious: 'They thought he still lived there.'[2]

No one is totally immune to the 'black poison of suspect'; it can corrode the healthiest of minds. Indeed, a touch of paranoia may be a socially desirable attribute in the successful management of life, and the agent engaged in espionage may find a highly developed persecution complex essential to survival. Most of us stand neatly balanced between two poles: the excited mind that perceives the 'engine of Satan' in the design of human events, a demonic rationality in every thread and pattern of the fabric of history; and the dispassionate, if unimaginative, soul who senses little more than accident, coincidence, ambiguity, and the perversity of the gods behind the shadowy facade that makes up the shape of historical reality. A.A. Milne caught the essence of this polarity in Pooh and Eeyore's marvellous conversation when Pooh informs his asinine friend that his tail is missing. 'With a long, sad sigh', Eeyore exclaims:

> 'I believe you're right.'
> 'Of course I'm right,' said Pooh.
> 'That Accounts for a Good Deal,' said Eeyore gloomily. 'It Explains Everything. No Wonder.'
> 'You must have left it somewhere,' said Winnie-the-Pooh.
> 'Somebody must have taken it,' said Eeyore. 'How Like Them,' he added, after a long silence.[3]

To view history as a vast cosmic conspiracy, to be weighed down by the conviction that 'hell's black intelligencers' stand in our midst constantly contriving the overthrow of the righteous, to be for ever on guard against the enemy at the door, and to find in the loss of a tail an explanation for 'Everything' has an irresistible attraction born of the need to impose order upon chaos, and it is as old as the human species itself. No occurrence in history is too tangled or far-reaching to confound the paranoid explanation; no group or individual is too insignificant to escape suspicion. The Abbé Barreul was convinced that 'everything in the French Revolution, even the most dreadful of crimes', was 'the consequence of the most profound villainy' on the part of men 'who knew how to choose and to hasten the favourable moments for their schemes'.[4] On an even grander scale, Senator Joseph

McCarthy during the 1950s saw the Communistic 'bottled spider' of evil secretly set free in 'a conspiracy of infamy so black that, when it is finally exposed, its principals shall be forever deserving of the maledictions of all honest men'. In the Senator's estimation the responsibility 'for our present situation' lay with 'men high in this government' who were plotting 'a conspiracy on a scale so immense as to dwarf any previous such venture in the history of man'.[5]

The political right has had no monopoly on the paranoid cast of mind or its insistence on overestimating the power, rationality, and deliberate self-interest of evil individuals or groups in authority. The Communist proposition that the state is the 'executive committee of the ruling [capitalistic] class', or the more common view that Wall Street, Madison Avenue, advertising agencies, and oil cartels singly or in collusion are manipulating events like so many marionettes on strings are manifestations of an approach to human affairs that perceives sinister logic, demonic control, and ruthlessly clever protagonists at the core of world history.[6]

In more recent years, even the plodding humanist has been cast as the fallen angel who, in the opinion of Pastor Leo Wine of the Moral Majority, controls not only the Ford Foundation and the Rockefeller Foundation but also 'the television, the radio, the newspapers, the Hollywood movies, magazines, porno magazines, and the unions'. Two hundred and seventy-five thousand strong, humanists have infiltrated 'every department of our country' and eventually 'hope to name their own dictator who will create out of the ashes of our pro-moral republic a humanistic utopia, an atheistic, socialistic, amoral humanist society for America and the rest of the world'.[7]

If the twentieth-century addled-headed humanist can be clad in the conspiratorial garb of Satanic rationality and be numbered among the devil's disciples, then why isolate paranoia as that characteristic of the sixteenth century that provides a unique signature to Tudor politics? The answer may have more to do with perception than reality, for Tudor England imagined political life to be so exposed to naked villainy and so devoid of true friendship and loyalty that only a James Bond could have hoped to have survived. It postulated not only for that sewer of perfidy and deception, the royal court, but also for the kingdom at large, an intensity and quality of malice that makes Pastor Wine's malevolent influences appear as bungling and amateurish incubi. No matter the source — from the advice offered to the young and treatises on friendship to the pre-ambles of government statutes and the moralistic warnings presented to Tudor theatre-goers — the message was the same: 'Whoso taketh in hand to frame any state or government ought to presuppose that all men are evil, and at occasions will show themselves so to be.'[8]

'Ever Fear the Worst'

Despite a façade of noble sentiments, 'very pleasant and profitable to read', setting forth 'the omnipotency of God, the frailty of men, the inconstancy of fortune' and 'the good which moral men ought to pursue',[9] most of the counsel tendered in Tudor England crawled with 'lizard-lipped paranoia'. Advice is probably the most abundant commodity in the annals of human history, and very likely old Adam himself sought to direct Cain along the path of righteous-ness, but never was good counsel packaged in greater profusion or delivered with greater confidence than in the sixteenth century, for which, no doubt, we have human nature and the printing press to thank. Fathers inflicted upon their offspring the voice of genera-tional experience; editors and translators gathered together the wisdom of the past in capsulated and quotable form; educators pon-tificated upon the rules of acceptable conduct; professionals instructed neophytes; experience lectured innocence, and youth was besieged from every direction with moral caveats and useful reflections.[10] Tudor England believed whole-heartedly with Robert Greene that 'men that write of moral precepts or philosophical aphorisms are more highly esteemed than such as write poems of love and con-ceits of fancy'.[11] What started out as a trickle with the first Eng-lish advice book printed in 1450 became a torrent of admonitory and didactic literature; William Baldwin's *A Treatise of Morall Philosophie* (1547) went through twenty-three editions by the end of the century, Nicholas Ling's *Politeuphuia, Wits Commonwealth*

(1597) reached twelve editions by 1630, and Raleigh's *Instructions to His Son and to Posterity* (1632) was reissued five times in four years.[12] Every word of this deluge of 'stately phrases and pithy precepts'[13] was sustained and invigorated by one of the most determined triumphs of hope over experience: sixteenth-century England was sublimely confident that moral instruction actually influenced the minds and actions of the young. James I spoke for his century when he warned his 4-year-old son that if his fatherly advice were not followed, he would 'take the great God to record' and 'procure to be ratified in heaven, the curse that in that case here I give unto you'.[14]

The advice offered was rarely firsthand, and even when presented as sage parental hints on how to succeed in society, it was largely plundered from the classical and Christian reservoir of moral precepts collected in the countless commonplace books of the century. Almost without fail the literature commenced with the stock adage: 'The fear of God is the beginning of wisdom', and the equally hallowed admonition to the young that patience and obedience to authority were the true paths of righteousness and happiness. Lord Burghley's three-and-a-half page *Memorial* (1561) to his son Thomas on how to use his time while travelling in Europe is characteristic of the weight assigned to the 'commandment of the Lord your God'; three pages were dedicated to his son's spiritual welfare and exercise, while only the concluding seventeen lines dealt with 'your journey and order thereof'.[15] The proportions are extreme, but Cecil was only too well aware of Thomas's need for divine forgiveness, and later he had cause to write to his son's tutor that he was 'used to pains and troubles, but none creep so near my heart as doth this my lewd son. I am perplexed what to think. The shame that I shall receive to have so unruled a son grieveth me more than if I had lost him by honest death.'[16]

Grieved but undaunted by younger generations that paid scant heed to their elders' words, fathers continued to flood the realm with Poloniusque advice. Moral edicts loomed large: 'let all untruth be far from you'; 'let no ambition entangle your mind'; 'let not cruelty, but mercy and pity overcome you'; 'speak truth and shame the devil'; 'pain and danger be great only by opinion and...in truth nothing is fearful but fear itself'; and 'hell gates and a whore's apron are ever open for wicked guests'. Behavioural instruction was even more abundant: build not 'castles in the air'; 'converse not with fools'; 'take heed of knaves'; 'think before you speak'; 'kneeling ne're spoiled silk stockings'; 'phantastical attire be a confirmation of an unsettled mind'; 'delight to be cleanly'; and 'go a hundred miles to see a wise man [rather] than five to see a fair town'. Then there were the economic admonitions: 'eschew prodigality'; 'be moderate in all things and frugal in expenses, for wasters and proud men be very fools'; leave no 'possessions for promises or assurances for hope'; and 'no lover of his bed did ever yet perform great and noble things'. Finally, there were those two perennial warnings: 'use great providence and circumspection in the choice of thy wife' and stay out of debt.[17] Such chestnuts are familiar to any parent who pays the piper and expects to dictate the tune and who knows that 'the world be like a well with two buckets, that when one falleth another riseth, yet the fall is much swifter than the rising and [for] good reason, because the one goes down empty and the other comes up laden'.[18]

Advice, no matter how platitudinous, is a reflection of the real, or at least the perceived, world. It is a composite of *ad hominem* caveats about how to thrive in the jungle of life, and inherited perceptions about human nature and the ultimate scheme of the universe. Although Tudor advice books mouthed the usual Christian virtues, sixteenth- and early seventeenth-century authors felt compelled to counsel their young to be prepared for evil to a degree that the twentieth century would find shocking. The waters were filled with sharks; 'all men', it was said, 'are liars', and 'even the courses of the strictest saints have their crackings'.[19] Sir William Wentworth spoke for the entire century when he informed his son always to 'be suspicious of the conscience of any that seem more saintly than others and smooth like oil, having many times God and conscience in their mouths when their hearts are far from Him'.[20]

Tudor society was an 'old muckhill overspread with fresh snow',[21] and the three pieces of counsel that were reiterated *ad nauseam* by experienced fathers, worried educators, and observant social philosophers were first, trust no one; second, watch out for the enemy; and third, beware of appearances. The 'black poison of suspect', admitted Sir Francis Bacon, clouded the mind, destroyed friendships, and disposed 'kings to tyranny [and] husbands to jealousy'. It was, he warned, dangerous to procure a 'magic glass wherein to view the animosities, and all that malice which is any way at work against us'; nevertheless, he had no doubt that the 'evil eye' of envy 'walketh the streets', that the 'curious man' is by definition 'malevolent' and 'that a habit of secrecy is both politic and moral'.[22]

The voice of the turtle was not to be believed; and commonplace book after commonplace book echoed and re-echoed Ben Jonson's furious words: 'Love no man: trust no man.'[23] In mid-century William Baldwin urged his readers to 'trust not the world, for it never payeth that [which] it promises'; 'doubt them whom thou knoweth and trust not them whom thou knoweth not'; 'be secret in council and take heed what thou speaketh before thine enemies'; and 'beware of spies and tale-bearers'.[24] Fifty years later Nicholas Ling was quoting the same sources and advocating the same caution: 'He that never trusteth is never deceived'; 'a man's look is the gate of his mind, declaring outwardly the inward deceit which the heart containeth'; 'it is better to suspect too soon than mislike too late'; and 'silence is more safety than speech when our enemies be the auditors'.[25] Noblemen were counselled not to 'tell all that you think' and always to remember that 'although all men promise to help you if you had need, yet nevertheless, trust not too much thereunto...[for] if occasion be offered [they] will be the first to strike you [and] to give you the overthrow'.[26] Lord Burghley informed his younger son Robert to 'trust not any man too far with thy credit or estate'.[27] Lady Margaret Hoby praised the advice she had been taught as a child: 'Take heed' from whom you 'received gifts' lest you betray yourself 'unawares' to 'wicked companions'.[28] Lady Anne Bacon, an even more paranoid female, warned her son Anthony to beware of 'pot-fellowship companions' and not to believe 'everyone that speaks fair to you at your first coming. It is to serve their turn.'[29] Sir Francis Walsingham concurred; he wrote to young Anthony that 'the number of evil-disposed in mind is greater than the number of sick in body', an

estimate which, given the health of society, must have included
almost everybody.[30] If evidence was required, history could prove
that 'it is better to have an open foe than a dissembling friend'.[31]
In the *Mirror of Magistrates,* the fate of the second Duke of Buckingham is presented as a lesson in misplaced trust. By trusting his
servant and his King, the Duke was betrayed and executed.[32] Even
the graffiti scribbled on the prison wall spoke the same message:
'Wise men ought. . . to beware whose company they use; and above
all things, to whom they trust.'[33]

Secrecy was a social and political obsession which was regarded
as one of the basic laws of nature, for the whole world knew that
'wild beasts dwell in dens, fishes bed in mud, and birds in nests;
and a wise man is wrapped up in secrecy'.[34] Sir Thomas Elyot
warned his noble reader to take great care 'whom he may use as
his familiars and safely commit to them his secrets',[35] and that
elderly Puritan William Higford advised his grandson that 'a prudent disguising of your purposes' was the most effective way of
achieving 'your designs'.[36]

In such an atmosphere the advice offered by the three most
ruthlessly pessimistic fathers of late Elizabethan society — Sir William
Wentworth, Sir Walter Raleigh, and Henry Percy, ninth Earl of
Northumberland — can no longer be regarded as deplorable oddities
of the age, but must be accepted as highly quotable confirmation
of the paranoid climate of opinion held by all parents, educators,
and moralists. The three men not only shared a devastatingly low
view of human nature but they also urged a common theme upon
their offspring: 'Ever fear the worst.'[37] Wentworth advised his
son to 'be very careful to govern your tongue, and never speak in
open places all you think' and 'in matters of great importance trust
none'. It was, he added, his policy to pen as few letters as possible
because 'it is common custom to keep letters, and years later produce them for evidence against you in court or elsewhere'. Sir
William had a clear picture of the evil that stalked the earth, for
he categorically stated that 'whosoever comes to speak with you,
comes premeditate for his advantage'.[38] Raleigh was in agreement.
'Be advised', he told his heir, 'what thou dost discourse of, what
thou maintainest whether touching religion, state, or vanity; for

if thou err in the first, thou shalt be accounted profane; if in the second, dangerous; in the third, indiscreet and foolish.'[39] Northumberland assured his 9-year-old son that it was far easier 'for many men to deceive you than you to deceive yourself, since men's ends are secret to themselves, and combinations will deceive the wisest men'. The world, he said, was filled with adventurers who 'love their own cases and themselves best' and will 'puff and speak big...not to yield you any great returns but to use your means at home for them to get somewhat abroad'.[40]

On the subject of human nature, Sir Walter was even more pessimistic than the Earl and wrote in his 'Cabinet-council' that 'whoso laboureth to be sincerely perfect and good shall necessarily perish, living among men that are generally evil'. The world was a jungle and 'he that is weakest must always go to the worst', for 'men are far more mindful of injuries done unto them, than of benefits received', and they are only good if 'no respect of profit or pleasure draws them to become evil'. Only force will make men good.[41] Sir William Wentworth could not have agreed more and informed his offspring that 'people are servile, not generous' and 'nothing but fear of revenge or [law] suits hold back men from doing wrong'.[42] The potential for malice and deceit was endless, and all three cautioned: never trust your servant, your tenant, and above all others, a reconciled enemy, 'for secret poison is like invisible in his heart'.[43] As for your friend, always remember, said Wentworth, that he 'may become your enemy, a thing very common in these days'.[44] Raleigh had the same message: take 'especial care that thou never trust any friend or servant with any matter that may endanger thine estate' because 'thou make thyself a bond slave to him that thou trustest'. To make matters worse, it was also impossible to know the flattering enemy from the true friend, and it was essential, he told his namesake, to remember that 'as a wolf resembles a dog, so doth a flatterer a friend'.[45] Tudor England clearly discerned the ring of truth in Richard Taverner's translation of Erasmus's *Proverbes* when he wrote in 1545: 'It is wisdom in prosperity when all is as thou wouldest have it, to fear and suspect the worst.'[46]

The friend fascinated and repelled Tudor society. No other human

relationship received so much attention and, if we can believe
sixteenth-century moralizers, no other concept was honoured so
much in the breach as friendship: 'your friend today, your enemy
tomorrow'.[47] Most of the ideas were stolen from Cicero's
Amicitia, but originality was never a highly prized quality of Tudor
philosophizing, nor did a concern for plagiarism prevent authors
from capitalizing on a subject of universal social interest. Essays,
chapters, poems, aphorisms, epigrams poured off the press.[48]
Entire books and even plays were devoted to the subject, and Raleigh
began his *Instruction* to his son with the statement: 'There is nothing
more becoming a wise man than to make choice of friends...'[49]
Courtiers spoke of the political and economic usefulness of the friend,
philosophers extolled the idea of true friendship, educators thundered
against the false deceiving friend, and traitors lamented the fatal
consequence of blind adherence to friendship.[50]

To a society that was rapidly divesting itself of the ancient ties
of lordship and kinship but had not as yet developed a sense of party
loyalty and membership, the friend was a peculiarly important person. He kept your cashbox when you travelled, looked after your
interests in your absence, lent you money in your need, gave you
advice in your confusion, introduced you to contacts in political
life, protected you from your indiscretions, supported you with his
patronage, and acted as your executor and family protector when
you died. Friendship, as both Sir Thomas Seymour and Lord
Burghley realized, made the political world go round. 'Three steps',
Seymour confessed, were necessary 'to raise a man to observation:
some peculiar sufficiency, some particular exploit, [and] an especial
friend', for 'sufficiency and merit', he warned, 'are neglected things
when not befriended'.[51] Cecil's advice to his son was equally
unsentimental: 'Be sure ever to keep some great man thy friend...for
otherwise in this ambitious age thou shalt remain as a hoop without a pole, live in obscurity, and be made a football for every insulting
companion to spurn at.'[52]

True friendship involved far more than 'the benefit that one man
reaps from another'.[53] Perfect friendship, according to the social
ideal, was 'to make one heart and mind of many hearts and
bodies'.[54] It was the creation of 'a second self', to whom a man

might disclose 'the secrets of his heart and recount to him all his grief, trust him with things touching his honour and deliver him to keep his goods and treasures...'[55] The sixteenth century expected much of the friend, for not only was he to be 'in prosperity a pleasure, in adversity a solace, in grief a comfort, in joy a very companion' but also 'a true friend, seeing or hearing his friend in danger...ministers to him of his goods', takes 'long and painful voyages and hazards his person to help and release his friend out of peril'.[56] Friends, in the doubtful doggerel of Richard Edwards's *Damon and Pithias,* are 'alike in joy and also in smart...for in two bodies they have but one heart'. There, of course, was the rub, and the play concludes that friendship is:

A rare and yet the greatest gift that God can give to man;
So rare, that scarce four couple of faithful friends have been,
    since the world began.[57]

The 'faithful friend' was crucial, but unfortunately he was scarce, and Tudor England could never rid itself of the suspicion that behind the hand of friendship lay a heart filled with malice. It was with this fear in mind that Thomas Breme wrote his preface to *The Mirrour of Friendship: both how to Knowe a Perfect friend, and how to choose him, with a brief treatise or caveat not to trust in worldly prosperitie* (1584): 'Good reader, considering that in these days there is such unsteady friendship amongst many, that it is hard to find a perfect and true friend: for now friendly words are common but when friendship cometh to the touch of proof, the alteration is marvellous: yea, and sometimes so dangerous that of friends in words they will become enemies in deeds.'[58] And so the warning went out: distrust your friend, test him in the summer of your prosperity before the autumn of your adversity, and beware of those 'glow-worms' and parasites, the flatterer, the hypocrite, and the con-man who hide behind the mask of friendship.

Friends, Northumberland assured his son, are 'weak hearted in cases of adversity'.[59] William Cornwallis warned that 'under this name of friendship...is included much danger'. Nicholas Breton rhymed 'thus much for thy assurance know; a hollow friend is but a hellish foe'.[60] And Nicholas Ling collected a string of depressing quotations in the same spirit: 'We ought to use a friend like gold, to try him before we have need'; 'friends ought always to be tried before they be trusted'.[61] William Baldwin was equally pessimistic: 'Put no trust in friends in thy present prosperity'; 'flattery from friendship is hard to be dissevered'; and 'they that trust much to their friends know not how shortly rivers be dried up'.[62]

The Truth of Our Time, revealed and written by Henry Peacham, stated the bald reality of late-Tudor-early-Stuart society: 'Ordinary friendship is but mere acquaintance . . . so that if among one hundred of your acquaintance, yea, five hundred, you meet with two or three faithful friends, think yourself happy. Such is the world in our cunning age.'[63] William Martyn in his *Youths Instruction* (1612) put the case more metaphorically: 'For as a barge-man turning his face one way, roweth another, so a dissembling friend hath honey in his mouth, but poison in his heart.'[64] The situation, according to Richard Paice's *Howe one may take profit of his Enemyes,* was so serious and friendship had so lost her speech, while 'flattery hath tongue enough', that 'we must hear the truth' about ourselves not from our friends but from our enemies who make a point of knowing our every defect. An enemy, assured Paice, 'in seeking occasion of slander, prieth and peereth always on thy living, perceiving with his sight like a linx not only the timber, the covering, and the walls of thy house, but also thy friend, thy servant, and whom so ever keepeth thee company . . . He will know what thou dost, piercing and trying all thy secrets.'[65] Society was agreed: 'There is so little difference between our enemy and our friend, and so hard to know the one from the other, that there is great jeopardy lest we defend our enemy instead of our friend or hurt our friend instead of our enemy.'[66] Sir Francis Bacon presented the situation in its most quotable, if not most original, form; he cautioned his reader to 'love your friend as if he were to become an enemy, and hate your enemy as if he were to become your friend'.[67]

If friends were scarce, enemies, alas, were ubiquitous. It was not sufficient to distrust your friend; it was also necessary to know your enemy so as to confuse neither 'thine enemy for thy friend nor thy friend for thine enemy'.[68] No one — parent, statesman, moralist, educator — doubted that the enemy was for ever knocking on the door. 'And now for knowing of thine enemy', urged Nicholas Breton, 'let this suffice for reasons true direction':

> Who doth intrude into thy company,
> And make a show of too too much affection:
> Such nimble wits have ever in rejection.
> And by a serpent's hiss and bear-whelp's eye
> Mistrust the treason of an enemy. [69]

The Marquis of Winchester had much the same grim message, and on the subject of 'Evill and Wicked Men' he waxed metaphoric: 'Under the crystal stone lieth oftentimes a dangerous worm; in the fair wall is nourished the venomous coluber [snake]; within the middle of the white tooth is engendered grief to the gums; in the finest cloth is the moth soonest found; and the most fruitful tree by worms doth soon perish: so under the clean body and fair countenance are hid many and abominable vices.'[70]

The friend and the enemy were the pivots upon which all human relations, and therefore politics, depended, and Sir Francis Bryan expressed no more than a cultural reflex of his age when he warned in a didactic poem of doubtful quality, but of noble sentiments, that 'in things displeasant an enemy is spied, and in adversity a friend is tried'.[71] Behind all the outpouring of sententious counsel stood the spectre of the enemy concealed in a jungle of evil. Moral philosophy itself was predicated upon the knowledge that the 'men among whom we be born be of so evil disposition, the world with whom we live so fierce and cruel...that they [will] hurt us with their feet, bite us with their teeth, scratch us with their nails, and so swell us with their poison that the passing of this life is nothing but the suffering of death'.[72] The lament was universal, and scarcely a word of wisdom to the young did not perceive the existence of the enemy.[73] Even the emblemist, who contrived and collected those immensely popular Elizabethan conceits, the 'speaking picture', was caught up in the same warning:

Latet anguis in herba.

Of flattery with sugared words beware,
Suspect the heart, whose face doth fawn and smile,
With trusting these, the world is clogg'd with care,
And few there be can scape these vipers vile;
    With pleasing speech they promise and protest
    When hateful hearts lie hid within their breast. [74]

The forest of malcontent was thickest and the 'black poison of
suspect' strongest at court where, according to Mr John Husee,

there was 'nothing but every man for himself'.[75] The writer of
these pessimistic sentiments was Lord Lisle's man-of-all-works in
London, and oddly enough, one of life's optimists. When he roused
his employer's alarm by describing 'that great courtesan, the court',
as a cesspool of 'back-friends', 'secret enemies', 'harm-doers', and
flatterers possessed of 'a fair face and double dissembling heart',
he felt obliged to curb His Lordship's mounting paranoia. In 1538
Husee begged Lisle to cast off 'such fantasies', for 'God is the best,
and as long as the King is good and gracious lord unto my lord
and your ladyship', no one need give 'a halfpenny for the rest'.[76]
Unfortunately, 'the rest', so happily dismissed by Husee, could not
be ignored, for Tudor politics thought it most unlikely that the
condition contained in the proverb 'take away the wicked from before
the king and his throne shall be established in righteousness' (Proverbs 25:5) would ever occur. It was a fact of political life that the
wicked were omnipresent, and to the question 'what is a courtier
most to take heed of?' the answer was self-evident: 'envious ambition, malicious faction, palpable flattery, and base panderism'.[77]

The literature dealing with political survival was immense.
Baldassare Castiglione's *Il Cortegiano*, translated into English in 1561
by Sir Thomas Hoby, with its high-minded exhortation to purchase royal favour by deserving it, was standard reading. More cynical
was Sir Thomas North's adaptation of Guevara's *Dial of Princes* with
its advice on how to win the confidence of kings and protect yourself
from your enemies.[78] There was also available in English after 1607
Lorenzo Ducci's *Ars avlica or the courtiers arte* with its endless varia-
tions upon the twofold theme — 'how to know the nature and
affection of the prince' and how to handle one's enemies and enviers.
Ducci's cynical counsel to watch carefully the prince's actions even
'in his most retired places', but to be careful not to be 'taken as
a spy', and the equally Italianate dictum to place informers in the
houses of 'malicious enviers' because 'none liveth without sin',
must have struck Elizabethans as depressingly continental but nevertheless highly practical advice.[79]

The most outspokenly paranoid counsel, however, did not appear
in England until 1622 when first John Reynolds and then Edward
Walsingham translated an anonymous French how-to-do-it treatise

entitled *A Practical Guide for Ambitious Politicians*. The manual was without a doubt the creation of an intimate of the court of the last of the Valois monarchs. The author may have been Eustache du Refuge, a minor French governmental official who, despite the villainy of sixteenth-century French politics, was able to keep his sense of honour and self-respect.[80] For all of its Machiavellian realism and paranoia, the guide was a profoundly moral book. Unlike other commentaries on monarchical politics, it argues that even though 'the vicious are always in court in greater throngs' and 'wanton love, cruelty and avarice' are 'those passions that are of greatest sway in princes' minds', the true courtier must try to foresee and prevent these 'unjust desires and the unlawful designs of the prince'.[81] Well intended or not, the successful courtier was warned always to discover the truth that lies behind appearances, and to realize that politics is composed of friends and enemies. 'Our young courtier', advised du Refuge, 'must observe well the manners and conditions' not only of the prince himself but also 'of such of his followers as he most trusts and relies upon'. Unfortunately 'wary princes', the author cautioned, 'will endeavour to conceal and smother' their true inclinations; however, 'since all their actions are so exposed to the eyes of men', and 'they are so oppressed and vexed with the weight of business', they will forget their artifices and 'betray their dispositions'. In the struggle to know and influence the prince, the courtier needs constantly to keep a close watch on two kinds of people, 'those that may help and advantage us' and 'those who are likely or able to hurt us'. The interests and power of both must be carefully weighed, especially our potential adversaries, of whom 'there are three kinds: either those that are our enemies, or those that envy us, or lastly, those that are our competitors'. Those who are our enemies 'hate us for our own or our friends' sake', and according to du Refuge, there is little that can be done about unadulterated hatred directed against us personally except to guard ourselves as best we can. Nevertheless, he spends an entire chapter on 'How we are to treat with those enemies that hate us for our own sakes'. Enmity aroused through association is more easily handled; it is best mitigated by staying clear of all 'friendships of the court', which are 'for the most part factious and cruel, compelling us to break off all friendships and familiarities that may bring us into suspicion'.[82]

Englishmen did not have to turn to the example of foreign lands to learn about the 'lean and vicious people' who haunted the households of princes, or how to succeed in the court of kings. There was plenty of domestic advice available. Sir Thomas Wyatt and the Earl of Northumberland both warned that the political arena was crawling with 'detraction', a 'vice very ugly and monstrous', which operated 'under the pleasant habit of friendship and good counsel'.[83] Francis Bryan in 1548 translated and adapted from the Italian a short piece entitled *A Dispraise of the Life of a Courtier* in which he presented the standard warning that the court not only abounded with those who 'will do off with their bonnets to you that gladly would see your head off by the shoulders' but was also a hellhole where 'there be gentlemen so rooted in vengeance and hatred that by no means, request nor gentleness a man may direct them from their evil intents'. The single original opinion Bryan had to offer had to do with retirement: 'The wisest being[s] in the court may say every day that they die and at their houses in the country they live... but I dare affirm that for X pounds weight they have of honest will [to leave] they have not half an ounce of honest liberty... There is no liberty to depart hence. The yoke of the court is hard, the bonds fast tied.'[84] Seventy years later Bryan's words were happily plagiarized and enlarged upon in *The Court of the most illustrious and most Magnificent James, the first... With divers rules, most pure precepts and selected definitions lively delineated*, the most practical precept being the commonplace: 'Take heed whom thou trusteth for in trust is treason. And in this regard let every courtier be... quick sighted and watchful... having eyes both behind and before... [Do not] put confidence in a glavering, crouching and deeply protesting or swearing friend.'[85]

Lord Burghley and the Earl of Northumberland had practical counsel to tender their offspring on the importance of receiving credit for services rendered and on how easy it was for thanks 'cunningly to be turned from your hands'. 'If', said Cecil, you 'have cause to bestow any great gratuity, let it then be some such thing as may be daily in sight'; never, admonished Northumberland, give freely like a god, but 'give as one that expecteth a return'.[86] In a similar vein, James VI urged his son always to be wary of choosing his companions and servants lest they labour for their own profit and advantage, and he pronounced the golden rule of effective government: 'Govern your subjects by knowing what vices they are naturally most inclined to.'[87]

Sir Francis Bacon, as usual, had the most to say about success, and he offered his countrymen a collection of court-weary observations presented as advice for 'the self-politician or the art of rising in life'. The most successful men, he noted, were 'continually plotting their own rise and advantage', and the wise man always reserved 'a window open to fly out or some secret back-door for retreat'. Bacon, like du Refuge, sensed that the 'words of men are full of deceit', and that the 'surest key for unlocking the minds of others, turns upon searching and sifting their tempers and natures, or their ends and designs'. Bacon bubbled over with sententious counsel about the choice of friends and dependants, and the need to know yourself as well as others, but he concluded with the chilling advice that in the end appearances count the most. 'The self-politician' must 'show, express and fashion himself' so as to be noticed, and at the same time he must hide his defects, because concealment is as important as the 'artful manipulation of [one's] virtues'.[88]

Most of the manuals on political success were cribbed from or influenced by French, Italian, and classical sources, but the most unusual and soundly English how-to-do-it essay was Robert Beale's 'A Treatise of the office of a Councellor and Principall Secretarie to her Majestie' (1592).[89] Written in the tradition of older instruction manuals reaching back all the way to Richard Nigel's *Dialogue of the Exchequer* (1177), Beale's work recounts in detail the duties and function of the office of Principal Secretary, but unlike its predecessors, his description emphasizes the dangers inherent in the office, and he gives excellent advice on how to succeed as Principal Secretary. When there was unpleasant news to impart to the Queen, Beale urged that the Secretary avoid having 'the burden be laid on you alone but let the rest [of the Council] join with you', a tactic well known to Lord Burghley who once urged the young Earl of Bedford that if he had to report anything 'misliked or tedious' to her Majesty, to 'procure others also to write thereof, and in no wise write thereof alone'.[90] The secretaryship was not an enviable position, for 'if anything be misliked, it will be said' by the rest of the Council 'that it was the Secretary's doing, that they signed for company [or] that the letter was brought to them' by the Secretary himself. 'Be not too credulous', Beale advised, 'lest you be deceived', and be sure to 'have a special cabinet' whereof you 'keep the key' for your 'secret intelligences, distinguishing the boxes or tills rather by letters' than by names. Always keep a friend in the privy chamber and be sure you have foreknowledge of her Majesty's disposition before you bring her any business, and if she is 'angry or not well disposed, trouble her not with any matter which you desire to have done unless extreme necessity urge it'. Also take care that you do not 'addict yourself to any faction that you may find among the councillors. You shall find they will only use you for their own turns and that done [will] set little by you afterwards.' And finally, he concludes with the warning, never fall to the temptation of bribery, for 'your *enemies* shall have less occasion to seek your discredit and overthrow, who most commonly, in the supplantation of men, look rather to some part of the spoil or prey than either to just matter or the service of God, prince, or country'.[91]

Possibly no piece of advice dramatizes the essential quality of sixteenth-century success literature and emphasizes its contrast to modern how-to-do-it business counsel as do Beale's parting words. On the surface, the two approaches to success are brutally similar. Modern success counsel postulates a corporate world just as ruthless and carnivorous as any sixteenth-century court; the path to the top in business is strewn with just as many bodies of those who mistakenly placed their trust in loyalty, friendship, honour, and gratitude. The twentieth-century prescription for success is every bit as blatant in its acceptance of, need for, and delight in distrust and intimidation, and like Tudor England it also insists that appearances — a pleasing countenance, a firm handshake, and a winning smile — are more important than either hard work or a high I.Q.[92] The ethics of loyalty today have little meaning for the upwardly mobile success hunter, for loyalty can 'be too easily simulated or feigned by those most desirous of winning'.[93] Where the twentieth and the sixteenth century part company, however, is in the concept of the enemy as the villain who seeks the destruction of his opponent for his own sake. In Robert Ringer's *Winning Through Intimidation* no holds are barred, and 'the game of business is played in a vicious jungle', but that jungle is filled with impersonal types, not with depraved and personal enemies. There are for Ringer 'only three types of people who exist in the business world': the avowed opponent who does not attempt to conceal the fact that he is out to replace you; the hypocritical adversary who speaks with a forked tongue and stabs you in the back; and the most common and dangerous of all, the man or woman who is filled with good but deadly intentions. This third type 'wants to see you get a "fair shake," but because of the reality of the laws of non-altruism, he is "forced," by any one of a number of "reasons," to attempt to grab your chips. Because he is really and truly sorry for having to hurt you, it's very difficult to reach the level of sophistication where you're able to view a Type Number Three as a dangerous opponent in the game of business.'[94]

Not only is the phraseology of Ringer's approach to the business world alien to the sixteenth century, but so also is his essential hypothesis. Business is a 'game', not necessarily with Queensberry rules, but nevertheless with rationality, order, and laws, and 'Type Number Three' is subject to those laws. He is 'forced', not by internal vice or innate sinfulness but by the system itself, to 'grab your chips'. In contrast, the sixteenth-century enemy was a free, demonic spirit, unfettered by his own limitations or the 'toils of the vast mechanism of history'.[95] Robert Beale could not conceive of an adversary as either a 'type' or a legitimate rival, seeking to engineer the Principal Secretary's downfall for respectable reasons, such as disagreeing with his politics, sensing his ineptitude, or perceiving his vices. Instead, the enemy looked 'to some part of the spoil or prey' and not to 'the service of God, prince, or country'. Beale's villain is motivated by an inner fire. His intentions are not good because he is evil and, being evil, he delights in his rival's misfortunes. Ringer's type number three is soulless and therefore evilless, and when his victims are destroyed, nobody particularly cares. But in sixteenth-century life — be it in the court of kings or in the counting house of merchants or simply in the daily encounters of society — the enemy was deeply, viciously concerned for his rival's personal survival or destruction. The existence of an enemy brought to Tudor politics a quality of paranoia almost totally lacking in the modern 'game' of survival. Individual businessmen and politicians can today be hopelessly paranoid, but the system itself is not based on a paranoid response to society.

Underlying all Tudor advice literature, giving it an intensity and character peculiar to the century, is a third assumption about the woof and the warp of human events. The counsel to 'ever fear the worst' was probably a sensible precaution in an overly litigious society; a belief in the existence of a personal enemy was undoubtedly a useful working hypothesis; but the conviction that things are not what they seem to be was a fundamental cultural prejudice that tainted, distorted, and corrupted every human relationship. If there was a single lesson that Tudor England sought to instil within the minds of young and old alike, it was the paranoid advice to look behind every facade and not to be sold a bill of goods, be it the fair face and decorous manners of a prospective wife, the word of a deceiving papist, clipped coinage or falsely weighed bread. 'Every virtue and fair quality has its counterfeit,' cautioned the Earl of Carbery for the benefit of his son; don't be 'deluded with appearances', Northumberland told his heir; and William Baldwin assured his tender readers that 'glory, honour, nobility, and riches are to cloak maliciousness'.[96] Nicholas Breton thought that 'under simplicity is hidden much subtility'.[97] Do not be deceived by the external and outward appearance of the papists 'who are fair without and all rotten within', educator James Cleland warned his young noblemen; and William Vaughan in *The Golden Grove* wrote that a man was 'like unto a tree which in outward appearance seemeth to be most beautiful and is full of fair blossoms, but inwardly is rotten, worm-eaten and withered'.[98] 'The world', confessed William Higford to his grandson, 'is a stage and everyone is to act his part before that great spectator, God Almighty', who alone knows whether the actor is playing his true self or some dissembling part.[99] Deceit, fabrication, hidden meaning were the grist of survival, and when the conviction that things are never what they seem was conjoined with man's normal suspiciousness and instinctive tendency to portray any opponent as a villain and to espy an enemy in anything unpleasant, the result was a deeply atavistically paranoid approach to life.

To brand Tudor England as paranoid raises a problem. The urge to generalize, to present the muddle of history in some coherent form, is essential to the historian's craft. Unfortunately, the habit of mind that seeks to impose stereotypes and common characteristics upon the fragments of the past is all too often the victim of its own clarity and at the same time bedevilled by bias born of the need to be selective. Consciously, or worse unconsciously, historical data can be rigged, words misrepresented, events given anachronistic importance, and evidence taken out of healthy, normal context. Sixteenth-century advice literature was paranoid, but it is well to ask what else could be expected? What child has not regarded his parents as being ridiculously suspicious and told them not to worry? What privileged social group has not sensed the presence of the unwashed multitude, snapping at its heels, envying its wealth, and seeking to destroy its political power? What moralizer has not deplored the depravity of mankind and society? What collection of quotable precepts for human behaviour has not had its share of pessimistic and paranoid maxims? And what centre of political power is not eaten with suspicion and filled with secret enemies, back-friends, and flatterers?

The warning is well taken. Nevertheless, the conviction that organized and deliberate evil stalked the kingdom was not simply cant carefully edited to intensify its paranoid effect and unique to the articulate pens of obsessive parents, fanciful schoolmasters, and depressing moralists. Paranoia in the sixteenth century appeared in two other areas: in the conspiracy theory of human behaviour that was imposed upon all political activity and in the depiction of evil in all its perverted fascination, which was presented upon the Tudor and early Stuart stage.

The Conspiracy Theory of Politics

Politics in the sixteenth century was not a rational, socio-scientific 'game' populated by Ringeresque 'types' and governed by hypotheses about the predictability of social behaviour and institutional function. Instead, it was a moral encounter between good guys and bad guys struggling upon a forum designed and sanctioned by God. Those who held authority were legitimate in every sense. They were enlightened by divine grace; they administered only what was just; they were open and sincere; they knew the right and sought to enforce it; and they invariably spoke for the overwhelming majority of God-fearing, right-thinking people. Those who were on the outside resided in total darkness. They were motivated not by public good but by private profit. Only in the sense that they represented the Antichrist did they possess group identity; otherwise, they were a collection of wrong-headed individuals, allied in their greed, who were seeking to overthrow the established order, not to improve or reform it. They were private, conspiratorial, and totally illegitimate. They were the enemy who sought nothing but discord. 'Let us see', asked Nicholas Breton early in the seventeenth century, 'where is the fault, what is the cause [of disunity], and why it should take place? In God? No, he loveth unity. In the King? No, he would have a union. In the subjects? No, they would be obedient to their King. In the godly? No, they would be obedient to God's will. In whom then? Surely in none except in some private persons or some private causes, to some private ends.'[100]

Ninety years earlier Sir Thomas More had come to the same conclusion: political rebellion and social turmoil were the work of wilful individuals bent on personal maliciousness and gain. Sir Thomas was committed to the conspiracy theory of history,[101] and when asked to investigate the evil May Day riots of 1517, which modern historians explain as being the result of rising prices, instinctive dislike of aliens, and a natural tendency to blame foreigners for domestic economic distress, he discovered 'that all that business of any rising...began only by the conspiracy of two young lads that were prenticed in Cheap[side]'. According to More, their 'ungracious invention', whispered into the ears of silly London apprentices and ignorant journeymen, caused an upheaval that ended 400 Londoners in prison and at least one on the scaffold, and to Sir Thomas's outrage the 'lewd lads', like all true *agents provocateurs* and conspirators, 'fled away themselves and never came again after' the rioting began.[102] More was incapable of thinking in terms of modern theories of mob psychology, class identity, or economic determinism and, had he or anyone else in the sixteenth century known the expression, More would have argued that the incident was the work of 'some pathological agitator'.[103]

Once the Reformation broke out, conspiracy took on more sinister and far more cosmic proportions, but nevertheless the conviction prevailed that heresy and its even uglier stepsister sedition were the product of tiny groups of conspiring individuals determined upon private profit. Despite the extraordinary speed with which Protestant ideas spread and their obvious association with the basic economic, political, and psychological needs of the century, More and most of his society continued to view the religious upheaval as the work of a handful of evil men and women set upon corrupting innocent but, alas, gullible subjects.[104] Few religious or political leaders ever asked why the Reformation was so attractive, except by way of disparagement and scorn: the licentious doctrine withdrew the yoke of restraint and good order from all who sought to do evil, stripping humanity of its responsibility to live charitably, humbly, and obediently. It catered to every kind of greed — to the covetous landlord who wanted to work his peasants harder by cutting down the number of holy days (holidays), to the gluttinous servant who wished to eat meat on Fridays and during Lent, to the lustful priest who hoped to marry his harlot, and to the licentious husband who desired to live in bigamy.[105] There was nothing legitimate about the movement and, for Sir Thomas, Protestantism remained the work of 'pot-headed apostles', a handful of dissembling brethren who went about the country changing their names and spreading the poison of discontent — an active conspiratorial, untrustworthy minority scheming to overthrow the moral majority. The aim, he warned, of these conspirators was not what they claimed — to gain recognition, to achieve toleration, and to reform legitimate abuses. Instead, it was the plundering of the clergy, the destruction of the nobility, the subversion of the commonwealth, and the total destruction of society for their own benefit, and he told the parable of 'Tom Truth' whose lands were claimed by a 'wiley shrew'.[106] Tom, overconfident fellow that he was, believed that the justice of his cause was so obvious that no court would decide against him, and he assured his lawyer that 'all the whole country knows it, the matter is so true and my part so plain'. His subtle enemy, however, 'for lack of truth...put all his trust in craft' and forged himself false evidence, bribed the sheriff, and arranged for a rigged jury. When the case came to trial, negligent Tom brought no witnesses into court and left his deed box at home, and consequently Truth in its innocence was overcome by Evil in its cunning.

The language of debate lends itself to paranoid fantasizing, and More and his chief polemical rival, William Tyndale, did not hesitate to indulge in paranoid hyperbole. A conspiratorial approach to human affairs was just as central to Tyndale's thinking as it was to More's. Tyndale viewed the Catholic doctrine as a diabolically clever simulation of the true faith on the part of the Antichrist, whose ability to counterfeit God's word was the source of his power and attraction. When confronted and defeated by divine truth, the Antichrist would steal off the stage 'for a season' in order to disguise himself anew and would then 'come in again with a new name and a new raiment'.[107] Tyndale in good paranoid style gave Mistress Rose of Rome high marks for satanic rationality and organization, for he was certain Catholics had spies in every parish, 'in every great man's house, and in every tavern and ale house. And through confession know they all secrets, so that no man may open his mouth to rebuke whatsoever they do, but that he shall be shortly made a heretic.'[108]

Catholic or Protestant, conservative or reformer, each side depicted the opposition as a small band of evil men and women dressed in the cloak of conspiracy and carrying the dagger of sedition. Each group attributed to the other Mephistophelean powers of destruction, calculated cunning, and dissimulation. Stephen Gardiner, the wily Bishop of Winchester as Protestant reformers described him, thundered in March of 1546 against those 'abandoned men, the very dregs of humanity' who, 'putting on the semblance of virtue. . . and a theatrical mask of piety, want to appear to be vigorously banishing vices and renewing and restoring religion'.[109] A year later, he warned against the anabaptists who, he claimed, were seeking 'to overthrow this royal power and get rid of kings'. He was not, he said, imagining or feigning the danger, and if 'someone should say that I am fearful, suspicious, prophesying, or auguring ill from my own imaginings in a manner not permitted by charity', or that 'it is not necessary or expedient to talk of these matters' because all commonwealths have 'some corrupt and unhealthy members' who do but small harm, 'this I shall assert': it is 'not only what must be looked to at the present moment which is to be considered. . . but what has been at any time or what can possibly be in the nature of things'. Do not wait, Gardiner urged, until it is too late. Although he did not know the future, he was certain that 'if something happens, something will follow'.[110] The Bishop's logic, from the paranoid perspective, is impeccable — nothing happens by chance and everything has a consequence.

Stephen Gardiner's approach to the enemy was matched by friend and foe alike. His master, Henry VIII, admonished his ambassador to Rome not to believe a word that traitor Cardinal Pole said, for 'as such deceitful traitors be commonly hypocrits', their 'fair and pleasant' words must be distrusted because 'howsoever the head thereof be coloured, the tail thereof is always black and full of poison'.[111] The final irony of Pole's life was that he lived to be the target of an even more paranoid attack from the leader of the Church for which he had given so much. By the end of 1557 Pope Paul IV was 'convinced that Pole had been for years the mastermind behind a great conspiracy against the church', and that the Cardinal had been from the start a secret Lutheran.[112] Belief in conspiracy was not, as is sometimes suggested, a matter of being old-fashioned or ill-informed; it was built into the thinking of the age, and the act declaring Queen Mary to be of legitimate birth dismissed the entire Reformation as the work of 'the malicious and perverse affections of some, a very few persons', for 'their own singular glory and vain reputation'.[113]

Religious controversy engendered the most extreme fears, and Protestant John Bradford spoke 'nothing but that I know perfectly', when he avowed in 1554 that Spanish papists were determined on massacring all the 'godly youth of England' and at the very least were planning to drive them into exile or sell them in slavery to the Moors.[114] James VI of Scotland was equally earnest when he assured his young son that he should never trust Puritans whom 'neither oaths or promises bind', and who breathe 'nothing but sedition and calumnies, aspiring without measure, railing without reason, and making their own imaginations . . . the square of their conscience'.[115] When James coined the *bon mot* 'No bishop, no king', he was simply applying Gardiner's logic — 'If something happens, something will follow' — to the dangers of Puritan control of society. But the most revealing example of the paranoid style of thinking was the encounter between Cardinal William Allen and William Cecil over English policy towards the Catholics, in which both men developed the conspiracy theory of politics to its fullest.

During the late 1570s and early 1580s a relatively cold, but nevertheless intensely ideological, war between resurgent Catholicism and English Protestantism was heating up. The international struggle — involving a crippled and divided France, a rebellious Netherlands, a commercially restless and aggressive England, and a Spanish colossus fed from the wealth of the Indies — was becoming entangled in a religious ordeal, in which God's Englishmen fancied themselves as predestined to slay the papal dragon and destroy Philip of Spain, who had elected himself as the chosen instrument and champion of militant Catholicism. What alarmed the English government was the fear that Catholicism was winning the war for Christian souls, not simply in Europe where the Counter-Reformation was in full swing, but also at home in England. No one knew exactly how many Catholics there were within the kingdom — the guesses ranged from one-third to two-thirds of the population — but the exact number mattered little as long as Catholics kept their religious opinions to themselves, placed allegiance to their Queen above loyalty to Rome, and turned a deaf

ear to the siren voice of conscience, magnified a hundredfold by
Jesuit and seminary priests who were stealing into the kingdom
to encourage the weak and admonish the apathetic.

As the decade of the 1580s advanced, however, militant, international, and papal Catholicism seemed to be luring more and more
English subjects away from their obedience and duty to the sovereign.
The old Church was no longer disorganized and leaderless, and
when Edmund Campion arrived in the country in June of 1580,
the government, in a panic, passed legislation to force, by heavy
fines and threat of imprisonment, English Catholics to conform
to the established faith. And the Council declared all-out war on
what was regarded as a papally financed and inspired fifth column
— the underground Catholic clergy recently reinforced by Jesuit
and secular priests trained at the English seminary college at Douai.
These storm-troopers of the Counter-Reformation were in the eyes
of the government a military élite, although paradoxically it described
them as 'a rabble of vagrant friars...running through the world
to trouble the church of God'.[116] Presumably they had been sent
to depose England's Protestant Deborah and to publish the Pope's
tyrannical bull of excommunication, blessing and urging rebellion
and treason.

In 1583, partly as a propaganda move, partly to defend itself against
the Catholic accusation that the government was conducting a heresy
hunt, the Council issued a manifesto directed against 'certain stir-
rers of sedition', denying that Edmund Campion and his kind had
been tracked down and executed for their faith. Written by William
Cecil and entitled *The Execution of Justice in England,* the treatise
starts off with a blanket affirmation of the conspiracy theory of
history. 'It hath been in all ages and in all countries a common
usage of all offenders...to make defence of their lewd and unlawful
facts by untruths and by colouring and covering their deeds...with
pretences of some other causes of contrary operations or effects,
to the intent not only to avoid punishment or shame but [also]
to continue, uphold, and prosecute their wicked attempts to the
full satisfaction of their disordered and malicious appetites.'[117] A
band of 'hell hounds', trained in seminaries designed 'to nourish
and bring up persons disposed naturally to sedition', had 'under

secret masks' crept into the kingdom to stir up the politically and economically malcontent of the land. 'Like hypocrites they colour and counterfeit' their true aims with professions of Christian religion, but in fact their purpose was to lead a conspiracy aimed at murdering the Queen and massacring 'great multitudes of Christians'. God, however, had been merciful and had, 'for all their secret lurkings', given 'His handmaid and dear servant ruling under Him' the means to discover and punish these 'sowers of rebellion'. 'For their practices and conspiracies both abroad and at home against the Queen and the realm', and 'for no other causes or questions of religion', they had been condemned and executed as traitors.

In language that would have done justice to Pastor Wine and his outraged and moral majority, Cecil warned that words could be just as dangerous as swords and that misguided intellectuals were the 'seedmen of sedition'. 'Let these persons be termed as they list: scholars, schoolmasters, bookmen, seminaries, priests, Jesuits, friars, beedmen, romanists, pardoners, or what else you will, neither their titles nor their apparel hath made them traitors, but their traitorous secret motions and practices; their persons have not made the war, but their directions and counsels have set up the rebellions.' This group, although it pretended to keep its fingers bloodless, was in fact weaving a vast spider's web of treason and was conspiring to shed the blood of all the Queen's faithful subjects, turn the country over to foreign invaders, and disinherit 'all the nobility, the clergy, and the whole commonality that would...defend their natural gracious queen, their native country, their wives, their children, their family, and their houses'.

The Catholic answer to Cecil's fulminations was not long in coming, and in 1588 Cardinal William Allen published *A True, Sincere and Modest Defence of English Catholics*, which like *The Execution of Justice* was quite incapable of picturing the confrontation in any other guise than an illegitimate conspiracy of evil in which deceit, the machinations of the enemy, and satanic legerdemain predominated. Allen's purpose was to deny that Catholic priests were traitors. They were instead God-fearing pastors seeking to bring men and women closer to God and to reconcile their souls and consciences to a Truth which had been guarded and preserved over the centuries by the Holy Church. Say what he might, Cecil was fooling no one when he maintained that the English government executed only traitors. Campion and the other holy martyrs were loyal subjects of the Queen, and it was sheer hypocrisy to pretend that they were not dying for their faith or that Elizabeth's government had not determined on the extermination of Catholicism.[118]

Having pictured the Catholic revival in England as a spontaneous upsurge of conscience on the part 'of the greatest number, noblest, and honestest sort of the realm', which no amount of treason legislation written in the blood of the martyrs could withstand, Allen then proceeded to indulge in one of the most blatant examples of the pot calling the kettle black. No more than Cecil could he conceive of a legitimate religious revolution or of spiritual needs that transcended Church or creed. The Reformation had been, in the eyes of the Cardinal, the work of factions, self-interested 'private' individuals who even after a generation in power numbered only 'the third man in the realm'. This band of wicked men had 'put their conscience, reason, and religion to silence to be partakers of the pleasures and commodities which. . .the world yieldeth by the spoil of infinite Catholics and honest innocent men of all sorts'. In the face of mounting Catholic fury, the 'politiques of our country, pretending to be Protestants', had become fearful lest they lose what they had seized and were now enjoying. Following their 'own deceitful wills and uncertain opinions', therefore, they were now seeking to maintain themselves in their vicious life by seducing the kingdom with a religion that flattered 'all fleshly lusts and turpitudes'. 'What conscience, honour, or equity', the Cardinal demanded, 'can be in this course?' The answer was self-evident: 'None at all, surely.'

'All the World's a Stage'

Dissembling, deceitful men and women determined upon corrupting and subverting God's truth and all public order walked the streets and attended upon the manifold weaknesses of humanity, and they were unanimously decried as the devil's disciples by monarchs and statesmen, parents and educators. But upon the stage the prince of villainy, free from the fear and disgust generated by his followers in real life, could be enjoyed by all. In the theatre the paranoid style assumed its most visible and colourful guise, and the sordid politics of distrust were translated into a cosmic drama involving Lucifer himself.

Scarcely a Tudor playwright did not try his hand at depicting and interpreting evil, and the Tudor stage crawled with brilliant artists of dissimulation, with false, self-indulging friends, and with masters of hypocrisy and intrigue, all of whom played upon and were themselves dark confirmation of the paranoia that beset society.[119] From the simple morality plays of the early decades of the sixteenth century, in which Vice appeared as a stock, two-dimensional personification of the black hordes of hell, to the demonic personality of Iago wrapped in the laughing, triumphant attire of amorality, Tudor theatre-goers recognized and delighted in the dramatic representation of the malice that they sensed in real life. Again and again the warning was voiced: 'All Vices mask themselves with the vizards of virtue' and 'borrow their names, the better and more currently to pass without suspicion.'[120] The deceitful faces of Satan were without limit as Isabella in *Measure for Measure* learned to her sorrow about Angelo who 'in all his dressings, characts, titles, forms, be an arch-villain'.[121] 'Avarice' in *Respublica* (1553), by disclosing that he travelled under a multitude of aliases,[122] played to his audience's conviction that only those who had something to hide changed their names (like the villainous Dr William Parry). One of Bishop Gardiner's most telling points in his debate against the Protestant reformer William Turner was the fact that Turner wrote under the pseudonym of William Wraghton.[123] And after John Lambert confessed during his trial for heresy in 1538 that 'my name is John Nicholson, although of many I be called Lambert', Henry VIII spoke for all loyal subjects when he retorted: in that case 'I would not trust you, having two names, although you were my brother'.[124] Only troublemakers sought to conceal their identity, and Iago's statement 'I am not what I am' was simply a brazen affirmation of what everybody already knew: 'The world descends into such base-born evils that forty angels can make four score devils.'[125]

'The black poison of suspect' was the essential ingredient in the hundreds of recipes for human destruction concocted upon the stage, and Marlowe's propaganda piece, *The Massacre at Paris* (1593), deliberately catered to the paranoid fears of a generation who did not have to be told that secret armies were being readied throughout Europe, that papal dispensations for murder were being issued cut-rate to every would-be assassin of the Queen, and that the citadel of righteousness was being infiltrated and undermined by Jesuit and Spanish demons from hell.[126] The playwright's message that a St Bartholomew's Day massacre of Protestants could happen in England found fertile soil in an audience that along with William Cecil was ready to see a conspirator and 'seditious seedman' behind every scholar and bookman. 'Cloaked Collusion' in John Skelton's *Magnificence* (circa 1513) avowed that 'division, dissension, derision' were his aims, and boldly admitted: 'I sow seditious seeds of Discord and debates.'[127] King Henry VIII in Shakespeare's play of that name is just as knowledgeable as the real sovereign when he tells Archbishop Cranmer 'your enemies are many and not small; their practices must bear the same proportion... You are potently opposed and with a malice of as great size.'[128] Malice and hatred, those same enemies of whom du Refuge in his *Practical Guide for Ambitious Politicians* warned, were the heart and soul of evil's assault upon the holy bonds of virtue, duty, and affection, which held society together. 'Politicke Persuasion' in *Pacient and meeke Grissill* (circa 1561) is happy to admit to the true viciousness of his personality when he says:

> The Scorpion forth will fling his poison to annoy,
> And passengers that pass him by with Venom to destroy,
> So those whose malice doth abound, thy sting dost now
>   prepare,
> To vex and harm those wightes [people], whose lives most
>   virtuous are.[129]

The Tudor stage villain for all his soliloquizing was no mere lecturer on the *modus operandi* of evil nor a raconteur of the endless traps that the devil baits with good intentions. Nor was he solely a sermonizer on the wages of sin and the consequences of human frailty and folly. In the hands of Shakespeare, evil attempted far more than simple garden-variety domestic and political malice or conspiracy. It is not enough for the great Shakespearean villains — Richard of Gloucester, Iago, bastard Edmund, and Aaron the Moor — to play on human greed by spreading their choking, corroding cloud of lies and suspicions or to make fools and dupes of mankind with their consummate playacting.[130] They are not of a kind with the simple-minded rascals who, in the words of the Marian statutes of 1554, sought to disrupt a 'happy, flourishing commonwealth' for the benefit of their own private 'glory and vain reputation'. They are instead infinitely more satanic in their ultimate designs. Nor are they victims of the tawdry human sins of vanity and pride. They are in no way trapped into evil by their own greed. Richard III is so inhuman and impervious to corruption that he does not even seek the comfort of the side-effect of his villainy — the achievement of immortality in the bloody annals of recorded time. Revenge, and the sins of resentment and envy, are for Iago little more than sops offered to Tudor conventionality and camouflages for his real motive: evil for its own sake. The true traitor needs no purpose; the act of destruction by itself is sufficient reason for his actions.

Shakespeare's evil operates at every level of existence, but in *Richard III, Othello, King Lear,* and *Titus Andronicus* it reaches cosmic proportions and builds upon the basic element of all paranoid thinking — the conviction that primordial hatefulness and concentrated evil stalk the universe in both time and space. The villainy directed against love, virtue, duty, and good order is so pervasive that it takes on McCarthyistic dimensions, and Tudor England would have had no hesitation in agreeing with the Senator that such infamous conspiracy 'deserves the malediction of all honest men'. Lucifer, as Henry VIII warned his brother sovereign of Scotland, 'can never be [the] author of unity but [only of] discord',[131] and when Satan assumed the face of a Richard III or an Iago, he was seeking to create that 'divinity of hell' in which he could attain what he desired most and what Tudor society feared most: the negation of all unity, order, love, and beauty.

Iago has yet another dimension that makes him infinitely more dangerous than either Vice — that composite personification of Envy, Avarice, Ill-report and all the other human failings found in the medieval morality drama — or the modern criminal enacting his sociologically and environmentally conditioned, and therefore predictable, villainy. Iago not only strikes at the root of God's universe; he is also the enemy incarnate who cannot be detected, and who hides behind the mask of service, loyalty and friendship. He is neither a rival nor a worthy opponent against whom honourable men such as Othello can guard themselves; he is instead the mealy-mouthed enemy who is out to corrupt and destroy for no other purpose than the malicious enjoyment of it. He is the 'eternal villain'. Consequently, *Othello* is much more than simply a study in the nature of evil; in a sense the play belongs to the advice-book genre: a dreadful admonition against innocent trust of a friend who is in fact the enemy in disguise — the viper amongst the flowers. Iago is sly, talented, and charming; nevertheless, Shakespeare makes it perfectly clear his villain should never have been trusted. It is blind trust, Othello's, Cassio's, even Roderigo's, that makes possible Iago's treachery. Almost to the very end, when the audience is itching to cry out and warn the noble Moor not to be so gullible, Iago remains 'my friend...honest, honest Iago'.

Fear and distrust, the commitment always to believe and look for the worst, the urge to extrapolate from the loss of a 'tail' the loss of a kingdom, and the desire to find proof of a conspiracy of demonic proportions were not the products of overwrought imaginations on the part of dramatists set upon selling their wares to gullible, unwashed, and uneducated audiences. Foreign observers also sensed the same cultural paranoia, and although neither foreign ambassadors nor casual visitors are to be overly credited with objectivity or profound psychological insights into the Tudor frame of mind, it is worth noting that Charles de Marillac, the French Ambassador between 1538 and 1543 to the court of Henry VIII, described that foxy sovereign as being plagued by 'distrust and fear'. The King, he said, 'knowing how many changes he has made and

what tragedies and scandals he has created, would fain keep in favour
with everybody, but does not trust a single man...' As a consequence, 'subjects take example from their prince, and the ministers
seek only to undo each other to gain credit, and under colour of
their master's good each attends to his own. For all of the fine words
of which they are full', concluded Marillac, 'they will act only as
necessity and interest compels them.'[132] Half a century later, an
Italian visitor was even more sweeping in his portrayal of English
paranoia. 'The English', wrote Andrea Trevisano, have no 'sincere
and solid friendships amongst themselves, insomuch that they do
not trust each other to discuss either public or private affairs together,
in the confidential manner we do in Italy.'[133]

In as much as Italy was in the eyes of all sixteenth-century
Englishmen a veritable sink of Machiavellian vices and Catholic
intrigues, it may be wise to accept with caution Trevisano's observations on things English. Nevertheless, the evidence gleaned from
advice literature, political manuals, theories of political and historical
behaviour, and dramatic productions clearly indicates that
Englishmen did in fact view their society from a deeply pessimistic
and paranoid position. The pervasiveness of this evidence and the
importance assigned to it is, of course, largely a matter of the dexterity with which the historian is able to dress historical reality in
plausible psychological attire. If cultural paranoia is not to be
dismissed as yet another example of the emperor's new clothes,
woven out of invisible thread which no amount of twentieth-century
Freudian preconditioning can make visible, it is necessary to expose
the cloth to careful inspection and to investigate what Clifford Geertz
has called the 'control mechanism' which governs human behaviour,
identifies and defines what a society regards as being important in
life, conditions its response to the mystery of existence, and deter-
mines how it will interpret the actions and interactions of its
individual members. Since signatures, be they psychological or
calligraphic, must be learned, the first step in making visible what
is in effect invisible is an analysis of how Tudor school children were
taught to organize and evaluate the human and cognitive worlds
around them.

III

'THE AGREEMENT OF ITS MINDS'

For it is an old saying. The pot or vessel shall ever savour or smell of that thing wherewith it is first seasoned.

Richard Whitforde, *A Werke for householders...*, 1530

The sixteenth-century pedagogue was a man with a mission, an intellectual warrior willing to take on those twin dragons of educational dissension — how to shape a child's character and what to teach him. Tudor schoolteachers aimed at nothing less than the total indoctrination and impregnation of young minds and tender hearts with the moral, spiritual, and social Truth. They were fully aware of the magnitude of such a task and insisted not only that the process had to start in the cradle but, such was the 'deceitful, cruel', and 'most proud beast' that lurked in every youthful breast, it also had to be a collective enterprise of the schoolmaster, parent, priest, and employer, heavily reinforced by the persuasion of the rod.[1] The sixteenth century operated from a twofold vantage point denied the twentieth century; although there was debate over the precise definition of the Truth, nobody denied its existence or the need to teach and enforce it; and nobody questioned that the goal of education was first and foremost to turn out virtuous and godly subjects and only secondarily to create individuals possessed of self-understanding and equipped with the technical means to realize their own potential. Characteristic of their species since the day that Socrates irritated almost everybody by boasting of an infallible method for improving the youth of Athens, Tudor educators offered a panacea for most of the social ills of the century. With an assurance that would make any modern child psychologist shudder, Thomas Starkey announced in 1533 that 'the good education of youth in virtuous exercises' is 'the chief key' for 'the remedying [of] all other diseases in this our politic body'.[2]

What for the twentieth century have become well understood and often ruthlessly applied sociological principles — political and economic might are far more effective when dressed in the respectability of religion and moral right, and submission bred of fear is less dependable than obedience owed as a moral duty — were for the sixteenth century largely instinctive social responses to the needs of the emerging nation state. Those responses found theoretical expression in the writings of educators who hopelessly underestimated the ability of small boys to defeat even the most inspired or brutally enforced curriculum and to remain their own self-centred and intransigent selves. Possibly at no time in human history has the gulf between the educational goals of society and the reality existing outside the classroom been so great. Nevertheless, Tudor educators, animated in part by Protestant zeal to direct young souls along the pathways of righteousness, in part by an over-conscientious reading of Plato's *Republic,* and in part by a naivety bred of inexperience, continued in their sublime optimism that the security of the state lay in the virtuous upbringing of its citizens.

Throughout the century, theorists reiterated the classical doctrine that 'the unity of the state exists not merely in its houses or its streets but...in the agreement of its minds'.[3] Juan Vives, the Spanish educator and tutor to Princess Mary Tudor, called upon the authority of Xenophon to argue that it is more efficient to prevent crime by raising virtuous citizens than by imposing furious punishments.[4] A kingdom, it was said, was 'held together by natural affection', every individual doing 'his duty to [the] other with brotherly love,...loving one another as members and parts of one body'.[5] To call your parents 'father and mother' was not enough; true obedience 'requireth also that you reverence them in heart and mind'.[6] Tudor society accepted the axiom that the loyal heart was a far more willing defender of the established order than the bended 'knee, whose duty is deceivable and false', for 'when children are well instructed in their childhood, they busy not their brains afterwards with innovations; they plot nor conspire not against their country, but submit themselves and cleave to the government of the higher power, as the bees to their honeycombs in winter'.[7] Put more succinctly, the aim of education was to make treason impossible by making it unthinkable. Schools were far more than 'seminaries of the state', as Ben Jonson called them. A more felicitous and accurate metaphor would be to say that they were the crucibles out of which were forged those links, lighter than air but stronger than iron, of affection and obedience that formed the chains of social hierarchy and political authority.[8] In the hands of Tudor political alchemists, might was not so much transmuted into divine right as moral authority was metamorphosized into the substance out of which power itself was created.

The optimistic conclusion that the child most likely to become a loyal subject was the one who 'in his tender age showeth himself obedient to school orders'[9] was a logical inference, which grew out of Tudor confidence in the interconnectability and natural order of all things, and the conviction that evil, if not tightly imprisoned during childhood, would burst its fetters and grow into a monster of wrongdoing and malcontent. Moralists and educators never wearied in their efforts to demonstrate the relationship between the physical microcosm of this life and the moral macrocosm of the universe. The base seed, they asserted, unbridled by a virtuous and disciplined environment, would inevitably produce the evil man; wantonness was sure to lead the mind into false opinions; corrupt manners in living would breed false judgment in doctrine; and ill brought-up children, who turned from God and His true doctrine, would shortly run from 'their lords, masters, and all duty', and in the end would defy 'their prince, country, and all due allegiance'.[10] Such conclusions grew naturally out of the prevailing 'want-of-a-horse-shoe' style of argument: 'Of slouth cometh pleasure, of pleasure cometh spending, of spending cometh whoring, of whoring cometh lack, of lack cometh theft, of theft cometh hanging, and there an end of this world.'[11] With such a logical progression as part of society's mental baggage, it made perfect

sense for Roger Ascham to argue that 'he that can neither like
Aristotle in logic and philosophy nor Tully [Cicero] in rhetoric
and eloquence will...mount higher to the misliking of greater
matters; that is, either in religion to have a dissentious head or
in the commonwealth to have a factious heart...'[12] Disobedience, wilfulness, pride, no matter how slight, led to greater consequences. 'If something happens something else will follow,'
Bishop Stephen Gardiner had said, and in 1545 Gardiner, as
Chancellor of Cambridge, perceived clearly the full significance
of undergraduate rebellion when students defied his edict banning
the 'new' pronunciation of Greek. He wrote to Dr Edmonds, the
Vice-Chancellor, that 'if fear is removed, what is there that can
command respect among those of less mature years, utterly irresponsible as they are at that period of life?' The issue was particularly
pressing, for in advocating the new pronunciation, 'they are learning to condemn and make light of my office as well as your
authority'. It might appear, he admitted, to be 'a trifling matter'
if taken in isolation, 'but it paves the way for more serious things'.
The bishop then concluded with the comment: 'The writer who
declared that innocence deserts a man step by step was not lacking in discernment, taking note as he did of a characteristic of
human nature.'[13]

Stephen Gardiner was convinced of the utter irresponsibility of
college undergraduates, and almost no one in the sixteenth century would have disagreed with him. The natural propensity for
disobedience within the child and young adult was bottomless,
and it behoved educators to correct that inclination as soon as possible. The moment of birth was none too soon, and Thomas Elyot
in writing his book on *Bringinge up of children* thought it 'most
expedient to take the beginning at their procreation'.[14] Although
some educators preferred the metaphor of soft wax ready to take
'the best and fairest printing', all scholars agreed that the child
was 'like an empty new vessel being void of all learning' but 'apt
to receive that which is first taught'.[15]

What gave concern, however, was the fear that the vessel itself
might contaminate the virtuous instruction and good learning
poured into it. Schoolteachers could not make up their minds about

the exact balance between environment on one side and heredity on the other.[16] Vice could slip in from a multitude of sources. The sins of the father could descend upon his offspring, for everyone knew that 'of an evil father cometh never a good child; of the evil raven an evil egg'. Bad blood, as James VI warned, could be transferred 'from the parents to the posterity'. And since the physical and moral worlds were interconnected, the child could suck 'the vice of his nurse with the milk of her pap', for 'out of our mother's teat together with the milk' flowed 'not only love, but also conditions and dispositions'. Children, therefore, could quite 'literally' become 'what they ingested'.[17] A good environment was equally important; it was not enough to seclude the infant from 'barbarous nurses'; he also had to be safeguarded from 'clownish playing mates and all rustical persons', for everyone agreed that children in general and small boys in particular were naturally inclined to corruption.[18] It was the cross that humanity bore that 'the good is more quickly forgotten than the bad'.[19] As a consequence, only by the most vigilant control of the child's total environment, guarded by a high 'wall of discipline', could the educator hope to curb the instinct of depravity, engrave the soft wax with virtue, and perform what Erasmus regarded as the chief 'duty of forming boyhood': 'that the little tender mind imbibe impregnations of piety'. Thereafter, the remaining goals of the Erasmian educational formula could follow with reasonable expectation of success — be taught to 'love and master liberal disciplines', be 'instructed in the duties of life', and 'from the very first beginnings of life...be habituated to civility of behaviour'.[20]

Training in piety and humility, as Erasmus suggested, was far too difficult to be left solely to the schoolroom. It required the total and continuous education of the young by every instrument available. Church and family shared responsibility with the school, and the authority and teachings of the master were expected to be constantly reinforced by those of the father and the priest. The obligation, thought pedagogue William Kempe, to keep a boy in 'good order even when he is under a school master...must after a sort be extended to everyone that hath the like charge or opportunity, be he tutor, governour, school master, or host'.[21] As a consequence, the child was brow-beaten, terrified, manipulated, cajoled, and disciplined from all sides. The father had to 'keep his fatherly authority over his child and jointly with the [school]master prescribe unto him a good order for manners and behaviour, for repairing home, for attendance, for diet, for apparel [and] for exercise in learning [so] that his behaviour be godly and honest, in serving God, in keeping His church, in humility towards his superiors [and] in humanity towards all men'.[22] And if there were trouble in the home, the Bible graphically reminded the young rebel of the unpleasant fate in store for those who defied parental authority: 'The eye that mocketh at his father and despiseth to obey his mother, the ravens of the valley shall pick it out and the young eagles shall eat it.'[23] The family was indeed 'a school wherein the first principles and grounds of government and subjection are learned',[24] and Thomas Elyot recommended that a gentleman's home be decked with 'painted tables and images containing histories, wherein is represented some monument of virtue, most cunningly wrought with the circumstance of the matter briefly declared'. Not an hour of the day, not a corner of the house was to be wasted in the endless indoctrination of right-thinking, whereby men, women, and children could be 'to virtue persuaded'. Even a gentleman's 'plate and vessels' should be 'engraved with histories, fables, or quick and wise sentences, comprehending good doctrine or counsels...'[25]

Wherever youth turned, the purpose was the same: 'to catechize him in religion truly, frame him in opinion rightly, fashion him in behaviour civilly...'[26] The courtesy books that glutted the sixteenth-century market were not simply manuals of etiquette; they were primarily instruments of social and moral indoctrination, designed to combine virtuous behaviour with minimal social graces. Hugh Rhodes's *Boke of Nurture and schoole of good manners for men, servants and children* united admonitions to 'dread God', 'rise early', 'pay your respects to your parents', 'do them reverence', and do not answer them back with such profitable tips on sound domestic observances as 'make your bed', 'clean your shoes and buttons', 'walk demurely', and 'wash your hands'. Added to these excellent instructions were such basic social prohibitions as 'don't dip your meat in the salt cellar', don't 'belch near a man's face',

'don't scratch your head at meals', 'don't blow your nose on the
napkin', 'don't spit over the table', don't 'break wind', and 'don't
look at what comes out of your nose'.[27]

The 'wall of discipline' did not stop in the home, and parental
authority could on occasion follow a young man to court, as the
17-year-old Marquis of Dorset discovered when he arrived in London in 1534. His mother, the Dowager Marchioness, sought to
keep a firm hand on the boy and teach him proper manners through
the aid of Master Thomas Cromwell, the King's Principal Secretary,
to whom she wrote asking him to stand *in loco parentis*. Wisely
accompanying her letter with a £10 tip, the formidable lady begged Cromwell that if he saw 'in my son Marquis either any large
playing or great usual swearing or any other demeanour unmeet
for him to use', to 'rebuke him thereof'. The Dowager, true to
her type, was more than a little pessimistic about her son's character,
and she concluded her request by saying that if her offspring had
'any virtue or grace' in him, he would remember Mr Secretary's
'goodness now showed unto him' and would be bound to 'him
at his further years of knowledge and discretion'.[28]

Lower down the social order the same training held true, and
another 17-year-old, John Smyth by name, who served in the
household of Lady Katherine Howard, discovered that escape from
home did not mean escape from discipline and absolute deference
to rank, not even under the most trying circumstances. He was
hurrying down the long gallery, balancing a covered dish of food
in his hand, when, in passing the seated Lady Katherine, he made
only a perfunctory bow. She immediately called him back and made
him kneel before her a hundred times. Despite Smyth's breach of
deference, he had been well brought-up, and he reported that 'such
was her great nobleness to me (then a boy of no desert, lately come
from a country school, and but newly entered into her service) that,
to show me the better how, she lifted up all her garments to the
calf of her leg that I might the better observe the grace of drawing
back the foot and bowing of the knee'.[29]

John Smyth was fresh from 'a country school', and under the
keen eye and swift rod of the schoolmaster he, as a member of the
'better part' of society, had been imbued with the essential attributes

of a properly brought-up young man: 'right opinion in faith', 'civility towards men and right judgment in behaviour'.[30] Since the primary aim of Tudor education was to implant those moral reflexes which would eventually lead to right opinion and judgment, and therefore to approved social and political conduct, educators gave careful attention to the formation of behaviour and thought patterns by means of early, prolonged, and total exposure to what was regarded as being morally right. Because all schoolteachers agreed with Plato that children could 'be moulded to take the impression one wishes to stamp' on them, and with Plutarch that 'the virtues of character' are tantamount to 'the virtues of habit',[31] they believed that tender minds should be bombarded from every direction with good examples. Not only must the master himself be of exemplary character but every educational instrument he used must also possess a moral meaning and teach a moral lesson. Books of rhetoric, exercises in grammar and translation, reading selections from the classics, and above all history were regarded less as vehicles of instruction designed to train and inform the mind than as vast reservoirs of morality, carefully selected and constructed to expose the young to examples of virtuous living and thinking.

Education was a holistic enterprise in which religion, the liberal arts, good manners, and citizenship were taught simultaneously, and no subject, not even arithmetic, was regarded as being devoid of moral meaning. Consequently, Robert Recorde did not hesitate to combine good-natured indoctrination in degree, priority, and place with instruction in fractions and percentages. The problem he posed for his students involved four men who were required to divide 'a booty or prize in time of war'. The value was set at £8,190, and 'because the men be not of like degree, therefore their shares may not be equal, but the chiefest person will have of the booty the third part and the tenth part over; the second will have a quarter and the tenth part over; the third will have the sixth part; and so there is left for the fourth man a very small portion, but such is his lot (whether he be pleased or wroth) he must be content with one-twentieth part of the prey. Now I demand of you, what shall every man have to his share?' Recorde clearly suspected that his students understood the morality better than the mathematics, for he has the student respond with the refreshingly honest answer: 'you must be fayne [willing] to answer to your own question, else it is not like to be answered at this time'.[32]

Thomas Wilson in his immensely popular *Arte of Rhetorique* (1553) also sought to combine sound technical training with instruction in the great chain of social and physical being that held the universe together. 'I know', he wrote by way of introduction to his discussion on the 'Disposition and Apt Ordering' of an oration, 'that all things stand by order and without order nothing can be, for by an order we are born, by an order we live, and by an order we make our end. By an order one ruleth as head and other[s] obey as members... Yea, by an order the whole work of nature and the perfect state of all the elements have their appointed course. By an order we devise, we learn, and frame our doings to good purpose. By an order the carpenter hath his square, his rule, and his plummet... and everyone according to his calling frameth things thereafter.'[33] Not only did an oration or schoolboy's theme have a correct order of interconnected parts but so also did the words of a sentence, and Wilson warned that some untutored writers 'will set the cart before the horse as thus: "My mother and my father are both at home," even as though the good man of the house wore no breeches or that the grey mare were the better horse'.[34] Like Stephen Gardiner, Thomas Wilson knew that out of tiny grains of correct word order and the pronunciation of the Greek alphabet were fashioned the mighty empires of right-minded men.

More patent in its purpose to inculcate good habits was the first-year text book in which children learned to translate English into Latin. There 6- to 8-year-olds read and translated such morally uplifting and often highly practical sentiments as 'help thy friends', 'abstain from other men's things', 'try thy friends', 'respect thy kinsfolk', 'follow concord', 'hate slandering', 'fear cozenage', and 'drunkenness makes men mad'.[35] More advanced students were presented with Corderius's *Dialogues* for translation into Latin. In one of the conversations between the master and his pupil, the iron fist of duty was only faintly concealed behind a light-hearted interchange in which the master begins by asking his student a series of questions about the day's sermon — did he attend, who preached, when did it start, what was the text, and what did the boy learn from it? All goes well until the last question, when the pupil confesses that he has learned nothing and can remember nothing. The dialogue continues with the outraged master asking:

Not so much as a word?
Nothing at all.
. . .
. . . Come, what was the reason why you committed nothing to memory?
My negligence, for I did not hear diligently.
What did you do then?
Now and then I slept.
So you use; but what did you do in the rest of the time?
I thought of a thousand fooleries, as boys are wont.
Are you so much a child that you ought not to be attentive to hear the Word of God?
If I were attentive, I might profit something.
What then have you deserved?
Stripes [a thrashing].
You have deserved indeed and that very plentifully.
I confess ingenuously.

In the end the pupil begs for mercy and promises to 'do my duty hereafter'. In return for such humility and deference to authority, the master forgoes the rod.[36] As an exercise in Latin translation, the dialogue may have been adequate; as a moral whip with which to chastize tender consciences, the exchange was a spectacular success, for there is no more tireless a custodian of the temple of truth, honesty, and obedience than a sense of guilt implanted at an early age. And should the child ever doubt the wages of sin, his imagination was jogged in a peculiarly artful fashion. In Robert Whittinton's Latin grammar schoolboys read as examples of the genitive construction the following vivid reminder of the fate in store for wrongdoers and traitors:

Upon London bridge I saw three or four men's heads stand upon
  poles.
Upon Ludgate, the fore-quarter of a man is set upon a pole.
Upon the other side hangeth the haunch of a man with the leg.
It is a strange sight to see the hair of the heads fase [fall?] or moose
  [mould] away, and the gristle of the nose consumed away.
The fingers of their hands withered and clung unto the bare
  bones.[37]

Of all the pieces selected for translation, *Aesop's Fables* were the
most popular, but here again the Latinizing was secondary to the
moralizing. 'Wherefore, in the teaching of them', Sir Thomas Elyot
wrote, 'the master diligently must gather together those fables
which may be most accommodate to the advancement of some
virtue whereto he perceiveth the child inclined, or to the rebuke
of some vice whereto he findeth his nature disposed.'[38] Erasmus
concurred: 'When the little fellow has listened with pleasure to
Aesop's fable of the lion and the mouse...and when he has finished his laugh, then the teacher should point out the *new*
moral.'[39] The same attention was given to those compilations of
historical, moral, and philosophical information, known as commonplace books, from which schoolboys of all ages gathered their
information, ideas, and authorities for their endless themes and
orations. John Brinsley recommended Nicholus Reusnerus's *Sym-
bola* because it was so 'full of most singular precepts and instructions concerning duties and virtues, and for framing and ordering
the whole course of our life, and managing all our affairs with
wisdom, safety, and commendations'.[40]

Commonplace books, brimming as they were with 'wise directions for all occasions of life', were still deficient in moral philosophy compared to history, the ultimate 'mirror of man's life',
which 'ought never to be out of our hands'.[41] History was valued not just as a light into the darkness of the future but, more
important, as a treasure-store of examples 'convenient for every
man...in his degree', displaying obedience and its virtues and
rebellion and its consequences.[42] No reading gave greater delight,

'imprinting a thousand forms upon our imagination'; no discipline was more profitable, warning us 'by the evils which have befallen others' and kindling the mind with 'an ardent burning desire of imitating. . . the most glorious attempts of the greatest and most excellent'; and no subject had such medicinal potential, helping those who studied history to recover their health. On one occasion, it was credibly reported that the reader of history was cured 'of a very dangerous fever'.[43]

This cannonade of moral injunctions had but a single target, the formation of a young man's character; for in a society where political and economic success depended on birth, kin, and patron rather than on innate ability, it was more useful to the child to be trained in a sense of propriety than to be possessed of a vast store of technical information. Character building for the offspring of a group that had walked off with the lion's share of the prizes in life involved three interrelated steps — discipline in obedience, exercise in self-control, and education in decorum.

Obedience, Self-Control, and Decorum

Habit, as Plutarch suggested, may have been the wellspring from which flowed an abundance of virtue, but the quality that Tudor England admired most, 'the principle virtue of all virtues, and indeed the very root of all virtues, and the cause of all felicity', was obedience.[44] William Baldwin began the third book of his *Morall Philosophie* with the axiom that 'all order standeth in ruling and obeying', and schoolmaster Mulcaster considered that learning 'to govern and obey' was second only to a proper knowledge of God Himself.[45] Ruling and obeying were the essential and inseparable characteristics of good order in an hierarchic society, where every natural leader was both master and servant. The child, no matter how exalted his lineage or great his inheritance, had to be drilled in a sense of subordination and humility and in the proper social symbols of deference — bending the knee, doffing the cap, and those words of address owing to one's betters — for service was a duty expected from all sections of society. 'Amongst what sort of people', asked one late-Elizabethan observer, 'should then this serving-man be sought for? Even the duke's son [is the] preferred page to the prince, the earl's second son attendant upon the duke, the knight's second son the earl's servant, the esquire's son [expects] to wear the knight's livery, and the gentleman's son [is] the esquire's serving-man.'[46] At some time in every man's life as well as in every child's career, Robert Cleaver and John Dod's moralizing on the fifth commandment was germane: the master of the household represents 'the authority of God, standing in Christ's place as His viceregent in the family'; and the main duty of the servant is to obey 'not principally because his master commands, but because God commands; not because his master's eye is upon him, but because God's pure eyes behold him, either to punish him if he do not his duty, or to reward him if he do it faithfully... As God bindeth the inferior to his duty, so He requireth that the superior be careful in his place and calling.'[47] Sir Philip Sidney pronounced a social as well as psychological verity when he directed his 9-year-old son to 'be humble and obedient to your [school]master, for unless you frame yourself to obey, yea and feel in yourself what obedience is, you shall never be able to teach others how to obey you'.[48] Every child had to learn the truth of William Gouge's description of sixteenth- and early seventeenth-century society: 'Even they who are superiors of some are inferiors to other[s]... Yea, God hath so disposed everyone's several place, as there is not anyone, but in some respect is under another. The wife, though a mother of children, is under her husband. The husband, though head of a family, is under public magistrates. Public magistrates are under another, and all under the King. The King himself [is] under God.'[49] The authority of a Tudor gentleman and landowner, as a Stuart civil and revolutionary war would eventually make manifest, was Janus-faced, looking upwards as well as downwards; authority, if it were to be effective, had to presume not only the willingness of inferiors to obey but also the existence of a higher power, be it noble, royal, or divine, to which deference was due.

Obedience went far deeper than a proper respect for parental and educational authority or learning from books of etiquette how to behave to adults, how to lay a table, or how to prepare my lord's chamber. It involved self-control: the subordination of will to reason or what the sixteenth century preferred to call the construction of a 'well-fashioned mind'.[50] Tudor educators based their instruction on three simple psychological premises — the existence within the child of will, reason, and imagination. Will was a baffling quality. Sometimes it was described as obstinacy, disobedience, and a natural proclivity to give way to one's appetites, and at other times as determination and will-power. The destructive influence of wilfulness could only be transformed into the constructive force of will-power when it had been severely disciplined by reason aided by imagination. Useful and necessary as imagination was, it was also viewed as an unreliable agent that was quite capable, unless carefully controlled, of leading reason astray.[51] Only in childhood could the Beast of Will be tamed, could fetters be placed upon Appetite, and Will be brought under command and made serviceable to 'religion, virtue, and honour'.[52] Such self-mastery was possible only if it had been preceded by self-knowledge, for no man could govern his baser appetites or place limits upon imagination without first understanding himself. Early in the century self-knowledge was viewed largely as a form of spiritual exercise, but by the century's end a more secular attitude prevailed — 'He is unmeet to rule others that cannot rule himself' was William Baldwin's stricture to his young readers, and Sir Walter Raleigh in his *Maxims of State* affirmed that 'a man must first govern himself, ere he be fit to govern a family; and his family, ere he be fit to bear a part in the government of the commonwealth'.[53] Self-control, no longer achieved through medieval mortification of the flesh but now developed through the doctrine of moderation, was the prescribed means to the 'well-fashioned mind'. The ultimate aim, according to the Earl of Northumberland, was the construction of that 'groundwork of tranquillity which will ever free us from hate, teach us never to love with passion, never [to] despair with disquiet, never to hope with folly, [and] never to sorrow with repentance...'[54] Reason, self-understanding, and moderation, these qualities could transform the rude personality of youth into the controlled, modulated, and rational character of manhood. Like the horse that had been 'well broken in youth' and had become a 'gentle and easy' mount, the sixteenth-century child had to learn the truth of Plato's warning that youth 'was not born for self alone, but for country and for kindred, claims that leave but a small part of him for himself'.[55]

What then of Renaissance individualism and self-identity, those much proclaimed badges of the liberated, creative, egocentric personality in which the century is said to have abounded? The answer has to do with decorum, which operated under a host of different aliases — seemliness, comeliness, decency, appropriateness, fitness. Next to piety to which it was closely related, decorum was the cardinal goal of Tudor education.[56] No concept was more central to character building and no word contained such a richness of meaning or breadth of application. Decorum was the knowledge, inculcated by strict discipline, virtuous example, and the development of good habits, of what was proper in relationship to 'the thing said or done, the end in view, the persons involved, the time and the place'.[57] Possibly no educational ideal has ever been so wildly optimistic in what it expected from both master and pupil, for decorum assumed that a suitable response existed for every conceivable situation and that it was possible for students to catalogue, learn, and apply the formula.

In education, decorum represented the triumph of reason over appetite. It was the ultimate achievement of the man who knew himself and had mastered himself according to a prescribed set of rules of thought and conduct. Such a man had attained John Colet's educational ideal of being able 'with good providence and discretion [to] see the where, when, how, why, or wherefore thou speakest, doest, or biddest any thing to be done'.[58] Applied to language, decorum meant that a privy councillor should not choose his metaphors 'from a dicing table', 'a justice of the peace draw his similitudes' from mathematics, or a divine speak the language of the 'bawdy-house'.[59] Society was expected to maintain at all times a harmonious balance between thoughts, words, and actions, or what Thomas Nashe meant when he wrote: 'Let our speech accord with our life.'[60] Decorum was the foundation upon which the study of rhetoric rested. Thomas Wilson's insistence upon a

proper order for structuring all themes and orations in accordance
with the order of the universe and his requirement that word structure conform to social hierarchy — the father precedes the
mother — were illustrations of the basic principles of rhetoric, first
sanctified by Cicero and thereafter endlessly repeated throughout
the intervening years. The function of rhetoric was obvious to all:
it was to consider 'what are the means suitable to produce a particular effect in relation to a particular place and time, having regard
to the particular speaker and listener'.[61]

'The decorum of place and persons, the seasonableness of time,
[and] fitness of opportunity', these were the building blocks of
propriety.[62] Sir Thomas Wyatt observed that 'times, persons, and
circumstance' were essential to 'knowing when to speak and when
to hold his peace'.[63] Roger Ascham urged his students to be
aware of the 'right framing of words and sentences...fit for every
matter and proper for every tongue'. James Cleland advised his
readers not to dispute 'with every man upon every light subject
but [only] in considering time, place, and persons...to answer
soberly'. Thomas Elyot described decorum as that 'majesty' which
is 'the foundation of all excellent manners'. The man who was
possessed of majesty, he said, had 'a beauty of comeliness in his
countenance, language, and gesture apt to his dignity and accommodate to time, place, and company'.[64] With pardonable if
somewhat blatant self-interest, John Bury, the sixteenth-century
translator of Isocrates' *Orations,* praised Isocrates as the model from
which we can 'learn how to behave ourselves to all degrees, and
how in all times and tempests also to dispose us. How to God,
how to our prince, how to our parents and kindred, how to our
friends, how to our enemies...' Everything in this reservoir of
moral philosophy teaches 'us to live either wisely or virtuously'.[65] Knowledge itself was the maidservant of decorum, for
information was pumped into young minds less to prepare students
for a particular career than to supply them with conversation suitable
for every occasion. The final educational product was the young
man whose 'manners in word, look, and gesture, as the time
requireth', had been 'ordered by measure'.[66]

Decorum went deeper than simply insisting on the necessary

politeness that enables strangers of different ranks to meet and converse on the basis of shared public signals or to communicate and
co-operate with one another without exposing 'their inner-most
secrets'.[67] Nor was decorum solely the ritualistic fancy-dress that
tricks the mind and senses into believing that menial service and
subordination to authority are not enforced responses to naked
power but are instead dignified and ennobling activities worthy
of all men and women no matter their rank. Above all else, decorum
was a style of thinking, a system of cognitive organization which
maintained that 'ill-doings breed ill-thinkings', and from 'corrupted
manners spring perverted judgments'.[68] Roger Ascham maintained that only an absolute mastery of words could prevent 'a
divorce betwixt the tongue and the heart', and he insisted that
the fate of Greece and Rome was sufficient proof of what happens
when language becomes deficient in decorum. 'Mark all ages, look
upon the whole course of both the Greek and Latin tongue and
ye shall surely find that when apt and good words began to be
neglected and properties of those two tongues to be confounded,
then also began ill deeds to spring, strange manners to oppress
good orders, new and fond opinions to strive with old and true
doctrines...'[69]

Style, wrote Raleigh, 'is the man', by which he meant a great
deal more than the 'spirit of perpetual dressing up' or reference
to the sumptuary laws of the century, whereby 'it was comely
that every estate and vocation should be known by the differences
of their habit'.[70] Raleigh was voicing the belief that the secret of
civilization was the ability to enact in an agreeable fashion that
role which God had destined the individual to play. George Puttenham concurred: 'The thing that may well become one man
to do may not become another.'[71] 'Walk', James Cleland
admonished his young noblemen, 'man-like with a grave civil pace,
as becometh one of your birth and age.'[72] 'For a king do like a
king' was Sir William Paget's advice to the Duke of Somerset
who, as Lord Protector, was expected to fill the seat of majesty.[73]
'There are', wrote the Earl of Northumberland for the benefit
of his son, 'certain works fit for every vocation; some for kings;
some for noblemen; some for gentlemen; some for artificers; some

for clowns; and some for beggars: all are good to be known to everyone, yet not to be used by everyone. If everyone played his part well that is allotted him, the commonwealth will be happy; if not then will it be deformed...'[74]

'Play his part well': no metaphor was so common in Tudor England as 'all the world's a stage', and the higher the actor's rank, the more public and demanding his performance.[75] James VI of Scotland, whose faults were legion but whose advice was invariably excellent, reminded his 4-year-old son of 'a true old saying that a king is as one set on a stage, whose smallest actions and gestures all the people gazingly do behold; and therefore...the people [who] seeth but the outward part will ever judge of the substance by the circumstances and according to the outward appearance...'[76]*

The purpose of Tudor education, it is often said, was to train the future servants of the state who, when 'called forth in the execution of great affairs in service of their prince and country', would 'be able to use and to order all experiences, were they good, were they bad, and that according to the square, rule, and line of wisdom, learning, and virtue'.[77] Roger Ascham's sentiments, which could be duplicated in the works of other educators many times over,[78] are sufficient evidence that Plato's admonition that children were not born for themselves but for their country was well heeded. But Ascham's words, although perfectly in accord with the principles of decorum, convey too limited a goal to the ultimate purpose for which the child's character was being framed. The aim of Tudor education was never career training in the modern sense. Instead, it sought to coach students in how to perform upon a public stage. Lord Herbert of Cherbury in the next century caught this theatrical flavour of the educational goals when, writing for the benefit of those about to complete their formal

---

*As usual his cousin Elizabeth of England expressed it better. 'For we princes,' she told a delegation of both houses of Parliament on November 12th, 1586, 'I tell you, are set on stages, in the sight and view of all the world duly observed: the eyes of many behold our actions: a spot is soon spied in our garments: a blemish quickly noted in our doings.' Holinshed, *Chronicles,* vol. IV pp. 933–35.

education, he argued that it was 'fitting to debate and resolve beforehand what you are [going] to say or do upon any affront given you, lest otherwise you should be surprised', and he concluded that once a young man had acquired from the study of moral philosophy all 'that wisdom and goodness which is requisite to direct you in your particular actions, it will be fit now to think how you are to behave yourself as a public person or member of the commonwealth'.[79] In other words, like any good trooper, you needed to know your lines beforehand, so as never to be surprised and always to be prepared to perform upon a public stage.

Central to acting is, of course, deceit, disguise, timing, and lighting. It is the ability to make things appear differently from what they actually are, to transform premeditation into artful naturalism and spontaneity, and to extract every ounce of credit and recognition from both the role to be played and the circumstances under which the performance is taking place. Thus in *The Courte of Civill Courtesie,* which possessed the optimistic subtitle *fitly furnished with a plesant porte of stately phrases and pithie precepts assembled in the behalfe of all younge gentlemen and others that are desirous to frame their behaviour according to their estates, at all times and in all companies,* it is not enough to act the role of a gentleman; you must also get credit for it. When a man of rank finds himself seated lower down the dining table than his station warrants, he is not to make a fuss about the insult; nevertheless, he must let it be known that he is aware of the slight but is letting it pass. The same decorum applies to the order in which a young gentleman enters a door when accompanied by an older but lower-born companion. He is instructed to back away and announce: 'I pray you go, for I love to follow the steps of mine elders.'[80] Role playing is a difficult feat, especially when it takes place before an audience of other actors, and Francis Bacon was probably correct when he wrote in his treatise on 'The art of rising in life' that 'it is hard to find so great and masterly a dissembler' who can 'carry on an artful and counterfeit discourse without some way or other betraying it'.[81] Nevertheless, role playing was what decorum demanded, and courtesy books, manuals of court behaviour, and texts on rhetoric catered to this need, for they were all 'essentially handbooks for actors, practical guides for a society whose members were nearly always on stage'.[82]

In a world beleaguered by ideological war and exposed to ill-understood economic forces that were making a mockery of time-honoured medieval notions about the proper association between birth, land, and political power, an all-out educational effort had to be launched to mass produce a socially acceptable pattern of cognitive responses by which personal behaviour could be integrated and co-ordinated into an ordered, ordained, and hierarchic society. The educational purpose then was not the self-fashioning of the individual in any modern sense, but instruction in how to live, think, and act that role suitable to one's station in life.[83] It was to supply the training, example, and information needed so that the young could fashion themselves, control their passions, and as adults enact the part assigned them by birth and circumstance.

In the tradition of Castiglione's *Courtier* and Giovanni della Casa's *Book of Manners*, most of the educational literature of the century attempted 'to fashion a gentleman'* in a self-conscious manner that would have been inconceivable in England a hundred years before, when creation and self-fashioning belonged to God and when man had to make do with divine grace as the sole path to self-improvement. But the sixteenth-century model for the fully self-fashioned individual remained highly medieval in one impor-tant particular: it was closer to a Platonic ideal, fixed, universal, and timeless, than to the nineteenth-century model of an inner-directed individual who. contrary to Donne's dictum, is an island unto himself, and who justifies his actions solely on his own identity

---

*Decorum applied to both sexes. Lady Jane Grey wrote that her parents insisted that 'whether I speak, keep silence, sit, stand, or go, eat, drink, be merry or sad, be sewing, playing, dancing, or doing anything else, I must do it, as it were, in such weight, measure and number even so perfectly as God made the world...' (Ascham, *The Schoolmaster*, p. 36). Early in the following century Margaret Hoby wrote in her diary that her 'father could not abide to see a woman light or unstable in her carriage, to hold her head one way, her hands another, and her feet a third...and her features disfigured by an evil countenance; but he liked a woman well graced, with a constant and settled countenance, and a good behaviour throughout all her parts, which presenteth unto all men a good hope of established mind and a virtuous disposition in her'. (*Diary*, p. 51)

and integrity. The sixteenth-century public man played a role, and as Richard Taverner wrote in *The Garden of Wisdom* in 1539, he was not to 'play with his sophemes and quiddities but fashion himself to the manners of men'.[84] In other words, he learns decorum. The goal of education, therefore, was fundamentally different from today's gospel of self-fulfilment, for the sixteenth-century ideal was lacking in the modern therapeutic ethos of learning to blend into the group, of cultivating a sense of team participation, of developing a sensitivity to others, and of discovering the 'real you', which presumably is better than, or at least different from, the socially indoctrinated and artificial 'you'. Sixteenth-century educators used many twentieth-century terms — self-knowledge, self-understanding, self-control, judgment making — but they supplied them with a very different meaning. What they sought was to present society with carefully prepared scripts or models with prescribed attributes that could be learned and enacted by an exercise of self-will and reasoning.

'Self', one's inner identity, could still be defended ferociously, but it was seen more in terms of the honour and reputation of one's role in life than as something generated out of ego. Indeed, when 'self' did become involved with the ego, it was universally condemned as pride. For Henry Peacham, pride was a cardinal sin; nevertheless, he pronounced that only two things were the true mirrors of nobility: 'evenness of carriage and care of reputation, without which our most graceful gifts are dead and dull'.[85] Tudor and early Stuart gentlemen would rather die than lose face, and next to the warnings and forebodings about the presence of malicious enemies and the unreliability of friendship, Tudor parents, moralists, and educators urged their young to protect their good names and be true to their stations in life. Decorum may have had a negligible effect on decreasing the total amount of violence in society, but it did harness and set limits to bloodshed and disorder. There was a proper time and place for violence, as part of the role being enacted. Fury itself was subject to decorum, and Samuel Rowlands informed his honour-soaked and aspiring young readers in *The Courte of Civill Courtesie* that 'as no man is disgraced by giving (of his courtesy) place to whom he list, so to have it taken from him by others being his right, is an abasement not to be suffered...'[86]

Artistry, acting, decorum, role playing then were the means by which society sought to restrict autonomy and increase behavioural predictability while at the same time permitting freedom of action, self-expression, and self-fulfilment. In a sense, after space had been reserved for country, for kindred, and above all else for role-playing, there may not have been any room at all left for 'self', except as it could identify with the role it had been assigned to play.

Assigning the proper role at an early age was crucial, for the higher up the social ladder, the greater the potential for successful treason, disruptive violence, and contagious malcontent. Therefore both pedagogue and magistrate concentrated their efforts upon the politically and economically powerful. Thomas Elyot in *The Book named the Governor* was explicit on this point: 'To the poor man mercy is granted, but the great men shall suffer great torments... The stronger...is the person, the stronger pain is in him imminent. Therefore to you governors be these my words, that ye may learn wisdom and fall not.'[87] Gently born lads, Henry Peacham informed his readers, undoubtedly 'ought to be preferred in fees, honours, offices, and other dignities of command and government before the common people', but the price for preferential treatment was heavy.[88] It entailed more and harsher education in order to curtail and discipline appetites and desires potentially dangerous to society. Inclination, aptitude, and even talent[89] were matters of far less concern to the schoolmaster than the social standing of the young mind to be trained in piety, obedience, and decorum. It was, as Elyot acknowledged, necessary 'to encroach somewhat upon the years of children and especially of noblemen that they may sooner attain to wisdom and gravity than private persons'.[90]

Tudor educators, of course, faced an inescapable dilemma. Their future masters obviously had to be trained in virtue, but even an elementary education — the ability to read, write, and to make rational judgments — can be a dangerous weapon with which to arm the intellect. Education shapes but it also opens the mind, and some sixteenth-century educators feared that too much knowledge in the hands of 'private persons' could lead to the very social unrest and discontent that schoolmasters sought to wash from the fabric of society.[91] The careers of Botolf and Parry, as the ruling élite were well aware, contained terrible examples that too much education too far down the social order could lead straight to treason. The only solution was to emphasize the civilizing and restraining side of education and to teach obedience, deference, and godliness appropriate to the child's station in life, and as far as possible to prevent education from becoming a device to short circuit those pillars of social stability and order — degree, priority, and place.

The underlying élitist orientation of Tudor education was expressed by George Puttenham in his *Arte of English Poesie* when he wrote that 'in every degree and sort of men virtue is commendable but not equally: not only because men's estates are unequal but for that also virtue itself is not in every respect of equal value and estimation'. Continence in a king, he argued, 'is of greater merit than in a carter', because royalty has the power to satisfy its appetites while those of base estate, lacking the means and fearful of the law, are 'not so vehemently carried away with unbridled affections'.[92] The well-born child carried a triple burden: he needed to be drilled vigorously in virtue, self-control, and decorum because he had greater occasion to satisfy his passions; being nobly bred, he was expected to achieve more; and heaviest of all, he had less excuse for failure.[93] Only 'sluggish minds live in corners and content themselves with private life, whereas very noble hearts ever desire to govern and rule' over 'the whole multitude'.[94] Willynilly the child had to be educated to lead, his sluggish mind excited with good examples, his appetites disciplined, and his imagination inflamed by histories of courageous deeds that 'maketh private men worthy to become rulers over others'.[95] The strains, physical and emotional, that a well-born boy suffered as he was coerced and cajoled into learning his leadership role in life are only hinted at, but the documents overflow with information on the curriculum that Tudor schoolboys endured from the moment they set off for petty school, aged six to eight, to be branded with the mark of superiority: a thorough knowledge of Latin.

'Small Latine and Less Greek'

Throughout the century the curriculum[96] to which children were exposed was the subject of increasing attention on the part of church and state officials who were seeking to establish quality, or more accurately, indoctrination, control over the entire elementary and secondary school system; especially the licensing of schoolteachers. By the second decade of Elizabeth's reign standardization of curriculum had been largely achieved, and even the informal sector of education — the household schools organized in the homes of the wealthy around my lord's son, his cousins, neighbourhood friends, and his father's wards – were being carefully scrutinized and their schoolmasters tested for 'soundness of religion'.[97]

At its most rudimentary and universal level, education in Tudor England had nothing to do with reading or writing, and everything to do with virtue, piety, and the soul's welfare, for every child as a minimum requirement was expected to be able to recite by rote the Ten Commandments, the twelve articles of the Apostles' Creed, and the Lord's Prayer, because it was felt that 'he that understandeth these three hath the pythe of all those things which Holy Scripture doth contain'.[98] The process of selection only began when the child took the next step and learned how to read 'the pythe' of Holy Scripture for himself. Entrance into grammar school was limited to those who had mastered these basic religious materials, and consequently, when children of both sexes entered petty school, they were confronted with instructional devices geared to teaching the rudiments of religion. The horn book, or wooden paddle, covered with a translucent horn, on which was written the alphabet, vowels, and syllables, also contained the Lord's Prayer and the words of the Trinity written as an exorcism to drive the devil out of young scholars.[99] The more advanced ABC was often combined with a simplified catechism. Henry VIII's primer, which came into use during the 1540s but was later replaced by the Book of Common Prayer, contained all the essentials of religious faith. From the start an English or English-Latin grammar was also required, and by mid-century arithmetic, or what was called casting accounts, had been added as a regular part of primary education. Writing was not always taught in petty school[100] — ink, paper, and quill cost money and often became part of the economic selection that determined if a boy went on to grammar school — but again the purpose of primary schooling was less to train children in the three 'Rs' than to bring them up 'in the knowledge of their duty towards God, their prince, and all other[s] in their degree'.[101]

Having learned to read his primer and passages from the Bible, and having mastered a certain amount of writing and possibly having been introduced to Latin grammar, the 'abcdarian', as the child scholar was called, was ready to enter the man's world of the grammar school where the process of selection took a giant stride by limiting secondary school education to the male of the species.[102]*

At the age of seven to ten the boy commenced the process by which he became not only a man but also a gentle-man possessed of the two essentials of his station — a thorough knowledge of Latin along with a nodding acquaintance of Greek, and extensive training in the queen and mistress of all the liberal arts, rhetoric. The process took from five to eight years, the norm being six years of strenuous and disciplined drilling, memorizing, and regurgitating from 6 a.m. to 11 a.m. with a fifteen-minute break for breakfast, and from 1 p.m. till 6 p.m. In the winter an hour was cut off at each end of the day to save on the cost of candles which the boys paid for themselves.[103] The first three years, or the lower school, presided over by an undermaster, were concerned almost exclusively with the mastery of Latin. The first grade was transitional; a child learned by heart the rudiments of English grammar but also began translating short phrases of English into Latin. Thereafter, greater and greater attention was given to the speaking, reading, and translating of Latin by means of Cato's verse maxims and Aesop's *Fables,* both edited and collected by Erasmus, and supplemented by selections from the Bible, especially Proverbs and Ecclesiasticus, the two books of Scripture most directed to shaping young minds by practical and moralistic admonitions about

---

*There were exceptions to this restriction, especially in the private household schools of the wealthy where the daughters of the well-to-do could and did receive a grammar school education.

how to get on in this world and the terrible consequences of disobedience.

If Erasmus dominated the lower school, Cicero ruled the upper, where students were introduced to the truth of Erasmus's statement that 'almost everything worth knowing has been set forth in the Greek and Latin tongues'.[104] For the final three years of their education under the direction of the headmaster, boys were immersed in the great classical philosophers, poets, and historians, were trained in writing prose and poetry, and were introduced to rhetoric, the art of persuasion or the 'artificial declaration of the mind in the handling of any cause, called in contention that may through reason largely be discussed'.[105]

Rhetoric, logic, dialectics — the words were technically distinct but by the sixteenth century had become almost interchangeable — were divided into two parts: *dispositio* or disposition, the organization of thought into coherent propositions and arguments; and *inventio* or invention, the discovery of material in order to amplify, adorn, and exemplify a particular topic, discourse, or theme.[106] A third division, which was limited to rhetoric in its oratorical sense, was *elocutio* or eloquence or style, which involved not only the ornamentation of language but also the expounding of the significance and meaning of both the written and spoken word.[107] Rhetoric, like decorum to which it was intimately related, was firmly grounded upon a slavish preoccupation with form and structure — every theme or oration, even of twelve to sixteen lines, had in most sixteenth-century manuals exactly five parts to it — and with style in which richness, variation, and profusion of words, images, metaphors, comparisons, and examples were, at least in theory, strictly regulated by rules of usage and propriety.

Cicero's *De Oratore* was the gospel from whence flowed all rhetorical knowledge.[108] His Latin prose became the model for every student to emulate, and his *copia* or copiousness, the ability to vary word structure and supply a cornucopia of illustrative and ornamental material with which to enhance and illuminate a subject, was demanded of every schoolboy's theme, letter, or oration. To achieve copiousness, students were first exposed to all that was stylistically pure, doctrinally sound, and ethically edifying in the

great classical authors, and then they were required to keep notebooks
or commonplace books of anecdotes, 'clever expressions and weighty
judgments', proverbs, 'names of well-known men of high birth,
famous towns, animals, plants, and strange stones', all plundered
from the prose and verse of their Latin readings, and organized either
generically or under such topics as love, family, honour, ambition,
and marriage.[109] For those boys who had difficulty deciding what
was memorable in what they read, or who could think of nothing
to write about, professionally collected and printed commonplace
books existed to aid them in their endless quest for *copia*. The pre-
digested source from which almost everybody stole was Erasmus's
compilation of quotable material, which in 1500 started off with
a modest 818 items but grew by 1508 to 3,260 entries designed
to stimulate thinking and adorn schoolboy themes and orations.[110]
This huge reservoir of copiousness had, however, serious drawbacks;
it was neither indexed nor organized by subject, and consequently
in the years following 1508 Erasmus and other collectors of wise
sayings were further digested down into commonplace books of
various lengths and on various subjects, and were finally translated
into English for the benefit of schoolboys with a shaky command
of Latin.

Consequently, when asked to write an essay, the young scholar
could discover a marvellously rich supply of ideas by turning to
the table of contents of a commonplace book possessed of the mind-
boggling and generous title: *The Welspring of wittie Conceites: containing, A Methode, aswel to speake, as to endight aptly and eloquently
of sundrie Matters: as (also) see great varietie of pithy Sentences, vertuous
sayings, and right Morall Instructions: no lesse pleasaunt to be read, then
profitable to be practised, either, in familiar speech, or by writing, in Epistles
and Letters*. Under the general heading 'the manner how we rejoice'
were useful subdivisions on 'health, of health recovered, of dignity
obtained, of dignity promised, of inheritance gotten, of goods gotten, of reconciliation'. There were also topics on 'how to wish or
pray' and 'how to lament or be sorry', which included among other
subjects sections on imprisonment, exile, and 'reputation lost'.
Under the category of 'how to advertise' the student had a rich
choice: 'to beware of errors, of traitorous dealings, of enmity, not

to fall into an evil opinion, not to speak amiss, to be circumspect in writing, to know himself, to administer justice, to conserve and maintain health'. Finally, if the schoolboy were feeling down on life, he could turn to 'how to blame, and what it is', and read: 'To blame is properly of the demonstrative kind... It comprehendeth in it all sorts of evil speaking, as to reproach, to find fault, to note, to disfame, to carp and rail at; also to reprove, but to reprove doth properly grow of love: on the contrary, to [blame] groweth commonly of hatred.' Then if he decided to write his theme on the evils of current manners, he was supplied with a number of suitable but varied quotations from approved classical authors to be incorporated into his essay: 'our country is spoiled and wasted through corruption of evil manners (Cic. Lib. 2)'; 'the doing of injury unto others is in two sorts, either by deceits or by force: the one, of which is the practice of the wolf, the other, of the lion, and both of them are most far from humanity (Epist. f 5)'; 'those things that are evil and filthy are always filthy, whether they be kept secret or made manifest (Diogenes)'; and 'who so is deformed of countenance and of evil manners, he doth naturally bring forth nothing but evil, like as out of one viper springeth another viper (Ecdorus)'.[111]

Young theme writers in search of copiousness required more than a sixteenth-century version of Bartlett's *Familiar Quotations* to help them. They also needed help in how to vary and enrich their word structure and diction, and early in the century manuals appeared offering clarification and illustrations of different types of figures of speech, especially the metaphor and the trope.[112] Finally, boys had to know how to utilize this abundance of literary, moralistic, and exemplative material, and they were often supplied first with Erasmus's *De Copia,* a relatively simple and generally lower school manual on how to achieve copiousness in phraseology, and then with the *Progymnasmata* of Aphthonius, the much translated and plagiarized fourth-century Greek rhetorician who presented the formulas upon which invention, disposition, and eloquence rested. Aphthonius supplied fourteen specimens of different kinds of theme writing, among which were examples of how to tell a fable, expand a proverb, write a rebuttal or defence, compose an essay on virtue or vice, organize a eulogy or defamation, write fiction, and marshal all the evidence first for one side of an argument and then for the other.

Composition writing entailed more than training in rhetorical organization and education in propriety so schoolboys would not 'wander from decorum or say unsuitable things'.[113] It also involved the development of two other talents prized by Renaissance educators — morality hunting and literary role-playing. What every child was expected to attain was the ability to expound at length upon the link between the universal principle and the concrete example, thereby extracting the moral meaning hidden within an event or statement. 'Of a truth', wrote Erasmus, 'from some single story...many themes may be drawn.'[114] Equally important was exercise in the art of manipulating words, ideas, and arguments to achieve a desired effect, particularly to dazzle the mind with various 'forms and fashions of speech'. Every word was studied and weighed for its metaphorical and symbolic as well as literal meaning; every sentence was scrutinized for its shape, balance, and design in accordance with the position or role the writer had assumed.[115]

Emphasis on copiousness and rhetoric resulted in the development of two conflicting traits. Early in life the child acquired a variety of magpie instinct, an obsessive desire to collect in copybooks and to memorize for some future use a mountain of phrases, images, examples, sentiments, and trivia, rather like the obsessive-compulsive personality who labours diligently to gather every bit of information about the relative standing of universities with some dim, but rarely obtained, purpose of going to the best.[116] At the same time, such profusion of knowledge and richness of expression had to appear natural and uncontrived. Therefore, the Tudor schoolboy worked equally hard at spontaneity and extemporaneousness, or what both courtesy books and textbooks called *sprezzatura*.[117]

Out of this crucible of rhetorical-Latinate education the final product, aged anywhere from thirteen to seventeen, that emerged was a young Prometheus whose soul had been preempted by society, whose personality had been bound by chains of decorum and role-playing, and whose mind had been seared for eight to ten hours a day with the importance of imitation, conformity, and obedience to the rules of rhetoric and the authority of the past. His brain had been packed with highly quotable and reproduceable wisdom encapsulated in a host of commonplace books, and he had been steeped in a rhetorical mode of thought that would henceforth dictate his response to life, colour his attitude towards friend and foe, and determine the way he organized the world around him. In brief, his grammar school experience had trained him in a paranoid style of thinking.

Education in Paranoia

The things a child carries away from school are legion — memories, habits, information, ideals, and social reflexes. Despite its rigours, Sir Philip Sidney recalled his grammar school days, if not with fondness, at least with respect, and he asked: 'Who is it that ever was a scholar that doth not carry away some verses of Virgil, Horace or Cato, which in his youth he learned, and even to his old age serve him for hourly lessons?'[118] Schooling instilled in Sidney the decorous rules of gentility and role playing, which he followed so consummately in living and dying, but it also served him with those 'hourly lessons' that Tudor gentlemen knew so well and sought to pass on to their descendants: appearances are not to be trusted, the enemy is close at hand, and conspiracy and evil fill the world.

William Wentworth, Walter Raleigh, Henry Percy and others who recorded their views on human nature and social relationships did not come by their paranoia either by accident or by the unique circumstances of their lives. Instead, it emerged like Athena fully armed from the head of the educational curriculum, which had shaped their thinking and which was steeped in paranoid literature and logic. Nor were Wentworth and his generation particularly original in the quality or content of the advice they offered the young. It was largely borrowed from Jeshua, the son of Sirach. The Wisdom of Sirach or Ecclesiasticus is seldom read today and rarely appears in the Protestant Bible, but along with Proverbs it

was the most important literary influence that shaped a child's
psychological development as he moved from the protective environment of the home into the larger and more dangerous world of
the petty and grammar schools. Ecclesiasticus was read in English
by schoolboys as early as seven or eight; it was translated into Latin
and back into the vernacular at ten; and along with the other books
of the Bible it was listened to every day at dinner and supper. Roger
Ascham regarded it and Proverbs as admirable devices for the 'brid-
ling of youth'. John Cheke recommended it to his royal pupil
Edward VI; Thomas Elyot thought both Ecclesiasticus and Proverbs to 'be very good lessons'; and there is overwhelming evidence
that Shakespeare was profoundly influenced by both books.[119]

Ecclesiasticus is the genesis of all advice books — a frank and highly
effective effort at conveying the wisdom of the father to his offspring.[120] Sirach starts with the approved acknowledgment to
God — 'All wisdom cometh of God, the Lord' — and then moves
immediately to the two matters uppermost in his mind: the duty
owed a parent by a child and the means of survival in a wicked
world. Parental authority comes from God: 'The Lord will have
the father honoured of the children', and the wages of duty are
clear: 'My son, make much of thy father in his [old] age and grieve
him not as long as he liveth.' Having admonished his offspring,
Sirach proceeds to anticipate what Tudor sons would hear so often
from their parents: 'Hear your father...and do thereafter that ye
may be safe.' On the subject of friendship, he is filled with gloom.

> If thou getteth a friend, prove him fast,
> And be not hastie to give him credence.
> For some man is a friend but for a time,
> And will not abide in the day of trouble.
> And there is some friend that turneth to enemitie,
> And taketh part against thee and if he know any hurt
>   by thee he telleth it out.
> And some friend is but a companion of the table,
> And in the day of need he continueth not...
>   . . .
> Depart from your enemies,

Yea, and beware of your friends.

Then follows a long list of 'do not's' designed to avoid trouble in a deceiving and unequal world.

> Strive not with a mightie man,
> Lest thou fall into his hands.
> Make no variance with a rich man,
> Lest he happen to bring up an hard quarrel against thee.
> . . .
> Lend not unto him that is mightier than thyself:
> If thou lendest him, count it but lost.
> . . .
> Go not to law with a judge
> For he will judge according to his own honour.
> Travel not by the way with him that is brainless lest he
>   do thee evil,
> For he followeth his own wilfulness, and so shalt thou
>   perish through his folly.
> . . .
> Take no council before a stranger
> For thou canst not tell what will come of it.

The world was a dangerous place, and it was Sirach's considered opinion that it was best always to stay away from anyone who had the 'power to slay'. If, however, contact had to be made with the politically strong, then he warned 'make no fault, lest he happen to take away thy life. Remember that thou goest in the midst of snares, and [walk exposed] upon the bulworks of the city.'

An understanding of the nature of politics and the dangers of power was not enough; it was also necessary to keep a sharp watch out for treachery.

> Bring not every man into thine house,
> For the deceitful layeth [in] wait diversely.
> Like as a partridge in a maunde [decoy basket],

So is the heart of the proud, and like as a spie that
    looketh upon the fall of his neighbour.
For he turneth good into evil and slandereth the chosen.
Of one spark is made a great fire:
And a ungodly man layeth wait for blood.
Beware of the deceitful,
For he imagineth wicked things to bring thee into a
    perpetual shame.
. . .
When thou wilt be good, know to whom thou doest it,
So shalt thou be greatly thanked for thy benefits.

After warning against treachery, Sirach turns to enmity.

Trust never thine enemy,
For like as an iron rusteth, so doth his wickedness.
And though he maketh much crouching and kneeling,
Yet keep well thy mind, and beware of him...
Set him not by thee, neither let him sit at thy right hand,
Lest he turn him[self], get into thy place, take thy room and
    seek thy seat.
And so at the last remember my words,
And be pricked at my sayings.
. . .
An enemy is sweet in his lips;
He can make many words and speak many good things.
Yea, he can weep with his eyes,
But in his heart he imagineth how to throw thee into the
    pit.
If he may find the opportunity
He will not be satisfied with blood.
If adversity come upon thee, thou shalt find him there first,
And though he pretend to do thee help, yet shall he undermine
    thee.
He shall shake his head and clap his hands over thee for
    very gladness,
And while he maketh many words, he shall disguise his
    countenance.

For a hundred pages and more, Sirach pours forth his wisdom in ever increasingly shrill strictures, interlocking paranoid caveats with excellent economic warnings about the inequality between the rich man and the poor man, heavy-handed advice that the father who loves his son will continually beat him, and counsel on how to behave at the dining table. What Tudor parents had to say to their offspring was essentially redundant; by ten years of age a son had heard it all and even translated it into Latin.

What the child learned from Ecclesiasticus was amply reinforced throughout his petty and grammar school years, for everything he read from Cato's couplets and Isocrates' orations to Richard Rainolde's *Foundacion of Rhetorike* and the multitude of collected aphorisms and proverbs from which schoolboys scribbled the substance, if not the form, of their essays, contained not only moral lessons but also practical warnings on how to protect one's self from the evils of this 'Wiley world'. Cato's distichs had been standard reading for centuries and could be had in endless critical editions and translations, which second and third year grammarians dutifully translated back and forth from English into Latin. There they found such rhyming counsel as:

Change not known friends for those thou doest not know;
Tried friends are sure, untried may not be so.

To all friends give freely of thy pelf [wealth]
But always duly mind the needs of self.

Observe what's past and what may next ensue;
And Janus-like keep both ways under view.

Deem soft cajoling speech an empty cheat;
Truth naked is, but flatt'ry cloaks deceit.

Praise not o'er much: one day's enough to show;
If he, oft claimed thy friend, is really so.

The final domestic warning, which was presumably lost upon 10- and 11-year-olds, may have been remembered in later life:

> Having a wife, be watchful of thy friend,
> Lest false to thee, thy fame and goods he spend.[121]

Often combined with Cato were the model letters and orations of Isocrates, whose examples of proper rhetorical style brimmed over with useful nuggets of advice about the human condition and with courteous but practical teachings on that Tudor favourite, friendship.

> Neither prove your friends with your annoyance; nor yet be ignorant of their conditions. And this you may do, if you feign to have need of them when you have no need at all; and commit unto them for great secrets, matters which may without danger be discovered. For albeit contrary to your expectation they bewray you, yet shall you not be endamaged thereby; and if they satisfy the trust and confidence you had in them, then have you a better trial of their manners...[122]

The schoolboy encountered further advice on friendship when he turned to William Baldwin's *Treatise of Morall Philosophie*, originally dedicated in 1547 to the 9-year-old Edward Seymour, one of Edward VI's schoolmates. Baldwin was just as sceptical as Isocrates: 'Allow them for thy friends that be as glad for thy prosperity as they seem sorrowful for thy misfortune: for there be many that lament a man's misery, that would envy to see him prosper.'[123] On the subject of the world at large, he was even more pessimistic: 'The world is so malicious that if we take not good heed to prepare against his wrinches, it will overthrow us, to our great loss and hurt.'[124]

Similar statements for use in theme writing and further confirmation that nothing was to be trusted were available in Nicholas Ling's *Politeuphuia, Wits Commonwealth*. Under the heading of 'vices

in general' and 'of deceit' in particular, young scholars were confronted with a cluster of highly quotable but profoundly paranoid
sentiments: 'Craft putteth on him the habit of policy, malice the
shape of courage, rashness the title of valour, lewdness the image
of pleasure; thus dissembled, vices seem great virtue.' 'Every vice
hath a cloak and creepeth in under the name of virtue.' 'A man's
look is the gate of his mind, declaring outwardly the inward deceit
which the heart containeth.' And finally, 'deceits are traps to catch
the foolish in'.[125]

Thoroughly conditioned in the inequities of the world and on
his guard against false appearances, the schoolboy would not have
been in the least surprised to discover in *The Welspring of wittie
Conceites* materials for writing an essay on 'traitorous dealing' that
included the warning 'take heed above all things to betrayings,
forsomuch as the hatred is universal which is even at your elbow's
end . . .' and under the heading 'Enemitie' the advice to: 'Take as
good heed as ye can that you foster not enmity near yourself: for,
as long as men shall live upon earth, so long will enemies
remain.'[126]

These cautionary sentiments could be reinforced with the
authority of no less an educational giant than Erasmus himself,
who in Richard Taverner's translation of the *Adagies* counselled
his young readers to 'trust no man unless thou hast first eaten
a bushel of salt with him'. Erasmus also had an unusual, if practical, interpretation of the Biblical exhortation to love thy neighbour.
Assuredly, he said, this did not require us 'to communicate our
secret counsels and the affections of our heart to all men alike. . .
It is wisdom in prosperity when all is as thou wouldest have it,
to fear and suspect the worst.'[127]

In a more practical, if no less paranoid, vein, the grammarian
had at his disposal Richard Rainolde's translation and adaptation
of Aphthonius's manual of rhetoric, in which he could read, as
an example of an essay based on a fable, the story of the shepherds
and the wolves.

The wolves on a time persuaded the shepherds that they would
join amity and make a league of concord and unity. The demand

pleased the shepherds, [and] forthwith the wolves requested to have the custody of the band dogs because else they would be as they are always, an occasion to break their league and peace. The dogs being given over, they were one by one murdered and then the sheep were wearied [attacked].

From this brief beginning Rainolde fashions a six-page treatise on political and social morality, in which he starts by arguing that originally wolves received their unpleasant personalities from a man of particular lupine quality who, for his manifold sins, was turned into a wolf by the gods and consequently became the father of the species. Mythology leads Rainolde directly into political pedagogy, and he lectures his young readers strenuously on the important role which the prince, his councillors, and the nobility play as shepherds of the commonwealth, and the need to obey, serve, and honour them. The discourse ends with a triple warning to beware all who come bearing gifts. 'Wolves, under a colour of friendship and amity', are compared to men who, 'under a feigned proffer of amity', seek their own profit; 'dissimulation in mischievous practices' is said to begin 'with friendly words' but 'end perniciously'; and the final conclusion is that 'feigned offers of friendship are to be taken heed of and the act of every man [is] to be examined, proved, and tried'.[128]

The Tudor grammarian had firsthand knowledge of the need to beware false friendships and the operation of 'dissimulation in mischievous practices', for he was surrounded by spies. Early in his educational career he learned that even a comrade could not be trusted. Indeed, the lesson was built into his exercise books, and in Petrus Mosellanus's *Paedologia* (1518), which was read and translated by almost every young scholar including Henry VIII and Edward VI, students received instruction in the realities of school life. Julian and Damian are conversing in one of those dialogues so highly approved by medieval and early modern pedagogues.

JULIAN: Today each one of us is compelled to pay the penalty

for all the offences he has in any way committed during the
entire week.

DAMIAN: Can the instructors know what we have committed?

JULIAN: In some way they find out everything so that nothing
can be concealed from them.

DAMIAN: How so? Are they skilled in divination?

JULIAN: Not at all, but they find it out in another way, for
they give this duty to a few secretly chosen for reporting
and accusing us, their own comrades, so that we can't do
anything at all safely. It is always to be feared lest someone
of this kind of *Corycaei* [spy] may overhear us; and be the
wolf of the fable, present among us without our knowledge,
to report to the preceptor like a hired traitor.[129]

The spectre of the enemy was not solely the product of a long
exposure to fakery and evil in advice literature, decorum, role-
playing, and school life. It was also the unconscious result of an
educational system which structured and presented information
in a confrontational manner. The learning process itself conditioned
children to a paranoid style of thought, for it was predicated upon
the existence of an opponent, and it predisposed young grammarians
to think in terms of hidden meanings which had to be investigated
and revealed.

Sixteenth-century education was fundamentally verbal and
agonistic — Professor Ong would argue that it was in fact an exten-
sion, intensification, and partial distortion into the written word
of a much older medieval-classical oral conception and organization of knowledge.[130] Despite humanistic invective against dialec-
tical debate, which was so characteristic of medieval-scholastic
education, sixteenth-century rhetoric retained its essentially
argumentative emphasis. The competitive character of rhetoric was
deeply disturbing to many humanists, and Juan Vives stated that
dialectics and rhetoric were so 'contentious from their very nature,
being provocative of strife and obstinacy', that he thought 'a youth
of quarrelsome and contentious disposition', and inclined to evil,
should not be exposed to such a combative art lest he 'twist

everything to that end'. More serious, rhetoric promoted deception and trained young minds not so much in sound logic as in
how 'to dazzle and persuade' which, claimed the critics, was simply
'a way of making the worse [appear to be] the better reason'.[131]
Like decorum, rhetoric placed high value on appearances, chicanery, and the manipulation of ideas, words, phrases, and gestures
to achieve a desired and artful effect: what Thomas Wilson in his
Arte of Rhetorique described as 'a privy twining or close creeping
in to win favour...called insinuation'.[132] No one was more
dangerous than the actor-rhetorician who could cover 'craft with
eloquence'. Unfortunately rhetoric was the queen of the liberal
arts, and Vives had to confess that it was 'the cause of the greatest
of the goods and evils of life'. He conceded that boys should be
'permitted to have slight contests on small matters of debate' so
long as the arguments did not 'grow to hatred and quarrels', but
boys with malicious minds and inclined 'towards acting deceit-
fully [should] be denied instruction in so dangerous a discipline'.

Since rhetoric by nature was a disputive discipline, argument
and confrontation — despite Vives's plea for moderation — understandably became the central feature of Tudor education. Essays,
according to Erasmus, should be exercises in contraries: what
students 'have persuaded, they again dissuade'; 'what you bear
into heaven with praises, that you hurl to the lower regions in
vituperating'; and 'what you have exhorted', you again decry. The
proper subject for a theme, therefore, had to be conceived in the
form of a debate: 'for letters, against letters; for riches, against
riches; for the monastic life, and against'.[133] Such subjects
required a child to take a stand and, since essays with two sides
were parcelled out to different boys, themes became written debates
that gave training in preparing for the full-fledged oration, which
was 'the capstone of the prose system'.[134] Further training was
achieved when boys of ten to twelve were required each morning
to debate in Latin before the class various points of grammar. The
formula for such classroom confrontations was carefully set, and
students were expected to follow faithfully the 'order and witty
conceits' of John Stockword's manual on the fundamentals of gram-
matical disputation. Asked to debate whether five declensions of

nouns were sufficient to cover all types without exceptions, Stockword gave his readers the following model in forensic decorum:

QUESTOR. My ability is not such that I can sooth your ears with a polite and elegant form of speech, nor is it my purpose to do so at this time. For the question itself demands exact proofs rather than rhetorical periods. Say then clearly, and without dissimulation what you think about the truth of this question.

RESPONDENT. The more briefly you speak, omitting circumlocutions, the more pleasing you will be to me and clearer, and I promise you, and engage to observe most heedfully, to use the same brevity in answering, as you in propounding. I say therefore there is nothing in this question that I would not dare to defend most truthfully and certainly.

QUESTOR. All is then well. I will anon cause danger to your forces, and I hope I shall so deal with you that it will soon appear to all how unequal you are to setting forth that which you have so rashly and boldly undertaken.

RESPONDENT. You err, and do not know me, my good sir, if you think you can put me to flight with your harsh words. You have, as it happens, a spirited adversary, and one whom you will not conquer as easily as you think. Were you Hercules himself, or stouter than Polyphemus, or more boastful than Terentian Thraso, I neither stand in awe of your forces, nor shall make light of the bombast in your words.

QUESTOR. Thus then I rise against the first question. There are many nouns which can be referred to no declension, therefore the first proposition is false.

RESPONDENT. The mountains labour, and a ridiculous little mouse is born...[135]

Francis Bacon had nothing but contempt for such empty infantile brains indulging in 'childish sophistry and ridiculous affectations', but schoolteacher John Brinsley had only praise for those argumentative exercises that, he said, improved a schoolboy's Latin, prepared him for disputations at the university and the Inns of Court, created 'audacity', and provoked young scholars 'to an ingenuous *emulation* and *contention*'.[136] No two words are more central to a rhetorical education, and headmaster William Hayne sought to encourage his students 'by sowing amongst them matter of all honest contention and laudable emulation' to 'excell one another...'[137]

A mind conditioned to an agonistic style of organizing, memorizing, and presenting information,[138] and to a polemical-partisan approach to knowledge, may, as Joel Altman has maintained, always 'look for at least two sides in every question', and thereby attain greater vision, 'making every man not only a devil's advocate but also a kind of microcosmic deity'. Or the educational system may, as Vives feared, breed hatred and malice. Or it may, as Walter Ong has argued, make the life of the mind more exciting because the intellect is 'framed in conflict'.[139] It may do all of these, but assuredly it does something more: it postulates the existence of an opponent who must be overcome. In fact, the aggressiveness and competitiveness engrained into the Tudor educational process suits well the capitalistic spirit and makes one wonder which was the chicken and which the egg.[140]

The possibility that partisan-argumentative thinking may have contributed to growing upper-class willingness to act first and ask questions afterwards has been suggested, at least tentatively, by more than one historian.[141] More important, however, is the relationship between cultural paranoia and the existence of a personality trained never to be neutral or objective and 'predisposed to approach any subject by taking sides'.[142] The mind that instinctively organizes information so that there is a right and a wrong answer, supporters and opponents, friends and enemies, suits nicely a political and social world that organized society into the defenders of right and truth on one side and traitors, malcontents, and conspirators on the other. Neither Tudor education nor Tudor politics had room for or respect for a consensus structure of politics or frame of mind.

Paranoia, in its insistence that appearances are not to be trusted and that events and actions contain a greater significance than meets the eye, is related to the rhetorical orientation of mind in one final way — the ability to speak and write at different levels of meaning. The mark of the master rhetorician was first, the ability to interpret, manipulate, and control his material, and second, an equal skill in ornamenting his thoughts with figures of speech that 'deceive the ear and also the mind'.[143] For the benefit of school children in need of an example of that quickness of wit so prized by the trained orator and writer, Erasmus and Sir Thomas More together composed a dazzling display of interpretative and forensic agility. In their translation of Lucian's *Tyrannicida* they give Lucian's story of the man who demanded a reward for having rid society of a tyrant, and they then proceed to reinterpret it. In the original tale the protagonist says that he entered the tyrant's palace, overcame his guards, killed the tyrant's son in hand-to-hand combat, and deliberately left his sword in the boy's body so that the father, when he discovered his son's corpse, would in his grief seize the sword and use it to kill himself. Events turned out as planned and the clever fellow now expected a reward for removing both the father and his heir. Erasmus and More, however, by rearranging the same facts demolish the man's argument and prove that, far from being a public benefactor, he was a common criminal and deserved death.

What actually happened was this: By good luck, you penetrated the citadel and chanced upon the son, who was alone and unguarded and in a drunken slumber. Him you killed. Fearing discovery, you fled, not even pausing long enough to pull your sword from his body. You hid in your house, trembling in terror until, hearing that the tyrant was dead, you suddenly stepped forward with your impossible fiction of being the author of his death and demanded the reward decreed for tyrannicides. You did not kill the tyrant, because you were afraid to try to do so.[144]

Skill in discovering the hidden truth behind the facade of words and appearances became even more important when the trained rhetorician was himself a master of verbal deception and double meaning. The ability to 'speak one thing and think another' so that 'our words and our meanings meet not' was essential to political survival, and according to George Puttenham, 'not only every common courtier but also the gravest councillor, yea and the most noble and wisest prince of them all' made use of *allegoria* and other figures of speech to dissemble their thoughts and protect themselves.[145] Anyone who has read Elizabeth's speeches to her Lords and Commons knows the truth of Puttenham's assertion, for the Queen was a master at 'speaking obscurely and in riddles' with 'a duplicity of meaning or dissimulation under covert and dark intendments'.[146] Gloriana was not only adept at verbal chicanery: she was also constantly on the look-out for it in others, especially in playwrights, whom she suspected of writing about those two prohibited subjects that so closely touched her person and prerogative — her marriage and the succession.[147] In March of 1565 the Spanish Ambassador wrote that he had been awarded a display of the Queen's talents at deciphering concealed allusions to her marriage when he had sat through a dramatic performance at court and had listened to Elizabeth's interpretation of what he saw.[148] Ten years later at Woodstock during a theatrical display put on for the Queen's entertainment and benefit, the hidden meaning of the performance was made manifest: 'If you mark the words with this present world or were acquainted with the state of the devices, you should find no less hidden than uttered and no less uttered than should deserve a double reading over...'[149]

Suspicion of the true purpose and meaning of words and the correct interpretation of events and outward appearances was in no way unique to the Queen. It was a national characteristic, bred in part of political necessity and in part of rhetorical training. Thomas Nashe complained that it was impossible for an author to mention 'bread' without it being interpreted as a reference to 'the town of Breden in the low countries'.[150] Shakespeare's 'Rape of Lucrece' was transformed into an attack on Sir Walter Raleigh

by 'readers, incurable in their search for hidden meanings', and
Willobie His Avisa was avowedly a rebuttal on the part of Raleigh's
political friends.[151] 'In short', to use the words of G.B. Harrison,
'the Elizabethan reader was accustomed to look for a hidden meaning in most of the books which he read.'[152]

The counsel and educational training that the Tudor schoolboy
received during his April years in the expectation of preparing him
for adult survival was unusual in two points. Unlike the advice
·books popular in the eighteenth and nineteenth centuries — the
Benjamin Franklin style of exhortation to be virtuous in the midst
of a corrupt and wicked world and to live up to the internal standards befitting a Christian and a rational human being — sixteenth-
century advice literature was obsessively absorbed with the existence
of evil and the intrigues of malicious people. It offered not only
endless paranoid warnings about the schemes of the wicked, but
also practical guidance on how to subvert their plots and distinguish
the true from the false, the real from the feigned. Even more
unusual, at least from a twentieth-century perspective, was the
enemy to whom the schoolboy was introduced. The enemy was
not simply an adversary, instead he was a villain. The opponent
in today's commercial and professional war for survival and for
economic and political success is just as dishonest, cunning, and
ruthless as his sixteenth-century counterpart, but he is not usually
pictured by parents and educators as being evil. Equally important, he tends to be portrayed as being epicene and faceless; he
remains in the minds of the young as an abstraction, chained within
the system itself and driven on by sociological imperatives and competitive instincts, which the economic structure itself is said to
generate.

In contrast, the Tudor schoolboy was prepared for a far more
personal and emotional, and therefore more paranoid, encounter,
because his enemy had a face, or more accurately a mask, which
might be the image of a business competitor, a political rival, or
even that of a friend or relation. The sixteenth-century enemy was
far more dangerous because he was so much more ubiquitous. Tudor
Englishmen did not live in a compartmentalized world in which
their business and public careers were divorced from their family

and private lives. What transpired in the country affected what happened at court; marriage, domestic affairs, religious convictions, and attendance at church, all had public overtones to them. In a society that demanded right opinions as a condition for right actions and which did, in effect, make windows into men's and women's souls, it was almost impossible to cast up barriers or to isolate one facet of life from another. As a consequence, the enemy, the spy, might be anywhere: amongst one's personal friends, in the midst of one's household, or in the ante-room of the monarch's privy chamber. No one was immune from his Iago because the unbeknown enemy could be hidden behind a dozen guises. The mask that evil wore made it much more difficult to detect and much more frightening to live with.

Whether such cultural paranoia should be viewed as a healthy and practical educational reaction to a society that was in fact a jungle of ingratitude and cut-throat political and economic competition, or whether the educational process itself, by generating a paranoid style of thinking, succeeded in modelling society in its own image, is impossible to say. In either case, the schoolmaster did not stand alone. The state of mind that converted the adversary into a personal enemy, the belief that a conspiratorial web of wickedness existed which magnified the most trivial and innocent remark and action into a grand design of infamy, the knowledge that hypocrisy, personal enmity, fakery, and conflict were the natural and normal order of the world, and finally the conviction that evil was possessed of the features of individual men and women and that malcontent, be it in the form of heresy, treason or economic malfeasance, was the fruit of personal sin, these were not solely the by-products of formal education. Instead, their roots went deep into the ideological atmosphere of society, and must be looked for in the cultural air the child breathed.

Formal education was not enough; good subjects had to be introduced to God's cosmos and ultimate purpose. 'Let the boys know that God is the Rewarder of all right actions; and that our minds and thoughts are manifest to Him, so that...they may become accustomed to do nothing for the sake of human gain, but rather for that divine and eternal reward.' The moral precepts that children learned in school were not to be read and forgotten but were to be 'chewed, digested, and converted into the substance of the mind'.[153] The process of conversion involved both an educational and cosmic encounter in which the exorcism stamped on every child's horn book — 'God the father, God the son, God the Holy Ghost, Amen' — was a crucial step in shaping his instincts and preparing his mind for God's eternal design in which order, harmony, unity, and love were for ever being assaulted by a conspiracy of evil organized by the hellhounds of Satan. The exorcism was necessary because even an innocent child was possessed of evil which had to be expelled. In the ultimate cosmic scheme of things, as in the affairs of mankind, paranoia prevailed as God and Lucifer struggled for a small boy's soul and in so doing augmented and confirmed the paranoid signature of Tudor England.

IV

TUDOR COSMOLOGY AND COMMONALITY

> There are some people and I am one of them, who
> think that the most practical and important thing
> about a man is still his view of the universe. We
> think that for a landlady considering a lodger, it
> is important to know his income but still more
> important to know his philosophy.
>
> G.K. Chesterton, *Heretics*

Tudor England believed firmly in the existence of evil in small boys
and in the necessity of exorcizing it. The twentieth century in contrast accepts the presence of normal psychological and glandular
imbalance in the child as he moves from adolescence into adulthood
and the need for society to be understanding and long-suffering
in the face of youthful wilfulness and deviant behaviour. Both
methodological assumptions, however, belong to that class of genera-
tional and cultural presuppositions that, in the words of Arthur
Lovejoy, ought 'to be traced connectedly through all the phases
of men's reflective life'.[1] Evil both in its moralistic sense of man's
persistent urge to do wrong and in its cosmic role in the eternal
duel between God and Satan was for the sixteenth century a palpable
and measurable reality which vastly magnified and reconfirmed
society's already highly developed paranoid traits. The devil's
signature was emblazoned across the entire Tudor cosmos and could
be encountered in every nook and cranny of the universe — even
in a child's heart — and Satan's conspiracy to undermine and overthrow the forces of divine order and love was a documented drama,
the truth and certainty of which could not be doubted.

If Lucifer today has lost his empire over the minds of men and women and his control over the operation of evil, his demise has had little to do with the advances of astronomy and the replacement of the Ptolemaic-earth-centred arrangement of the firmaments by the Copernican-heliocentric universe. Instead, it has been the result of the collapse of that venerable and atavistic habit of thought that views the cosmos as an interconnected and purposeful totality in which man, as God's unique creation, supplies the crucial link between the base mutability of animal and material existence and the divine immortality and purity of celestial life.[2] Nothing reinforced the sixteenth-century paranoid response with its faith in the logic of evil and in the existence of conspiracy so much as the presence of the devil's black intelligence. Satan was not simply the wanton destroyer of the good and godly; he was essential to the logic of God's creation. His very existence was predicated upon a rational universe of ordered and interconnected parts in which chance and coincidence were unthinkable, and every effect had both a moral and a logical cause.

The sixteenth-century cosmos,[3] according to the wisest and most accepted authorities, both classical and Christian, was born out of the peace and order imposed by God upon the boundless, timeless, shapeless 'eternal anarchy' of unformed matter in which the elements were in a perpetual state of war and confusion. Out of chaos God had forged a harmonious and rational system that was interconnected, hierarchical, and infused with moral purpose. This creative act was infinitely varied and exquisitely structured, with a primacy of ranking whereby every part instinctively maintained its appointed place and motion, and every element — fire, air, water, earth — was apportioned within the universe according to its worth and nearness to God. There was a place for everything and all things had their place. The Tudor heavens, therefore, were less an arrangement of astral space based on observation than an imaginative ordering of virtuous parts according to a divine design in which every division, be it spiritual, material, or animal, was related by a chain or ladder of existence which assured to the universe a tripartite unity: moral, physical, and spiritual. From the most sublime seraph guarding the throne of the Most High through the various grades of celestial beings down to the humblest living organism and the basest piece of matter, the holy bonds of concord and order held God's plenitude together in a hierarchy of innate nobility that guaranteed the rule of 'degree, priority, and place' throughout the cosmos. It was an indisputable astrological as well as moral fact that 'among the heavenly bodies . . . the nobler orbs' were raised the highest. Of the elements, 'fire, the most pure and operative', held the chief place; and within the animal kingdom the lion was 'king of beasts' and the eagle prince of the skies. 'Jupiter's oak [was] the forest's king'; the rose reigned as queen of the flowers; and of all the stones, the diamond was most valued. God had 'set degree and estate in all His glorious works', an arrangement 'beginning at the most inferior or base and ascending upward . . . according to the merit or estimation of the thing that is ordered'.[4]

The doctrine of primacy and plenitude bound the Tudor universe into a comprehensible and satisfying vertical totality. A web of interlocking correspondences held it together horizontally and supplied the sixteenth century with its most distinctive habit of mind. The frame of thought that organized perceptions and occurrences conceptually and that saw sympathetic associations or correspondences between events and ideas, which the twentieth century would insist bore no relationship to one another, was part of a cultural heritage stemming from the medieval past and beyond. From Thomas More to Francis Bacon, the age of the Tudors and early Stuarts instinctively tended 'to see similarities more readily than it did differences', and to assume the existence of a system of correspondences between the spiritual perfection of God and the heavens and the material imperfection of man and his physical environment. Although often baffling and mysterious and perceived only through the aid of analogy and allegory, sympathetic associations were as real as any more 'rational' cause-and-effect relationship. 'Nothing', wrote Francis Bacon, 'can be found in the material globe which has not its correspondence in the crystalline.'[5]

A world addicted to making connections on the basis of correspondences and which rarely thought in terms of generic classifications was to modern logical sensibilities hopelessly untidy in its rhetorical organization and wildly improbable in its social and political assumptions.[6] Erasmus's letter persuading a young man to marry is to twentieth-century eyes an attic of miscellany, but to Tudor schoolboys, who sought to emulate it, the epistle was a model of *copia* and structure in which 'the sky and firmament that...play the part of the husband' and 'puffeth up the earth' are linked both with the concubial laws of nature and mankind and with manliness, honour, and the obligations a young man owes his family and posterity.[7] Tudor sumptuary legislation whereby clothing was prescribed for different estates of society, the medical conviction that the complexion, colour, and habits of a patient revealed his inner temperament, and Henry VIII's stern admonition to his brother sovereign of Scotland to forgo the profits of sheep farming because such behaviour 'cannot stand well with the honour of his estate', were all based on the correspondence, not the causal relationship, of ideas.[8] The same sympathetic and cosmic logic lay behind Lord Hungerford's execution for treason in July of 1540 for having committed sodomy. To Tudor minds the link was clear: treason was a universal perversity; buggery was an unnatural act; therefore, buggery was treason.[9] There was for the sixteenth century always a hidden, sometimes symbolic, sometimes causal, connection and meaning which held the disparate parts of the universe together, thereby associating sodomy and sedition. 'The outward things', wrote William Baldwin, 'which the eye of man only beholdeth are but weak and uncertain tokens of the inward secrets.'[10]

The trick of mind that sees similarities, correspondences, and patterns of hidden meaning in widely diverse ideas and actions was reinforced by the rising tide of Neoplatonic thinking that captured the sixteenth-century's ontological imagination and transformed metaphysical abstractions into sensible and living realities. The Good, the Courageous, the Virtuous, and the Evil were for the Platonic mind not intellectual or moral classifications but God's eternal ideals, which had their shadowy and imperfect correspondence and similitudes on earth. Sin, in the sixteenth century, was far more than simple wrong-doing; it was a pulsating reality on a par with — but a terrible perversion of — those other ontological conceptions, love, justice, and duty, or those idealized social stereotypes so important to role playing: the honourable gentleman, the grave magistrate, the courageous soldier, and the perfect courtier whose portraits bedecked the long galleries of Tudor manor houses. It is no accident that Elizabethan portraits appear like so many heads of John the Baptist on ruffled platters, for the artist was hired not simply to preserve the individual identity and true features of the subject but also to commemorate his station in life by associating it with those expressions, costumes, and stances suitable to and corresponding to his social ideal. What was true for subjects was even more true for the Queen. Elizabeth was 'transformed into a kind of philosophical masque in which everything stood for some vast idea and nothing took place unburdened with parable'. Gloriana was Wisdom, Chastity, Beauty, Purity of faith, Peace and Safety upon the sea. Under the circumstances, it is not surprising that her portraits, though they change over time, are devoid of humanity and tend to be two-dimensional tabloids depicting the permanence and potency of majesty, not a faithful representation of the ageing process.[11]

A universe interlaced with correspondences and infused with divine purpose had by definition to be permeated with signs that either foretold or interpreted events on earth, for the Creator was neither a philosophical first-cause nor a dispassionate eighteenth-century clock maker, who stepped aside from His work and permitted it to operate without benefit of miracles, judgmental interference, or sense of responsibility. Divine indifference, benign or otherwise, was unthinkable. God did not sit 'as an idle Spectator'; instead He interposed 'Himself as a chief Actor on the theatre of worldly actions'.[12] The Lord was an activist, and although He might abide by His own laws of nature, He was nevertheless still Jehovah of the Old Testament, a 'consuming fire [and] ever a jealous God', who had cleft the waters of the Red Sea, had 'destroyed the seats of poor princes', and could still 'break the pride of your power' and 'make your heaven as iron and your earth as brass'.[13] The age of miracles had not passed. The miraculous was in no way regarded in its modern sense as a violation of the immutable laws of the universe; it remained as it had always been, simply an 'unforeseeable but not otherwise surprising' event.[14]

The Tudor cosmos had been made in God's image and as a consequence it was a highly active production, vibrating with moral meaning, filled with tokens and directional indicators, and overrun with a multitude of extraordinarily interfering agents ranging from the Creator Himself and the forces of His arch-enemy Satan to the legions of celestial citizens who inhabited God's heavenly mansion. When in October of 1532 Thomas Cranmer went on diplomatic mission to Germany, he viewed a magnificent astronomical display — a flaming sword and horse's head in the sky and a blue cross over the moon. 'What strange things these tokens do signify to come hereafter', he wrote, 'God alone knoweth.' Yet he was sure they did not appear lightly 'but against some great mutation'.[15] William Vaughan, almost three generations later and with the benefit of historical hindsight, knew exactly what such cosmic spectacles foretold, and he thought it meet to list those 'heavenly signs' that had taken place during the century. In 1500 a comet had appeared 'after the which followed many and strange effects' including plague and war in Germany. Eclipses and comets had been observed in 1506, 1514, 1518, and 1527 with consequences ranging from an outbreak of the sweating sickness in England to the death of the Emperor Maximilian in Germany. 'In the year of our Lord 1533 was seen another blazing star whereupon a little while after, King H. the 8 was divorced from his brother's wife.' Four eclipses occurred in 1544 with the inevitable results: England sent a fleet to Scotland and burned Edinburgh, and 'King Harry the eight went himself in person to France with a great army and conquered Boloigne'. 1572 was a particularly portentous year, for in 'the north a strange star, in bigness surpassing Jupiter, and seated above the Moon', appeared after which 'succeeded... the bloody massacre and persecution of the Protestants in France'. 1596 was equally active. Following the appearance of a 'comet northward', both Lord Chamberlain Hunsdon and Sir Francis Knowles died, and the Earl of Essex and Lord Admiral Howard 'burned the Spanish navy and sacked the town of Cales. Moreover, there continued here in England a great dearth of corn, with strange inundations of waters.'[16]

Not only did astral commotion and 'the planets in evil mixture' correspond to calamities, successes, and deaths on earth but also God could strike 'immediately from Heaven with his own arm, or with the arm of angels'. At the same time, He could buffet men 'with their own hands' and destroy them 'by the revenging sword of an enemy' or by 'the fist of His dumb creatures'.[17] God's judgment was everywhere — both in answer to prayers and in punishment for ill-doing. He warned 'men by dreams and visions in the night and by known examples in the day'.[18] He chastized transgressors of His law with bad luck, sickness, and sudden death; and Lady Margaret Hoby spoke for her society when she wrote in her diary that she 'neglected my custom of prayer for which, as for many other sins, it pleased the Lord to punish me with an inward assault'.[19] History itself was a gigantic and grisly moral commentary upon the wages of sin and the consequences of provoking God's wrath. That immensely popular collection of princely tales of wrongdoing, the *Mirror of Magistrates*, painted a picture of human treachery unsurpassed, if not in brevity, in tear-stained and lengthy regrets for the evils of this life which end in hell and God's retribution upon mankind. If there was a single certainty in Tudor society, it was the knowledge that God 'beareth the kiss of life and death', for 'nothing happeneth without Him which is the first and principal mover, either health or sickness, prosperity or adversity, riches or poverty'.[20] Every fortune, good or bad, of divine necessity had a moral cause, for, to adopt Keith Thomas's words, the 'implied link between misfortune and guilt was a fundamental feature of the mental environment' of the century.[21] The logic was devastatingly clear:

> Every sinner is subject to condemnation,
> Every man is a sinner. Ergo
> Every man is subject to condemnation.[22]

Divine providence was ubiquitous and absolute, and nothing separates the twentieth century further from the sixteenth than modern man's willingness, albeit reluctant, to accept the juxtaposition of two events as purely coincidental and not to rush to the conclusion that significant and coherent patterns exist within the operation of what are in fact fortuitous relationships. In an age when men searched for similarities in all things, and in a teleological universe where God played a dynamic role, coincidence was impossible. 'Search for the cause of everything', wrote William Baldwin, by which he meant not the modern scientific and myopic approach to inquiry — the study of what can be isolated and controlled — but quite literally 'the cause of everything'.[23]

The concept of coincidence in any society is difficult to accept, for it goes against the most fundamental and distinctive quality of the human species, the ability and need to impose rational order and control on chaos. The temptation, even in the twentieth century, to perceive a causal relationship between, for instance, the movement of Uranus in the heavens and the number of earthquakes on earth is overwhelming. It goes against every human instinct to dismiss such an alignment of astral motion and earthly disasters as an accidental and meaningless association of two unrelated sequences of events.[24] Should a houseowner step out of his home, slip on a banana peel and break his leg, two questions leap to mind: why was the banana peel located in front of the house in the first place, and what had the owner done to deserve his fate? The possibility that both questions are unanswerable and that there is no causal connection between the position of the peel and the person who happened to step on it, other than the coincidental overlapping of two quite separate occurrences in time and place, is alien to minds that require and see unity and purpose in the universe. Either the peel was placed at the doorstep by a human agent set upon harming the houseowner, or God in His infinite wisdom had permitted the arrangement of events because of some moral defect in the victim.[25]

The sixteenth century was highly susceptible to 'patterns of similarities', and it insisted that every natural disaster had to have a moral origin. The use of such terms as fortune and chance, warned William Baldwin, 'proceeded first of ignorance and want of true knowledge, not considering what God is, and by whose only foresight and providence, all things in the world are seen of Him before they come to pass'.[26] Margaret Hoby was quite certain that when Mr Bell fell from his horse and broke his leg, God was punishing the blasphemous young man for having profaned God's Church by bringing a horse to the font and 'christening him with a name'.[27] Chance was nothing but an appearance, the result of failing to discover William Baldwin's 'cause of everything'.

The Tudor cosmos not only possessed moral cohesiveness and divine accountability, it was also a geographic unit which was better mapped than most of the regions of man's terrestrial orb. The universe consisted of a series — the most popular calculation was eleven — of transparent, crystalline spheres upon which were attached the various astral bodies and in which resided the serried ranks of the celestial population. Around the core of the earth, the stationary and focal point, circled first the elements in their order of ascending merit — earth, water, air, and fire, where meteors filled the sky on a summer's night — and then the vaults of heaven: the moon, Mercury, Venus, Sun, Mars, Jupiter, Saturn, and the sphere of the fixed stars, all rotating about the earth in majestic progression every twenty-four hours. Beyond the view of human eyes came two more circles, the primum mobile which, though motionless itself, imbued the entire system with the necessary drive and desire to sustain its endless circular course, and finally the abode of God, beyond space, beyond time, beyond imagination, 'a circle whose centre is everywhere and whose circumference is no where'.[28]

Unlike its modern counterpart, the ancient universe was neither insensate nor inhospitable: it was filled with the warm light of the sun and the indescribably soothing music of the spheres, and it was inhabited by a celestial host divided into Seraphs, who stood closest to God; Cherubs, who included Dominations, Virtues, and Powers; and finally Thrones, the lowest of whom were the angels who on occasion appeared to man's eyes and interceded on his behalf in the eternal battle against the fiends of hell. Cosmic darkness and silence were mere illusions. The invisibility of sidereal inhabitants was no ground for disbelief in the reality of higher forms of existence; talk of divine indifference was nothing but the prattling of men afflicted with the curse of doubt; and any belief in the soullessness of the universe had to be the ravings of mad men and perverts. God's universe could only be like God Himself: ordered, rational, and purposeful.

Nobody doubted the immensity or complexity of God's creation. It was estimated that a stone dropped from the nearest star
would fall for one hundred years before reaching the earth, and that
a cosmonaut walking at forty leagues a day would take nearly 8,700
years to reach the summit of the sphere of Saturn, a distance of
approximately 380 million miles. The earth was nothing compared
to the vastness of the heavens, a mere 'prick in the middle of... the
greatest circle that may be made on the earth'. What the human
species was relative to the universe as a whole surpassed the imagination and led the twelfth-century philosopher Maimonides to wonder why man could 'think that these things exist for his sake, and
that they are meant to serve his uses'.[29] Man, however, had not
filled the empty voids of time and space with meaning only to have
them divorced from his psychological and social needs. Despite its
size, the inherited universe for most Tudor English men and women
remained profoundly animistic, anthropomorphic, and egocentric.

Man was a cosmic paradox. He was the heaven-descended master of the earth, 'the head and chief of all that ever God wrought,
the portraiture of the universal world' and a 'marvellous and cunning piece of work'.[30] Yet he was also 'nuzzled in sin', a monstrous and spiritually deformed creature 'subject to a thousand
discommodities' and 'void of beatitude'. Far from living in the place
of honour, he had been assigned to the cesspool of existence, 'the
worst, the deadest, the most stagnant part of the universe, in the
lowest storey of the house and the remotest from the celestial
vault'.[31] Man and his vile abode were victims of a double fall.
Lucifer for his insatiable pride had been cast out of heaven; Adam
and Eve because of their susceptibility to Satan's evil temptations
had been evicted from the ordered perfection of God's residence
and imprisoned in that sink of vice, death, suffering, and mutability
called earth, where not even the elements knew their proper place,
and life limped to its appointed end.

Devoid though he was of virtue, man was possessed of a surfeit
of imagination with which he more than compensated for his lowly
place in the eternal scheme of things, for he not only created heaven
and hell in the image of his own society and endowed nature with

his own intelligence, but he also placed himself at the most critical point in the great ladder of being. Man may not have been God's chief or most important creation, but he was His most unique, for man alone supplied the crucial bridge between the lower material and animal levels and the higher spiritual rungs upon which the entire progression depended. Man was 'a little world', not because he was 'composed of the four elements' but because he possessed 'all the faculties of the universe', especially and uniquely the gift, and therefore the responsibility, of free choice to do right or wrong, which, although not easy to reconcile with absolute divine providence, not even the most fervent Puritan totally denied.[32] Alone among the kingdoms of the universe, man's world was populated with creatures capable of reasoning and endowed with the miracle of birth. Only on earth were new souls created which could be claimed by God or Satan and over whom the forces of good and evil struggled. 'Man', wrote Bacon, if not the final cause, 'may be regarded as the centre of the world', for if he 'were taken away . . . the rest would seem to be all astray, without aim or purpose . . . and leading to nothing'.[33]

An egocentric view of existence, although it imposed a heavy burden upon medieval and early modern man not matched until his twentieth-century descendants acquired the means of genocidal self-destruction, was accompanied by the anthropomorphic conviction that heaven conformed to the rules of human society: the angels existed 'in marvellous and inconceivable numbers, because the honour of a king consists in the great multitude of his vassals and his disgrace or shame consists in their paucity'.[34] Even more anthropomorphic was the belief that hell was a perversion and grotesque caricature of all that was good and orderly in human life. In the hands of the devil, soft couches became beds of nails, loving endearments turned into loathsome embraces, and degree, priority, and place degenerated into the nine orders of hell over which the spirit of evil presided. Quite literally the cosmos echoed with the clash of highly corporeal abstractions: God took 'jealousy for His armour', 'uprightness for a corselet', 'unfeigned justice for a helmet', 'holiness for an invincible shield', and 'stern anger for a sword'. The heavens were a battleground where:

Well-aimed flashes of lightning will fly,
And will leap to the mark from the clouds, as from a well-bent
  bow,
And from a catapult hailstones full of wrath will be hurled.[35]

Much of the emotionalism of the century was related to this
animistic-anthropomorphic view of the world, where virtues and
vices were endowed with tongue, mind, and body, and Richard
Cox could tell his young pupil, Edward VI, to do battle with
Ignorance, conquer Captain Will, and curb Captain Oblivion.[36]
There is, Clifford Geertz has noted, an 'ingenerate tendency of men
to anthropomorphize power', and in the sixteenth century war and
diplomacy and functions of state took on human features which
could be directly and personally experienced.[37] War was not
viewed as a conflict of insensate social systems but as the clash of
heroes and villains, animated and accompanied by Hatred, Virtue,
Courage, Honour, Justice, and Evil. Despite Machiavelli, diplomacy
was still perceived far less as the delicate balancing of political goals
and economic means than as a dynastic encounter and spiritual clash
of right versus wrong. Institutional authority devoid of human
features and personal responsibility was almost unimaginable; and
few men in Tudor England would have had the courage to accept
the challenge of the vicar of Ticehurst who, when pointing to King
Henry VIII's image embossed upon a silver groat, asked: 'How
darest thou spit upon this face? Thou darest not do it...'[38]

Of all the personified forces that buffeted and beset the sixteenth
century, the image of the devil with his unholy band of vices, the
seven deadly sins, and his kingdom of demonic agents was the most
active, threatening to replace God Himself as the prime mover on
earth. His aim was not simply to thwart the successes of mankind
and purchase souls for hell. His speciality was the destruction of
all unity and love by sowing the seeds of discord and exercising
his greatest talents — dissimulation, seduction, and intrigue. The
devil was 'the father of liars and the chief author of deceit' who
sought to 'shatter every corner of the house of God'.[39] He walked
about the land 'like a roaring lion', leaving in his wake sickness,
failure, sterility, bankruptcy, and death, and although sceptics

endeavoured to remove him from nature, claiming that he had no power to raise the tempest and was only a symbol of the evil that resided in humanity as a whole, most sixteenth-century Englishmen agreed with the Essex clergyman who said that 'when there are any mighty winds and thunders with terrible lightnings...the Devil is abroad'.[40] The world as it had been from early Christian times was a perpetual battlefield in which the pious with God's battalions on their side fought 'with avarice, with immodesty, with anger, with ambition'.

Men's minds were for ever 'besieged, and in every quarter invested with the onsets of the devil', and that redoubtable spiritual warrior Lady Margaret Hoby happily reported that she had 'continued in bodily health, not withstanding Satan hath not ceased to cast his malice upon' her.[41] The military metaphor was peculiarly apt in this struggle against the forces of evil, for life itself was seen as a dangerous 'warfare' filled with enemies. The 'wise man forged upon the anvil of God's grace...the only weapons either to foil these enemies or withstand their never ceasing assaults'. 'Auxiliary soldiers' were needed to combat sin and had to be kept from mutiny. 'Guards' had to be maintained lest 'ambassadors and other impediments...obviate you in so dangerous a march', and provisions had to be made for your camp.[42] The reality of evil as a corporal and highly militant entity was as fundamental to Tudor England as the 'millions of spiritual creatures' that everybody knew walked 'the Earth unseen, both when we wake and when we sleep'.[43] The battle with Satan and his hierarchy of demons, Keith Thomas has written, was 'a literal reality for most devout Englishmen', and so essential was 'the belief in the personification of evil that the dogma' became an important argument 'for the existence of God' Himself.[44]

Lucifer and God were entwined in a duality from which neither could escape; moral conflict and rivalry were built into the cosmic system itself; and, when in the vastness of a universe that was an interconnected totality, good and evil clashed, they sent reverberations throughout the entire structure. God and Satan both interfered in the affairs of man. In a sense, they were conducting a titanic conspiracy, which was often obscure and difficult to follow but was generally devastating for mankind, who was for ever being punished with wind, storm, and personal disaster.

The cruelties, inequalities, perversities, and catastrophes of this world, complained William Baldwin in his *Treatise of Morall Philosophie,* were without end.

> Alas, alas, what a host of divers evil chances, how strangely they happen to us in this life! One bewaileth the loss of his children, his wife, and goods: another weepeth for lack of health, liberty, and necessary living. The work-man maimeth himself with his own tool...the gamer breaketh his leg in dancing, his stones in vaulting...or neck in wrestling. The adulterer consumeth himself with botches and leprosy. The dicer is suddenly stabbed in with a dagger. The student wrung continually with the rhewme or the gout. Who is free from the strokes and murder of thieves, or from the wounds, rapine, and slaughters of soldiers... Innocent men are oftentimes wrongfully punished, imprisoned, banished, and cruelly put to death: children are smothered in the cradle, fall into the fire, are drowned in the water, over-run with beasts, poisoned with spiders, and murdered or plagued with infection of the air...[45]

Neither the natural human desire to blame others for the misfortunes that befall us nor the knowledge that the universe was filled with purpose and linked by a web of correspondences to the world of man could tolerate the thought that such disasters could be devoid of meaning, mere flotsam and jetsam floating aimlessly upon the sea of misfortune. Nor was human conceit, although severely chastened over the centuries by the whip of Christian humility, ready to accept the vicissitudes of life solely on the basis of merit. A scapegoat was necessary. Rather than finding a failing — moral or otherwise — in one's self, it was far easier and infinitely more satisfying to look for the cause of life's catastrophes and personal failures in witchcraft, the evil eye, the interference of demons, and above all in the conspiracy of an enemy.[46]

Paranoia in the sense of the willingness to assume the existence of an outside agent endowed either with demonic powers to injure

or with rational cunning to lead the innocent and unwary astray
was part of the psychological signature of the age. It was an instinctive reaction to look for and, therefore, to find evil in whatever
shape it cared to assume. Such a response to life's calamities was
inherent in the mental habit that assumed the existence of the interconnectability of all things — buggery and treason, maledictions
and bad luck, wax images pierced with pins and political assassina-
tions, ravens and the approach of the plague,[47] dreams of the loss
of a tooth* and the death of a kinsman, the birth of Siamese twins
and the death of Edward VI,[48] and 'a blazing star' and Henry
VIII's divorce from Catherine of Aragon, culminating in the break
with Rome.

Man's Commonweal

'This inferior world' in which the descendants of Adam and Eve
had been destined to live obeyed the universal law of preeminence
which, according to William Vaughan, like 'light heat...issueth
down from the celestial essence and spreadeth itself through the
lump of this huge body to nourish all things under the moon'.[49]
As the sun was the 'principal minister of this celestial virtue, a monarch among the planets', and as every category — animate and
inanimate — in heaven and on earth recognized within itself a
superior, so kings and emperors were God's attested leaders among
men. It was written for all to read: 'God wills all subjects, [on]
pain of eternal damnation, to obey their princes.'[50] Divinely
ordained authority and merit, therefore, descended throughout the
ranks and estates of society, transforming the atomized anarchy and
'Babylonical confusion' of the human condition into a spiritual and
organic whole corresponding to the degree and order existing

---

* Thomas Hill, *The Moste pleasaunte Arte of the Interpretacion of Dreames* (1576) has five
pages on teeth: to dream of wax teeth meant 'a speedy death'; to have teeth of tin indicated
that shame and infamy would shortly descend; teeth of glass or wood portended violent
death; but dentures of silver indicated forthcoming wealth, etc. (fol. K v (pencil 76).)

throughout the macrocosm of God's creation. Society was no human contrivance designed to foster security and material well-being. Instead, it was as great a miracle and testimony to God's creative genius as man himself, and the metaphor so beloved of Tudor political theorists — 'a public weal is a body living' replete with all its organs and functioning as a biological totality — possessed an ontological reality that not only satisfied sixteenth-century fondness for similarities and correspondences but actually shaped political activity. It was part of and essential to the spiritual, physical, and symbolic unity of the cosmos.[51]

Within the prison of man's social existence on earth, evolutionary time stood still. True, the seasons and generations came and went, and the years marched by upon 'the inaudible and noiseless foot of time' in endless and uniform ranks. But change that is driven by some secret mechanism within the structure of life itself, whereby tomorrow becomes, if not an improvement, at least a transformation of today, was almost incomprehensible to a society that viewed 'this inferior world' as a fixed and eternal forum upon which man fulfilled his preordained role of generating those priceless souls for whose possession good and evil struggled. The caged, repetitive, and unswerving quality of history was caught by Sir Walter Raleigh when he wrote: 'Whoso will know what shall be, must consider what is past; for all worldly things hold the same course they had at first.'[52] The 'end of all government' was clear and unchanging; it was, as Henry Peacham informed his readers, 'the observation of laws' whereby 'might appear the goodness of God in protecting the good and punishing the bad...'[53]

Although divinely inspired, man's society was far from perfect — nothing 'in this inferior world' was — but it was suitable to man's nature and to the eternal scheme of existence. As part of God's creation, society could not be improved upon, for 'as long as each thing performeth only that work which is natural unto it, it thereby preserveth both other things and also itself'.[54] Consequently, when change occurred, it was seen as being retrogressive and satanic, a deliberate drawing away from God and an unnatural, indeed traitorous, act on the part of man. 'Let any principal thing', wrote Hooker, 'as the sun, the moon...or [the] elements but once

cease or fall or swerve...the sequel thereof would be ruin, both
to itself and whatsoever dependeth on it.' What applied to
astronomy applied equally to human society; the doctrine of correspondences required that any transgression by man of 'the law
of his nature' brought all 'manner of harm after it'.[55]

Partly because of the depressing corruptibility of human nature
and the necessary political presupposition that 'all men are evil and
will declare themselves so to be when occasion is offered';[56] partly
because society, being an organic and integrated unity, was peculiarly
vulnerable to the spread of evil and malcontent; and partly because
the sixteenth-century mind was conditioned to perceive in the loss
of a horseshoe the loss of a kingdom; the supreme social virtue
reiterated by every political theorist, playwright, educator, and minister was unity. It could only be achieved through a harmonious
submission of all estates to divinely ordained authority and a willingness on the part of each individual to fulfil his allotted function
within the social organism. The ideal, as Nicholas Breton wrote,
was 'one law, one love, and one life, one voice, one heart, and one
people'.[57] In the organic society, as in the human body, it was difficult to isolate evil and social disease or to conceive of limited political
or religious aims, let alone accept the good intentions of the agents
of change. No matter how small the disruption, men assumed that
it interlocked with something greater. Stephen Gardiner, when he
warned of student rebellion at Cambridge and perceived in such
'a trifling matter' the inevitable collapse of all social and political
authority, was making a cultural assumption. The logic was not
simply that 'if something happens, something will follow', but
more important that events will accelerate and something worse
will occur. The Bishop argued for exactly the same reasons that
the destruction of religious images by iconoclastic radicals 'containeth an enterprise to subvert religion and the state of the world
with it; and especially the nobility, who, by images set forth and
spread abroad...their lineage [and] parentage' emblazoned upon
family coats of arms.[58] In linking religious images with family
heraldry, Gardiner may simply have been making an astute observation upon psychological and cognitive habits of thought and their
relationship to social solidarity, but in so doing he was speaking

for an entire society that was unable to separate the parts from the whole or view events in isolation. When the Earl of Hertford in 1589 asserted that as the Puritans 'shoot at bishops now, so will they do at the nobility also, if they be suffered'; or when Archbishop Matthew Parker complained to Lord Burghley in 1573 that 'if this fond faction [of Puritans] be applauded to, or borne with, it . . . will be the overthrow of all the nobility'; or when James I succinctly quipped 'No bishop, no king'; they were expressing the instinctive response of the century to any form of change.[59]

Satan always presented his case piecemeal. Corruption 'creepeth in by little and little' and 'alteration and change' bred 'of light and trifling things' had dire and unexpected consequences throughout the entire realm. Therefore, it was essential 'to have a great regard of mischiefs and evils at the first budding, how small so ever it be'.[60] Thus, Nicholas Breton with perfect logic could write of those people who complained or wished for a change in this divinely ordained society that 'if thou be a man, and murmurest against God, thou art a Devil, if thou be a Subject and murmur against thy King, thou art a Rebel [and] if thou be a Son and murmur against thy Father, thou showest a bastard's nature'.[61]

The same paranoid leap to conclusions is evident in that strange Tudor governmental aberration, the determination to chase down every political rumour to what was always presumed to be its evil source.[62] Today we recognize that rumours need not have a source, evil or otherwise, nor do they necessarily possess a purpose. We are willing to accept the possibility that rumours grow, that in all likelihood they are corruptions, misunderstandings, and misapplications of what start as perfectly innocent remarks. The sixteenth century, however, inevitably assumed the worst: rumours emerged fully developed from someone's evil mind into which Satan had entered; for everyone knew, since society was a spiritual totality of interconnected organic parts, that 'every sin is conceived first in the heart, and afterward finished in word or fact'.[63] Rumours by definition had sinister origins, were evil in their purpose, and constituted a threat to society. The government was convinced that whosoever would 'be authors or settersforth of any such rumours, may appear rather desirous of sedition than of quiet and unity, and

may therein show themselves rather devisers how to put men in
trouble and despair...than how to reform that [which] is
amiss...'[64] Tale-tellers and 'counterfeiters of news', the government charged in 1534, went about only to 'extirp love, concord,
and quiet whereby any commonwealth flourishes, and to sow in
their place sedition, disorder, variance, and trouble'.[65] Four
generations later Francis Bacon was still quite sure 'that seditious
tumults and seditious fames [rumours] differ no more but as brother
and sister, masculine and feminine'.[66] Only potential traitors were
complainers and carriers of tales, and the truth or innocence of their
stories was no defence, as the bailiff of Exeter discovered to his horror:

> Good people, I am come hither to die, but know not for what
> offence, except for words by me spoken yesternight to Sir Stephen,
> curate and preacher of this parish, which were these: he asked
> me, 'What news in the country?' I answered, 'Heavy news.'
> 'Why?' quoth he. 'It is said', quoth I, 'that many men be up
> in Essex, but, thanks be to God, all is in good quiet about us.'
> And this was all, as God be my judge.[67]

'In our country', Sir John Mason noted in 1554, 'talking is
preparatory to doing',[68] and it made excellent sense to nip treason
in the bud by tracing the evil thought, no matter the cost, lest it
spread and corrupt the rest of society. As a result, in May of 1554
there began one of many long and generally fruitless rumour chases.

> One Lawrence Hunt of Diss came unto Robert Lowdall, chief
> constable, and told unto him that he did hearsay that the Queen's
> Majesty was with child, and that his wife did tell him so. And
> when his wife was examined before the said Robert Lowdall and
> others, she told him she heard it of one Sheldrake's wife. And
> when Sheldrake's wife was examined, she said she heard it of
> her husband. And when her husband was examined, he said he
> heard it of one John Wilby... And when the said Wilby was
> examined, he said he heard it of one John Smith, the elder of
> Cokkestreet. And when the said John was examined, he said

he heard it of one widow Miles, which came to his house and told it him two times. And when she was examined, she said she had heard it of two men but what they were she could not tell nor where they dwell... [69]

Before the authorities gave up the hunt, twelve people in all were interrogated and an inordinate amount of time expended on what the twentieth century would dismiss as a matter of little political importance. Who could possibly care that idle tongues were gossiping about whether or not the Queen was pregnant? Clearly Tudor England did. The fecundity of a reigning sovereign was an issue heavy with political and religious implications, and, more important, it was assumed that the gossip was being disseminated for a political and presumably malicious purpose. The evil intent, not the rumour itself, had to be scotched by tracing it to its source. The same paranoia was found in libel suits. The slanderer, even when his information proved correct, was punishable on the grounds that only an evil person would have spread the information in the first place. Indeed, the truth of a malicious statement only made matters worse, for an accurate allegation could prove to be more unsettling to the peace and security of the commonwealth than a false one. [70]

Rumours and treason, Bacon had written, were siblings. They shared a common parentage of evil that went to the root of the sixteenth century's perception of society and historic change, for no one in Tudor England doubted that 'the chief cause of all evils that happen to man is man himself, for...his greedy lusts and desires troubleth both himself and all creatures'. [71] The social organism was innocent, for it was only a host body, a container and stage necessary for the drama of salvation and damnation. If society displayed a weakness or malaise, the cause lay not in any sociological disfunction or imbalance within the social system itself or in any historical theory of glacier-like social drift based on economic and demographic change. There could be for the sixteenth century no record of society because history was composed of the actions of heroes, saints, and villains; history was a moral lesson and not a storehouse of evidence on which, *à la* Marx, to predict future change and progress. Nor could there be any real social analysis, for Tudor understanding of society was humanistic, animistic, and individualistic, not socio-scientific. Malfunction stemmed from 'humours corrupted' that had to be purged, from 'the mischievous malice of such men as be desirous to break the public unity', and from 'vices' that were the sole 'undoers of all commonwealths'.[72] The failings of society resided in man individually, not collectively. The health and welfare of society also depended on the virtuous thoughts and actions of individual men and women. 'Let the Prince be gracious,' wrote Nicholas Breton in his *Dialogue... Upon the Dignitie or Indignitie of Man* (1603), 'the Courtier virtuous, the Soldier merciful, the Lawyer conscionable, the Merchant charitable...the Labourer painful, and the Beggar thankful, and then will the Commonwealth of the world, be such a kind of heaven on the earth, that the very Angels of the heavens will commend the beauty of the world...'[73] No one thought it was necessary to reform a society that required soldiers or produced beggars, let alone lawyers.

Treason invariably started from within the traitor's evil heart. Sedition was the result of pride, envy and greed that drove men of weak character and evil disposition to look for a short, albeit dangerous, route to riches and power, and to embrace the devil. 'Whensoever we are out of our place and calling, Satan hath a fit occasion of temptation.'[74] Breton did not hesitate to describe the murmuring malcontent of society as a 'senseless wretch fretting in melancholy'. Why, he demanded, did such a complaining critic 'offend thy God, thy King, thy State, yea thy self, and thine own soul, with the wicked humour of Ingratitude which, grown out of Ignorance, bred in Envy, grows up in Ambition and shall die in Ignominy?' The answer was patent: his 'inhuman nature' fed only 'upon Evil'.[75] Sixteenth-century evil, be it personal or social, could not be the product of a thoughtless or mindless urge to act; the bureaucratic 'rule of Nobody', as Hannah Arendt has described it, where responsibility for wrong is diffused and dissipated throughout the group.[76] Playing a role designed and dictated by the system was essential to Tudor England, but the script was never allowed to become an excuse for evil; that responsibility rested solely with the individual, whose creator had endowed him with the central characteristic of his humanity — freedom to choose between right and wrong and, therefore, to assume responsibility for his own actions. Even for Sir Thomas More in his *Utopia,* social analysis consisted largely of a chronicle of those human vices which contained the seeds of civil evil: avarice that leads to inflation, vanity that results in theft, and pride that ends in treason.

The cure for social evil was almost invariably the same — root out and destroy the wrongdoer; rarely did it encompass the mitigation or reform of the forces that stood behind social malfunction and tension. Full bellies, it was discerned, produced contented and peaceful subjects while scarcity and war bred crime. Consequently, Tudor society took steps to control prices, prevent hoarding, and allay the worst effects of a static and immobile social structure. But in a world where nothing happened by chance and where everything was imbued with moral meaning, all rebellion, crime, and popular discontent had to have human — not soulless, mechanistic and environmental — causes to which men responded without recourse to choice or reprieve. What almost all Tudor social commentators insisted upon was that people, not society, required correction, and therefore it made perfect sense that edicts 'be written in blood', that a handful of malcontents be destroyed lest 'a whole kingdom perish with their malice', and that seditious persons, who were 'rotten and festered' members, be cut away by the skilled surgeon for the sake of 'the whole body'.[77] Human or even mechanical mishaps divorced of a human agent and responsibility, what the twentieth century means when it speaks of the natural perversity of events to go wrong if they possibly can, were completely alien to the sixteenth-century mind. When today the improbable happens, and, for instance, all three boilers of the *Q.E. 2,* which had been designed to assure maximum safety and reliability, broke down simultaneously in mid-ocean on a perfectly calm sea, we do not (necessarily) shout treason. We shrug our shoulders and perceive Murphy's law at work. The sixteenth century, in contrast, would have been alert for foul play and would have insisted on assigning responsibility either to man or to Satan.

What was true of mechanical waywardness was even more true of human perversity. What might be called a Watergate mentality, where responsibility for evil is assumed by society as a whole, would have been incomprehensible to Tudor England: no one would have sought to excuse Richard Nixon on the grounds that the imperial presidency, itself the product of history and subject to sociological laws of growth and change, was responsible for the misuse and abuse of presidential power. Instead, society would have insisted that, like Iago and Richard III, the tree had to be judged by its fruit, not by the climate or environment in which it grew. Evil actions stemmed from evil minds. Nixon would have been judged absolutely responsible; otherwise he would have been without a figleaf of respect or interest, scarcely a man at all. The play *Richard III* is about an evil and, therefore, fascinating man for whom the audience has a horrified, but reluctant, respect. It is not about the corrupting nature of an historic office. Shakespeare's message is not that 'power corrupts and absolute power corrupts absolutely', but that Richard of Gloucester was corrupt from birth. His evil was personal to himself and not a consequence of the crown he wore.[78] The devil in the sixteenth century retained a firm hold over the imaginations of men, and evil wore the face of Satan, the betrayer, the destroyer, the perverted mind that turns from God and embraces the father of lies and discord. The 'villain fatal, bleak, and ominous'[79] was more than a dramatic ploy appealing to the paranoid instincts of the age. He was comforting proof of the existence of God's ultimate design, and an adversary to be discovered, rooted out and destroyed.

What gave to Tudor treason its fascination and diabolic quality was not its frequency but its urgency and potency. With no sense of change, except as retrogression, and no concept of destiny or direction, except in terms of the fate reserved for indivudal men and women whose struggles for good and evil might indeed bring about the collapse of kingdoms, and with every device at society's command designed to nip treason in the bud even before it had taken cognitive shape, the traitor stood as a kind of Judas, a social and cosmic pariah, inwardly tortured and driven on by evil but necessary as the only instrument through which God and providential change could operate and, at the same time, perversely responsible for his crimes and richly deserving of his horrible end. Even when linked to and swept on by ideological forces and international conflict, the traitor remained in the eyes of society responsible for his actions. What Wallace MacCaffrey calls William Cecil's 'bland refusal to deal with the fact of religious revolution'[80] in his *Execution of Justice* and the Lord Treasurer's inability to comprehend the reality, let alone the legitimacy, of spiritual anguish, was not a failure on Cecil's part of social insight or sensitivity but the product of cultural conditioning. Cecil saw only a conspiracy of evil led by avaricious and seditious men, because no other view was possible in a world where society was ordained by God, and where evil was the work of man in league with the devil. Only in the twentieth century has Satan become anonymous and outgrown his human dimensions[81] or has change, impelled by demographic and economic impulses, become a clearly articulated and legitimate concept that statesmen must ponder and which they ignore at their peril.

Given Tudor England's view of human nature, the purpose and organic structure of society, the existence of an active and interfering deity and a universe of interconnected and corresponding parts, it is not surprising that William Cecil and his entire century should have been disposed to dismiss chance and coincidence in the affairs of life and to discount subterranean economic and social laws of human behaviour as an explanation for change. They searched always for the human factor and self-interested evil, which was for ever plotting behind the events of history. Paranoia, often quite healthy, was built into a system where the men who succeeded, as well as those who failed or were destroyed, were incapable of conceiving of religious dissent or economic and political discontent, let alone social malfunction, in any other fashion than as the evil intent of overly ambitious and wrong-headed individuals who were seeking to violate God's divinely ordered universe, and who, incidentally, were also endeavouring to seize for themselves the good things of political life. And there's the rub: paranoia was not of necessity the figment of a deranged and overactive imagination, nor was it solely the product of educational and ideological conditioning. It was also spawned by and thrived upon the real world of politics, especially at the court of kings where the 'profession' of the courtier was, in George Puttenham's 'plain terms, cunningly to be able to dissemble'.[82]

V

'THE WORLD IS QUEASY'

I would I were a man of greatest power,
  That sways a Sceptre, on this world's great Mass,
That I might sit on Top of pleasure's Tower,
  And make my will, my way, where ere I pass,
That Law might have her being from my breath,
  My smile might be a life, my frown a death.

And yet I would not: for then, do I fear,
  Envy and Malice would betray my trust:
And some vile spirit, though against the hair,
  Would seek to lay mine honour in the dust.
Treason, or Murder, would beset me so:
  I should not know, who were my friend, or foe.
                    Nicholas Breton, *I Would, and Would Not* (1614)

A cosmic and educationally conditioned penchant for viewing the macrocosm of God's universe as well as the microcosm of man's commonwealth as an arena for a vast confrontation between the conspiratorial forces of evil and the soldiers of righteousness was no cultural aberration devoid of practical implication. Education, despite the window dressing imposed by different cultures and eras, has as its chief end the security and survival of the species; and Sir John Bonde delivered the educational creed of his generation when in 1536 he urged Lady Lisle, 'Madam, for the love of God, keep' her son 'to his learning, substantially. I hear say that he shall have need of cunning in time to come.'[1] Parent, priest, and schoolmaster may have instilled in the ruling élite a susceptibility for paranoia, but the political structure itself supplied the necessary venom for the 'black poison of suspect'.

It is a psychiatric premise that pathological traits often display 'a certain consistency' with the attitudes, endowments and occupational environment and requirements of the patient.[2] The paranoia of the President's psychiatrist, for instance, seems to fit the nature of his professional duties. By the same token the Tudor schoolboy, who was already burdened with paranoid tendencies and a stultifying dependence upon cognitive and social directives resulting from rigorous training in rhetoric and decorum and soul-searing, self-regulating obedience to authority, tended to become even more paranoid the moment he entered the realities of political life. There he found massive evidence with which to substantiate his fears. The court was filled with real enemies and not simply with imaginary shadows; 'these are dangerous days, full of itching ears, mislying minds, and ready to forget all obedience and duty'.[3] To make matters worse, the rules of rhetoric and decorum, by which there was always a where, when, and how for every occasion, could not be relied upon. In the real world, the politic man crept 'like a snake in public' but posed 'as an angel in private'.[4] At the court of kings only survival counted, and the role-playing learned at school became either an infuriating cage that trapped and encumbered the actor, or a polite, but deceitful, facade behind which, as everybody suspected, lurked self-interest and cut-throat competition. The first lesson the fledgling courtier had to learn, according to that expert on courtly behaviour, George Puttenham, was to dissemble 'his conceits as well as his countenances' and never to 'speak as he thinks or think as he speaks' so that 'in any matter of importance his words and his meaning' would 'very seldom meet'.[5]

No one doubted that the court was a 'great courtesan' and her gallantries nothing but a 'sly disguise'. Poets, clergymen, educators, parents, and even those who had successfully negotiated the greasy pole of monarchical politics joined together in a chorus of condemnation against the 'gilded misery' that encrusted royalty. The court was a sink 'full of pride, envy, indignation, and mocking, scorning and derision'; and, as John Husee warned, it crawled with 'back-friends', 'secret enemies', and time-servers possessed of 'a fair face and double dissembling heart'.[6] 'This place', wrote the Eliz-

abethan Sir William Knollys, using improbable but nevertheless
effective mixed metaphors, was filled with 'the wolfish cruelty and
fox-like subtlety' of purportedly 'tamed beasts' who, 'when they
seem to take bread at a man's hand will bite before they bark; all
their songs be siren-like, and their kisses after Judas' fashion'.[7] In
more restrained language, William Cecil echoed the same sentiments;
the court, he wrote in 1566, was continuously torn by 'emulations,
disdains, back-bitings and such like'.[8] From every direction the
warning went out: stay away if you treasure honour, honesty, and
peace of mind. 'O happy thee that never saw the court, nor ever
knew great man but by report', rhymed John Webster. There are
'so many spies and enemies' who seek 'to entrap and mesh us',
warned George North, that no courtier could 'withstand them,
whereby [for the] most part men are deceived'. Elizabeth's godson, Sir John Harington, acknowledged that 'he that thriveth in
a court must put half of his honesty under his bonnet'. Robert
Cecil concurred: it was, he admitted, 'a great task to prove one's
honesty, and yet not spoil one's fortune'.[9] Innocence, honesty,
and trust were qualities fit only for the rural and rustic life, and
William Cornwallis summed up the wisdom of his century when
he recorded: 'Against no life doth the force of vice oppose herself
and make so strong a preparation as against the life of a statesman',
for 'she assaults with the weapons of Power, Self-love, Ambition,
Corruption, Revenge, and Fear'.[10]

No one had a good word for the court, but everybody was frantic to play a part upon that 'great theatre' of the world where the
drama of politics and power was enacted. Second and third sons
of the well-to-do might on occasion go into trade; peers might profit
from mercantile adventures; and not even the oldest families disdained merchant blood so long as it was dignified by a great deal
of money or, better yet, at least one generation removed from the
counting table; but for the clean-fingered gentleman fresh from
grammar school or university, politics with its focus at court was
the accepted path to prestige, power, and wealth. Only amongst
the restless throng of courtiers in their 'gorgeous habilliments' could
the answer to the most fundamental of all political questions be
found: 'Who gets what, when, where, and how?'[11] 'The right to

come to court', as G.R. Elton has observed, 'formed the clearest visible barometer of politics', and, one should add, of economic success.[12] Only the extraordinarily incompetent or the dangerously alienated stayed away. To remain in private retirement was to exist without the Crown's economic and political generosity upon which the aristocracy increasingly depended and to violate the code of service to which every Tudor gentleman had been educated. 'They hardly are to be admitted for noble', stated Henry Peacham, 'who, though of never so excellent parts, consume their light as in a dark lantern in contemplation and a Stoical retiredness.'[13]

Not all educated children looked towards the palaces of kings; only the best connected, the richest and most unscrupulously ambitious aimed so high. The majority had to make do with the outer peripheries of the political structure. John Smyth, learning deference at the feet of Lady Katherine Howard, and Sweet-Lips Gregory, fighting over protocol at Lord Lisle's banqueting table, had to endure the boredom, obscurity, and domestic malice of the semi-private households of their betters. Hope, however, then as now springs eternal, and every well-bred lad dreamt that some day, somehow, he would find his way to court and attract the attention of those who attended upon the sovereign. But whether to the manor born or only endowed with 'small Latine and less Greek', the young man starting off in life needed a patron. He had been baptized into a political world held together by bonds that enmeshed the length and breadth of society — the ties of patronage and paternalism, or, in more functional terms, the cords of cousinage and friendship, and the obligations of those fortunate few at the top to filter down the profits of priority and place to those below.

'The Remembrance of Noble Friends'

The sixteenth-century political world was small, intimate, and insufficient to meet the needs of a growing and hungry multitude of gently born aspirants ready to claw their way into the warm and profitable sunlight of political power surrounding the prince. Depending on how far down the social ladder one cares to go in determining the lower limits of the ruling élite — whether one includes a William Parry, Gregory Botolf, Clement Philpot, and Edward Corbett, not to mention the offspring of those close allies of the landed gentry, the clergyman, the lawyer, and the merchant — the political nation probably numbered at any given moment throughout the century no more than 3,000 to 4,000 individuals who sought to hold or capture the profits of office. 'Bounty', remarked Robert Cecil towards the end of the century, was 'an essential virtue of the king', by which he meant essential to the financial well-being of the ruling elements.[14] Open to their economic and social greed were various dignities ranging from the 200 or so great offices of state, positions on the Privy Council, and coveted household posts and sinecures orbiting directly around the sovereign to an indeterminate number of governmental jobs requiring varying degrees of administrative and legal expertise. Outside the central and royal administration but still within the Crown's 'gift' and linked by influence and prestige to the court were positions of power and social status within the shires, especially the justices of the peace, those dutiful satellites through whom the prince and Council reached out to the rest of the kingdom. Competition was not limited to office only; even more lucrative were the pensions, annuities, leases, monopolies, and reversions that supplied the economic sinews of aristocratic political strength. The total number of dignities and incomes available or suitable to the social and economic needs of the ruling 3,000 is incalculable. Historians, however, are agreed that even early in the century there was scarcely enough royal bounty to satisfy the financial requirements and political goals of a governing minority that was reproducing itself at a rate considerably in excess of the population as a whole. By the end of the era the ratio of aspirants to acceptable positions had risen alarmingly, certainly reaching two to one and possibly considerably higher.[15]

When the economic stakes are high and public competition is stiff, the individual with the greatest private connections is the winner. The name of the political game in Tudor England was the influence of the patron who could unlock the royal bounty and put pressure on his friends, relations, and political acquaintances.

The principle worked at every level. John Husee wrote to Lord Lisle to recommend to the Deputy's service Clement Philpot, the third son of his Lordship's old friend and Hampshire neighbour, Sir Peter Philpot. Edward Vaughan begged the newly ennobled William Paget in February of 1547 trusting 'that your Worship will not forget that I was of your preferment' and 'that you will not see me defaced and put out of countenance and reputation', and praying that 'you remember to help to make me a justice of the peace as you said you would'. And Mr Edward Dyer entered the Earl of Leicester's service in 1565 as a gentleman secretary and arranged through the Earl's influence an introduction to court.[16]

Sixteenth-century patronage was closely related to and descended from an older, medieval concept of lordship whereby the bonds of private and personal allegiance and mutual obligation held the public structure together. Except for its intimacy, however, Tudor client-age had long since lost the two distinctive qualities of medieval lord-ship — personal and binding loyalty on the part of both lord and vassal, and the responsibility of military service. Early modern patronage was a marriage of convenience in which both sides encountered risks and expected in return a good deal more than the elusive benefits of mutually supporting and interacting self-esteem — the client profiting from his benefactor's reputation and the patron displaying proof of his high position by surrounding himself, like God in His heavens, with a 'great crowd' of depen-dants. Private, paramilitary organizations consisting of friends, retainers, servants, and tenants all in livery were on the decline in sixteenth-century England.[17] The instruments of power had become both less obvious and less crude; and although the number of those beholden to the great magnates and political wielders of power remained a matter of honorific significance, great hordes of retainers could no longer be used effectively to influence the sovereign, wreak vengeance upon an enemy, or bend the law. Instead what counted in patronage was money and a financial *quid pro quo* whereby both sides expected to profit.

Advancement, noted one Elizabethan experienced in the ways of politics, could only be 'obtained by mediation and remembrance of noble friends'.[18] Consequently, throughout society the 'friend' was never forgotten. The gift — a brace of quail, a hogshead of imported wine, a basket of oysters, a set of spurs, a silver goblet, a dappled gelding — was the universal language of politics. Although John Lyly's complaint — 'in every place all for money' — has a crass flavour to it, and to modern ears smatters of corruption, the gratuity acted as a constant and necessary reminder of promises pending, thanks rendered, and investments to come.[19] Thomas Cromwell extracted a high price from Lord Lisle for his control of what the King heard and read, and he guarded his position jealously, for it was the basis of his political influence, and he successfully fleeced the Lisles out of valuable manors in return for being their mouthpiece to the King.[20]

Lord Lisle was at a terrible disadvantage. He was isolated in Calais and could not approach the King directly for all those essential favours a great magnate required: the preferment of his step-daughter as one of the Queen's maids, the exchange of monastic land for less profitable estates, or an annuity of £200 a year with which to pay off his clamouring creditors. Even permission to come to court or to meet Henry when he travelled on progress to Dover had to be negotiated through an intermediary, who alone knew when the King was 'in a good mood' or had time to respond to the crush of petitioners who sought to tap the munificence of royalty. The Lisle correspondence is a monument to the delays, frustrations, and deviousness of having to operate through channels guarded by courtiers who were determined to prevent any short-circuiting of the system. Lord Lisle had a number of 'very good friends' at court, but one of them, Sir John Russell, made the position of the intermediary perfectly clear: 'I have delivered the King your letters, marvelling that your lordship wrote not to me of your mind, that I might have been a solicitor unto the King's Highness therein.'[21] Even when Lisle won an audience, he made the mistake of failing beforehand to receive the necessary expert advice — you should always ask the King for more than you expect to receive. Unfortunately, his Lordship had asked for an annuity of only £200 which he immediately realized was not enough, but when Cromwell was approached to raise the ante to five or six hundred pounds, Lisle was told through John Husee that 'had you been earnest with the King, it was not to be doubted but you might as well have had a thousand marks as a hundred...'[22]

Advice, favours, bestowing of positions, arranging for entrance into the court, all cost money, for the swarm of petitioners about the sovereign was so thick that only the experienced and favoured few could reach the King, let alone persuade him to listen or read a petition. Lady Lisle, when she finally got to court, had to give up the attempt. Even when Cromwell had 'commanded' her to deliver Lord Lisle's letter personally to the King, she was unable to 'come unto his grace's speech', and she was obliged to give the letter to Sir John Russell 'who hath delivered the same to the King's Majesty'.[23] Princes lived in 'such a degree of eminence above others' and were 'so hedged in with the number of peers and train of veteran courtiers', that 'a stranger can hardly thrust in among the throng that stand in his way, unless either there be someone to take him by the hand and make his passage, or else that himself, by some extraordinary enterprise, do attract the eyes of all men upon him and, among others, those of the prince'.[24]

The success story of Christopher Hatton was evidence enough that once at court a young gentleman with few prospects except his wit and a well-turned calf could be rocketed to greatness in a twinkling of the royal eye. As one of Elizabeth's pensioners, the 23-year-old Hatton attracted his 31-year-old sovereign's attention by the gracefulness of his dancing; thereafter there was no curbing his rise to political power. Under the circumstances the price extracted from Edward Dyer by the Earl of Leicester — an entire manor in return for a position where he could be seen at court and meet the Queen — may not have been exorbitant. Dyer paid for 'someone to take him by the hand'; that was the essential first step. 'Some extraordinary enterprise' was next. Unfortunately, it was not as easy as Christopher Hatton's career appeared to make it. Extraordinary enterprises necessitated a precarious balancing act: 'If he had done nothing', Thomas Audley, Henry VIII's Lord Chancellor, quipped, 'he had not been seen; if he had done much, he had not been suffered.'[25] Recognition was the all-important goal, but the price could be high, for 'the nature of man', as Sir Walter Raleigh warned, and he had firsthand experience, 'is such,

as beholdeth the new prosperity of others with an envious eye, and
wisheth a moderation of fortune nowhere so much as in those we
have known in equal degree with ourselves'.[26]

In such a competitive world, the selection and keeping of a patron
was crucial. If, as William Cecil commented in 1568, offices like
'fishes are gotten with baits', then a man was 'a fish on the dry
shore when the tide of his master's love hath left him'.[27] There
were no options; the frustrations of the system had to be endured:
the delays, the costs, and above all else the grovelling before those
who could do you a favour.[28] Two of the greatest poets of the century sang in unison of the humiliation and boredom suffered by
those who waited in the antechambers of the prince or upon those
who controlled his bounty. Wyatt bemoaned 'The Courtier's Life'
under Henry VIII:

> Praise him for counsel that is drunk of ale;
> Grin when he laugheth, that beareth all the sway;
> Frown when he frowneth, and groan when he is pale;
> On others' lust to hang both night and day.[29]

Spenser was even sharper in his complaint of the 'suitors' state'.

> What hell it is, in suing long to bide:
> To lose good days that might be better spent;
> To waste long nights in pensive discontent:
> To speed today, to be put back tomorrow;
> To feed on hope, to pine with fear and sorrow;
> . . .
> To fawn, to crouch, to wait, to ride, to run,
> To spend, to give, to want, to be undone.[30]

In prose the same dirge can be heard with increasing regularity as
the century progressed. Edward Dyer spoke for all his kind when
he wrote to Lord Burghley that 'we that live in Court, do much
observe countenance, in personages of the greatest honour, and as
they show it favourable or strange towards us, so we reckon more

or less upon our reputation'.[31] Thomas Nashe maintained that a
suit for a pension or office to an earthly king was harder to obtain
than the kingdom of heaven, for 'though a man hath twenty years
followed' it and 'hath better than three parts and a half of a promise to have [it] confirmed, yet if he have but a quarter of an enemy
in the court, it is cashiered and non-suited'.[32] Henry Peacham
warned that political friends were no friends, for their vows 'vanish
into air' and the suitor's labour and expense 'in writing, soliciting,
and attending them at their house and chambers' were wasted.[33]

On the other side of the ledger, the patron's life was equally uncertain. The number of his clients knocking at his door might be a
gratifying sign of political status and favour with his sovereign,
and the flow of gifts from those who wanted to tap his patronage
was useful, but unless the patron could come up with the favours
his 'friends' demanded, they would assuredly leave him and turn
to his rival. Rather like the modern upwardly mobile executive advan-
cing through the corporate ranks, the patron's success depended
upon convincing his followers that he possessed 'the attributes of
a winner'; then as now 'information about the personality of the
players' as much as 'task-mastery' was the key to political and
economic success.[34] Consequently the patron had to study
carefully his clients before helping them. It was unwise to 'be too
prodigal of sharing' the prince's favour with others, and it could
be downright dangerous to 'introduce or commend any to the prince
who are not in some measure known to him, as well as to ourselves,
whose deserts we ought first carefully to look into'. The patron
had to be sure that his client neither shamed him by his failure nor
sought to replace him by his success.[35] Loyalty was never to be
depended upon.

Wits, good looks, luck, and patronage were all necessary to a
successful career at court, but the exact proportions were difficult
to judge and had to be just right, for advancement, as both Raleigh
and Bacon realized to their regret, had less to do with quality of
mind than with that special alchemy which could win the prince's
favour. 'Let no man that cometh to serve in court assume himself
by his wisdom to be advanced,' warned Raleigh.[36] 'Men of depth
are held suspected by princes,' counselled Bacon with clear

autobiographical bias. There was, he said, 'no virtue but has its shade, wherewith the minds of kings are offended'. Clever men were suspected of being able 'by their strength of capacity' to manipulate princes 'against their will and without their knowledge'. 'Popular men' were 'hated as standing in the light of kings'. 'Men of courage' were 'generally esteemed turbulent and too enterprising'; and 'honest and just men' were 'accounted morose, and not compliable enough to the will of their masters'. In the long run, only the problem-solving servant thrived. He 'alone in executing' his masters' commands did 'nothing displeasing to them', for the minds of princes were 'impatient of delay' and they thought 'themselves able to effect anything', and imagined 'that nothing more is wanting but to have it done instantly'.[37] Not even the most august birth conjoined with an average reserve of intelligence could guarantee, as the fourth Duke of Norfolk discovered, anything more than a token place at court, devoid of real power. The ranking peer of the realm under Elizabeth complained bitterly that his royal cousin 'hardly thinks anything well bestowed on me, be it never so small'.[38]

What was true for royal servants was equally true for the entire social structure, which was still sufficiently medieval to account service as the highroad to economic success and which suffered from a surfeit of gently born men and women who were willing to conform to the rules of a deferential and hierarchical society only so long as it paid well. The Earl of Northemberland understood the system when he told his son that suitors, clients, and servants spent most of their time discoursing on 'what you are' and 'how you must be managed'. 'If these be so', he added with surprising understanding and compassion for those frantic to clamber up the ladder of economic and political success, 'can you blame them, or think them unreasonable, to duck, to bend, to observe, to bribe, to flatter, to gain an intercessor that hath a power with you?' The Earl's advice was to be 'yourself, absolutely your own giver of your gifts, and none of these things can be feared'.[39] Unfortunately, the higher up the hierarchy the more difficult such counsel became in practice, for Tudor kings were not in fact free agents. They spoke largely through channels, and the minister or favourite who could

gain access to the channel's source — the royal closet — and direct
the ebb and flow of the King's generosity was in effect an *alter
rex*. Under the circumstances Cromwell and Sir John Russell were
astute to monopolize as far as they could the person of the prince,
and the conclusion offered by the *Practical Guide for Ambitious Politicians* proved absolutely correct: it was 'very necessary in courts to
think all kinds of men, even the meanest, useful unto you', even
those who waited 'upon the emperor at his stool' and were in 'charge
of his shoes'.[40]

In a political structure in which ceremony and ritual were aimed
primarily at protecting the monarch and metamorphosing him into
a semi-divine symbol of state possessed of the power to make or
break all who came close to his person, the winning of entrée into
the privy chamber was not sufficient. The successful politician also
had to remain alert lest a rival seek to displace him in the prince's
favour by spreading falsehoods and insinuations. Absence from the
privy chamber, even from the ante-room of kings, could prove fatal,
for the household of the prince was no different from that of lesser
personages throughout the kingdom: malice and tale-bearing
permeated them all. Envy, suspicion, enmity, and lies were reported
at all levels of society as clients and servants sought to win favour
by discrediting or destroying their colleagues and adversaries.
Thomas Whythorne, who was himself a servant-cum-music teacher,
reported that any domestic who won the special approval of his
master also earned the envy of the rest who would 'seek all the
means and ways that they can imagine' to disgrace their rival. At
a higher level the Earl of Northumberland concurred. Those who
attended upon him were for ever multiplying the 'faults in those
that are their co-rivals'.[41]

The 'malice domestic' found belowstairs in every household intensified in proportion to the stakes involved, and the fear of displace-
ment grew accordingly. It was universally understood that 'we ought
as little as may be, [to] be absent from the prince', for 'love abates
towards those that are absent', and 'a jealousy being once put into
the prince's head, in time, through the many suggestions of the
accuser, . . . takes such footing at last that oftentimes the prince hates
the person accused, before he examines the crime'.[42] Bacon agreed:

'The greatest subject that is or ever was greatest in the prince's favour' could not afford to be long from the source of royal bounty lest his absence breed 'forgetfulness which gives way to wrath; and the wrath of a prince is as the roaring of a lion'.[43] Put more simply: out of sight meant not only out of mind but also out of pocket or, even worse, out of office; and Raleigh bluntly announced that 'whoso serveth a prince far from his presence shall with great difficulty content him; for if he commit any error, it shall be aggravated'.[44] Only occasionally, and in nicely timed amounts, did absence ever make the royal heart grow fonder,[45] and it was a well-understood political device, artfully practised in what the Spanish Ambassador somewhat unfairly called that 'hatchery of falsehoods', the court of Elizabeth, to arrange for a rival to be sent abroad on diplomatic mission.[46] Early in the reign many people, including Cecil himself, thought his mission to Edinburgh would lead to his downfall 'considering that the absence of a great man from the person of the prince is a principal advantage to his enemies and found by common experience to be the first degree in declination to speedy and certain downfall'.[47]

'Win the Queen; if this be not the beginning, of any other course I can see no end.'[48] Bacon's formula functioned throughout the century and well into the Stuart era. No subject with political ambitions, no matter the antiquity of his title or the extent of his estates, could exist for long without the profits of royal favour, either directly from handouts or indirectly from patronage mongering.[49] As the fourth Duke of Norfolk warned, once Elizabeth's favour was lost, a man would lie at court unnoticed and 'unsatisfied', unable to 'attain to himself that he would' and 'do for his friends as his heart desires'.[50] Norfolk wrapped his laments in overly virtuous phrases for the benefit of his sons. What he really meant by doing for 'his friends as his heart desires' was acting the part of a political patron on whom sixteenth-century power rested. Without the Crown's support, patronage simply could not operate.

The expenses of the aristocracy — titled and untitled — were prodigious. The cost of the semi-feudal hospitality and display, still required of the great nobles, was more than most peers could afford in an era of rapid inflation, declining real incomes from land, mounting ceremonial and military obligations owed the monarch, and rising standards of living expected of those who attended upon kings. By the end of the century almost every politically active peer was in debt to the Crown — Norfolk borrowed £2,000 in 1560 to outfit himself in a style becoming the Lord Lieutenant of the North; the first Devereux Earl of Essex in 1573 received £10,000 to defray his military expenses in Ireland; Leicester was given over £16,000 in 1585 for similar costs in the Lowlands; and Christopher Hatton, Leicester, Warwick, Hertford, and Essex father and son, all died hopelessly in debt to the Queen.[51] The Lisle letters earlier in the century are a testimony to the lavish livery, social and political obligations, and economic irresponsibility of the aristocracy, and his Lordship's correspondence is filled with two refrains — John Husee's appeals that 'I may have money sent to pay the grocer and chandler, for they never leave crying and calling upon me for it'; and the Deputy's equally vocal lament to the King that he had to have a pension to keep himself from financial collapse.[52]

What applied to peers also afflicted the lesser figures at court. Edward Dyer had sacrificed a 'substantial portion of his patrimony' to gain admission to the court, and for a while it paid off.[53] Within four years he received, as a mark of the Queen's special regard, the stewardship of the manor and woods of Woodstock for life, along with the rangership and portership of the park. It took, however, William Cecil's direct intervention to persuade Lord Treasurer Nicholas Bacon to implement the Queen's generosity; Bacon clearly had an eye on the revenues for his own offspring. At twenty-six Dyer seemed to be securely on the road to political and economic eminence, but 'the love of kings is like the blowing of winds, which whistle sometimes gently among the leaves, and straightways turn the trees up by the roots'.[54] The next year Dyer, for reasons unknown, earned Elizabeth's extreme anger, and he was banished from the court. It took every trick in the courtier's bag — playing on Gloriana's compassion by sickness both real and feigned, and wooing her with costly pageantry and elegant poetry, plus five years of waiting for his opportunity — before the royal bounty again began to flow and he was accepted back into favour. In 1576 he received one of those lucrative licences to permit manufacturers to ignore (for a fee) government regulations controlling their industry. Dyer's monopoly was in the tanning trade, and it was a godsend to his declining fortunes, but even so, by 1580 he owed the Crown the sum of £3,000, and at the end of his life he died £11,200 in debt, more than the entire value of his estates.

Anthony Cooke was even less fortunate.[55] Possessed of an inheritance potentially worth £2,000 a year and of a Cecil uncle who was the Queen's Lord Treasurer and chief minister, Cooke came to court aged twenty with wealth, family influence, and expectations almost unrivalled. But young Anthony never gained entrée to the privy chamber. Instead, he lingered for a lifetime in the anteroom, bewailing that his 'sinister friends' had stripped him of his patrimony and had 'unfaithfully' led him astray. In only five years he succeeded in going through fifteen manors and £10,500 — William Parry in a period twice that long had only squandered 10,000 marks on the courtier's will-of-the-wisp, the Queen's economic indulgence — and like Parry he fled to Europe in order to escape debtor's prison. In Europe, without a licence 'whereof my enemies may take advantage', he was immediately suspected of treason and only escaped the consequences of his flight because of the influence of his Uncle Cecil. For the final three years of his life, Cooke existed in that coffin of last resorts, Ireland, commanding a company of fifty horse, and attempting to subdue 'this miserable, uncivil, and (as I fear) accursed nation of the Irish'. When not campaigning he besieged his cousin Robert with letters of reproach, comparing Cecil's 'great power and means to satisfy my poor requests with the small effect of goodness I have as yet received, contrary to the desires your Honour seems willing and ready to afford others your friends'.[56]

Anthony Cooke was destroyed by his own outstanding incompetence. He was clearly one of those economic malcontents who were 'not able to live at home but in beggry', and whom Lord Burghley instinctively suspected of potential treason. Cooke, however, like most of his generation, blamed his failure not on ineptitude but on the enemy who was ever ready to take advantage of his mistakes and to slander him in his absence, misrepresenting his actions. Paranoia was indigenous to the starkly competitive environment surrounding the court where there was not enough to go around, where success depended more on friends whom you could not trust than on talent, and where fortune was never 'so favourable to anyone in court as not to afford him as many enemies as friends'.[57]

Politics in the Raw

It is difficult to catch the emotional flavour of Tudor politics, the inner and hidden spasms that gripped the bowels, the sleepless nights of worry, and above all the unpredictable oscillation between frantic haste and endless waiting demanded of those who served the mulish whims and inconstant humours of the powerful. John Husee complained to Lord Lisle that he could not be expected to write regularly 'for sometime one hour missing attendance upon my Lord Privy Seal may hinder a month's suit. And further, to write unto your lordship when I have no direct answer to your causes, it shall but unquiet and disturb your mind.'[58] Behind the glitter of the court stood the stark reality caught in the cry of anguish: 'Oh; Whilst their heels cool, how do their hearts burn!'[59] Unquiet of mind was endemic in a political system which was still largely built upon personal attendance and the need to cater to the moods and caprice of authority. Delay with her two neurotic stepsisters — boredom and frustration — laboured overtime in the ante-rooms of kings and ministers to gather a rich harvest of imagined fears, which were even more unsettling than the presence of real and recognized enemies. 'As in paranoia so in politics', Philip Rieff, interpreting Freud, has written, '"the importance of one particular person is immensely exaggerated and his absolute power is magnified to the most improbable degree."'[60]

Only rarely do the official documents or correspondence of those in power reveal psychological reality. They tend to record only the reasoned, apparently rational exterior of politics and diplomacy, an emotionally emasculated portrait devoid of fear and confusion. The successful people of society carry off the major prizes in the economic struggle for survival; they receive the recognition they crave; they are adept at associating their own self-interest with that of society as a whole; they do not dwell unduly upon their failures or weep for what-might-have-been; and they skew the historical records in their own favour by leaving behind them private and official documents that enshrine and justify their actions and ideas. As a consequence, they rarely have much to say about the functional and psychological strains under which they operated with such ease. The unsuccessful, however, flounder and lash out, and thereby reveal in their lives the political pressures and emotional tensions that beset all the leaders of society.

It is, of course, just as dangerous to harken to the laments of the malcontents of Tudor England as to those who could manipulate the system to their own advantage, and when Wyatt and Spenser, plus a host of others, spoke against court politics with its infuriating delays and humiliating obsecrations offered upon the altar of priority and place, their bias is transparent. They had all been hurt by the system and were hitting back. Nevertheless, when in 1585 Lord Burghley, whose entire career was a study in astute politics and successful management, could be smitten with something akin to hysteria and write that he was so 'maliciously bitten with the tongues and pens of courtiers' that 'if God did not comfort me, I had cause to fear murdering hands or poisoning pricks,'[61] it may be well to accept William Vaughan's evaluation of a minister's life at court. 'They languish in mind: whereas poor men but weary their bodies, which easily might be recovered again. The consuming of the vital spirits [however] is in a manner irrecuperable.'[62] The first half of the century was no better. 'Who knows', lamented the third Duke of Norfolk, 'the cares that go to bed with statesmen'; the political world, sighed his contemporary John Husee, was a 'queasy' place.[63] The Tudor courtier in general and the minister in particular operated under strains almost unimaginable to modern politicians and bureaucrats in the West, for their insecurity, and therefore their fears and their paranoia, were magnified by three factors: the presence, sometimes real, sometimes imagined, of the informer; the dangers involved in finding one's self in opposition to the official policy; and the doctrine of the evil councillor.

The informer conjures up the spectre of a police state replete with

calculated reigns of terror and the brutal enforcement of a single
political truth. For years historians have been tilting at semantic
windmills and indulging in a quixotic debate over whether or not
a Tudor despotism in fact existed. At one time a scholar could en-
title a book *The Making of Tudor Despotism*,[64] but in more recent
years the balance has tipped heavily in favour of a more constitu-
tional description. The impressive and persuasive scholarship of G.R.
Elton, the mounting evidence that both at court and in the shires
privilege, patronage, paternalism, and administrative ineptitude and
confusion blunted the instruments of governmental coercion, and
finally the time-honoured and highly romanticized image of
Elizabeth as a queen who ruled through the magic of her subjects'
love have made the term 'despotism' sound increasingly harsh,
simplistic, and inaccurate. Nevertheless, the social historian continues to have his doubts, and is oppressed by a lingering suspicion
that Tudor England may have been totalitarian in aim if not in function. Renaissance dynamism and intellectual ferment had to operate
in a world almost devoid of any sense of personal privacy or concept of individual human rights, and the organic body politic, which
required its various parts to think and act according to a learnt and
indoctrinated script, had as its ideal the beehive — a society of right-
thinking, right-acting members who were all programmed to a
divinely ordained social directive.

There may have been no reign of terror or systematic governmental spying on and reporting of the conversations and actions
of sixteenth-century Englishmen, as Professor Elton so vigorously
argues,[65] but no one denies a Big Brother mentality existed that
was nourished and encouraged by statute and government policy.
'My duty', acknowledged one loyal country gentleman in 1533,
'binds me to disclose' seditious speech; indeed, failure to do so warranted life imprisonment.[66] Seventy years later the good subject
still thought of himself as being his brother's keeper, and the Duke
of Stettin-Pomerania noted on a visit to England in 1602 that 'in
England every citizen is bound by oath to keep a sharp eye at his
neighbour's house...'[67] 'One gets', concluded Lawrence Stone,
'the impression of a society in which privacy was non-existent',
and in which 'spying and prying and questioning' were universal

pastimes.[68] Most of this inquisitiveness, Keith Thomas has pointed out, took the form of village curiosity about who was sleeping with whom, and the interval between marriage and birth,[69] but, as Gregory Botolf discovered, anything unusual — his trip to the University of Louvain in the company of another man's servant — could arouse suspicion and might be reported, as indeed it was by Frances, the government courier. Moreover, there is clear evidence that the state, although it was far from systematic in its efforts, maintained informants in the establishments of the politically sensitive. Under Mary, spies were placed in various parishes to report on religious troublemakers, and throughout the century the posts were regularly opened and inspected, although whether or not on official orders is far from clear.[70] An accepted axiom of careful government, as Raleigh stated, was 'to have certain officers to pry abroad, and to observe such as do not live and behave themselves in fit sort agreeable to the present state, but desire rather to be under some other form or kind of government'.[71]

If the government and, for that matter, an enemy were not observing 'such as do not live and behave themselves in fit sort agreeable to the present state', everybody thought and acted as if they did. Anthony Bacon in a letter to the Earl of Essex concluded that, since official letters between a king and his minister were 'laid in wait for and opened, how much more letters betwixt private friends' must be exposed to scrutiny.[72] Three generations earlier John Husee refrained from writing to Lord Lisle on the grounds that he 'thereby might put myself in danger of my life and also your lordship to displeasure, for there is divers here that hath been punished for reading and copying, with publishing abroad of news'.[73] Lady Lisle's daughter, Jane Basset, was quite convinced that 'but few letters that cometh unto me' from her mother were not opened before they 'cometh into my hands'[74] — a remark that probably relates more to the young lady's state of mind and her suspicions about her household servants than to the security of the mails.

The spy was presumed to be everywhere.[75] Tyndale accepted as fact the existence of a vast papal network of espionage. So also did Cardinal Allen in his *Admonition to the Nobility and People of England*

(1588) in which, for propaganda purposes, he accused Elizabeth of placing in Catholic 'houses and chambers, traitors, spies, delators [informers] and promoters that take watch for all of their [Catholics'] ways, words, and writings'.[76] Bacon warned against the client who penetrated a household only to 'inquire the secrets of the house, and bear tales of them to others'.[77] And Sir Thomas Wilson, presumably on nothing but hypothesis, confidently asserted that 'in all great offices and places of charge, they do always place two persons of contrary factions. . . to the end, each having his enemy's eye to overlook him, it may make him look the warilier to his charge, and that if anybody should incline to any unfaithfulness. . .it might be spied before it be brought to a dangerous head'.[78] William Vaughan vented his fears when he warned his readers to 'beware whom they accept into their favour and houses, for it may be, their guests will become as grateful unto them as the adder, whom the husbandman, finding almost dead in the snow, brought home and cherished'.[79] And in the mid-seventeenth century Richard Vaughan Earl of Carbery, who had learned his politics and paranoia under Elizabeth, urged his son to consider that 'so many waiters at the table are so many spies; and what may fall from you merrily and innocently, may be maliciously taken up, and long after reported to your disadvantage'.[80] Given Sir Thomas Seymour's useful informant in the Earl of Rutland's London house, who supplied him with the evidence of his 'friend's' defection, Carbery's advice may have been extremely realistic.

As in industrial espionage today, so in domestic spying in the sixteenth century it was useful to maintain 'a politique doormouse' and a 'servant fee'd' in the establishment of the politically and socially powerful.[81] A gentleman in Tudor England was not totally a private, let alone autonomous, person who could do and say what he wished. His life was not solely his own, nor could he be allowed the luxury of that 'indifference of privacy' that is so essential to freedom.[82] The well-born man — and to a lesser extent the gently bred woman — was bred to public responsibility. He had a network of dependants about him; his private, religious, and family connections were deeply entwined with his political and economic standing; and he knew it was of cardinal importance, especially if

he possessed great birth or wealth or held public office, for friend
and foe alike to have an observer in his midst. Even the eligible
bachelor thought it advisable to plant a 'good scout' in order to
circumvent the well-known efforts of cunning mothers to conceal
the defects of their marriageable daughters, and to discover the truth
about his prospective wife. 'Time and envy', counselled the Earl
of Northumberland, when well paid, would reveal everything.[83]
In excruciatingly bad doggerel, Thomas Whythorne described the
behaviour of the serving man when he rhymed:

> I heard of late how one did prate
> And search of all things to know.
> As though that he had had a fee
> To spy, to sift and show.[84]

Under the circumstances, the Abbot of Peterborough's reaction upon
learning that one of his servants wished to enter Thomas Cromwell's
service is understandable: 'What will ye do with him, be one of
his spies? Shall we never be rid of these spies?'[85] As Elton has
argued, the Abbot's words are not necessarily evidence of a spy
system. More likely, they are a reflection of a society that accepted
espionage as a part of the social structure.

The more elevated the rung on the social ladder and the higher
the political and economic stakes, the more profitable informing
became and, therefore, the wider the margin for malice. Tudor society
abounded with ambitious and cynically loyal individuals, such as
Dr William Parry's good friend Mr Edward Neville, who, as Parry
learned to his grief, was only too willing to win favour or strengthen
the obligations of patronage by bearing tales. Except in foreign parts,
there was no real need for a paid spy system; self-interest and duty
united to unleash a flow of information to government officials.[86]
The secret in Tudor England, as a consequence, was extremely difficult to keep, which may in part explain why the age was so security
conscious and why treason so rarely prospered.

Those fortunate but highly insecure few at the political pinnacle,
where 'all rising to great place is by a winding stair' with enemies

standing on every step ready to cast you down, were peculiarly vulnerable to the informer.[87] Their peril stemmed not just from the garden-variety malice of a William Williams, who kept his uncle's treasonous remarks to himself for eighteen months in the hope of benefiting from him, but when his relative and potential benefactor accused him of stealing money and a horse, decided out of self-interest and revenge to reveal all.[88] Far more dangerous were the 'drudges' and hangers-on who wormed their way into the establishments and favour of the political and social élite, and who, according to Thomas Nashe, whenever anyone spoke out against them, twisted their opponent's words 'to the name of treason'.[89] In the privy chamber of kings, a courtier's enemies were 'wont to supplant him' either by endeavouring 'to remove him from court under an honourable pretence', or by seeking to 'render him suspect and hateful to the prince', for with 'half a word', the clever competitor could 'make a legend of lies'.[90]

The political nation 'at the top of the hill' was brilliantly visible in the colourful accoutrements of power. The élite had been placed by birth and training upon a public stage where the 'smallest vices' were 'readily spied, talked of, and severely censured; whilst in an ordinary man, they would either have lain concealed, or been easily excused'.[91] Politics, Sir Thomas More said, was a king's game* 'for the most part played upon scaffolds'.[92] The risks as well as the stakes were high, and the ruling sort paid with their lives for their mistakes 'in numbers disproportionate to their total'.[93] Widow Margaret Towler recorded what was in all probability the sentiment of her century when she reported the opinion of a Mr Thomas

---

* In Spain under Philip II 'most courtiers were obsessed by the twin problems of boredom and promotion, obsessions that were neatly reflected in a special game...played on a board with dice and tokens, and it combined elements from Monopoly and Snakes and Ladders. The board was divided into sixty-three squares to represent the years of a man's life, some of the squares representing hazards to his progress, others bonuses. Those who landed on square 15, entitled "the step of hope", paid the "bank" and advanced to square 26, "the house of the favourite". By contrast, those who landed on square 32, "the well of forgetfulness", lost a turn and had to pay all the other players to remind the favourite of their existence. Those who landed on square 40, "change of ministers", were sent back to square 10, "the house of adulation"; and those who landed on square 43, "your patron dies", had to go back to the start.' (Geoffrey Parker, *Philip II*, p. 170.)

Neville who had few doubts that wealth and political actuarial statistics were in inverse ratio to one another. Mistress Towler had been the housekeeper of the parson of Aldham who was jailed in 1537 for alleged anti-Reformation remarks. Would the parson, she asked, 'be put to death upon a false wretch's saying'? Mr Neville thought not, and assured her that the parson would only lose his benefice and be imprisoned for a few months, 'for he hath no lands nor goods to lose; but if he were other a knight or a lord that had lands or goods to lose, then he should lose his life'.[94] Twenty years later Étienne Perlin in his travels throughout England expressed much the same view. He would, he said, rather be 'a swineherd and preserve my head, for you will see these great lords in grand pomp and magnificence for a time; turn your head, and you will see them in the hands of the executioner'.[95] Whether the statistics actually support such an evaluation of Tudor politics is questionable; that the sixteenth century was fascinated by the notion of fortune's wheel being peculiarly temperamental and exceptionally dangerous for those who inhabited the courts of kings is undeniable. The wages of power were the presence of an enemy observing your every move, being supplied by informers of your every remark, willing to tear your every word out of context, and conspiring to achieve your destruction. Nicholas Breton's fear that, if his fantasy for 'greatest power' were realized, 'treason or murder would beset me so: I should not know who were my friend or foe' was more than an unpleasant dream born of indigestion; it was a nightmare that found its reality at court.[96]

The successful courtier endured yet another terror; he was in constant dread of losing what he had so desperately acquired. The more he had to lose, the greater the fear lest someone else might conspire to take it away. The author of *The Practical Guide for Ambitious Politicians* was particularly astute on this point. Fear, he said, was a far more potent impulse at court than hate. 'To discern who is most able and likely to prejudice us, we must consider not only their power, but also the nature of their malice towards us; for some have a desire of revenge, like a handmaid, always waiting upon their hate; others a fear, lest that having got what we aspire to, we should be more able to hurt them. Though the sting of his revenge is very sharp, yet the fear I mention is the most violent and frequent cause of our court oppressions, and far the most unavoidable.'[97]

When the courtier or statesman for reasons of ideology or self-interest found himself in opposition to the policies of the monarch — be they personal to the sovereign or embodied in a majority opinion on the Council or at court — he was in an even more vulnerable position. His political and economic existence now depended on his willingness to conform to and enforce policies which he disliked. Unfortunately, despite all the political platitudes about a royal servant's duty to speak only the truth to his prince, he could not risk for long antagonizing the ultimate source of power. There existed no legitimate channel to express political disagreement, for there was in Tudor England no institutional concept of a loyal opposition; dissent always carried with it the smell of treason, which, of course, one's enemies were the first to detect.

Dissent in an organic and right-thinking community, blessed by a watchful and activistic deity and governed by a prince who claimed semi-divine status, could assume with devastating suddenness the face of treason. When sovereigns spoke 'with God's help' and 'a king's word was more than another man's oath', subjects were well advised to bend their own fond fancies to the will of the monarch.[98] Quality, not quantity, gave weight to the royal opinion, for as Henry VIII bluntly stated: he was right 'not because so many saith it' but because he knew 'the matter to be right'.[99] Princes, of course, possessed the institutional means to sustain and enforce their obstinacy, but what cut the ground out from under those who dared to disagree was that the voice of royalty was by the definition of all, except the thankless traitor, inspired by God. Shakespeare's Henry V expressed the conviction of all Tudor sovereigns when on the eve of his sailing to France he proclaimed:

> I doubt not that, since we are well persuaded,
> We carry not a heart with us from hence
> That grows not in a fair consent with ours;
> Nor leave not one behind that doth not wish
> Success and conquest to attend us.[100]

Not that ministers did not speak their minds; they disagreed and told their princes nay. Despite the bowing and ceremonial deference before God's viceroy on earth, who expected to be addressed 'with fearful bending' of the knee, Tudor monarchs put up with a surprising amount of disobedience, argument, familiarity, and irreverence.[101] The state papers for the entire century are filled with evidence that Crown servants cajoled, manoeuvred and pressurized their sovereigns. Elizabeth's Parliaments were notoriously rebellious and factious. Both Robert Carey and the Earl of Essex dared to suggest to the Queen's face that she was spiteful and unfair. And George Neville, fifth Lord Abergavenny, who took his title from the Welsh manor of Burgavenny but had recently mortgaged it, did not hesitate to risk Henry VIII's wrath in a none too tactful duel of wits. When confronted by the royal quip, 'God morrow my lord of Burgavenny without Burgavenny', he countered: 'God morrow my liege Lord, King of France without France.'[102] The point is not the amount of freedom of speech countenanced by Tudor kings and queens; what produced the tyranny was that there were few rules to the game and what rules there were could be changed without notice;[103] so much depended upon the sovereign's mood and who was interpreting and editing the flow of information. Burghley was banished from court for his role in engineering Mary Stuart's execution, and Mr Secretary Davison almost paid with his life. 'Her Majesty,' the Lord Treasurer wrote to Sir Walter Mildmay in something close to a frenzy, 'I know not how, is informed by her prerogative she may cause Mr Davison to be hanged and that we may all be so convicted as we shall require pardon...'[104] Several months later the Queen was still so angry that Burghley was sure his enemies now presumed the Queen's 'ears to be open to any calumniation to be devised' against him, and he confessed in a long and typically unpunctuated letter to Christopher Hatton that:

I am so wounded by the late sharp and most heavy speech of her Majesty to myself in the hearing of my Lord of Leicester and Mr Secretary Walsingham, expressing therein her indignation...[that] I am most careful how by any means to me possible,

I may shun all increase of this her Majesty's so weighty offence, knowing it very true that was said by the wise king, *Indignatio principis mors est* [the king's wrath is death].

Clearly what upset the Lord Treasurer most was the public nature of his scolding: Leicester and Walsingham heard all. And significantly he added: 'I have cause to fear that this increase groweth more by means of some secret enemies than of any hard influence of her own princely nature.'[105]

'No kind of slander', warned *The Practical Guide for Ambitious Politicians,* 'does subvert more great men than that which accuses us of conspiring against the prince's person or his empire, or else of contempt or disdaining to obey, with detraction and derision towards the prince.'[106] Political opposition could so easily be coloured to look like treason, and words spoken years before on public service could so readily be recalled and used against you, that George Puttenham's courtier was well advised never to 'speak as he thinks or think as he speaks'.[107] Such dissembling was no mere meaningless decorum; it was a matter of survival, as Sir Thomas Wyatt years earlier had known. When imprisoned in 1541 for allegedly treasonous words spoken while on diplomatic mission to Europe, he wrote in anguish — 'God knoweth what restless torment it hath been . . . perusing all my deeds to my remembrance, whereby a malicious enemy might take advantage by evil interpretation.'[108]

Power is friendless; no prince could be absolutely sure that loyalty and duty were devoid of self-interest, and most Tudor sovereigns were no more paranoid than their office warranted. Trust, unfortunately, is a fragile commodity and easily crushed by doing too little or too much, and the Imperial Ambassador was probably on the mark when he wrote to his master in 1536 that Cromwell was doing his best to promote a pro-imperial policy but that neither he nor any other privy councillor dared 'attempt to shake off the opinion of the King or persuade him to follow a different course in politics, unless the idea comes from him first'. Should Cromwell and his colleagues 'originate any measure, the King is sure to suspect them, and dissent from their opinion, even if he should otherwise deem it acceptable, and in conformity with his own views'.[109] When, as under Mary, ministers and their sovereign became so totally estranged that the Queen spent much of her time remonstrating and shouting at her councillors, no one felt secure, and another imperial ambassador confessed that 'the confusion is such that no one knows who is good or who is bad, who constant, or inconstant, loyal or treacherous'.[110] Under the circumstances, the counsel of one foreign observer of the Reformation upheaval in England made excellent sense and applied to the entire century: 'Those who serve kings ought to dissemble in some matters so as to gain at least a part of their object.'[111] To survive at court, noted a mid-seventeenth-century father for the benefit of his son, it was safer to 'appear a fool than a malcontent'.[112]

The political malcontent bore yet a further burden. There was no escape from politics, for in a social structure where economic power in large measure depended upon political success, retirement was neither financially nor politically possible. Today in the Western industrial world, when the politician retires from public office, he sacrifices little. The private sector can be every bit as attractive as public life, and in certain circumstances carry greater social status and financial reward. The Tudor courtier, however, once he was caught up in the costly web of patronage and competition for political recognition, had no retreat. Neither silence nor retirement were a defence against royal or governmental wrath. Sir Thomas More attempted both, only to be informed at his trial that 'even though we should have no word or deed to charge against you, yet we have your silence, and that is a sign of your evil intention and a sure proof of malice'.[113] Sir Thomas Smith found himself in a similar predicament during the protectorate of the Duke of Somerset upon whose patronage and goodwill he depended. 'For my part', he cried out, 'I am in a most miserable case, I cannot leave the King's Majesty, and him [Somerset] who was my master, of whom I have had all; and [yet] I cannot deny but I have misliked also some things' he did.[114] As Thomas Fuller observed years later, 'it was present drowning not to swim along with the stream'.[115]

Although the *Practical Guide for Ambitious Politicians* counselled voluntary retirement — 'Why dost thou weary tired fortune so? Depart the court, before thou art forced to go'[116] — William Cecil discovered it was not all that easy. Elizabeth's chief minister was for ever threatening to obtain 'licence to live an anchorite or some such private life whereunto I am meetest, for my age, my infirmity, and my daily decaying estate'.[117] But when, as one contemporary historian observed, 'by a letter written with his own hand to the Queen in very earnest manner, he offered to resign...his offer was not accepted; howbeit, whether in that point the Queen's will or the policy of his friends in court prevailed more, I will not take upon me to ensure'.[118] The price of efficiency and royal favour was indispensability. For twelve years Sir Roger Manning begged to be excused his duties at court as one of the esquires of the Queen's body. Even when he deliberately neglected his duties in order to drive his request home, the best he could achieve was a deputy so that he could 'take my ease and wait [upon the Queen] when I list or when her Majesty herself shall command me'.[119] Elizabeth's father could be equally difficult. Henry wrote to his ageing and ailing deputy of Ireland, who had begged for permission to retire, that 'we be not so moved with your age, sickness and debility, which no doubt be no small impeach unto you...as we will yet in respect thereof remove you from the room, honour and authority which we have committed unto you within that land'.[120]

A permanent retreat into private life for a Leicester, Essex, Seymour, or, for that matter, a Lord Lisle was not only socially and politically unthinkable, it was financially impossible. Sir Walter Raleigh sensed the economic chains that crippled and imprisoned the courtier and statesman when he wrote that it was prudent to retire from court to avoid 'the inconveniences of contempt', but 'true it is, that whoso hath lived a prince, or governed as a public person, cannot expect security in a private estate'.[121] The retired and/or disgraced minister was too dangerous: Sir Thomas More was too well known, the fourth Duke of Norfolk was too powerful, and William Cecil knew too much and was too useful both to his Queen and his friends to be allowed the luxury of private life. Worse, Bacon explained, retirement only gave advantage to one's enemies, and he strongly urged the Crown's servant not to quit his post in the face of royal disfavour on three grounds: 'Our enemies and enviers are more emboldened to hurt us'; the anger of the prince would be increased by such a public display of dissent; and 'resigning carries something of ill-will with it, and shows a dislike of the times, which adds the evil of indignation to that of suspicion'.[122] For the courtier who dared to dissent there were only limited alternatives. He could come crawling back on hands and knees to ask forgiveness — Norfolk described himself as an 'unworthy wretch, lying prostrate at your Highness' feet', 'a dead fly'; and Essex begged to kiss his Queen's 'fair correcting hand'. He could play the traitor; or, as so often happened, he could combine the two.[123]

Without a concept of loyal opposition, let alone of political toleration, living in an ideological world coloured either black or white — 'no papist can be a good subject'[124] — and denied the safety valve of retirement, the dissenting politician had only one course open to him: to maintain the fiction of the evil councillor, the satanic grey eminence who shaped and poisoned the royal mind and directed it against him and his friends.

The belief that evil was engaged in a vast historic and cosmic conspiracy against good, and the instinctive paranoia of a society in which even the most well adjusted and successful courtier presumed the existence of enemies set upon his destruction, joined forces with practical and psychological governmental needs to create in Tudor England a political figment — the evil minister. The confidant of kings stood in double jeopardy. The office of Principal Secretary, William Cecil explained, was 'dreadful' not only because 'he that liveth by trust' was at the mercy of his sovereign and therefore must be very 'careful in the choice of his master', but also because the chief minister was envied by all for the ease and freedom of his access to the prince and was maligned by all for whatever 'a prince has cause to delay or deny, to search or punish...'[125] The servant who guarded the door, vetting the flow of information that reached the royal ear and determining the order and time in which the King spoke to the throng outside his chamber, could be as powerful as — historically on occasion even more powerful than — the master he served. His existence fulfilled an important psychological role; he supplied one of the faces of the Janus of power, the evil profile of authority, while the monarch represented the good.

Government officials in the sixteenth century were individually, not collectively, responsible for evil or benign policies. There had to be someone to blame because power, and therefore responsibility, possessed a human face. Today we like to believe that we know so much about the subterranean and perverse nature of authority — interlocking directories, behind-the-scene committees, accommodation to wealth and influence — and about the dialectics of policy-making, whereby rulers become the victims of earlier decisions either made by others or reached on the grounds that some kind of action is required, that we have almost ceased to think in terms of individual rulers. Authority is conceived as a collective non-being called the Establishment, and the twentieth century makes do with such nebulous, epicene, and expressionless expressions as 'they' or 'them' in its efforts to identify power and responsibility. We condemn the system; Tudor England accused the King's evil ministers. In 1525 Cardinal Wolsey complained that 'it is the custom of the people, when anything miscontenteth them, to blame those that be near about the King; and when they dare not use their tongues against their Sovereign, they, for colouring their malice, will not fail to give evil language against [me]... Howbeit, I am not sole and alone therein.'[126] Subjects 'cursed the Cardinal' and praised Henry as 'the gentlest prince and of the most gentlest nature and the most upright that ever reigned among men'.[127] Sixty years later the same double vision existed among members of the Privy Council. Sir Francis Walsingham wrote to the Earl of Leicester that despite his and Burghley's best efforts, Elizabeth had 'had a sudden change of heart' and was now adamantly opposed to the Earl becoming governor general of a combined Dutch and English army in Holland. 'She grew so passionate in the matter as she forbid him to argue any more.' 'Surely', he concluded, 'there is some treachery among ourselves, for I cannot think she would do this of her own head.' A few weeks later Sir Francis was reluctantly forced to confess that Gloriana's veto stemmed not from secret advice supplied by an enemy but from 'her Majesty's own disposition'.[128]

The reflex to blame the evil councillor, however, was far too useful

both to princes and commoners to give way before reality because
it supplied a justification for and a degree of protection from the
obstinacy, spitefulness, and ill logic of kings. In 1587 Robert
Devereux, the young Earl of Essex, found what solace he could
in the myth of the evil councillor when he clashed with his sovereign
lady over her treatment of his sister, Dorothy Perrot. Dorothy had
earned the Queen's extreme annoyance and had been banished from
court for flouting all the rules of social decorum and royal authority
by eloping with Mr Thomas Perrot. Elizabeth had a long and
cankered memory, and when she was on progress visiting her old
friend Lady Warwick at North Hall, she discovered Dorothy as one
of the houseguests, and promptly ordered Lady Warwick to con-
fine the wretched girl to her room. What outraged Essex was not
only the public and obviously deliberate slight to his family name
but also the fact that Gloriana had known all along Dorothy would
be one of Lady Warwick's guests; the Earl had informed her himself
in an effort to forestall a scene, and had been led to believe that
the matter was of no concern to the Queen. In his fury Essex wrote
a passionate letter to his friend Edward Dyer in which he gave an
outraged description of the subsequent confrontation with his royal
mistress.

> Her excuse was, first, she knew not of my sister's coming; and,
> besides the jealousy that the world would conceive, that all her
> kindness to my sister was done for love of myself. Such bad excuses
> gave me a theme large enough, both for answer of them, and
> to tell her what the true causes were; why she would offer this
> disgrace both to me and to my sister, which was only to please
> that knave Raleigh, for whose sake I saw she would both grieve
> me and my love, and disgrace me in the eye of the world...[129]

The presence of knaves about the Queen supplied Essex with
a safety valve for his anger and humiliation. It did something else:
it protected from calumny a political idol, who clearly possessed
most of the least attractive qualities of the human species, and it
permitted Gloriana to indulge her royal spite while maintaining
her Junoesque image. 'This strange alteration', as Essex described

Elizabeth's unforgivable behaviour, was 'by Raleigh's means', not
the result of any flaw in the perfect mirror of majesty. 'If', as Bishop
Gardiner maintained, 'we desire the name of king to be sacred, which
all good men desire...we must take care lest any stigma be cast
upon this name by others.'[130] The mechanism that protected the
monarch against stigma, however, imposed upon those who served
the idol an ironic burden. 'Great men', Francis Osborne in the seventeenth century irreverently observed, were like puppets; they were
'managed by their servants' and the ones dearest to them were those
who could 'make them appear less fools than in truth they are',[131]
a hypothesis that may explain why both Cardinal Wolsey and
Thomas Cromwell were destroyed exactly at that moment when
they caused Henry VIII to look ridiculous in the eyes of the world.

Good counsel might preserve the prince from his own folly, but
evil counsel was the necessary scapegoat to safeguard his reputation and to remove him from the nastiness and partisanship of politics. If kings as God's deputies on earth could do no wrong, and
if the system of society was divinely ordained and governed, then
responsibility for the mishaps and mistakes of government by a process of elimination had to rest with ministers bent on subverting
public good to private interest. Elizabeth herself did not hesitate
to place the guilt for her sister's calamitous reign where it so
obviously belonged — on the evil counsel of her Catholic prelates.
Early in Gloriana's reign she confronted them with a question to
which the answer was manifestly clear: 'Was it our sister's conscience made her so averse to our father's and brother's actions,
as to undo what they had perfected? Or was it not you, or such
like advisers, that dissuaded her, and stirred her up against us?'[132]

Ministers could err but 'the princely seat and kingly throne' constituted by God could not. The principle was essential to the image
of kingship as the cornucopia of bounty, justice and love. To sustain the illusion, the truth had to be neatly packaged. Monarchs
could not be publicly revealed levying unpopular taxes, following
disastrous policies, denying a patron seeker, or refusing a pardon,
especially if Bacon's axiom for political stability was to operate.
'It is a certain sign', he said, 'of a wise government' to 'hold men's
hearts by hopes, when it cannot by satisfaction'.[133] The contem-

porary historian John Clapham explained Elizabeth's success on
the grounds that she suffered 'not at any time any suitor to depart
discontented from her; and, though oft times he obtained not that
he desired, yet he held himself satisfied with her manner of speech,
which gave him hope of success in a second attempt'.[134] To sustain that confidence when there were three hopefuls clamouring
at the door for every scrap of royal bounty, someone other than
the monarch had to say no; a scapegoat had to be found to preserve
the fiction that if the sovereign could only be reached or preserved
from evil counsel, he would say yes to all that was asked of him
and would rectify whatever was amiss. Those 'caterpillars of the
commonwealth', Bushy and Greene in *Richard II*, who had misled
their prince, 'a royal king, a happy gentleman in blood and
lineaments, by you unhappied and disfigur'd clean', were no
figments of the playwright's imagination.[135] By Shakespeare's day
the political function, if not the institutional theory, of the evil
councillor who acted like a kind of malignant *alter rex* was clearly
understood and utilized by commoners as well as kings.[136] Bacon
said that 'the wiser sort of great persons bring in ever upon the
stage somebody upon whom to derive [turn aside] the envy that
would come upon themselves'.[137] A generation later the Earl of
Carbery cautioned his son 'as near as you can, remove from yourself
the envy of a hard answer'. It was, he said, preferable that 'displeasing
answers, vexing delays, and unwelcome denials, especially if they
be of small concernment, and to little people (which still are the
most clamorous) these should proceed from others, rather than from
yourself, partly to take off the envy, and partly, because it may not
become your person to take notice of such mean things'.[138]

The principle was even more essential to kings. Lord Burghley,
as Wolsey had done before him, acknowledged that it was her Majesty who 'throweth upon me a burden to deal in all ungrateful
actions...to give answer unpleasant to suitors that miss... My
burden also is this, that in all suits for lands, leases or such things,
her Majesty commands me to certify the state thereof... And if
the party obtain [the grant], I am not thanked; if not, the fault
(though falsely) is imputed to me.'[139] Cecil was not alone in his
predicament; all royal councillors were forced to play the part of

the evil minister whose flattering and forked tongue had befuddled the prince's mind. Raleigh urged that a king always 'commit the handling of such things as procure envy or seem grievous, to his ministers, but reserve those things which are grateful and well pleasing to himself'.[140] 'The ill success' of government policy, warned *The Practical Guide for Ambitious Politicians,* 'is always wont to be imputed to the unfortunate adviser, and the good to the fortune of the prince: not only by the vulgar, who judge all things by the event, but also by the prince himself, who is always glad to have someone upon whom to derive the envy of an unlucky undertaking, and scarce ever willing that anyone should share with him in the glory of a prosperous action.'[141] Little wonder Cecil cried out in desperation to Francis Walsingham in November of 1588 that 'all irresolutions and lacks are thrown upon us two in all her speeches to everybody. The wrong is intolerable.'[142] The wrong was intolerable but necessary to the system, and it reflected the paranoia that had become essential to the proper functioning of divinely inspired authority. As Cecil himself confessed, society would always blame the 'lacks and errors to some of us that are accounted inward Councillors, where indeed the fault is not', but 'they must be so suffered, and...so imputed, for saving the honour of the highest'.[143]

There are obvious dangers in suggesting that Tudor politics was not only improbably absurd, at least to modern eyes, but also bordered on the insane, a courtly madhouse inhabited by Robert Burton's melancholic man who suffered constant neurotic ill health and regarded the slightest setback as the work of enemies, counting 'honesty dishonesty, friends as enemies'.[144] Men learn to survive, even to accept as normal, the most austere and friendless environments. Known horrors are invariably less dreadful than unknown, and no sixteenth-century courtier would have advocated a fundamental change in the system. All he asked was a share of the spoils and a conspicuous place in the political sun commensurate with his expectations. There, of course, was the source of the trouble. Neuroses characteristic of a society, as Kai Erickson has said, are culturally conditioned and are signatures of a particular era, but when applied to individuals they are the product of an imbalance between aspirations determined by perceived talents and social status, and the recognition and power which society is willing to offer or the individual is capable of commanding. Paranoia was as much the child of mental strain born of frustration and incompetence and of tensions imposed by a political system that swarmed with real and imaginary fears as it was the culturally conditioned offspring of education and cosmology. When there is no acceptable alternative to political success — retirement, loyal opposition, achievement in some other occupation, or relief in direct action — mental anguish and neurotic behaviour are to be expected. And yet one still wonders why the sixteenth century in particular? What made Tudor England cosmologically, educationally, politically, and psychologically so different from the centuries that preceded or followed it, which also possessed many of the same elements that produced Tudor and early Stuart paranoia?

VI

A 'WONDER TO BEHOLD'

History is not what happened but what people
felt about it when it was happening.
G.M. Young, *Victorian England: Portrait of an Age*

Paranoia was a disease of the spirit, a 'subtle humour' that, in the
opinion of Cardinal Allen, was crucifying the soul of Tudor England.
The kingdom, he said, was tormenting itself with absurd and brain-
sick nightmares, and he ridiculed its ruling Protestant élite who
'even now in the vaunt of their wealth, peace, and prosperity...show
such extraordinary fears as is [a] wonder to behold'. Their misery
was so pathetic, and 'the perplexity which God hath driven them
unto so terrible, that there is not a poor priest can enter [the realm]
to say mass but they imagine he bringeth their destruction. There
cannot a ship appear in any coast, nor any prince's preparation for
his own affairs, but it is for invasion of the realm.'[1] Despite the
prelate's polemical language, Allen's evaluation of his countrymen's
state of mind during the 1580s contains an important kernel of truth:
something had happened in sixteenth-century England that no
amount of cosmological, educational, or even political analysis can
totally explain. By all rights medieval society should also have been
beset by paranoid fears. The sixteenth century had no monopoly
on an interfering God, and its view of society as a stage upon which
man wrestled with Satan and enacted the drama of salvation and
damnation was as old as Christianity itself. Tudor educational
theories and dependence on rhetoric and decorum, although directed
to the use of a new, enlarged and secular state, not a clerical caste
— the distinction is important — were nevertheless largely adapta-

tions of classical-medieval pedagogical principles and practices. And despite their tax collectors and bureaucratic record keepers, sixteenth-century kings were not noticeably more ruthless or capricious than their feudal confrères. Logically the Tudor enemy, spinning his ugly web of conspiracy and malice, should have been equally visible to medieval eyes. So what set sixteenth-century England apart from its past, branding a paranoid signature upon the face and personality of its body politic?

The answer has to do with social psychology and historical change. As Richard Hofstadter has observed, a disposition to view the world through paranoid coloured glasses, although always present in 'some considerable minority of the population', surges or retreats in the face of tensions and strains released by social conflicts that threaten cherished beliefs and time-honoured habits, and which bring in their wake passions that can only be resolved by violence and direct political action. 'Catastrophe or the fear of catastrophe is most likely to elicit the syndrome of paranoid rhetoric'; and Tudor society, if it was sure of nothing else, was certain that it lived on the brink of disaster.[2]

It is unnecessary to recount in detail the agonies of the sixteenth century. Although the precise chronological limits are subject to debate, almost without exception historians have marked the century as one of the crucial moments in the gestation of modern society. It was an age of profound foreboding born of vast but ill-understood demographic, economic, and spiritual upheaval that found only partial and inadequate expression in institutional change.[3] The population exploded with all its concomitant human misery and cancerous urban growth. Europe commenced that absolute upset of the world balance of power that for four centuries bestowed upon it the riches of the earth and their unregenerated offspring — greed, war, and inflation. The acquisitive spirit burst its Christian chains of moderation and charity, and with Cosmo de Medici claimed God the son, God the father, and God the holy ghost as debtors. The wages of cupidity were clear: as Europe spun its golden thread of trade and finance, the Turks battered unopposed at the gates of Christendom, swearing to turn St Peter's Cathedral into a stable for infidel stallions. Constantinople, the jewel of the Middle East and the capital of a millenium-and-a-half-year-old Roman Empire, had fallen in 1453; a century later Suleiman the Magnificent stood before the walls of Vienna. Instead of defending the ramparts of Christendom, early modern kings fought wars of territorial aggression and systematically sought to chasten and chastize the historic guardian of the faith — the feudal baron and the medieval prelate. Everywhere the venerable signposts, the historic methods, and the ancient loyalties were being distorted and corrupted by newer political and economic alignments and obligations. And most distressing of all, Christ's seamless cloak of religious unity that had given spiritual warmth and solace to all believers was in tatters, torn to shreds by Martin Luther's stand upon conscience, the 'captive of the word of God', and his appeal to a 'living God'. All had become unhinged, and change was on the march in raucous and atrocity-committing battalions unimaginable in the past. Although there was excitement, curiosity, and dynamism aplenty as man began to rival his creator as the measure of the universe, there was much to fear and to grieve. At one time or another, for one reason or another, everyone had occasion to agree with Erasmus's lamentation: 'Where now is gladness, where tranquillity of heart? Everything is full of bitterness and trouble; wherever I turn my eyes, I see nothing but what is melancholy and cruel.'[4]

Of all the viruses of change in England, the two most virulent and generative of a paranoid response to life were the profound spiritual ecstasy that in a single generation brought down with a mighty trumpet blast of righteousness religious walls that had stood battered but unbreached for 1,500 years, and the equally momentous new alignment of political loyalties, which converted a feudal confederation of overlapping and conflicting allegiances and obligations into the nascent nation state with its juggernaut champion and symbol — the divine-right monarch.

The saintly temper with its moralistic and didactic cruelty, for reasons never adequately explained, was on the ascent in the sixteenth century. The urge, especially on the part of the social and intellectual élite, to become my brother's keeper, the sudden heightened sensibility to cosmic signals heralding God's renewed concern for man's sinful ways, and an increased predilection for

questions dealing with the ultimate purpose of life, death, and universal creation were all part of a religious revival that initially found
expression in Martin Luther's message of spiritual exaltation
embodied in justification by faith alone, and later in the crusading
zeal of Puritanism. Heavily, often embarrassingly, supported by men
of Mammon who had their own earthly reasons for bringing Rome
to heel, those who felt upon them God's hot breath sought to bring
down the ancient ecclesiastical edifice of Catholicism which had
stood for centuries as the indispensible intermediary between God
and man. Even in England where Protestantism met with only partial
success, not so much bringing down the walls of Rome as nationaliz-
ing the citadel and secularizing its captain, the new Church was
deeply committed to the central tenet of the reformed faith. Man,
the sinful, fallen, rebellious vestige of his prototype in the Garden
of Eden, stood alone and unredeemable before his deity to face the
consequences of his sins without benefit of the magical formulas
and saintly intercessors of ancient Catholicism, warranting only
his just desert — eternal punishment in hell. Faith in God's
forgiveness was the Christian's sole solace, and in that hope he lifted
his eyes heavenwards, sang the Lord's praise, and sought to recast
this sinful world in God's image. Long ago it had been written
that the 'good things that are put in a closed mouth are like as
when meat is laid upon the grave'.[5] Only if men and women gave
themselves fully to the Lord could they partake of the spiritual
nourishment offered by a 'living God'.

Protestantism was a peculiarly demanding and immoderate creed.
In the name of ecclesiastical purity and theological logic, it reached
back into the attic of time and historic authority and selected for
disproportionate and special emphasis man's depraved and fallen
condition, God's absolute sovereignty to the exclusion of chance,
fortune and human will, and the cosmic, almost Manichaeistic,
struggle between good and evil. All three were inherent within
the Christian tradition, but all received a new urgency as Protestant
reformers set out to sanctify the world and do combat with 'that
triple-crowned monster and great Antichrist', the Pope in Rome.[6]
Of all people, Protestants were most prone to expect the worst,
for they knew the world in which they lived surpassed all previous

generations in sinfulness. Never before had men and women been 'so wicked, so froward, so perverse, so obstinate, so malicious, so hypo-critical, so covetous, unclean, untrue, proud, [and] carnal'.[7] The existence of unprecedented evil, instead of engendering cynicism and defeat, inspired a renewed challenge. As never before the hounds of hell were conspiring to infiltrate and overthrow the garrisons of righteousness; and they had to be met and conquered ere it was too late. As a result, there was in Protestantism throughout the century a sense of panic and extreme emergency, for two cosmic forces stood poised and ready for combat. There were, wrote one passionate reformer, two churches: 'the church of Christ militant, and the church of Antichrist; and. . . this church of Antichrist may and doth err; but the church of Christ doth not'.[8]

Anxiety bred of spiritual agitation and a sense of terror that the beast was at the gate took on institutional form when, under Henry VIII and his successors, dynastic politics and economic self-interest allied themselves with ideology to create the conditions of fear and instability in which paranoia for the next five generations could thrive. 'From the moment that Henry VIII entered upon his breach with the papacy', G.R. Elton has written, 'and thus opened the door to the Reformation, all political debate — all issues of domestic and foreign policy — acquired an ideological component.'[9] As Erasmus predicted the 'long war of words and writings' terminated in blows.[10] The spiral of domestic fear and distrust had begun, and henceforth the kingdom was confronted with enemies not only abroad but also at home, the numbers, determination, and military strength of whom nobody knew. Sir William Paget thought that the new faith, purged of papal venom, was 'not yet printed in the stomachs of the eleven of the twelve parts of the realm', and Bishop Edmund Bonner confessed that fear, not conviction, stood behind the lip-service loyalty offered to Henry's new Church.[11] Far into the next century, dread of a menacing fifth column dominated English minds and politics, and secret Catholics were accused of everything from kidnapping children and killing livestock to causing the Civil War.[12]

Protestants had cause for alarm, for their onslaught against the papal beast, instead of bringing the Antichrist to bay, had only given him renewed strength. The Catholic hydra was no imaginary monster. The same spiritual exaltation that filled the followers of a 'living God' began to intoxicate the old Church. Slowly, painfully international Catholicism with its gilded head in Rome, its tangled vested interests in every court and chancery of Europe, and its weary cynicism about the frailty of human nature reacted to the menace of the reformed faith, responded to the inner cry of conscience and the outer voice of authority, and sought the path of martyrdom in the spiritual war of rival truths. Half a decade after Elizabeth had secured her throne and irrevocably linked England to the Protestant star, Philip of Spain set the tone for the Counter-Reformation and gave expression to what Englishmen feared most — a vast international conspiracy of resurgent and militant Catholicism willing to take advantage of every domestic weakness and potential traitor within the island citadel. In 1564 Philip instructed his new ambassador to England to publicly compliment Elizabeth 'with the fairest words you can use' but in private to contact and aid the many thousands whom he was sure remained faithful to the 'only true ancient Catholic religion'. Then he added a crucial codicil: 'This, however, must be done with such secrecy, dissimulation and dexterity as to give no cause for suspicion to the Queen or her advisers, as it is evident that much evil might follow if the contrary were the case.'[13] All the political and economic elements opposed to the emerging nation state found a rallying point in the defence of the old faith the moment that the second Tudor committed his dynasty to religious revolution but failed to supply the means for a lasting solution to the question of the succession. Every loyal Englishman knew that Cardinal Allen spoke the truth not just for Elizabeth's reign but for the entire century when he evoked the curse of the Tudor dynasty and warned of 'the most dreadful and most desperate case our whole country, every order and each particular man thereof, is in by the uncertainty of the next heir to the crown; yea, by the certainty of most bloody civil and foreign wars among such a number of competitors, such diversity of religions, such ambitious spirits that already make their packs and complots for the same'.[14]

Protestantism needed no public proof of Rome's villainy, for the nature of Antichrist was deceit. Had he not deceived, with earth-shattering consequences, the parents of mankind, assuring them 'you shall not die...but shall be like unto God Himself knowing good and evil'?[15] Unsatiated and unbridled, Satan was once again at his old tricks. For a thousand years he and his arch ally, the papal whore of Rome, had been hoodwinking Christians with their worthless rituals and idol worship. God, however, had met trickery head on and had made His Truth manifest in Scripture for all to read in English and thereby had offered His followers a method for discerning the artifice of priests and bishops. 'Now', thundered William Tyndale, 'thou partly seest the falsehood of our prelates, how all their study is to deceive us and to keep us in darkness, to sit as gods in our consciences, and handle us at their pleasure...'[16] A century later little had changed; James Cleland was still warning young noblemen not to believe Catholic 'promises and offers otherwise than the Song of Sirens'.[17]

As revolutionary and ideological war heated up and the sides hardened into mutually suspicious extremes — 'whatever is contrary to the Catholic faith is heresy'; 'we must either [be] on God's party or else on the devil's'[18] — Protestant paranoia grew proportionately. There was but one 'true church', which could only be defended by going on the attack: 'It is impossible to preach Christ, except thou preach against Anti-Christ.'[19] God's verity could be neither multiple nor uncertain, and Henry VIII voiced the judgment of his age when he categorically announced that the Truth was 'so certain, so evident, so manifest, so open and approved' that it 'ought to be allowed' by all Christian men and women.[20] Only the devil's doctrine was obscure and manifold, for his method was always to confuse the issue with exceptions, cloud the truth with sophistry, blunt God's Word with the argument that every kingdom has its harmless lunatics, and deny that a vast conspiracy of evil was afoot.

Satan waxed strong and found new pastures to contaminate as religious hysteria mounted. Not only did every warring sect expand the devil's domain by picturing opponents as being in league with the forces of evil — Luther had been seduced into heresy by Satan's prompting; the Pope was Antichrist — but far more serious, the

fiend had discovered psychology.[21] His colourful and faintly com-
ical medieval antics, which were invariably outwitted and defeated
by the forces of good, gave way to a darker, more potent and subtle
agent of evil — man himself. The dark recesses of the human mind
became Lucifer's chosen abode where he taught and practised
'policy', or what he cleverly disguised as the sound application of
foresight and calculation to the acquisition of power and wealth,
but which the godly knew to be pride, dissimulation, and
Machiavellian cunning devoid of moral and religious standards, the
negation of legitimacy, honour, loyalty, love, and order.[22]

How important the Reformation was in creating Lucifer's
Renaissance is difficult to gauge; clearly other than religious forces
were at work as man divested himself of his medieval hallmarks
and claimed himself to be the measure of all things, including evil.
But Protestantism's insistence upon the intensely inner nature of
sin, and its imperviousness to magical and mechanical exorcism by
Catholic bell, book, and candle, gave to the devil a potency and
an immediacy that was unique to the sixteenth and early seventeenth centuries.[23] There can be little doubt that the Tudor
schoolboy who had been told a hundred times over that 'this life
is a perpetual struggle, fierce and vehement', between good and
evil,[24] and who had been schooled in the Protestant doctrine of
original sin, was possessed of a concept of internalized evil that made
him more sensitive than his medieval counterpart to the existence
of Iagoesque villainy, not only upon the stage but also in real life.

If Tudor England observed the devil to be on the rampage and
sensed the operation of secret enemies and traitors, it is tempting
to link such fears to Protestantism in the same fashion that Keith
Thomas relates the sudden and virulent outbreak of witch persecution in the second half of the sixteenth and much of the seventeenth
centuries to the collapse of medieval Catholicism and its 'protective ecclesiastical magic'.[25] In medieval society, witchcraft was of
little concern because the Church possessed an effective antidote.
Holy candles, signs of the cross, consecrated bread, sacred amulets,
and prayers directed to a host of saintly intercessors had for centuries protected men and women against the devil and those who
practised his 'malignant magic'. After the Reformation, this shield

was largely removed. Saint George and his heavenly associates and
the Church's magical powers of exorcism were dismissed as
superstitious nonsense. Unfortunately, however, the dragon of evil
remained, and society became increasingly disturbed by witches and
their black craft, demanding that they be punished and purged.
With the devil now unleashed and uncontrollable both at home
and abroad, and his allies and worshippers apparently on the increase,
Tudor England more than at any previous time in its history thought
there was reason to be afraid and felt the need to warn its children
to be on their guard against the presence of the enemy.

The Protestant doctrine of God's absolute providence may also
have had an effect on paranoia. The refusal to accept the operation
of chance or free will and the even more depressing logic that all
misfortune stemmed from the slug of depravity inherent in every
Christian soul, which, according to Keith Thomas, drove Tudor
England to seek an explanation and remedy for personal failure in
the existence and punishment of witches and warlocks, may also
have encouraged the conviction that the enemy with his sinister
conspiracies was for ever stalking innocent, unsuspecting and loyal-
hearted people.[26] When luck and fortune were removed from the
equation of human success and failure, and only God's merited
punishment of man's sins remained, the enemy as well as the witch
became the necessary scapegoat to preserve an Englishman's self-
respect and pride. Ironically, it was of considerable comfort and
satisfaction to believe, as did Robert Beale, in the menacing presence of an enemy who sought 'some part of the spoil or prey'
and who worked against 'the service of God, prince and country'.[27] There may be no measurable proof, but Protestantism and
paranoia were clearly linked if only in their insistence upon the
existence in society of demonic and rationally conducted evil and
their exclusion of chance, bad luck, and coincidence in the affairs
of God and man. Certainly the reformed faith helped to supply
that atmosphere of urgency and catastrophe that Richard Hofstadter
postulated as the essential condition for a paranoid style of life.

Protestantism may have helped supply that sense of 'diffuse
apprehension' which made it so difficult for Tudor society to 'put
its faith in the motives of others',[28] but paranoia could never have

flourished as richly as it did had it not been for the growing concentration of political and economic power orbiting about the person of the sovereign and his translation into a divine-right ruler.
The divinity that hedged the King, dazzling in its majesty and
mesmerizing in its ritual, was little more than the religious figleaf
and anthropomorphic trappings placed upon the naked realities of
power in order to make them more suitable to an age that was
undergoing an absolute shift of personal loyalties and a collective
identity crisis. From a semi-feudal cluster of highly idiosyncratic
loyalty networks based on kinship, lordship, and an atavistic
attachment to one's immediate locale, sixteenth-century England
was moving into something resembling a nation to which all subjects gave their undivided loyalty and from which they derived their
status as well as their security.

The Tudor formula 'obedience is best in each degree' was political
shorthand used to describe the essential nature of the emerging state
in which various medieval corporate entities were fused together
by the divinity of a monarch who was no longer the greatest baron
of them all or a lord among lords, but was now regarded 'not only
[as] a king to be obeyed on earth but [also as] a veritable idol to
be worshipped'.[29] Tudor Englishmen in their relations with Henry
VIII, wrote John Hales in the 1540s, had 'not to do with [a] man
but with a more excellent and divine estate'.[30] A qualita-
tive distinction was being made: all ranks and corporations were
imbued with divine right bestowed by God at the moment of
His initial creation of society, but once the prince had reinforced
his ancient medieval sacerdotal powers with the supreme headship
of the Church and had smashed all other rival authorities within
the kingdom, the King was elevated to a pinnacle from which he
could speak directly to God and demand a monopoly of service
and loyalty that reduced feudal barons and medieval churchmen to
the level of subjects, equal to all others in the eyes of the monarch. Not only did kings insist that their meanest servants had
'sufficient warrant to arrest the greatest peer of this realm', but
such was the divine majesty gracing their royal brows that it
could be said of Bishop Fox that 'to serve the king's turn [he]
would agree to his own father's death'.[31]

The medieval tripartite balance of Church, Crown, and baron-
age in which Christians rendered equally unto Caesar and to God
and gave their loyalty to both king and overlord in proportions
hallowed by time and circumstance had collapsed. The deity had
switched channels — 'the word of God is to obey the king and not
the Bishop of Rome'.[32] Sovereigns required of their subjects an
allegiance just as soul-engulfing as that demanded by Moses when
he charged the children of Israel 'if thy brother,...or thy son,
thy daughter, or the wife of thy bosom, or thy friend...entice thee
secretly, saying let us go serve other gods...thou shalt not consent...but thou shalt surely kill him'.[33] Tudor monarchs as
'God's lieutenants, God's presidents, God's officers, God's commissioners, God's judges, ordained of God Himself', were explicit.
The true subject should never hesitate 'to forsake father, mother,
kindred, wife, and children in respect of preserving the prince'.[34]
As with God, so with royalty; a double standard was claimed between king and subject, for the monarch was now the life-giving
symbol of a kingdom, beleaguered by the hellhounds of Catholicism,
in which a single attribute — even more binding than obedience
— qualified its citizens for membership: a sense of Englishness
especially blessed and protected by a Protestant God. By the end
of the century, Robert Greene felt no hesitation in putting the doctrine in its most extreme and political form:

> Why, Prince, it is no murder in a king,
> To end another's life to save his own:
> For you are not as common people be,
> Who die and perish with a few men's tears;
> But if you fail, the state doth whole default,
> The realm is rent in twain in such a loss.[35]

It is far too easy to accept Tudor monarchs at their own propaganda value and to become hypnotized by the rich verbiage that
hedged about the divinity of kings. The new leviathans of the sixteenth century were still infants compared to their later adult descendants, and they possessed dangerously immature feudal minds. The
prince might command paper divinity but he did not always receive

the respect due his office, and even Elizabeth put up with a degree
of waywardness and high-spirited disobedience among her beardless
boys that a modern head of state would never have countenanced.
To enforce their statutes and to mobilize their kingdoms, sixteenth-
century princes still had to rely on their great magnates, a number
of whom continued to harken back to the days when a king was
little more than a titular head, first among equals, and when barons
maintained private law, raised private armies, and commanded personal allegiance as great as — sometimes greater than — that offered
the King. Nevertheless, by the first decades of the sixteenth century an absolute upset in the political balance of power had occurred, and the two prerequisites for the growth of political paranoia
had been established — the concentration of political and economic
power at court, and the dependence of all worldly success upon
the favour of the monarch and his immediate entourage.[36] The
conspiratorial theory of politics simply could not function without that special brand of uncertainty and emotional stress that came
with a relatively rational and structured political organization which
permitted the belief that enemies abounded in close and evil prox-
imity to the wielders of power and that the enemy possessed the
economic and political instruments to achieve his wicked ends. Politics and paranoia have an affinity if only in that the one exaggerates
the power of authority and the other magnifies the rationality and
cunning of the adversary. When political authority became cen-
tred upon the person and symbol of a single individual, the conditions for politics by assassination were established to a degree
unimaginable in the medieval past. Henceforth, as Cardinal Allen
warned, the kingdom had to live in the fear that 'ambitious spirits'
were in fact making 'their packs and complots'.

The transformation of the King's household into a Renaissance
court and 'glittering misery' appeared in England with surprising
suddenness and in luxuriant form under Henry VIII as he reaped
the rich harvest of an expanding economy, of revenues that far
outstripped those of even the greatest barons of the realm, and of
policies laid down by his predecessors who sought to convert a torn
and fragmented feudal kingdom into a unified society of right-
thinking, right-acting subjects, who looked to and depended upon

the Crown's patronage for their sustenance and economic well-being. As the century progressed, much of that bounty began to dry up, courtly decorum stiffened into servile ritual whereby the prince was never spoken to or served except 'in adoration and kneeling', and space at the political top became increasingly scarce.[37] As a consequence, by the final decades of Elizabeth's reign political competition and paranoia had grown apace, producing, some historians have argued, a new, or at least an identifiable type — the disillusioned, unemployed, profoundly bored, and dangerously discontented failure known in literature as the 'melancholy malcontent'.[38]

The victims of the black bile of melancholy, who were branded by society as students of 'dangerous Machiavellism' and inventors of 'strategems, quirks and policies', and who suffered a 'meddling of evil angels' which caused them 'to foretell and forge very strange things in their imaginations', were not peculiar to the concluding years of Elizabeth's reign.[39] They were symptomatic and characteristic of the entire century in which boredom, frustration, anger, and uncertainty permeated the ante-rooms of the politically and economically fortunate and beset all who had to stand and wait upon the whims of others. Only during the final decades of the Tudor era, however, did literature catch up with reality and discover melancholia as a political and social affliction. Certainly Robert Burton's picture of the melancholic man, 'apt to mistake and amplify', ready 'to snarl upon every small occasion', on the alert for any sign — a laugh, cough, or gesture — that he is being criticized or ridiculed, and sure that when two or more talk or whisper together 'they mean him, [and] applies all to himself', was a perfect portrait of the paranoid mind and fitted neatly the profile of a century conditioned to 'fear the worst'.[40]

No one, of course, can say with surety whether those who were plagued with 'melancholy testiness' and the 'habit of malcontent' were pathological personalities, unique unto themselves, or whether they were the product of a paranoid cultural mould which conditioned society to imagine and therefore to find the enemy behind every friendly face. Certainly fear fostered by an agonistic and paranoid educational system, the conviction that conflict and evil were essential to God's plan, and the psychological strains produced by a social structure that sought to make treason unthinkable afflicted all but the most robust, optimistic, and healthy minded. The irrational and self-destructive treason to which the malcontents of Tudor society were drawn, when impelled by religious conviction, greed, bad luck, or the terrible logic of their lives whereby failure generated even greater failure, may indeed have been an expression of what has been called 'the maladjustment...of life itself to its environment'.[41] Conversely, the alarming tendency of traitors to lose control of reality and indulge in delusionary activities without concern for even the most basic safeguards for survival may have been personal and special to each one of them. The truth is that far too little is known about their motives, personalities and neuroses, cultural or pathological, to be sure.

A great deal, however, is known about one Tudor melancholic malcontent, for he was one of history's best documented butterflies. Therefore, on the grounds that it is impossible to count the number of angels on the head of a pin until at least one angel has been recognized and described, it is time to translate social and psychological theory into human and biographical reality and to recount the career of one of the most literate, vibrant, and paranoid traitors of the sixteenth century, Robert Devereux, second Earl of Essex.

VII

'WIN THE QUEEN'

> What psychoanalysis does assume, however, is that
> the psychological disturbances from which people
> suffer are related to the whole emotional climate
> in which they were reared, and that neurosis and
> psychosis in adult life are explicable in terms of a
> failure of the environment to meet the needs of
> the particular individual under scrutiny, at a time
> when those needs were paramount.
>
> Anthony Storr, 'The Man', in *Churchill Revised*

Robert Devereux, second Earl of Essex, is one of those elusive, mercurial figures who keep eluding the historian's grasp. Despite the
wealth and variety of documentation, he never quite adds up; some
crucial component of his character seems to have been mislaid, and
the deeper the analyst sounds the depth of his personality, the more
the truth evaporates into a mist of speculation. Essex was not, as
friends and foe alike so often depict him, a dazzling Icarus whose
soaring imagination and vaulting ambition lifted him to destruction. He was instead an explosive Proteus, a man of a thousand
moods, none of which were ever successfully hidden behind the
mask of dissimulation. He was, as his personal secretary Henry Cuffe
darkly observed, a victim of 'levity and inconstancy',[1] a
dangerously appealing but changeable charmer whose personality
lacked an anchor and whose public and private profiles were afflicted
by uncertainty, confusion, and suspicion stemming from the conviction that even the most trivial decision and trifling remark had
a hidden purpose directed against him.

Even the date of the Earl's birth is volatile, and there is uncertainty whether he was born on November 10th or 19th and whether
the year should be 1567, 1566, or 1565. Most historians opt for
November 10th, 1567,[2] but that calculation poses a further con-
undrum. Scholars agree that young Robert was damnably
precocious; but did he in fact enter Trinity College, Cambridge
at the age of nine and a half in May of 1577 and graduate, as the
college records maintain, Master of Arts four years later?[3]
Statistically it is just conceivable, for throughout the century at
least one other forward youth entered Cambridge at nine, but the
probability is not great.[4] Moreover, Sir Henry Wotton, another of
the Earl's secretary-cum-agents, remarked that Essex matriculated
at twelve, a statistic on which Sir Henry was not likely to have
been mistaken since he entered university at the more normal age
of sixteen.[5]

Essex was a child of Mercury, but he came from solid, stable stock.
The Devereux name stemmed from a Norman invader and cousin
of the Conqueror, Robert d'Evreux, who had been granted, by
his grateful prince, lands in the frontier county of Hereford.[6] For
fifteen generations the Devereuxs, defying all demographic and
actuarial predictions, survived with the male line intact, and in the
fifteenth century they commenced that series of fortuitous marriages that transformed a den of militant border barons into ranking peers of the realm. Once started, the process took little more
than a century. Shortly before 1446 Sir Walter Devereux married
Anne, the 7-year-old daughter and sole heiress of Lord Ferrers of
Chartley. She was dead at thirty, but not before Walter had been
summoned to Parliament as Lord Ferrers by right of his wife's
inheritance. Their son John projected the family another rung up
the aristocratic ladder by marrying, in 1488, Cecily, sister and only
heiress of Henry Bourchier, Earl of Essex, through whose veins
coursed the blood of half the royalty of England and Scotland. It
took three more generations for the Essex title to be resurrected
in the Devereux line, but family perseverance was eventually
rewarded. John's son Walter was created Viscount Hereford in 1550,
and twenty-two years later his grandson, another Walter and father
to young Robert, was elevated to the Earldom of Essex. That final

step had been immeasurably helped by yet another strategic alliance, for Walter Devereux in 1561 wedded the ravishing, if wayward, Lettice Knollys, grand-niece of Anne Boleyn and first cousin once removed to Queen Elizabeth.

The Devereuxs had made it to the top, but a fatal defect remained: the Tudors had been generous in their reward of service but they had singularly failed to conjoin land and revenues to titles, and as a result Walter, first Devereux Earl of Essex, found himself one of the most impecunious noblemen in the kingdom. To rectify this deficiency, he turned his thoughts across the Irish Sea to that emerald graveyard of so many English lives, reputations, and wallets, and in 1573 he mortgaged his Welsh estates to the Queen for £10,000, accepted his sovereign's gracious charter to seize and colonize large sections of south-east Ulster, and set sail at the head of 1,200 men to win wealth and honour. Dreams of conquest, however, rapidly evaporated as the Earl learned that campaigning against stubborn Irish chieftains involved a nightmare of disease, atrocities, and treacheries in which Devereux violated every code of chivalry by systematically putting old women and children to the sword and butchering his unarmed guests as they sat at his banquet table. The Irish in their turn murdered 'the Queen's subjects' whom they 'beheaded and then stuck their heads on poles with their privy members in their mouths'.[7] After three years of fruitless and barbarous slaughter, Walter had nothing to show for his brutality except an immense pile of debts and mortgages, and on September 22nd, 1576, after twenty-one days of agony, he died, aged thirty-five, 'in extreme pain, with flux and gripings in his belly'.[8] And so a stripling boy — Robert second Earl of Essex — came into an inheritance that was long on family name and blood but so impoverished that he scarcely had the means to pay for an education appropriate to his rank and lineage.

That young Robert's mind was sculptured according to the soul-searing Tudor educational standards whereby a boy was catechized in religion truly, framed in opinion rightly, and fashioned in behaviour civilly cannot be doubted. He was a ward of the Crown, and Lord Burghley saw to it that the 'Queen's children' were educated properly. The Earl dutifully purchased 'Isocrates in Greek' (four shillings) and 'Ramus on Tully's [Cicero's] orations' (four shillings). His imagination was inflamed by tales of heroism that 'make private men worthy to become rulers over others', and his moral character was fortified and elevated by reading about the rewards bestowed upon virtue and the dire consequences awarded disobedience found in that 'mirror of man's life', Holinshed's *Chronicles* (one pound, six shillings). And he memorized the wheres, whens, hows, whys and wherefores so necessary for enacting that role for which birth had cast him.[9] In later life, the Earl, heavily prompted by Francis Bacon, had nothing but praise for the educational goals of his generation. The 'end and scope' of learning, he told the young and impressionable Earl of Rutland, was 'the tilling and manuring of your own mind' to the 'sweetness' of decorous behaviour, to a 'freedom from passions' and to the 'power which maketh us perform good things and great things'.[10] Fluent in Latin, graceful in verse, conversant in French and Italian, Essex was thoroughly educated to perform upon a public stage. Only sluggish minds lived in obscure corners; the private life was an idle life, and he informed Lord Keeper Egerton 'that life I call idle' is that 'not spent in public business'.[11] Blood, training, and economic necessity, all dictated that as soon as he was of age he would be drawn to that centrepiece of Tudor society and politics — the court of Elizabeth I.

How well equipped young Devereux was for survival in the jungle of sixteenth-century politics is difficult to say. When he arrived at court sometime between his seventeenth and nineteenth year, he could claim political, physical, and mental advantages that seemingly would guarantee the fulfilment of every dream a young man might fancy. Tall of stature, fair of face, and blessed with reddish-blond hair; related by Boleyn blood to a sovereign who was known to be partial to a well-turned calf; directly descended from that wellspring of so much Plantagenet blood and genealogical confusion — Edward III — and possessed of a wit and pen that could match the best minds of his generation; Essex seemed to be preordained to achieve those 'good things and great things' that his educators had told him were the mark and obligation of privilege and rank.

And yet there were serious flaws, only barely noticeable in the golden hue of youth. In later life Essex liked to recollect that as a teenager just down from Trinity College and living on the family estate at Lampsie in Pembrokeshire, he acquired such a 'taste of the rural' life, he 'could well have bent his mind to a retired course'.[12] It was a pleasant dream on the part of a man weighed down by his misfortunes and the uncharitable actions of his enemies both real and imagined, and as Devereux knew, it was totally impossible. From the start he was drawn by education and financial necessity, without regard for talent or temperament, into that 'fatal circle' surrounding Elizabeth Tudor. There was simply no other option for a boy who had been born into a clan that had for generations made opportunism, advantageous marriages, and service to the Crown the instruments of its economic and political survival. But in retrospect, possibly it is not inaccurate to say that too much was asked of a sensitive boy who was for ever being judged not by what he was but by the high expectations due his noble status. Essex was never able to reconcile his knowledge of what was demanded of him, his public reputation and destined role in life, with his sense of self and individuality, and as a consequence he suffered from, and in the end was destroyed by, what contemporaries branded as insatiable pride but what the twentieth century tends to describe as an identity crisis.

Despite the best efforts of his educators to shape the soft wax of his personality to conform to a social ideal and to regiment it with godliness, decorum, and obedience, young Devereux never learned self-control or, until it was far too late, self-knowledge: the two hallmarks of the well-fashioned Tudor mind. His most endearing qualities — candour, enthusiasm, loyalty, integrity, sense of honour and disdain for hypocrisy — were fatally conjoined with excessive and almost psychotic touchiness, with mindless impulsiveness, with corroding melancholy, and with consuming egotism that could not allow him to share stage centre, not even with his Queen. The mixture proved disastrous at court, for Essex was incapable of following the most basic prescription for success in Tudor politics: to know 'when to speak and when to hold his peace'. In short, Essex never learned decorum. He invariably either overacted or overreacted; he could rarely fit his actions to the political occasion; and almost everyone agreed that he was never 'built or furnished for a courtier'. Henry Wotton described him as being 'a great resenter and a weak dissembler of the least disgrace', a man who could not keep 'his passions in his pocket'.[13] The contemporary historian William Camden called him a nobleman not 'made for the court,...of a soft and easy nature to take offence, but harder to remit it, and one that could not conceal himself'; and he quoted the Earl's secretary, Henry Cuffe, as complaining that Devereux carried 'his love and his hatred always in his brow'.[14] As a courtier, young Essex was a cripple, possessing only the last two of the four attributes prescribed by Nicholas Breton for success at court: 'concealing of discontentments, mitigating of passions, affability of speech, and courtesy in behaviour'.[15]

Worse yet, the boy who set forth to court in 1584, determined to 'exercise great and keen judgement, diligent watchfulness and care' not only to preserve the honour and reputation of his heritage but to excel it in courage and service to his Queen,[16] had no concept of, let alone defence against, failure. Tudor education had ignored what *The Practical Guide for Ambitious Politicians* presented as 'the best counsel that can be given to all courtiers': to 'prepare themselves for their fall'.[17] In the lexicon of noble youth there was no such word as 'failure'. As those stern pedagogical taskmasters of aristocratic expectations told all their noble pupils, the scions of privilege had less excuse for failure than the offspring of meaner folk. Essex as well as his mentors accepted as gospel the creed that a nobleman 'ought to be preferred in fees, honours, offices and other dignities of command and government before the common people'. Consequently, when in twelve short years fortune's wheel turned full circle and meteoric success was replaced by a series of escalating political débâcles, Devereux could only seek the explanation in sources outside himself. As his political career fell to pieces, the Earl found it far easier to populate his world with enemies hellbent on his personal destruction than to reckon with his own deficiencies.

Possibly no figure in Tudor history was ever so much a victim of and a symptom of the paranoia that beset late Elizabethan society as this impoverished, if charismatic, youth who came to court at the invitation of his newly acquired stepfather, Robert Dudley Earl of Leicester, to charm a bewigged, painted, and cantankerous sovereign lady, some thirty-five years his senior. The courtier who wore his heart on his sleeve and was desperate for the financial fruits of political office and favour was painfully vulnerable in the lair of an elderly female who invariably played politics with loaded dice[18] and gambled with the ambition, bravado, and paranoia of the beardless boys who sought to charm and manipulate her.

That 'deep and unscrutable centre of the Court, which is her Majesty's mind'[19] was, as it had been almost from the day Elizabeth ascended the throne over a quarter of a century before, the fulcrum upon which political and economic success and failure wavered and teetered with agonizing uncertainty. 'Win the Queen' had been the quintessence of Francis Bacon's famous advice to Essex. 'If this be not the beginning, of any other course, I can see no end,' except, he might have added, disaster.[20] The Queen's mind, which had been shaped by the experiences and memory of her majestic father who had known himself to be a 'god on earth', remained constant and unbending. Unfortunately, economic and biological conditions changed as the autumn of her reign turned into the winter of both her own and her subjects' discontent. Survival at court became an increasingly unpredictable game in which the stakes, though ever fewer in number, grew proportionately in worth as war with Spain and in Ireland dried up the Queen's bounty, and the years inevitably advanced her towards that moment when a new sovereign must sit upon the throne. 'Two weighty and watchful solicitudes', Henry Wotton noted, kept Essex as well as his entire generation tense with anxiety and expectation, 'like a bow still bent'. First, he had 'to wrestle with a Queen's declining, or rather with her very setting age'. And second, there was always the unmentionable, but ever-present, question: who would succeed a lady 'somewhat shy', to say the least, of thinking about, let alone naming, her successor?[21]

As Elizabeth aged, the magic upon which her reign relied began to falter. She could no longer satisfy every suitor's expectations with a smile. The metaphorically mixed but deeply sincere love offered 'upon the knees' of their hearts by the young gallants of her salad days was giving way to the frustration of a generation that found it increasingly embarrassing to live with, not to mention worship, an idol who survived on memories that grew more distant and less real with every passing year. Her court, as her godson Sir John Harington sighed, had become a stage where there was 'no love but that of the lusty god of gallantry, Asmodeus',[22] and Gloriana herself was forced to rely more and more upon deception and legerdemain to hold her audience. Cosmetics and false hair encroached upon nature; ritual replaced the spontaneity of youth; niggardliness seemed to triumph everywhere; and the myth that Bess could do no wrong fitted ill with the sharpening image of a royal scold whose 'ireful speeches', tongue-lashings, ear-boxings, and prevarications left her servants and subjects hurt, frustrated, and angry. The enmity, backbiting, and emotional strain that were inherent within the Tudor political system were magnified tenfold when proud, impoverished and ambitious courtiers could lament that 'no man is rewarded to his desert'.[23] The emotional atmosphere at court was electric with paranoia and the mirror of majesty shattered when an Essex could eventually be induced to cry out that his royal mistress 'was as crooked in her disposition as in her carcass'.[24]

Wrestling with the Queen's declining age, wooing and winning a sovereign in her fifties, was an uncertain venture. That Essex succeeded was largely because his faults were so endearing. It helped, of course, to have the great Earl of Leicester as a patron. Perversely, it even helped to have as a mother the one woman Gloriana thoroughly detested, for Lettice Devereux, now Lady Leicester, had dared to outqueen the Queen by appearing at court in gowns, bodices, and farthingales even more bejewelled and resplendent than Gloriana's own. For her lese-majesty, Lettice had been informed that 'as but one sun lighted the east', so Elizabeth 'would have but one Queen in England'; and she had had her ears boxed for her arrogance and been ordered never again to present herself at court.[25] It amused her Majesty to monopolize Essex's affections and capture his admiration if only because this was a means of detracting from his mother's influence. But above all, it helped that young 'Robin' Devereux was such a maverick, the antithesis of those stiff and conniving courtiers who studied the Queen's every mood with calculating intent and modelled themselves upon George Puttenham's 'courtly poet' who dissembled 'not only his countenances and conceits but also all his ordinary actions of behaviour... whereby the better to win his purposes and good advantages ...'[26] Instead, Essex 'dared to be open with her'. He disdained court etiquette and manners, and on most occasions cared little for sartorial finery, hardly knowing 'what he had on' even while in her Majesty's presence.[27] His very naivety, at least for a time, was an attraction to a middle-aged sovereign who seemed to delight in his moody sulks and temper tantrums, in his ostentatious determination to excel all others 'in valiancy of arms, in knowledge and dexterity in all honest things', and in his open jealousy of any rival for his royal lady's favour.[28] Finally, it helped that he entered Elizabeth's service during those euphoric years when an English David stood boldly against a Spanish Goliath, when God's chosen people knew themselves to be united against the papal dragon, and when the Queen's abundance of favours and offices, annuities and monopolies still overflowed.

Essex was an instant success, which was just as well since his estates were mortgaged to the sum of £25,473, the Queen still held his father's IOU for another £10,000, and he was soon confronted with the high cost of courtly and military life. In the autumn of 1585 he was invited to accompany his stepfather in Elizabeth's last-minute military effort to save the Low Countries from total defeat by the well-disciplined and seemingly invincible troops of Philip of Spain. The young Earl was delighted and, although his grandfather accused him of 'wasteful consumption', Essex immediately invested £1,000 outfitting a band of his own retainers in heraldic regalia appropriate to a gallant and eager young nobleman. Devereux had little chance to prove himself in the defence of the Lowlands except to get drunk, skirmish victoriously with Spanish musketeers and pikemen, be created knight banneret by Leicester, and inherit Sir Philip Sidney's 'best sword' after that legendary and perfect soldier-poet-courtier died from wounds received in the same engagement in which the young Earl won his spurs.

By November of 1586 both Essex and his stepfather were back

in England thoroughly disgusted with their Dutch allies. Leicester was to return within the year, but Devereux in his new-found role as royal favourite was regarded as being too precious to be risked on war. Throughout the spring and summer of 1587 the Queen and her newest, handsome toy were inseparable: 'when she is abroad, nobody [is] near her but my Lord of Essex; and, at night, my Lord is at cards, or one game or another with her, [so] that he cometh not to his own lodging till birds sing in the morning'.[29] As the association grew, so also did Devereux's expectations, and it was reported in mid May that 'he looked to be Master of the Horse within these ten days'.[30] The prediction was correct; the mastership with its revenues of £1,500 was bestowed on June 18th, 1587, and one of the central features of Essex's political existence was established: between his financial ruin and his sovereign's favour there could be 'no mean'.

Unfortunately Essex's financial sweet was not without its occupational and political sour sauce. He had to share his mistress's favour with that knave Raleigh. Worse, he had to struggle with the hidden eddies and dark currents of the Queen's mind, and in doing so he twice blundered — once in February and again in July — and revealed the defects of his personality that would in the end destroy him. He was devoid of any sense of timing; he was incapable of controlling, let alone concealing, his emotions; and he personalized politics, convinced not only that every setback was a deliberate affront to him personally but also that his enemies were for ever hard at work conspiring his undoing.

Essex had a gift for backing the wrong candidate for office at the wrong time, and his first attempt to influence court politics was a dangerous portent of disasters yet to come. On February 17th, 1587 Elizabeth allowed herself to be tricked into permitting the execution of that Catholic 'handmaid of iniquity' and daughter of all sedition, her first cousin and anointed Queen of Scotland, Mary Stuart. Bess faced an excruciating dilemma: either to spill the blood of a kinswoman and thereby violate the sanctity that enshrined the brotherhood of monarchs or to leave uncured a festering wound that imperilled her life and might soon destroy her kingdom. With that volatile mixture of hypocrisy and sincerity that passed for Gloriana's sense of political morality, she decided after months of procrastination to sign the warrant of execution but reserved the privilege of bursting into righteous indignation when her ministers carried out her orders. Mr Secretary William Davison was left holding the bag, for he had taken the signed warrant to the Council, and Elizabeth swore she would have the Judas hanged. Into this political and emotional thunderstorm, when every other sensible politician was running for cover, rushed Essex, bungling and innocent, to attempt to save the luckless victim of Elizabeth's guilty conscience. With unbelievable naivety, he wrote to James of Scotland that 'Mr Davison, fallen into her Majesty's displeasure and disgrace, [but] beloved of the best and most religious in this land, doth stand as barred from any preferment or restoring in this place, except, out of the honour and nobleness of your royal heart, your Majesty will undertake his cause'.[31] What Essex thought the son of the executed Mary Stuart could or would do for the man who had been as instrumental as anybody in arranging his mother's death and had been officially singled out as the scapegoat can only be sought for in the strange and muddled unreality that substituted for political acumen in the Earl's young mind. He never comprehended that the system required that the Queen's conscience, as well as her person, could do no wrong but that her ministers could, and they had to suffer the consequences.

The same miscalculation was apparent five months later when in July of 1587 Essex and Elizabeth had a public row over the presence of the Earl's sister, Dorothy Perrot, as a guest in the home of the Countess of Warwick. Devereux had leaped to the conclusion that Raleigh was behind the confrontation and was responsible for the Queen's humiliating order that the girl be sent to her room. Essex's reactions were overly theatrical and played directly to Gloriana's delight in baiting her young courtiers. He started by loudly venting his 'grief and choler' at Raleigh, who was eavesdropping at the door; his words, however, only led Elizabeth to defend Raleigh all the more and eventually goaded her into attacking Essex's mother. Hurt and embarrassed, the Earl haughtily announced he would immediately send his sister away from the house, and that for himself, he was 'loath to be near about' his mistress when he knew that his affections were 'so much thrown down and such a wretch as Raleigh highly esteemed of her'. He then stalked out of the room, took horse to Margate and hired a ship for Flushing and a hero's death in the Lowlands, informing his friend Edward Dyer that:

> If I return, I will be welcomed home; if not, an honourable death is better than a disquiet life... My friends will make the best of it; mine enemies cannot say it is dishonest; the danger is mine, and I am content to abide the worst.[32]

Already Essex's political style was taking on that emotional, almost suicidal, flamboyance that was to characterize his reaction to any personal setback or affront, and his political world was becoming populated with those personal enemies who sought to turn the Queen against him. For Essex, the evil minister and the conspiring favourite were more than convenient masks by which to shield the realities of the Queen's nastiness; they were realities in themselves.

Robert Devereux never got to Flushing and a chance for a memorable death in war in the style of Sir Philip Sidney. His mistress peremptorily ordered him back before he could even set sail, and all was forgiven. Elizabeth still delighted in and needed her moody, vibrant Earl; moreover, every soldier was required at home, for open military confrontation with Spain was scarcely a year away. The crisis came during the spring and summer of 1588 when Philip of Spain determined that the English citadel and cesspool of heresy would have to be breached and disinfected before he could subdue rebellion in the Low Countries. Essex, much to his chagrin, was not allowed to join Lord Charles Howard in that moment of glory when the Armada was destroyed by a combination of English determination and technological superiority and by Protestant winds that smashed Spanish men-of-war upon the reefs of Holland and the rocks of Scotland and Ireland. But he was allowed to prance gallantly beside his Queen at Tilbury, where the English army was encamped.

The following year, however, he nearly strangled his political career 'almost in the very cradle' by chasing off after 'the Portugal voyage' without the Queen's consent. The naval expedition of April to June 1589, designed to restore Don Antonio, the ex-King of Portugal, to his throne and prove to Philip that the war could be taken to his very back yard, was one of those magnificent but expensive military gestures from which commanders derived much honour but the Queen no profit. Worse, as far as Essex was concerned, Gloriana was not pleased by her favourite's disobedience, and she ordered her handsome Earl to return home in such strident and royal terms that he had no choice but to obey — 'Essex, your sudden and undutiful departure from our presence. . . you may easily conceive how offensive it is, and. . . we do therefore charge and command you forthwith, upon receipt of these our letters, all excuses and delays set apart, to make your present and immediate repair unto us.'[33]

Once again young Devereux escaped the consequences of his actions. His mistress chose to regard his defiance of her authority as just another 'sally of youth', and the Earl set himself to playing the proper courtier. Time spent winning the Queen was well worth the effort, for the Earl of Leicester had died in September of 1588 and two political prizes were available which Essex felt belonged in the family — Leicester's farm of sweet wine worth £2,500 a year and his position as General of the Queen's Armies. This time the young Earl played his cards deftly, and in 1590 he received the coveted monopoly and the economic means by which to transform himself from a privileged favourite into a major political power. The second prize took longer to achieve — two months of continuous nagging and two hard hours pleading on bended knee before his sovereign — but in June of 1591 the Earl of Essex was appointed General of the Queen's Armies destined for France when the centre of the Catholic-Protestant military struggle moved from the Lowlands and the English Channel to the gates of Paris. The assassination of the last Valois king on August 1st, 1589 had transformed Protestant Henry of Navarre into the Most Christian King of France. For once Elizabeth's conscience was at ease: she could support a legitimate sovereign and at the same time thwart her one-time brother-in-law, Philip of Spain, whose armies were seeking to defy God's will and place upon the French throne Isabella Valois, Philip's daughter by his second wife.

At first Essex was delighted by the course of events and took every occasion to display his army of 7,000 men, cavorting about France in search of fame and honour. Unfortunately, the operation shortly turned out to have less to do with chivalric one-upmanship, in which Devereux so delighted and excelled, than with broken promises, lethal sanitary conditions, inconclusive military engagements devoid of glory and, most frustrating of all, constant interference and criticism by Elizabeth and mounting fear on the part of the new commander that his political rivals were taking advantage of his absence from court. Essex had landed at Dieppe on August 3rd and four days later wrote one of those strange letters filled with over-optimism and paranoid fears that would soon become the hallmark of his literary style. 'Your Majesty's army is, I dare say, for the number, the finest troop in Christendom. I protest unto your Majesty, the French do more admire them than can be believed.' These brave words, however, were followed by fearful thoughts that 'another in mine absence should rob me of your gracious and dearest favour', and he confessed that he was 'jealous of all the world, and have cause, since all other men that have either open eyes or sensible hearts are my competitors'.[34] The Earl's forebodings were justified, and before his tour of duty was finished, he had learned at first hand the truth of Raleigh's dictum that errors on the part of distant servants, unable to defend themselves, were invariably exaggerated. In desperation the commander wrote to Sir Robert Cecil that 'I was blamed as negligent, undutiful, rash in going, slow in returning, undiscreet in dividing the horse from the foot, faulty in all things because I was not fortunate to please',[35] and he began to conclude his letters to the Queen with what would become a standard line in most future communiqués — he was ill, overworked, misunderstood, abused and melancholic; 'I have been sick all day and yet write at night till my dim eyes and weak hands do fail me...'[36]

The French campaign was a disaster from which Devereux learned nothing; it was too easy to blame French duplicity for his failings and to rely on his silver tongue to allay his mistress's growing annoyance over a totally ineffectual military venture and deflect her fury over his creation of twenty-four new knights, more knighthoods than Elizabeth had bestowed during the previous decade, including the Armada year. Devereux's standard response to any royal criticism was to put pen to parchment and produce one of those marvellously beguiling epistles upon which he depended to win his way back into Gloriana's heart. His letter of October 18th, 1591 was a model of elegantly phrased flattery:

> The two windows of your privy chamber shall be the poles of my sphere, where, as long as your Majesty will please to have me, I am fixed and unmoveable. When your Majesty thinks that heaven [is] too good for me, I will not fall like a star, but be consumed like a vapour by the same sun that drew me up to such a height. While your Majesty gives me leave to say I love you, my fortune is as my affection, unmatchable.[37]

The words, although profoundly prophetic, had their desired effect; the Queen was soothed, and Essex's good fortune remained 'unmatchable'. Mr Secretary Francis Walsingham had died shortly before Devereux left for France, thereby leaving vacant two political plums — the Principal Secretaryship and the Chancellorship of the Duchy of Lancaster — both of which Devereux coveted. Lord Chancellor Christopher Hatton had also gone to his grave, and in the musical chairs involved in filling his post, Essex felt sure that something was bound to come to him and his political friends. Best of all, six months after his return to court in January of 1592, the impudence of that knave Raleigh finally caught up with him: he put one of the Queen's maids up against a tree, got her pregnant, and ended up in the Tower for his violation of his sovereign's old-fashioned rules of propriety. With Raleigh in disgrace and the older generation fading away, only the Lord Treasurer, old Lord Burghley, and his crook-backed cub, Robert Cecil, stood between Devereux and absolute control of Gloriana's closet. That 'old Leviathan' Burghley was impregnable,[38] but the hourglass of his life could have little sand left. And although Essex might for the moment be outside the citadel of real power, time was surely on his side. As for dull, spindle-legged Cecil, 'his hands full of papers and head full of matters',[39] once his father was gone, he could scarcely compete with charming, flamboyant Essex, who could twist the Queen's emotions as he pleased.

Not only did the future look bright, but Essex also had the support of two of the best minds of the century, Anthony and Francis Bacon; the former constructing an international espionage system to keep the Earl alerted and well informed, the latter offering him counsel that would have made the author of *A Practical Guide for Ambitious Politicians* look like a simple-minded monk thrown into a palace of Machiavellian princes. Winning the Queen, according to Francis, was only the start. The trick was to know how to manipulate her, and Bacon proceeded systematically to enumerate each of the Earl's faults and to instruct him how either to conceal them or use them to his advantage in controlling the Queen. Essex, he pointed out, was too proud, too extravagant, too solicitous of public acclaim, too entranced by military strutting, and too hypnotized by the tinsel and trappings of power. Could there be, he asked, 'a more dangerous image' to present to any monarch, especially one jealous of her power and popularity? No combination of traits, Bacon cautioned, was better designed to persuade a sovereign of 'her Majesty's apprehension' to listen to those who would keep Essex's estates 'bare and low', misrepresent his actions, speak against his friends and dependants, and scheme to place him in 'odious employments and offices' and send him on 'perilous and desperate enterprises', thereby destroying his reputation, revealing his weaknesses and goading him into ruinous measures. If ever Elizabeth should become distrustful of her Earl, the court abounded in evil men who would be happy to spy out her 'humours and conceits, and second them: and not only second them, but in seconding increase them', and turn them to their own advantage and the destruction·of Essex.

Devereux's only defence, according to Bacon, was to emulate Puttenham's courtier, control his countenance, appear to be what he was not, and lull his royal mistress into a false sense of security. He should never remind her of past failures or irrevocable mistakes; he should model his approach to his coquettish and maiden sovereign upon the successes of past favourites, especially his stepfather; and when flattering the Queen, he should try to appear fresh, witty, and extemporaneous. He should always, Bacon counselled, have some 'particular afoot' which he could easily drop 'upon taking knowledge of her Majesty's opposition and dislike'; and he should deliberately support a candidate for office whom he was willing to give way upon in order to please the Queen and appear amenable to compromise and harmony, thereby avoiding the reputation of being opinionated and stubborn. Occasionally it was prudent to leave the court to attend to private business — it would make him look diligent and serious — but he should not go away too often or stay too long. And most important of all, he should shun all military positions such as the Earl Marshal or the Master of the Ordinance, and seek instead the office of Lord Privy Seal, 'a quiet place' worth a thousand pounds a year. Finally, Bacon warned, never seek to upstage the Queen: it smattered of kingmaking, denied the divinity of her office, and hinted at that Tudor anathema, personal popularity with the unwashed multitude. Sulking, storming, melodramatic withdrawals from court and constant nagging for favours were no ways to move Gloriana or win her respect. Such behaviour, Bacon cautioned, might be effective on occasion but it soon grew dull and lost its edge from overuse. In contrast, finesse, timing, insinuation, dissimulation, decorum, and 'obsequiousness and observance' were far more efficient instruments for shaping the fine grain of royalty to one's own image.[40] In short, 'princes may be led but not driven'.[41]

The advice was excellent, but the Bacon brothers did Essex no service by packaging their political observations in sinister Machiavellian wrappings, for their patron, although he was himself incapable of practising what they preached, was nevertheless convinced that everybody else was, in fact, doing so. Their analysis of court politics and how to sway the Queen simply played upon Essex's growing paranoia, which was nourished by a host of political associates and servants who viewed Tudor politics as an encounter between 'villainous enemies and...noble friends'. Wherever Devereux turned, he received a chorus of Cassandra-like prophesies, urging him to 'walk circumspectly' and 'fear the worst'. 'God grant you', wrote the mother of the Bacon brothers, 'safety from all crafty subtle snares whatsoever'.[42] Anthony Bacon was just as pessimistic and prayerful; not only was he convinced that Robert Cecil had become 'a mortal enemy, and will make me feel it when he can' but he also appealed to God to 'preserve her Majesty's royal heart, if not her ears, from the venomous infections of the two pestilent vipers, sovereign jealousy, and subaltern unquenchable envy'.[43] The Earl's secretary, Mr Reynolds, was equally alarmist and feared that his master's absence from court would 'give time, opportunity, and advantage to the cunning plotters and practicers of the court, who work at all times...but most of all in absence, upon the discontented humours of her Majesty'.[44] Given such an environment and the Earl's already highly developed paranoid leanings, it is not surprising that by January of 1597 he confessed that as a patron he felt himself to be totally hamstrung and dared not act without the written licence of the Queen, for 'knowing how carefully mine enemies lie in wait to carp at all my actions, and how many things are therefore censured to be ill done because they are done by me, I durst not, I say, without warrant from her Majesty, resolve anything or do anything in the matter moved unto me'.[45]

Paranoia may be the product of a sick and tortured mind, but it also possesses a self-fulfilling quality. The paranoid invariably finds the treachery he is looking for, and in late January of 1594 Essex 'discovered a most dangerous and desperate treason'. His worst fears were realized, and with brutal succinctness he reported: 'The point of conspiracy was her Majesty's death. The executioner should have been Dr Lopez; the manner poison.'[46] How much substance there was to the Lopez plot is impossible to ascertain. It may have been manufactured by Essex as part of a personal vendetta against the Queen's private physician who had earned the Earl's wrath by gossiping in public about his intimate medical problems. Equally possible, it may have been a politically motivated demonstration to prove to Burghley and the Queen the value of Essex's international espionage system constructed by Anthony Bacon. It is even conceivable that the conspiracy was in fact based on some shred of reality torn out of context from the murky and contradictory world of spy and counterspy. Whatever the truth — unadulterated fiction or partial verity — there is no doubt that the plot grew and blossomed in a political atmosphere that presumed the existence of evil, especially when it could be so neatly tied to Jewry, for Dr Roderigo Lopez was a Portuguese Jew who had fled to England in 1559 and had thrived as a fashionable London physician. Initially, and to Devereux's absolute fury, the Queen dismissed the evidence as a tissue of malicious fabrications and Essex as a 'rash and temerarious youth'.[47] Enraged and humiliated, the Earl stalked out of the royal presence, dashed at breakneck speed back to London and Essex House, and locked himself into his private bedchamber. For two days, oscillating between bouts of obsessive brooding and overwork, Essex examined, cross-examined, and re-examined everyone concerned with Lopez, and not surprisingly came up with a case that he claimed would make the villain's guilt 'appear as clear as the noon-day'.[48] And so it did; in February the unfortunate Doctor and two associates, all intermittently confessing and denying their crimes, were tried and horribly executed as the law and public expectation demanded.

Not only was the Earl preoccupied during the winter and early spring of 1593–94 with the spectre of evil directed against the Queen, but he was also growing increasingly concerned about another matter in which the enemy could be detected. Try as he might Devereux did not seem to be able to tap the source of his mistress's generosity for anybody except himself. This was a serious development, for if he were to be anything more than a gilded butterfly enmeshed in a golden net of economic dependence upon the Queen, he had to build up a patronage system of satisfied suitors relying upon his influence for their well-being. The son of the fallen Secretary William Davison, to whose defence Essex had rushed back in 1587, put his finger on the central issue of the Earl's political difficulties when in November of 1596, shortly after Essex's glorious return from the sacking of Cadiz, he posed the crucial question: whether Devereux 'shall be able to bring in any of his friends to strengthen him (of which all the world thinks he hath need) or keep out his greatest enemies, who will seek by all possible means to overthrow him, I now neither see nor hope for'.[49]

The first public indication of Essex's inability to control the

Queen's patronage involved the Principal Secretaryship which had been vacant ever since April 1590, for Elizabeth's shopworn solution to the factional struggle to capture various key positions in her government was to procrastinate. At first Essex had the poor taste to push again for the return of William Davison, but when Gloriana said 'no' in a way that even Devereux could understand, he backed off and began to recommend Sir Thomas Bodley, a worthy but dull gentleman in no way attractive to the Queen. The Earl's purpose was obvious; he was determined to block Lord Burghley's ambition to place his son Robert in the Secretaryship. In his usual intemperate fashion Essex so overplayed his hand, praising Bodley to the skies and detracting 'from Cecil's reputation with such odious comparisons', that he antagonized the Queen, who 'now began to disapprove of those men whom he most commended', and he so branded Bodley as an Essex follower that Burghley changed his mind about a possible compromise whereby he would have settled for Bodley and his son sharing the office.[50] Essex simply could not heed Bacon's admonition to drop a candidate 'upon taking knowledge of her Majesty's opposition and dislike', and as a consequence the office remained unfilled.

Ironically it was Bacon himself who was forced to suffer the disastrous results of his patron's ineptitude and lack of political decorum. Francis had been classified in Elizabeth's mind as a brash young troublemaker, for in the Parliament of April 1593 he had spoken out against the government's proposed heavy tax to pay for the defence of the kingdom. The Queen's manifest disapproval, however, did not in the least deter the Earl from supporting his protégé for the office of Attorney General. Essex set his heart, staked his political reputation and foolishly cashed in all of his chips with his royal mistress in order to attain the post for Francis. The lesser position of Solicitor General was also vacant, but Essex would not settle for second best in what rapidly escalated into a political battle between the Cecil and Essex factions at court, and in a conversation with Robert Cecil he made his position immoderately clear. When Cecil expressed surprise that Devereux 'should go about to spend your strength in so unlikely or impossible a matter' as to seek the Attorney Generalship for Bacon when the Solicitorship was 'of easier digestion to her Majesty', Essex was incensed. 'Digest me no digestions,' he stormed, 'for the attorneyship for Francis is that I must have; and in that will I spend all my power, might, authority and amity, and with tooth and nail defend and procure the same for him against whomsoever.'[51]

Devereux was as good as his word. He launched a campaign to wear Elizabeth down, announcing that 'what I cannot effect at once, I will look to do *saepe cadendo*'. When he encountered the Queen's delaying tactics, he assured the Bacon brothers he would 'take the first opportunity I can to move your suit', and would 'tomorrow take more time to deal with her, and will sweeten her with all the art I have to make *benevolum auditorem*'.[52] A more hysterical scene in which the Earl mixed politics with personal reputation was described in detail. '[I] urged her, that though she could not signify her mind to others, I might have a secret promise [of her intent], wherein I should receive great comfort; as in the contrary great unkindness.' Elizabeth was thoroughly annoyed by this blatant appeal to favouritism, and Essex reported that in a passion she 'bade me go to bed, if I would talk of nothing else. Wherefore in passion I went away, saying . . . I would retire myself till I might be more graciously heard.' Essex would never give up: 'Tomorrow I will go hence of purpose, and on Thursday I will write an expostulating letter . . .'[53] A few days later he was reporting that 'I went yesterday to the Queen' and 'had long speech with her of you, wherein I urged both the point of your extraordinary sufficiency . . . and the point of mine own satisfaction, which, I protested, should be exceeding great, if for all her unkindness and discomforts past, she would do this one thing for my sake'. In answer she retorted that 'if there were a yielding, it was fitter to be of my side'.[54]

In the end the Earl lost out to his 'mighty enemies',[55] and both the Attorney Generalship and the Solicitor Generalship went to Cecil supporters. In sorrow and bitter disappointment he made one of those marvellously sincere gestures that redeemed so many of his political idiocies and won men to him. Bacon had, he said, fared ill 'because you have chosen me for your means and dependence . . . I die if I do not [do] somewhat toward your fortune'; and he presented Francis with a handsome piece of property worth £1,800.[56] Essex could afford to indulge his honour and generosity. Even though he could persuade his sovereign to do nothing for Bacon, her bounty to her Earl continued unabated. On February 25th, 1593 he achieved his political goal: he was sworn in as a full member of the Privy Council, and the following year she presented him with £4,000, saying 'Look to thyself, good Essex, and be wise to help thyself without giving thy enemies advantage; and my hand shall be readier to help thee than any other.'[57]

Essex stood at the apex of his career. Even the elements seemed to be favourably inclined, for during the summer of 1596 the breezes blew fresh for a naval descent upon King Philip's homeland, and three of the most renowned, if temperamental, gentlemen at Elizabeth's court — my lord of Essex, Lord Admiral Charles Howard of Armada fame, and Sir Walter Raleigh, who had been returned to favour and commanded one of the battle galleons — set sail for Cadiz. The expedition, a combined Dutch and English venture consisting of over 13,000 sailors and soldiers and an armada of 150 transports, men-of-war, and lesser vessels, had been ready since April. Elizabeth, however, had been her usual capricious self, urging her military men forward, then abruptly cancelling their orders, unable to make up her mind where to send them or whether to risk her money on that most uncertain of all military operations, an amphibious strike against Spain. In utter frustration and growing criticism of his mistress, Essex raged that she 'wrangles with our action for no cause but because it is in hand'.[58] Eventually, however, Gloriana committed herself and her sailors to what she disliked the most: an irrevocable decision.

For once almost everything that could go right appeared to do so. Four immense Spanish galleons — the pride of Philip's navy — were burned or captured; the city of Cadiz and its citadel were assaulted and plundered; and a convoy of thirty-six undefended merchant ships was discovered in the inner harbour. Raleigh and Essex both had a chance to display their courage and honour. Raleigh met the guns of the Spanish galleons with scornful blasts of his ship's trumpets, and Essex, beating cadence on a drum, waded ashore at the head of 200 men, scaled the walls of Cadiz and fought his way to the central square. The only blemish to an otherwise storybook victory was a trifling oversight on the part of the English commanders: they were so busy winning glory and dividing up the plunder that they forgot about the merchant ships, which the Spaniards proceeded to burn to keep them out of English hands, thereby depriving Elizabeth of merchandise worth eight to twelve million ducats — easily sufficient to run her government for a year.

Gloriana was not pleased, and although she publicly acclaimed her wayward heroes on their triumphant return in early August, the more she learned about their irresponsible antics the more she scolded. Essex had anticipated trouble but not the form it took. To his intense mortification he discovered that in his absence the Queen had given the Principal Secretaryship to Robert Cecil, thereby commencing a disturbing pattern — no matter when Cecil entered the revolving door of Elizabethan politics, he invariably contrived to exit in front of Essex and to do so while the Earl was safely away from court attempting to win military laurels. Of more immediate concern, Devereux sensed a Cecilian plot to single him out as being financially responsible for the entire expedition. The Cadiz adventure had yielded less than £28,000 but had cost Elizabeth £50,000. The careless loss of the merchant fleet rankled deeply, and through her newly appointed Principal Secretary, Elizabeth began to pry into what she regarded as Essex's mishandling of the spoils of war which she felt rightfully belonged to her as the chief shareholder in the expedition. She even went so far as to suggest that he forgo the ransom of prisoners, which by the rules of chivalry belonged to him. Essex's reaction was typical. He could not believe that the Queen blamed him or that she was responsible for such a suggestion, and his anger fell as usual upon Cecil: 'I was more braved by your little cousin', he wrote to Anthony Bacon, 'than ever I was by any man in my life.'[59] The Earl's latent paranoia was heightened by Lady Bacon's warning to her son 'to be more circumspect' and 'walk more warily' now that Cecil was fully installed 'in his long longed-for Secretary's place'.[60] Essex himself was soon referring to Cecil's financial probings as 'these plots of his enemies' which, he boasted, 'instead of destroying' him had 'rendered him more agreeable to the Queen'.[61]

Essex may have bragged in public that he was more than ever 'agreeable to the Queen', but his actions belied his words, for in the face of political setbacks, the Earl's behaviour was becoming predictable; he sulked, feigned sickness and withdrew from court; and it was noted that 'his lordship is wearied, and scorneth the practices and dissembling courses of this place'.[62] There was, alas, no end to the 'dissembling courses' of the court, and when on March 5th, 1597 old Lord Cobham died and his two offices, the Lord Chamberlain and Warden of the Cinque Ports, fell vacant, Devereux again detected the sinister influence of his 'enemy' Robert Cecil. Instead of following Bacon's advice and directing his efforts at attaining for himself the civil office of Lord Chamberlain, Essex demanded the military post. He did so first for Robert Sidney, the younger brother of Philip, his dead friend and hero, but when Elizabeth balked, he made it known that he himself was a candidate for the wardenship. When the Queen announced that Henry Brooke, Lord Cobham's son and Robert Cecil's brother-in-law, would be appointed warden regardless of the Earl's pleas, Essex immediately became 'indisposed with melancholy', again retired from the court in high dudgeon, and announced that his enemies had once more triumphed and that his sovereign had been turned against him.[63]

Devereux as usual had leaped to the wrong conclusion, for in the same month Henry Cobham received the wardenship, Elizabeth displayed her continued favour by presenting the Earl with the Mastership of the Ordinance,[64] a military position of great importance since the kingdom was preparing itself for yet another descent upon Spain and for what was hoped would be an even more glorious and profitable repeat of the Cadiz triumph. Essex received what he desired above all else, absolute command, but the gods were unkind: this time everything that could go wrong did so, and the commander had no one to blame but himself. The weather was abominable and delayed the expedition for weeks; Devereux was unable to destroy Philip's warships stationed at Ferrol as he had been instructed to do; his own ships were dispersed and battered by further storms; when he sailed for the Azores, the Spanish treasure fleet eluded his grasp; and what might have been a consolation prize — an immense 1,800-ton galleon — was beached and burned by the Spaniards under his nose. There was no honour, no glory, no profit, only heavy charges against the Queen's exchequer, and the Earl sailed for home in October deeply bitter against those who 'sat warm and at home and descant upon us' and 'lacked strength to perform more' or 'courage to adventure so much'.[65]

Contemporaries and modern historians alike are agreed that Essex never recovered from the Azores fiasco: his psychological hold on reality began to slip, his mind more and more paralyzed by 'the black poison of suspect'. The Earl, it has been said, 'coarsened' and adversity 'deformed him'; 'his humours grew tart'; there was a 'physical deterioration of judgment and faculties'; and he began to commit 'strange mistakes'.[66] One modern historian has suggested that he suffered from syphilis, but this is little more than theorizing based on the flimsiest court rumours and the speculation that his vindictive and obsessive insistence that Dr Lopez had committed treason was spawned by the doctor's violation of professional confidence about the nature of the Earl's illness, which Lopez had been treating.[67] Syphilis in the sixteenth century ravaged both mind and body and is a convenient whipping disease for almost any variety of irrational behaviour. It is not, however, necessary to burden the Earl with Venus' curse; he had enough ailments already — rheumatic pains, fevers, dysentery, ague, and painful sensitivity to cold. Moreover, he was obviously afflicted with melancholia, his mental health fluctuating wildly between dizzy bouts of ungrounded optimism and spasms of black depression and psychosomatic illness.

The Essex of 1597 may have coarsened, but he was essentially no different from the youthful favourite of the late 1580s who had raged at his arch-enemy Raleigh and been obsessed with the fear that his royal mistress would fall victim to evil influence in his absence. Ten years had changed little; the knowledge that evil stalked the kingdom and that bands of conspirators were plotting his destruction remained a useful shield in the arsenal of his psychological defences. Devereux continued to view the world with a constant and preoccupying obsession that the key to politics lay in unearthing hidden motives and in seizing upon and correctly interpreting 'significant' clues. In searching for the underlying secret truth, Essex invariably discovered what he expected to find in the first place, be it the Lopez treason against the Queen or the Machiavellian plotting of that diabolical triumvirate: Cecil, Cobham, and Raleigh. Politics and the court consisted for the Earl of a set of indicators, especially the Queen's public display of favour or rebuke, which were personalized into signs that obscured for him the possibility that events could take place, accidents could occur, which were outside any pattern of rational conspiracy and had nothing to do with him. Robert Burton might well have had an Essex in mind when he wrote that victims of melancholia invariably 'misconstrue every word... and interpret it to the worst', and 'if they be not saluted, invited, consulted with, called to council, etc., or that any respect, small compliment, or ceremony be omitted, they think themselves neglected and condemned'.[68]

Essex not only interpreted the worst, he also tore actions out of their political context and attributed to his adversaries a rationality and determination they did not possess, transforming them into the objects of his fears and hatreds and turning them into scapegoats for his own inadequacies. He never felt free to 'perform good things and great things' partly because he lacked the inner strength and stamina to do so, but equally because he was careful to construct for himself a world where it was impossible for him to be great. Devereux was for ever being thwarted by his enemies who contrived in his absence to turn the Queen against him and to prevent him from realizing what he knew to be his full and true potential. As a consequence, he could never give in to others — Cecil, Burghley or even the Queen — without feeling both humiliated and inadequate: a failure. The harshly competitive environment in which Essex was born and educated and the bitter rivalries — both real and imagined — that existed at court, transformed an overly sensitive and naturally suspicious young man into a veteran paranoid. Under the strain of an escalating sense of vulnerability, his defence mechanism stiffened into what has been called an 'intense single-minded directedness' which produced in Devereux both an obsessive preoccupation with identifying the enemy and a conflict of wills in which he constantly tested himself not only against his political rivals but also against the Queen herself.[69]

VIII

'IF YOU HAVE ANY ENEMIES'

> We are all sufferers from history, but the paranoid
> is a double sufferer, since he is afflicted not only
> by the real world, with the rest of us, but by his
> fantasies as well.
>
> Richard Hofstadter, *The Paranoid Style in American Politics*

Essex's enemies had been doing more than sitting comfortably by their chimneys, descanting against the Earl; they had been hard at work capturing political plums and rewarding themselves with new honours while Devereux had been off suffering 'painful days, careful nights, evil diet and many hazards'.[1] Only days before Essex landed at Plymouth, Cecil had received the long-vacant Chancellorship of the Duchy of Lancaster and the Earl's old naval rival, Lord Admiral Charles Howard, had been elevated to the earldom of Nottingham. Then to add salt to the wound, on his return he learned that Nottingham's patent of elevation had singled Howard out for special mention as one of the victors of Cadiz, and the Lord Admiral had been appointed Lord Steward, thereby giving Nottingham ceremonial precedence over Essex. Devereux, already deeply hurt by his mistress's frigid reception, promptly succumbed to sickness, retired to his country house, and refused to attend Parliament or sit with the Council.

The Earl's sullen and voluntary exile was met with a barrage of advice, recommending his immediate return to court. Sulking at home was exactly what 'thy enemies wish, make use of, and rejoice in', and he was warned that 'whereas thou retainest many in thy Lordship's favour as thy true and secret friends, remember

that Christ had but twelve and one proved a devil'.[2] The analogy
did little except to fire the Earl's already inflamed martyr complex.
He was for ever being betrayed and expected that out of any twelve
friends one at the very least would emerge as a Judas. Even the
French Ambassador, who had arrived to discuss whether England
might join France in peace with Spain, concluded that 'the Earl
errs greatly, for he gives occasion to his enemies to calumniate him'.
The judgment of the whole court, he reported, 'is that he is ill-
advised' to stay away from the centre of power, for the Queen might
'grow suspicious, and if once that come to pass he has no means
of restoring himself'.[3]

Elizabeth was singularly devoid of the 'black poison of suspect',
and although her irritation with her moody Earl was manifest,
especially when he let it be known that his grievances were not
his alone but belonged to all 'gentlemen who have been ill
recompensed' and were resentful of 'their enemies', she evened up
the sides.[4] As a Christmas present for her Robin, she bestowed
upon him the office of Earl Marshal, the highest military honour
in the kingdom. The Earl was jubilant. The Cecils — father and
son — had been defeated; he now outranked the Earl of Nottingham;
and despite Bacon's dire prophecies, the broad sword of moral and
histrionic outrage seemed to have brought the Queen to her knees.
Equally satisfying, it was clear that his mistress once more needed
him, for the military situation in Ireland was rapidly deteriorating
and the advice of soldiers was again on the ascent. It was, however,
precisely the need for counsel and a decision as to whom to send
to Ireland that produced the confrontation between Queen and subject that irreparably damaged their relationship, planting in
Elizabeth's mind exactly what Bacon had most feared — suspicion
and apprehension — and leading Essex to formulate the one question that was guaranteed to place in jeopardy the fragile political
figment that God's vice-regents on earth cannot err: if kings were
really inspired with divine wisdom, why did they act unjustly and
listen to bad advice?

Neither the Cecil nor Essex faction wanted to send one of its
own party from court as Lord Lieutenant to that sepulchre of lost
reputations, Ireland. Sir Robert and the Queen proposed Sir William

Knollys, Essex's uncle and political ally; Essex favoured Sir George
Carew, a friend of Cecil. The Earl's factional malice in promoting
Carew was so transparent that the Queen laughed in his face and
jeered at his sudden praise of a man he thoroughly disliked. Highly
insulted, Essex spun on his heels and contemptuously turned his
back on his sovereign, who in a temper promptly boxed his ears
for his insolence and told him he could 'go and be hanged'. The
climax came when the Earl, having lost all control over himself,
committed the one gesture a subject must never make in front of
royalty — he reached for his sword. The Lord Admiral instantly
moved between the two; Essex stalked out of the room swearing
loudly that he would not have taken such an indignity even from
Henry VIII himself; and he dashed off to his country house to lock
himself and his wounded pride away in self-imposed banishment.[5]

Tudor society was scandalized and deeply troubled by Essex's
violation of the most sacred rules of decorum, and as the days of
his haughty silence grew, the sulking Earl received a cannonade
of letters begging him to come to his senses and return to court.
Posing as an impartial bystander and endeavouring to introduce a
modicum of reason into what he clearly judged to be a ridiculous
and highly explosive situation, Lord Keeper Thomas Egerton
warned: 'If you hold still your course,...there is little hope or
likelihood that the end will be better than the beginning.' He then
introduced a note of rational scepticism that revealed that the Lord
Keeper had no appreciation of the demons that plagued his colleague. 'If', he said, *'you have any enemies',* by absenting yourself
from court 'you do that for them, which they could never do for
themselves; whilst you leave your friends to open shame and contempt, forsake yourself, overthrow your fortunes, and ruinate your
honour and reputation'. In Egerton's estimation there was no
debate: it was Essex's 'indissoluble duty, which you owe to your
gracious sovereign, a duty not imposed upon you by nature and
policy only, but by the religious and sacred bond in which the divine
majesty of God hath by the rule of Christianity obliged and bound
you', to return and 'humbly to submit' himself. Finally, he went
to the root of the Earl's troubles. 'The difficulty, my good Lord,
is to conquer yourself, which is the height of all true valour and

fortitude... Do it...and God will be pleased, her Majesty satisfied...and your enemies (*if you have any*) shall be disappointed of their bitter sweet hope.'⁶ Essex's uncle William Knollys, over whom the quarrel started in the first place, was equally disturbed and wrote to his nephew that 'between her Majesty's running into her princely power, and your lordship's persisting in your settled resolution, I am so confounded, as I know not how nor what to persuade', and he begged him not to stand upon his honour but to remember his duty to the Queen.⁷ Even Essex's mother joined the growing chorus: 'I doubt not but you are wise and politic enough to countermine with your enemies, whose devilish practices can no way hurt you but one.'⁸ That one way was for the Earl to continue his stubborn refusal to serve his sovereign or even defend himself or his interests at court until he had received the Queen's apology.

Essex knew, whatever the Lord Keeper might say to the contrary, that the court was crawling with his enemies; the only question in his mind was whether he should include the Queen herself among them. Throwing all caution to the winds, he violated the most fundamental political advice of his century: 'Take heed what thou speaketh before thine enemies.' Ignoring Sir William Wentworth's warning that 'it is common custom to keep letters, and years later produce them for evidence against you in court or elsewhere', he bared his soul and poured forth in writing the full extent of his rebellious anger. He wrote the Lord Keeper a long, impassioned and defiant answer in which he defended his honour, painted himself as the injured party, and clearly demonstrated the intense pleasure he was deriving from his multitudinous misfortunes. Point by point he took up Egerton's arguments. By keeping himself to himself was he aiding and abetting his enemies? No; 'when I was in the court I found them absolute: and therefore I had rather they should triumph alone, than they should have me attendant on their chariots'. Was he ignoring his political friends and dependants? What difference did it make? 'When I was a courtier, I could yield them no fruits of my love unto them.' Was he by becoming a hermit overthrowing his fortune? At least now in retirement he had no cause to build 'a fortune of paper-walls, which every puff of wind bloweth down'. As for 'that indissoluble duty' he owed the Queen, he was ready to offer her his life and the 'duty of an earl and of lord marshal of England', but he denied absolutely her right to command his personal attendance upon her. Up to this point his words were filled with self-pity, neurotic but not dangerous, but the flow of his injured pride could not be stemmed and it swept him on to treason. The Lord Keeper was correct; Essex could not control himself. 'But, say you, I must yield and submit. I can neither yield myself to be guilty, or this imputation laid upon me to be just... Nay more, when the vilest of all indignities are done unto me, doth religion enforce me to sue? or doth God require it? Is it impiety not to do it? What, cannot princes err? cannot subjects receive wrong? Is an earthly power or authority infinite? Pardon me, pardon me, my good Lord, I can never subscribe to these principles.'[9]

The monster of sedition locked away behind polished walls of decorum and role-playing, fettered by years of educational and cultural conditioning in obedience and duty, and anathematized by God Himself, was rattling its chains. Essex wrote words that no divine-right monarch could long ignore or allow to go unchallenged, for Devereux had joined together the arrogance of male superiority and the pride of aristocratic lineage with a far worse evil — the sin of doubt. He was questioning the divinely ordered nature of government, of society, and ultimately of the universe itself. The Queen herself had become one of the enemy, her office a mere political contrivance capable of gross error. Essex, of course, remained pure and injured, and self-righteously he concluded: 'As for me, I have received wrong, and feel it.'[10]

Neither sovereign nor Earl would back down. Elizabeth in her fury announced that Devereux had 'played long enough upon her' and she meant now 'to play awhile upon him, and to stand as much upon her greatness, as he hath done upon [his] stomach'; and Essex made any reconciliation almost impossible by dumping the blame squarely in the Queen's lap — 'I was never proud till your Majesty sought to make me too base.'[11] In the end, Ireland came to both their rescues, providing the military crisis that made it possible for each to retire from the fray with dignity. The reconciliation took place as news began to reach London of an unparalleled military disaster. On August 14th, 1598 the rebel Earl of Tyrone had ambushed and slaughtered at Yellow Ford 2,000 English soldiers including the marshal of Elizabeth's forces and thirty of his officers. Essex wrote something approximating to an apology — 'As I had not gone into exile of myself if your Majesty had not chased me from you as you did, so was I ever ready to have taken hold of any warrant that your Majesty could have given me for my return.' True it was that he had waited in patient expectation only to learn that his Queen remained indignant and 'did willinglyest hear those that did kindle' her ire; 'yet when the unhappy news came from yonder cursed country of Ireland...duty was strong enough to rouse me out of my deadest melancholy'.[12] Then just as the Earl Marshal was rousing himself from his melancholy and offering to do his duty he fell seriously ill, thereby supplying Elizabeth with the occasion to appear forgiving and merciful.

By September the reunion was complete, and Essex was back at court, as confident and swaggering as ever. The reconciliation, however, was a patched-up affair, and contemporaries, looking back on that stormy summer of 1598, 'dated Essex's ruin' from those pregnant words, 'what, cannot princes err?' and they whispered that 'fortune rarely caresses a cast-off favourite a second time, and that princes once disobeyed, are seldom heartily reconciled'.[13] Elizabeth knew of her Earl's seditious letter to the Lord Keeper but chose for the time being to ignore it,* and Essex, as was his wont, made the mistake of interpreting his royal mistress's concern for his health as a complete capitulation, and he set about pestering the Queen for the most politically sensitive and financially profitable prize in her gift — the Mastership of the Court of Wards, vacant since the demise of Lord Burghley the previous month.

The death on August 4th, 1598 of the old Lord Treasurer, Elizabeth's devoted friend and chief minister for forty years, was symbolic. The Queen might live on but her palace guard had changed; an age was past, and try as she might to hold back time, Gloriana had no choice but to look squarely into the grave. No wonder Sir William Knollys wrote to Essex that 'her Majesty is so

*Essex's ill-chosen words to the Lord Keeper were used against him two years later during the public condemnation of his 'disobedient' behaviour in Ireland. See p. 258.

variable, so distracted in herself, as I know not what advice to give in this case'.[14] Part of her distraction was caused by grief at Burghley's death and part by what she hated most, decision making: somebody would have to be appointed to assume the old man's two chief titles, the Lord Treasurer and Master of the Court of Wards.

An early report seemed to indicate that Essex would receive the Mastership, a position that stood at the core of the Tudor patronage structure and that had generated out of gifts and gratuities some £3,000 annually for a relatively honest and scrupulous Burghley but that had the potential for far more in the hands of anyone determined to milk the system.[15] Certainly Devereux expected and needed the post. Why else had Elizabeth surrendered and come back to him; what better evidence could he supply to his clamouring creditors that his fragile financial house, mortgaged from basement to attic, was supported by the Queen's favour and bounty? Indeed, he was so sure of himself that he made discreet inquiries as to the profits of the office, especially 'how may the revenues of the Court increase', and he began receiving begging and expectant letters — 'I pray that we may hear that you are Master of the Wards, for then I shall hope that you will bestow a male or female upon me.'[16] All the political setbacks of the past years, all the fancied or real rebukes given him by his sovereign would be swept away by this single presentation which would give Essex the financial means to perform those 'good things and great things' for which he craved. Unfortunately, the Queen, when faced with a decision, ran true to form: she procrastinated and sought refuge in half measures. First she informed Devereux that he could have the post but she intended 'to geld or curtail it'; to that solution Essex indignantly answered that he would not take the position at all unless it was 'whole and unmaimed'.[17] Then to the Earl's growing mortification she let the office stand vacant, refusing to make up her mind one way or the other. Essex took these delaying tactics as a personal affront and accused her of publicly denying him 'an office which one of my fellows [Burghley] so lately and so long enjoyed'. 'If, therefore,' he wrote in anger, 'your Majesty give it not at all, the world may judge, and I must believe, that you overthrow the office because I should not be the officer.' His final recourse, as usual, was to shed tears: 'If your Majesty value me as you would do any man that had done you half that service, think again of the suit of your Majesty's humblest servant.'[18]

If Essex's unforgivable and unforgettable words — 'what, cannot princes err?' — planted 'the black poison of suspect' in Elizabeth's mind, her refusal to grant the Earl the Mastership of the Wards was the turning point in Devereux's association with his royal mistress. To his sick and seething mind it seemed to place her irrevocably in the Cecil camp and to slam shut the door to his political career.[19] The only course left to him was to seek solace in battle — the one area in which he knew he could prove his worth and teach his enemies and his Queen a lesson. He would find his salvation and his revenge in Ireland from whence came messengers 'daily (like Job's servants) laden with ill tidings of new troubles and revolts'.[20]

The potential for disaster in Ireland had existed for decades. But endemic racial and religious antipathy between Celtic Catholic natives and Anglo-Saxon Protestant intruders, and clan violence, periodically fostered by large infusions of Spanish gold, did not erupt into full-scale war to evict the English from Irish soil until an intelligent and diplomatic Ulster chieftain — Hugh O'Neil, Earl of Tyrone and paramount chief of the clans — emerged as Ireland's national hero and proved at Yellow Ford that ragtag Irish rebels could resoundingly rout Elizabeth's finest troops.

Yellow Ford was a national disgrace; equally dreadful, it was the signal for all of Ireland to burst into rebellion, the looting, burning and killing spreading to the very walls of Dublin Castle. All that was needed to make Tyrone king of the entire island was for Spanish troops and artillery to land and 'root out all remembrance of the English nation in this kingdom'.[21] The crisis catapulted the Queen into unaccustomed action — no matter the cost to her treasury she would see Tyrone hanged as a traitor — and throughout November and December the council debated who would lead her armies into Ireland and revenge Yellow Ford. Essex vetoed every name suggested, insisting that only 'some prime man of the nobility, considerable for his power, honour and estate, acceptable to and respected by the soldiery, [and] who had been general of an army' was worthy to lead.[22] No one fitted such a description except himself, and the Council had no other choice but to name him Lord Lieutenant of Ireland and General of the Queen's Army, and Essex had no other course but to accept the honour.

Why he arranged matters as he did remains an unresolved mystery, for Devereux was fully cognisant of the risks long before he accepted the command. Francis Bacon wrote him a letter that bristled with warnings of the dangers involved in campaigning in Ireland: 'a service of great merit and great peril' in which he was placing his reputation and fortune in 'greatest peril'.[23] The new Lord Lieutenant himself outlined the political and military dangers: 'Into Ireland I go. The Queen hath irrevocably decreed it; the Council do passionately urge it; and I am tied to mine own reputation to use no tergiversation [evasion]. . . I am not ignorant what are the disadvantages of absence; the opportunities of practising enemies when they are neither encountered nor overlooked.' Essex appreciated the risks and hardships, but he was also careful to establish a scapegoat for possible failure: 'All those things, which I am like to see, I do now foresee. For the war is hard; . . . the rebel successful; . . . the supplies uncertain; [and] it is safer for me . . . to show the world that my endeavours were more than ordinary, when the state that set me out must conspire with the enemy against me.' He then concluded with his usual lament: 'The court is the centre; but methinks it is the fairer choice to command armies than honours. In the meantime enemies may be advanced . . .'[24]

Whatever reasons Essex may have found to justify to himself his going to that 'moist, rotten country', contemporaries were darkly suspicious of his insistence that he alone was the Hercules capable of cleansing the Irish stables. Those least friendly whispered that 'he wished nothing more than to have an army at his command and to engage the sword-men to him'.[25] One cautious and sceptical critic reported that court opinion was divided on the question whether the Queen had in fact 'granted forgiveness' for the Lord Lieutenant's 'late demeanour in her presence', and he advised his cousin, Sir John Harington, to 'observe the man who commandeth and yet is commanded himself: he goeth not forth to serve the Queen's realm but to humour his own revenge'. And he concluded with the standard warning: 'Be heedful of your bearings; speak not your mind to all you meet'; and 'give not your opinion; it may be heard in England'.[26] More friendly observers interpreted the enterprise in Baconian terms: a conspiracy on the part of the Earl's 'subtle and close enemies' who, posing as his friends and admirers, sought to remove him from court and, extolling 'him to the sky', did 'in the meantime carry on their secret enmity most eagerly and violently, knowing well that the fierceness and heat of his youth would be his undoing'.[27]

Whatever the verdict — victim, hero, psychopath — the die, as Essex liked to say, 'was cast'; his appointment as Lord Lieutenant was officially announced on January 14th; eventually his commission and instructions were signed after months of hard bargaining with the Queen; and on March 27th he left London amidst cries of 'God save your lordship'.[28] He rode at the head of the largest English army ever to be sent into Ireland — 16,000 foot soldiers and 1,300 horse — and he had extracted from Elizabeth powers never before conferred upon a lord lieutenant and governor general. He was, in effect, Gloriana's viceroy. He could declare martial law, proclaim and pardon traitors and all other malefactors including counterfeiters of the Queen's coins; he was authorized, with carefully built-in limitations so as to curtail the Earl's well-known generosity, to award knighthoods; he could summon and prorogue the Irish Parliament; he could bestow at his own discretion all military and civil offices, even those in the Queen's gift; and if he saw fit he could return to England to discuss the military situation directly with the Queen and her Council. Finally, he was given authority to take that 'capital traitor', Tyrone, 'upon such conditions as you shall find good and necessary for our honour and safety of that kingdom'.[29]

On paper Essex was supreme; but as he had already learned, empires protected by 'paper-walls' were no safeguard against his royal mistress's interfering and contradictory whims. The Queen played with marked cards: yes, he had absolute authority to bestow all military and civil positions as he chose, but there turned out to be exceptions, and within days of his departure Elizabeth vetoed his appointment to the Irish Council of his close friend and second stepfather, Sir Christopher Blount. Essex, with considerable cause, was instantly goaded into writing a bitter denunciation of such treatment. He was maimed, he cried, even before he set out. He had only wanted his stepfather so as to have 'one strong assistant', but the Queen had denied even that small help; and he warned that if she refused him the means, Gloriana could not 'expect nor exact great performance'. Devereux was running true to form. It was not his fault if he could not perform 'great things' or live up to expectations, and he darkly predicted that 'if things succeed ill in my charge, I am like to be a martyr for her'. His tale of woe even before he landed in Ireland was endless: 'If I have not inward comfort, and outward demonstration of her Majesty's favour, I am defeated in England'; 'I spake a language that was not understood. . . to a goddess not at leisure to hear [my] prayers'; 'let me plead in any form it is in vain'; and 'it is not Tyrone and the Irish rebellion that amazeth me, but to see myself sent on such an errand, at such a time, with so little comfort or ability from the court of England. . .'[30]

Not even the weather co-operated, and Essex was delayed for days before he finally arrived on April 14th in a sodden condition in a land so wet it had 'bogs upon the very tops of mountains'. Once in Dublin Essex walked into a nest of corruption, both civil and military. Commissioners pocketed the Queen's money to pay her troops, who, as a consequence, went about in rags; soldiers sold military supplies to stay alive; and captains hired Irish rebels to fill their ranks when the muster master came to check the rolls. Worse, he was confronted with guerrilla warfare whereby Irish 'rogues and naked beggars' fought unfairly 'in woods and bogs where horse[s] are utterly unserviceable'.[31] Finally, the splendidly worked-out paper strategy so carefully drawn up by the Lords of the Council in London to attack Tyrone directly in Ulster proved to be totally impractical and was opposed by all Irish experts. There was insufficient cattle for such an excursion into enemy territory, and the few beasts there were at this time of year were not worth eating. It was impossible to forage off the land, and because of the foul weather the transport horses from England had not yet been shipped to Ireland. The specialists agreed that if Essex had to campaign anywhere, it would be better to secure his rear by moving south into Leinster and Munster where the Irish had built up formidable rebel forces, and wait until July to march north and attack Tyrone in his home county of Ulster.

The expedition south was a predictable disaster. Not even the Lord Lieutenant's secretary was sanguine of victory: 'What his Lordship's journey into Munster will effect, I know not. We hope the best, and you are like to hear the worst.'[32] The Irish refused to fight in the open but skirmished 'in passes, bogs, woods, fords and in all places of advantage' and held it 'no dishonour to run away'.[33] The Lord Lieutenant's army dwindled away from desertion and disease, and after two months of thankless sloshing about in the rain, Essex and his weary troops were back in Dublin with only 3,500 able-bodied foot soldiers and 300 horsemen out of an original invasion force of over 16,000. Nothing had been accomplished of military value; the army was decimated and demoralized; and Essex once again involved himself in a head-on collision with the Queen over ultimate authority.

Before Devereux left England, Elizabeth had made it clear that she 'misliked' his suggestion that his friend Henry Wriothesley Earl of Southampton be appointed to his military staff; the young nobleman was on her blackest list for having made one of her maids-in-waiting pregnant and then having had the impudence to marry her without royal sanction. The Lord Lieutenant regarded such bias as idiotic feminine caprice, an unwarranted interference into a man's world of war and a blatant violation of his legal right to 'make free choice of all the officers and commanders of the army'.[34] Ignoring the Queen's clear signal, the moment he landed in Ireland he appointed his friend General of the Horse. Elizabeth was not pleased, and cavalierly chose to construe her 'misliking' of Southampton as an absolute denial of his appointment. In a fury she instructed her Council to inform Essex that she had expressly prohibited the appointment from the start and that 'this commandment being by her Majesty so precisely delivered unto you, and the same being now so publicly manifested to the world to be broken, hath moved her Majesty to great offence in that respect'.[35] Devereux countered with one of his most tear-stained letters. Firing his friend at this stage (July), he pleaded, 'must discourage all my friends, who now see the days of my suffering draw near...and are some of them tempted to renounce me'; such an act 'must dismay the army, which already looks sadly upon me, as pitying both me and itself in this comfortless action'; compliance with the Queen's orders 'must encourage the rebels, who, doubtless, will think it time to hew upon a withering tree, whose leaves they see beaten down, and the branches in part cut off'. And he concluded with an ecstasy of sorrow — 'Oh miserable employment, and more miserable destiny of mine, that makes it impossible for me to please and serve her Majesty at once!'[36] Gloriana's retort was a blast of outraged majesty: it is 'strange to us that you will dare thus to value your own pleasing in things unnecessary, and think by your private arguments to carry for your own glory a matter wherein our pleasure to the contrary is made notorious'.[37]

Essex's cup ran over. In early June, while still on the Munster campaign, he received news of Cecil's appointment as Master of the Wards.[38] It had happened again: once Devereux was away from the Queen, his enemies had got to her, and clever, stay-at-home Sir Robert had come out ahead. Essex was trapped in a cursed land where nothing went right; his best efforts earned only scorn and criticism; and the 'unwholesome and uncertain climate' was raising havoc with his delicate health. How, he complained, could he 'talk of victory or of success' when he received 'nothing but discomforts and soul's wounds' from England? 'Is it not spoken in the army', he demanded of the Queen, 'that your Majesty's favour is diverted from me...? Is it not believed by the rebels, that those, whom you favour most, do more hate me out of faction than them [the Irish rebels] out of duty and conscience? Is it not lamented of your Majesty's faithfullest subjects both there and here, that a Cobham or a Raleigh (I will forbear others for their places' sake [i.e. Cecil and Nottingham]) should have such credit and favour with your Majesty' when they do nothing but conspire 'the ill success of your Majesty's most important action, the decay of your greatest strength, and the destruction of your faithfullest servants?'[39]

The more Devereux brooded, the more suspicious he became,

and on July 1st he wrote to the Lords of the Council hinting darkly at deliberate betrayal: 'I am armed on the breast, but not on the back. I armed myself with confidence that rebels in so unjust a quarrel could not fight so well as we could in a good [cause]. Howbeit, if the rebels shall but once come to know, that I am wounded in the back, not slightly, but to the heart, as I fear me... then what will be their pride and the state's hazard, your lordships in your wisdom may easily discern.'[40] Sixteen days later he gave full vent to his mounting paranoia. 'In professing myself unarmed on my back', he explained to the Council,

> I meant that I lay open to the malice and practice of mine enemies in England, who first procured a cloud of disgrace to overshadow me, and now in the dark give me wound upon wound.

He knew, of course, that those close to the Queen would deny their evil intent; nevertheless, it was common knowledge both in England and Ireland that they were conspiring 'in this my absence to supplant me in the favour of my sovereign'.[41]

The hapless Lord Lieutenant had evidence enough of his enemies' sinister influence. On his return to Dublin in early July he was confronted with a torrent of his Queen's most barbed and strident invective. She demanded that he 'compare the time that is run on, and the excessive charges that is spent with the effects of anything wrought by this voyage'. She had not supplied him with £1,000 'a day to go in progress'. Was it to be the fate of the Queen of England, who had defeated the greatest monarch in Christendom, to have 'a base bush kern' accounted 'so famous a rebel' that all her Majesty's forces and the entire nobility of her kingdom 'must be thought too little to be employed' against him? Embedded in Elizabeth's letter was a dangerous, if metaphorically obscure, threat on which her Earl would have done well to ponder:

> Whosoever it be that you do clad with any honours or places wherein the world may read the least suspicion of neglect or

contempt of our commandments, we will never make dainty to
set on such shadows as shall quickly eclipse any of those lustres.

Whatever the Earl may have made of the Queen's mixed metaphor,
her instructions were botanically precise: 'We must now plainly
charge you, according to the duty you owe us...with all speed
to pass thither [i.e. north into Ulster] in such order, as the axe may
be put to the root of the tree, which hath been the treasonable stock
from whence so many poisoned plants and grafts have been
derived.'[42]

In a second and even harsher letter dated July 30th Gloriana concluded her tirade with a paragraph that left Essex quivering with
anxiety and suspicion: she revoked her licence permitting him to
return to England at his own discretion, and she commanded that
'you do now in no wise take that liberty, nor adventure to leave
that State in any person's government, but with our
allowance...and our pleasure first known unto you...'[43] Essex
was in a frenzy. To the Queen he wrote one of his customary obsequious letters, grieving that, although he perceived 'nothing but
gathering clouds and foul weather after me, yet my duty, faith and
industry shall never alter'.[44] But in private it was reported that he
was 'highly discontented, especially with Secretary Cecil' and used
'speeches that might be dangerous to his own safety'.[45] To make
matters worse, he blatantly violated the Queen's precise orders and
during July and August created eighty-one new knights, not as
Elizabeth had commanded on the basis of their merits but, as it
was later claimed, to win the hearts of his captains and create for
himself a personal following of private swordsmen.[46]

The interpretation, if not totally unjust, was overstated; the
gentlemen adventurers who had rushed to Devereux's banner in
April began in July to wilt away, determined not to be 'wrecked
upon Essex's coast'.[47] If the Lord Lieutenant was to save himself
and the morale of his army, he had at all costs to keep the loyalty
of the military, and he sought to hold his officers with honours
and knighthoods. In an atmosphere of growing distrust and anxiety, Essex tended to isolate himself among military friends upon

whom he could depend. The opinion of soldiers, those tried and true veterans of past campaigns, not weaselly politicians and civilians, carried ever greater weight as the military and political crisis deepened. Tragedy was indeed in the making as the prediction of one contemporary was fulfilled: 'Soldiers are strong and sufficiently courageous', but 'being always among enemies and in a hostile place... they can never enter into dealings with others without suspicion. Suspicion, however, breeds hatred and hatred open war,... and in this way all love perishes.'[48]

Essex's love for his mistress was perishing, slowly and by degrees, but he still obeyed. Amidst dire warnings that his soldiers so feared 'a northern journey' that 'they disband daily' while 'the Irish go to the rebels by herds', and brave talk that Tyrone was surrounded only by 'a kennel of hungry, starved hounds', the Lord Lieutenant on August 28th marched forth with his sorely depleted forces to do battle with the enemy in Ulster, announcing that 'we will on one side or the other end the war'.[49]

On September 3rd the Earl encountered for the first time Tyrone's vastly superior army encamped on a wooded hill near Ardolph Castle. For two days the opposing forces jockeyed for position, and then on September 5th the unexpected occurred: the Lord Lieutenant was informed that the 'barbarous ungrateful rebel Tyrone' was ready to parley, make his submission, and seek the Queen's mercy.[50] Cautiously, fearing a trick, Essex consented on September 7th to a meeting and went alone to Ballaclinche Ford to discuss terms. He did so, he later argued, so as to minimize the threat of treachery — he alone taking the risk.

At the encounter, Essex approached to the water's edge; Tyrone rode half-way across to meet him and, with the stream coursing past his horse's belly, he 'took off his hat and, inclining his body, did his duty unto his Lordship with very humble ceremony, continuing the same observancy the whole time of the parley'.[51] The Lord Lieutenant was immediately captivated by this elderly, well dressed, urbane and highly cultivated nobleman, who had been educated in Essex's own stepfather's household, and who possessed the devil's tongue of sweet reason. They spoke for half an hour, and Tyrone's terms seemed deceptively reasonable and beguiling

— a truce to be renewed on a six weekly basis during the winter until May 1st and only to be broken on fourteen days' notice; the outline for a more enduring peace to be presented to the Queen personally by her Lord Lieutenant; and should Tyrone's allies refuse the temporary secession of hostilities, Essex had the right to carry on the war against them; otherwise the sides would remain in the existing military balance until spring. By way of a covenant, Devereux offered his word of honour and the rebel Earl of Tyrone gave his oath before God. The following day, what had been privately determined was publicly confirmed. Then on September 9th Essex sent the Queen a copy of the terms, referring only casually to his private conversation and leaving it unclear whether he had in fact committed himself to the truce. Finally, he headed back to Dublin, anticipating a warm welcome for having ended a fruitless and expensive war. What he found was mounting suspicion about what had really transpired at that private interview — had Tyrone actually urged Essex 'to stand for himself'; had the Irish rebel promised to help him in treason against the Queen; and had the Lord Lieutenant really 'utterly rejected' such a proposition?[52]

On top of growing suspicion came increasingly shrill letters from the Queen, which drove Essex near to panic. He was a 'double sufferer': he had to endure Elizabeth's invective, but even more painful, he had to suffer the fears and fantasies that those tirades engendered in his feverish mind. He had been back in Dublin less than a week when another royal thunderbolt from Nonsuch Palace, dated September 14th, descended upon him. What vexed Gloriana the most was that she had been tricked into purchasing a pig in a poke, and as usual had been 'won to expense by little and little, and by representations of great resolutions'. Those marvellous resolutions, however, had invariably vanished in the face of a multitude of excuses. She was tired of excuses. Essex's 'own proceedings' alone had begotten the mess that he was now in, and with clinical dexterity she proceeded to demolish his arguments:

If sickness of the army be the reason, why was not the action undertaken when the army was in better state? If winter's approach, why were the summer months of July and August lost? If the spring be too soon, and the summer that followed otherwise spent? if the harvest that succeeded were so neglected, as nothing hath been done, then surely we must conclude that none of the four quarters of the year will be in season for you . . .

It was a long letter, uncharitably based on hindsight and bristling with anger and indignation that she had been made a laughing stock among the crowned heads of Europe. Worse, she dared to accuse Essex of deliberate prevarication: 'We require you to consider whether we have not a great cause to think that your purpose is not to end the war . . .'[53] Such unfairness and perversity were more than a loyal subject and nobleman could stand. It was obvious his royal mistress was a captive of the enemy.

Exactly when Elizabeth's letter reached Dublin is uncertain, but Essex's mind, gripped in the coils of those twin serpents, suspicion and fear, and afflicted with a menagerie of paranoid monsters fed by ignorance about what was really going on at court and by the need to know what hidden forces were strewing obstacles in his path, was heading for an emotional crisis long before Elizabeth's letter arrived. Two weeks earlier on August 30th, he had written to the Queen in near suicidal hysteria:

From a mind delighting in sorrow; from spirits wasted with travail, care, and grief; from a heart torn in pieces with passion; from a man that hates himself and all things that keep him alive, what service can your Majesty reap? . . . The rebel's pride and successes must give me means to ransom myself, my soul I mean, out of this hateful prison of my body. And if it happens so, your Majesty may believe that you shall not have cause to mislike the fashion of my death, though the course of my life could not please you.[54]

Gloriana had one more explosive bolt left in her arsenal of scorn, penned when she learned on September 17th of her Lieutenant's dealings with the rebel Tyrone. Whether Essex ever read her epistle is not clear; if he did, it could only have fed his anxiety and sup-

plied his paranoia with further evidence that his sovereign was a
prisoner of his enemies. She suspiciously pointed out that his conversation with the traitor Tyrone had been held 'without anybody's
hearing; wherein, though we that trust you with our kingdom
are far from mistrusting you with a traitor, yet both for comeliness,
example, and your own discharge, we marvel you would carry it
no better'. She could not decipher from his report the substance
of the discussion and could only 'by divination' guess at what was
spoken, but if history were any precedent, she anticipated little success. She regarded his handling of the war so far to be 'dishonourable
and wasteful' and predicted that any truce would 'prove perilous
and contemptible', a 'hollow peace'. It was madness, she warned,
'to trust this traitor upon oath', equivalent to accepting 'a devil
upon his religion'. 'To trust him upon pledges' was 'mere illusory',
and she commanded him to conclude nothing 'till you do particularly
advertise us by writing, and receive our pleasure hereafter for your
further warrant and authority in that behalf'.[55]

Elizabeth's words struck home. Essex had indeed lost touch with
reality; not only was a pledge with the devil 'illusory', so also was
the vast conspiracy of evil that he saw creeping in upon him. The
only solution that his inflamed and unstable mind could conjure
up was to defeat the machinations of his enemies by appearing unex-
pectedly at court, rescue the Queen, and win her once again with
the magic of his charm, pouring forth the tale of his troubles,
wrought by his enemies, and the truth and innocence of his actions,
which his foes persisted in misrepresenting.

At what point sedition broke its bonds and emerged from the
inner dungeon of his mind, fully armed and articulated, is not
known. Camden argued it was the shock in early June of learning
of Robert Cecil's victory and Elizabeth's betrayal when she
appointed her Principal Secretary Master of the Wards. It was then
Essex began 'to cast himself into dark clouds and troublesome
storms, contriving in his heart' the 'wicked and unhappy design'
that led him to violate his sovereign's most dire command and to
return unannounced to England.[56] Later historians tend to date the
decision from his return to Dublin in September and the panic produced by the Queen's scornful letters.[57] The evidence, however,

points to a moment somewhere in between, for Essex was imagining treason even before he set out to meet Tyrone. In a very private discussion held in Dublin Castle with his two closest friends and military colleagues — the Earl of Southampton, and his stepfather, Sir Christopher Blount — he dared to suggest a military solution to his political troubles that was tantamount to high treason. 'He told us', they later confessed, 'he found it necessary for him to go to England', but, given the power of his enemies, 'he thought it fit to carry with him for his security as much of the army as he could conveniently transport [two to three thousand men] to go ashore with him in Wales, and there to make good his landing... till he could send for more, not doubting but that his army would so increase within a small time that he should be able to march to London and make his conditions as he desired'.[58]

The ultimate purpose of his proposal, as in the case of most Tudor treason, was left in studied vagueness: 'make his conditions as he desired'. The failure to face the future, to squarely establish his goals, was symptomatic of the entire plan, which was the product of a mind that fed not only upon phantom plots and villainous enemies but also on dreams of spontaneous popular support and the illusion that the justice of his cause, as he presented it to himself, was irrefutable. His design was no spur of the moment piece of youthful bravado on the part of a wayward and unstable nobleman who 'carried his love and his hatred always in his brow' and who found himself sinking into a quagmire largely of his own making. It was open revolution, the violation of the most fundamental political instincts of his society; and his two colleagues would have none of it. To invade England at the head of an army was sacrilege; worse, it was political suicide. Southampton spoke for both men when he said the scheme was 'altogether unfit, as well in respect of his conscience to God, his love to his country and his duty to his sovereign'.[59] Essex, however, persisted that he had to reach the Queen, to speak with her alone before her mind could be further corrupted and turned against him. And so the three soldiers devised an improbable alternative.[60] The Earl was to be accompanied only by a band of comrades, small enough to guarantee speed and secrecy but sufficiently large to secure him from arrest and from his 'private enemies' — the official version put the number at 200 swordsmen all sworn to Essex but the Earl himself admitted to only ten.[61] They would sail for England, gallop post-haste to London, surprise the Queen in her privy chamber, and give her Robin a chance to present his case, accuse his enemies, and regain his royal mistress's heart.

Even for a century that believed in miracles, the project was disobedient and dangerous idiocy; but it was not treason. For the time being at least, the dragon of sedition had been put back in its cage. Nevertheless, the unthinkable had been thought; treason had been formed into words, and once shaped it was not likely to remain long chained within the dark recesses of the Earl's mind. Within fifteen months of his unauthorized departure from Ireland on September 24th, sedition would emerge again and drag the Lord Lieutenant straight to the execution block.

IX

'GIVE LOSERS LEAVE TO TALK'[1]

> For instance, now, she [the White Queen] went
> on ... there's the King's Messenger. He's in
> prison now, being punished: and the trial doesn't
> even begin till next Wednesday: and of course the
> crime comes last of all.
>
> Lewis Carroll, *Through the Looking-Glass and
> What Alice Found There*

Treason for Tudor England was the invention of the devil in whose
clever brain were first conceived those seductive but rational
enticements that drew weak and susceptible subjects into rebellion.
Lucifer had no need for madness or psychosis; he corrupted men
and women with reason, logic and good intentions, playing on their
greed, ambition and pride, and dressing sedition up in a host of
attractive disguises. Wickedness never came 'better armed than with
the show of seeming sanctity'.[2] When the time came to present
the official version of Essex's overt treason, which followed so closely
upon his dangerous and disobedient return to England, it did not
suit the government's purpose — indeed, it did not even enter
anybody's head — to befuddle and cloud the purity of evil or the
villainous consistency and premeditated rationality of the Earl's
actions with the mitigating and confusing possibility that Devereux
was driven to disaster by the deliberate provocation of the Queen
or by a herd of chimeras bred of a diseased and tortured mind. Tudor
England would leave for later generations the suggestion that Essex
was trapped into treason, a victim of society and the paranoia that
it spawned. For the sixteenth century, Robert Devereux's crime

was clear and unadulterated, the work of an evilly logical and starkly ungrateful subject who 'had long ago plotted. . . in his heart to become a dangerous supplanter of that seat [of power and royalty] whereof he ought to have been a principal supporter'. Thus it was important for the Crown not only to advertise 'his last actual and open treasons, but also his former more secret practices and preparations towards those his treasons'.[3]

In a document penned by Francis Bacon, edited by the entire Privy Council and scrutinized and corrected by the Queen herself, the government systematically analysed and laid bare the monstrous truth of Essex's rebellion. Where the root of his sedition originated, the Crown confessed, only 'God that discerns the heart, and the devil that gives the instigation', could say for certain, but once Essex had set foot down the path to open rebellion, every step was premeditated and logical, and the government displayed immense ingenuity in fitting his every action into a treasonous pattern. It all started with the Irish venture which the Earl's 'high imagination' and corrupt heart perceived to be the means to 'his desired greatness in England'. With 'what appetite and thirst' had he conspired to obtain the place of Lord Lieutenant! His campaign to make it impossible for the Queen to appoint anyone but himself was so blatant that it 'far passed the bounds of decorum'. His bellicose counsel advocating the need to strike directly at the rebel Tyrone in his Ulster stronghold with an overwhelming force was nothing but a carefully orchestrated deception designed to persuade her Majesty to 'increase the list of her army, and all proportions of treasure and other furniture, to the end his commandment might be the greater'. Nor had he any intention of fulfilling his own prescription; his aim from the start was 'to get great forces into his hands' and 'to oblige the heads of the rebellion unto him, and to make them of his party'. Even his insistence on unprecedented authority in his commission as Lord Lieutenant was based on a lie; it was 'suspiciously strange even at that time with what importunity and instance he did labour' to persuade her Majesty to grant him power to pardon all cases of treason, even those directed 'against the person' of the Queen herself. As soon as he landed in Ireland his evil purposes had become clear: he had long planned to use such authority to pardon Tyrone and thereby obligate the rebel to him.

The 'whole carriage of his actions' in Ireland 'was nothing else but a cunning defeating' of his advertised purpose, and his true intent was to gratify Tyrone 'with a dishonourable peace, and to contract with him for his own greatness'. The 'unseasonable and fruitless journey into Munster', which had never been authorized by the Queen's Council, was a deliberate ploy to exhaust her Majesty's forces and make a successful invasion of Ulster impossible, thereby preparing the way for 'such a peace as might be for the rebels' advantage, and so to work a mutual obligation between Tyrone and himself'. Long before the fateful meeting at Ballaclinche Ford, the two traitors had been in communication, and the Irish Earl had offered to 'make the earl of Essex the greatest man that ever was in England'. In order to cover up their inequities, Essex made a pretext of marching north, claiming afterwards, as the government scornfully noted, that 'the very terror and reputation of my Lord of Essex's person was such as did daunt' Tyrone and 'make him stoop to seek a parley'.

Since it was odious, nay 'monstrous', that Essex should conspire with a rebel 'against whom he was sent', he managed a private interview 'under colour' of a peace treaty, 'no third person admitted'. Indeed, such secrecy was maintained that no person overheard 'one word that passed between' the two men, but what transpired could easily be surmised from their later actions. Tyrone, immediately after the Earl's return to England, began to boast 'that within two or three months' there would be 'the greatest alterations' imaginable, and that he 'hoped ere long to have a good share in England'. He had also written to the traitorous Earl of Desmond that by the terms of his agreement with Essex, Devereux 'should be king of England, and that Tyrone should hold of him the honour and state of viceroy of Ireland, and that the proportion of soldiers which Tyrone should bring or send to Essex [in England] were 8,000 Irish'.

As for the Earl of Essex, immediately after the parley, he set in motion a strange project which 'no doubt he had harboured in his breast before': to return to England and 'carry with him of the army in Ireland as much as he could conveniently transport' in the expectation of enlarging his forces and marching 'with his power to London, and make his conditions as he thought good'. Mercifully, not even Essex's two most desperate friends, the Earl of Southampton and Sir Christopher Blount, could stomach such appalling treason, and therefore as an alternative plot, it was decided to 'draw forth of the army some 200 resolute gentlemen', return to England, 'make sure of the court', 'execute the surprise of her Majesty's person', and, if necessary, rescue the Earl by force should he be thrown into the Tower for having come over 'expressly against the Queen's prohibition [written] under her signet'.

The Queen, however, was more than a match for the seditious Earl, and when on September 28th he arrived at court unannounced, his heart thus 'fraughted with treason', and barged into her bed chamber, 'it pleased God, in His singular providence', to guide Gloriana 'in a narrow way of safety between two perils'. Sensing Essex's underlying sedition, but not wishing to drive him to desperation — only seeking to correct, not ruin, him — she placed him under house arrest in the care of the Lord Keeper. In order to satisfy her honour and administer justice while at the same time letting the world know the truth and extent of his disobedience, her Majesty ordered a private inquiry into his actions in Ireland. He was found by a panel of his peers guilty of contempt, but not disloyalty, and was instructed to forbear the exercise of his various offices of state.

Essex, master dissimulator that he was, and 'infinitely desirous...to be at liberty to practise and revive his former purposes' transformed 'himself into such a strange and dejected humility, as if he had been no man of this world', protesting that 'the tears of his heart had quenched in him all humours of ambition'. This performance was cunningly contrived 'to make her Majesty secure, and to lull the world asleep, that he was not a man to be held any ways dangerous'. Her Majesty, blinded by her mercy, was for the time fooled by this devilish stage acting and granted him his freedom, but as soon as he 'felt the wings of his liberty', he began 'to practise afresh as busily as ever, reviving his former resolution, which was the surprising and possessing the Queen's person and the court'. The Earl and his associates in rebellion singled out those who were 'discontented or turbulent, and such as were weak of judgment' among the nobility and military. Promising all things to all men,

both Catholics and Puritans, and 'turning his outside to the one
and his inside to the other', he attracted to him a desperate and
dangerous crew of potential rebels. Care, however, had to be exer-
cised in bringing 'such persons as he thought fit for his purpose
into town together without vent of suspicion'. This was achieved
piecemeal, using one pretext or another, so that it would not be
'perceived that all moved from one head'.

As the moment of sedition approached, Essex ordered the leaders
to meet together in consultation 'at Drury-house, where Sir Charles
Danvers lodged, thinking...his own house to be under observation'. There five of the ringleaders — the Earl of Southampton,
Sir Charles Danvers, Sir Ferdinando Gorges, Sir John Davies, and
John Littleton — met to study a list of six score knights and
noblemen supplied by Essex and said to be favourable to his treason.
They also discussed three courses of action: to assault the court
directly and surprise 'her Majesty's person', to possess the Tower
of London and then bring in from Wales and elsewhere enough
troops to force the Queen to do their bidding, and finally to rouse
and hold the city of London in preparation for an attack on the
court. Possession of the court by force of arms, which had been
the original plot first devised in Ireland but rejected in favour of
the mad scheme to surprise the Queen and throw himself at her
feet, was deemed to be essential to the Earl's plans. Therefore, the
ringleaders determined that a small cadre of traitors, 'such as were
well known in court, and might have access without check or suspicion', would insinuate themselves 'into the several rooms in court,
according to the several qualities of the persons'. Sir Charles with
his company would occupy the great chamber and presence room;
Sir John would take over the hall; and Sir Christopher Blount would
hold the outer gate. When all had been prepared, Essex was to arrive,
accompanied by the 'noblemen of his party', force his way into
the royal closet and demand the removal 'of such persons as he called
his enemies' from about the Queen. Once possessed of the sovereign
and the centre of government, he intended to summon a Parliament, bring 'his pretended enemies to a trial upon their lives' and
divide up among his friends the profits of state.

Although Essex himself did not participate personally in the

Drury-house plottings, he was the 'directing voice', and he, along with his secretary Henry Cuffe and his stepfather Christopher Blount, refined and modified the decisions. The government in one of its longest run-on sentences in the entire document argued vigorously that Essex's eventual decision not to march directly on the court or to seize the Tower but instead to raise the city of London on his behalf was neither an act of desperation nor a departure from his original plan. The Earl all along had had a 'secret inclination' and 'special mind thereunto' and the move was merely a preparatory step to the eventual seizure of the court, his purpose being 'in all likelihood...that although he should have prevailed in getting her Majesty's person into his hands for a time with his two or three hundred gentlemen', he was fearful that 'the very beams and graces of her Majesty's magnanimity and prudent carriage ...would quickly break the knot, and cause some disunion and separation amongst' his followers, unless 'he should build upon some more popular number, according to the nature of all usurping rebels, which do ever trust more in the common people, than in persons of sort or quality'.

By early February of 1601 the pieces were in place and the conspiracy worked out to perfection; all that was lacking was 'the assignation of the day'. Fortunately, at this propitious moment — the evening of February 7th — 'God, who had in His divine providence long ago cursed their action' and had determined that Essex's treason 'should be like the untimely fruit of a woman, brought forth before it came to perfection', inspired the Queen to send Mr Secretary Herbert to require the Earl to appear before the Council to explain the crowds of armed men and commotion going on at Essex House. The Crown had no intention of restraining the Earl, 'but his own guilty conscience' panicked him into believing that his villainy had been discovered, and, fearing 'peril in any further delay, [he] determined to hasten his enterprise, and to set it on foot the next day'. Moreover, hearing that 'the guards were doubled at court' and 'so concluding that alarm was taken,...he thought it to be in vain' to attempt to surprise the Queen, and so decided to march upon the palace 'in strength, and to that end [resolved] first to attempt the city', relying upon the conceit that he was 'the darling and minion of the people'.

In order to spark the rebellion, Essex 'was forced to descend to the pretext of a private quarrel', claiming 'how that evening, when he should have been called before the lords of the Council, there was an ambuscade of musketeers placed upon the water, by the device of my lord Cobham and Sir Walter Raleigh, to have murdered him by the way as he passed'. This fabrication was spread throughout the city and used to entice the Earl's friends to come to Essex House next morning, where they heard various versions of the story — the Earl was to be murdered in his bed or on the water or by four Jesuits — and where they were told that Essex 'meant to go to the court and declare his griefs to the Queen, because his enemies were mighty and used her Majesty's name and commandment' to prevent him from reaching her. By ten o'clock the Queen had heard of 'this strange and tumultuous assembly', but in her princely wisdom, seeking 'to cast water upon this fire', she sent 'four persons of great honour and place' — Lord Keeper Thomas Egerton; the Earl of Worcester; Essex's own uncle Sir William Knollys; and John Popham, the Lord Chief Justice — to Essex House to inform the Earl and his followers 'that if they had any particular cause of griefs against any persons whatsoever, they should have hearing and justice'.

Essex's reply was to shout 'in a very loud and furious voice' that 'his life was sought, and that he should have been murdered in his bed, and that he had been perfidiously dealt withal'. The Lord Chief Justice answered reasonably that in that case Devereux should return with them to court and make known his grievances to the Queen. The Lord Keeper added that if the Earl would not declare his wrongs openly or did not wish to name his would-be murderers, he might do so privately, and he promised that all four of the Queen's officials would 'procure him satisfaction'. The throng about the Earl — some two to three hundred strong — seized upon these conciliatory and reasonable words, and shouted 'Away, my lord, they abuse you, they betray you, they undo you, you lose time.' Upon hearing such bellicose language, the Lord Keeper commanded the armed assembly 'upon your allegiance to lay down your weapons and to depart'. Instead of doing so, some of the traitors shouted 'kill them, kill them', and others of this 'disordered company' cried out to 'keep them as pledges, cast the great seal out at the window'. Essex immediately seized upon this last suggestion and used it to reinforce his treason. If he failed in forcing his way to the Queen, four high officers of state would be useful hostages; if he succeeded, their imprisonment would deprive her Majesty of their advice and counsel; and regardless of what happened, the surest way to commit 'his followers in the very beginning' was to imprison four privy councillors who were 'carrying her Majesty's royal commandment for the suppressing of a rebellious force'.

Once started upon the path of sedition and violence, events moved predictably to their divinely ordained and tragic conclusion. The deity had created kingship and He detested treason, and from the instant Essex locked away the Queen's servants and rode forth with his troops to rouse the city of London, it seemed that 'God did strike him with the spirit of amazement'. The moment he entered London 'he never had so much as the heart or assurance to speak any set or confident speech to the people...nor to do any act of foresight or courage'. Not one man of the entire city 'from the chiefest citizen to the meanest artificer or prentice' would answer the Earl's appeal. And 'his face and countenance' being 'moulten with sweat...by the perplexity and horror of his mind', the miserable nobleman came to the house of Sheriff Smith 'where he refreshed himself a little' and learned that throughout the city he had been proclaimed a traitor by the Queen's heralds. Now that he had been publicly denounced, his swordsmen began to melt away, leaving him with 'nothing but despair'. Not even the more monstrous lie that there was a conspiracy to sell the kingdom to Spain could hold men to him or persuade the citizens of London to arm themselves. And so, thoroughly dismayed by the news that her Majesty's forces were mobilizing against him and 'not knowing what course to take', he fled back to Essex House, hoping to use his hostages to protect him and to wait for nightfall when 'his friends in the city would gather their spirits together and rescue him'. Again, however, God interfered to thwart the Earl's villainy: one of Devereux's own followers, Sir Ferdinando Gorges, seeing 'my lord's case [to be] desperate', had rushed back from the city, and, hoping to save his own neck, had ordered and obtained the release of the four councillors. When Essex recovered his house, after a clash with the Queen's troops at Ludgate, there was nothing left but either to surrender or die fighting. And after an appropriate display of chivalry, whereby the Queen's forces permitted the ladies of Essex's household to leave unharmed, the traitors elected to capitulate, the Earl being granted three requests: he and his followers 'might be civilly used', 'they might have an honourable trial', and Essex might have Ashton, his chaplain, 'with him in prison for the comfort of his soul'. These being granted, the 'action, so dangerous in respect of the person of the leader . . . and the intent of the plot, broke forth and ended within the compass of twelve hours'.

The government's artful and immaculate presentation of the hideous but indisputable events that took place from the day Essex arranged to be appointed Lord Lieutenant of Ireland to his surrender at Essex House on the evening of February 8th, 1601 was carefully designed to attest to the logic, premeditation, and magnitude of Devereux's wickedness, but it contained one profound defect: why had such a privileged and gifted nobleman fallen prey to the devil's entrapment and committed treason? As with Thomas Seymour, Essex's sedition cast the entire system, educational, political and spiritual, into doubt. How could society have spawned such a pervert who spoke of his sovereign as a woman as 'crooked in her disposition as in her carcass', who questioned the infallibility of God's viceroy on earth, and who sought to impose his will upon his Queen? What had happened to those pedagogical pillars upon which society rested — obedience, decorum, and religion — that they had had so little influence upon an Essex? And most disturbing of all, how was it that a gentleman who had won the Queen's affection and bounty and had been acknowledged by all to be generous of spirit and noble of heart had fallen into filthy and perfidious treason?

The traditional explanation for sedition in the sixteenth century was to point grimly to 'pride, vanity and love of this wicked world's pleasures', and to blame ambition: 'When soever we are out of our place or calling, Satan hath a fit occasion of temptation.' And Sir John Harington, when he said of Essex 'the haughty spirit knoweth not how to yield', was offering no more than the customary Christian formula for the Earl's tragedy.[4] Self-esteem, however, was a tricky vice for Tudor society to handle. It obviously contained the seeds of sin but it was also a close relative of honour. It was, as Tamburlaine dramatized, a characteristic of greatness, and was accepted as a quality inherent in all nobility. To present Essex as a defeated Icarus whose uncontrollable ambition had brought him to destruction made the government uneasy, for such a role smattered of the fallen but still popular hero who thrives on adversity. The Earl was already far too popular with the multitude to risk turning him into an attractive Coriolanus whose sense of honour and noble pride engendered his disaster. A more politic solution to the mystery had to be found.

Two other possibilities remained. Robert Devereux was from birth the evil child of Lucifer, and like his satanic parent was a master of deceit and dissimulation, his entire career being nothing more than a colossal lie; or he possessed some fatal flaw through which the devil's poison had been able to penetrate, corrupting his virtues and blinding his reason to honour and duty. The first solution, although offered by the government as a possibility — he had feigned remorse and humility to make 'her Majesty secure and lull the world to sleep' — was never seriously developed. Essex was of royal blood, and despite what Elizabeth might privately think about Lettice Knollys-Devereux-Blount, it was unthinkable that the Earl had come from corrupt stock. Moreover, far too many people were agreed that if Essex had a fault it was the exact opposite of dissimulation: he was gullible, frank, and unable to 'keep his passions in his pocket'. A better and far more acceptable explanation for a world which remained convinced that evil resided solely in man, not God's divinely inspired society, was to discover the base, demonic personality that had led noble Essex astray, playing on his virtues and weaknesses, and cruelly leading him to rebellion and death.

Such a solution struck a responsive chord, and Essex's contemporaries were quick to paint him as a tragic and innocent victim of some villain of blackest hue, deceitful, cunning, revengeful, and cowardly. Sir Robert Naunton in his *Observations on the Late Queen Elizabeth, Her Times and Favourites* speculated that if only 'one honest man or other, which had but the brushing [of] his clothes, might have whispered thus in his ear: "My Lord, look to it, this multitude that follows you will either devour you, or undo you; do not strive to over-rule all"', the disaster would have been avoided. Unfortunately, the Earl was surrounded by evil and selfish leeches, who 'had sucked too much of their lord's milk, and instead of withdrawing, they blew the coals of his ambition, and infused into him too much of the spirit of glory; yea, and mixed the goodness of his nature with a touch of revenge...'[5] Later in the century Thomas Fuller, when he came to write his *Worthies,* used the same device: 'Revengefulness was not bred, but put into his disposition.'[6]

The problem, of course, was who was to be cast in the despicable role of Essex's Iago. There were a number of candidates who could qualify, but like Goldilocks and her porridge only one was 'just right'. Southampton was out of the question: he was of noble family. Sir Christopher Blount was, as he said, not to be condemned but commiserated with for the 'natural considerations' that tied 'him to the Earl, having married his mother'.[7] Gilly Meyrick, who had been with the Earl ever since university days, was too obviously a devoted servant, shaped in the historic mould of the feudal retainer — 'What his lordship's will is, I must obey it.'[8] Sir John Davies was clearly a professional military man, courageous and loyal, who could not be connected with the plot to seize the Queen until a week before the abortive march on the city of London. Finally, Sir Charles Danvers came from an excellent Wiltshire family and was deeply and personally obligated to Southampton, not Essex. The perfect villain had to be someone of inferior heritage who, like Dr William Parry, could be depicted as 'a man of very mean and base parentage but of most proud and insolent spirit', consumed with envy for his betters. He also had to be sophistical, a secret demon upon whom the unthinking Essex relied and trusted, a man privy to the conspiracy from its conception — Lord Burghley's 'seed-man of sedition' — who cowardly left it to others to take the risk. Only Henry Cuffe, the Earl's confidential amanuensis, could with any verisimilitude be typecast for such a role, and the government unhesitatingly selected him as the true villain of the drama in whose 'vindictive brain' the conspiracy had been framed and who had deliberately led Essex into treason.

Cuffe was the perfect candidate. He came from an upwardly mobile Somerset yeoman family who had disdained 'all good order' and sent its precocious youngest son first to grammar school and then in 1578, aged fifteen, to Trinity College, Oxford. There young Cuffe had been trained in Greek and rhetoric, becoming in 1590 professor of Greek, a 'great philosopher' who could 'suit the wise observations of ancient authors to the transactions of modern times'.[9] No one, of course, was more dangerous to society than the over-educated parvenu — shades of 'Gregory Sweet-Lips' and Dr Parry. No one was more cunning than the master rhetorician who could cover 'craft with eloquence' and ornament his thoughts with figures of speech that 'deceive the ear and also the mind'. Indeed, scholar Cuffe seemed to suit perfectly Vives's warning that youths inclined to evil should not be exposed to rhetoric lest they 'twist everything to that end'. Cuffe left Oxford shortly after 1594 to become Essex's private secretary, the confidant of his most intimate thoughts, the bearer of all his secrets and the go-between who was known to all the principals involved in the conspiracy. Best of all, he had travelled in Italy,[10] that sinful kingdom of Machiavellian corruption, and was, as the government pointed out, a cowardly 'book traitor' who had remained at Essex House locked in his chamber amongst his manuscripts while better men had been out staking their lives to execute the evil he had planted in their hearts.

In Henry Cuffe the government was able to have its cake and eat it too: to prove that Essex had planned treason from the start but that Cuffe was the actual villain, the 'chief plotter and inducer of the Earl'.[11] With marvellous dexterity the Crown wove the two ideas together. Essex, 'having long before entertained into his service' as 'his chief secretary, one Henry Cuffe, a base fellow by birth, but a great scholar, and indeed a notable traitor by the book, being otherwise of a turbulent and mutinous spirit against all superiors', had immediately after his liberty from house arrest in May of 1600 'set his engines' to work, and the two men had 'set down between them the ancient principle of traitors and conspirators, which was to prepare many and acquaint few'.[12] Cuffe was the

perfect 'Mephistopheles to Essex's Faust',[13] except for one detail
— a motive.

Sir Henry Wotton supplied, at least for history, the missing link
in the Secretary's perfidy. Wotton, as one of the Earl's learned clerks,
was in grave danger the moment his patron's treason was revealed,
but unlike Cuffe he had enough sense to disassociate himself from
the final débâcle and diplomatically went on a grand tour of Europe.
When it was expedient to return after the Earl's execution, he did
so, he said, to find the cause of 'such a prodigious catastrophe',
and he unerringly pointed to Essex's nearest attendant, 'one Henry
Cuffe, a man of secret ambitious ends of his own, and of propor-
tionate counsels smothered under the habit of a scholar, and slob-
bered over with a certain rude and clownish fashion, that had the
semblance of integrity'.[14] Five or six weeks before the fatal upris-
ing of February 1601, Cuffe, according to Wotton, was summarily
dismissed from the Earl's service because Essex sensed that his
secretary 'would prove the very instrument of his ruin', and resented
his 'sharp and importunate infusions', for Cuffe had accused the
Earl of 'cowardice and pusillanimity'. The secretary was reported
to have been struck dead by his master's actions, 'as if he had fallen
from some high steeple, such turrets of hope he had built in his
own fancy'. Cuffe, however, soon had his revenge. He contrived
to get the Earl of Southampton to persuade Essex to reinstate him,
and he so worked upon Essex, urging him 'to stand stoutly in his
own defence', and seek his return to the Queen's favour 'by some
desperate attempt' that he 'spun out the final destruction of his
master and himself. . .'[15]

Wotton's animosity towards his one-time colleague is blatant,
and Sir Henry has become the historical source for much of Cuffe's
villainy, but, in fact, long before Wotton's return to find the cause
of the catastrophe, the Crown had already singled out the secretary
for the role of Iago. Of all the men who plotted to raise the city,
seize the court and bend Gloriana to their will, only five were
executed, and each of them, except one, was a principal; the exception was Cuffe, who had never been a part of the treasonous discussions at Drury-house, was not in any way involved in the
imprisonment of the Queen's officials at Essex House, and did not

accompany the Earl on his fatal 'eruption into the city'. Instead, the secretary stayed quietly in his rooms, as he said, deep 'in very melancholy'.[16] Southampton, Littleton, Sir John Davies, Ferdinando Gorges, every one of whom had been leaders in the Drury-house plottings, escaped with their lives. But not Mr Henry Cuffe, for the Crown was determined that he should die. The Attorney General, Sir Edward Coke, set the atmosphere for the trial with his opening words. Cuffe was 'the arrantest Traitor that ever came to that bar; he was Poly [meddlesome]...the very seducer of the Earl', and since the traitor was a scholar, he would set him a syllogism and dare him to deny it: 'Whosoever commits rebellion intends the Queen's death; but you committed rebellion: *ergo,* you intended the Queen's death.' He then branded Cuffe a busybody, a 'cunning coiner of all plots', who had not only seduced his master but also by his sophistry and lies had entrapped Sir Henry Neville, the Queen's Ambassador to France and 'a worthy gentleman', into countenancing the Earl's treason.[17]

Robert Cecil interrupted the course of the trial to call Cuffe a 'subtle sophister' and said he wanted to 'speak of a difference he found between noble and generous-minded men and others baser born;...[with] the gentlemen of birth and of good house, all their confessions came freely and liberally...without concealment or covering any thing with untruths'. In contrast, Cuffe and other low-born traitors confessed nothing and 'shadowed their actions with untruths so far as their wits could do it'.[18] Cecil was exceedingly vexed because Cuffe was using his training in rhetoric to undermine the government's case and display its palpable bias. With considerable logic Cuffe complained that he had committed no act of treason yet 'the number of matters heaped upon me, and the inferences and inforcements of the same [were] used against me to make me odious, make me seem also as a monster of many heads in this business'. He hoped, he said, that being in Essex House on that fatal Sunday would not 'be construed as in the case of others'. 'If those who only had their being within the walls...and [had] no hand nor head in that action' were traitors, then the lion that was 'there locked up in a grate' must be called a traitor also. To this sophistry the Attorney was curt: 'In treason the very intent is treason, if the same can be proved', and there could be no doubt that the traitor Cuffe knew of the intended seizure of the court. Indeed, it was the government's argument that the secretary had contrived 'the plots for restoring the Earl to greatness' and had 'turned the wheel which else had stood' still and was 'the stirrer of his mind which otherwise had settled to another course'.[19] It was also deemed of no consequence that Cuffe had not been at the Drury-house conferences, for 'in treasons there were no accessaries, but all principals'.[20] The conclusion was forgone. Cuffe had to endure his execution 'as full of ignominy as terror', because the Crown was bent on publicly exterminating the evil that had led the great Earl into treason and had so deeply embarrassed the government and its Queen.

As for Essex himself, he joined in the chorus of condemnation, eager to exculpate himself and exorcise his sins through the vilification of the helpless Cuffe. Devereux had never really been at fault; the guilt lay elsewhere in those who had misled him. And shortly after his trial and sentence to death, the Earl accused 'most of his confederates for carrying malicious minds to the state', and he singled Cuffe out as the arch-deceiver, calling him to his prison cell and bluntly stating:

Henry Cuffe, call to God for mercy, and to the Queen, and deserve it by declaring truth. For I, that must now prepare for another world, have resolved to deal clearly with God and the world; and must needs say this to you: you have been one of the chiefest instigators of me to all these my disloyal courses into which I have fallen.[21]

And thus Essex helped give birth to an Iago, only three years before he was to appear on stage. Not until the final scene did the performance falter or Cuffe fail to enact the part assigned to him. In life he was exactly what the plot required: the demonic prince of villainy. In death, however, he failed to supply society with a culmination to his evil appropriate to his villainy. Instead of dying as did Iago in tight-lipped and unrepentant silence, Cuffe squealed to high heaven, and desperately sought to save his skin by turning state's evidence. And his scaffold confession, true to Tudor bias about low-born scholars, was a verbose and tiresome affair in which his fervent appeal to God's angels and his own conscience that he was in no way involved in the 'wild commotion' of February 8th earned the sheriff's cold rejoinder not to 'palliate his crime by specious pretences', but to allow the executioner to get on with his grisly work.[22]*

The historic Cuffe was patently a sacrificial lamb offered up upon the altar of Tudor snobbery, social prejudice and paranoia: the knightly ideal still prevailed, insisting that swordsmen and noblemen were preferable to yeomen and scholars, and evil for ever stalked the kingdom and was by definition low-born and sophistical. Nevertheless, for all its manifest unfairness, the Crown did its work well; like all well executed specimens of propaganda, its case was soundly grounded on verifiable events and its version has endured. Henry Cuffe, the man, has been unable to break away from Cuffe, the villain. The Oxford don who left the security of academe and succumbed to Essex's devastating 'spiritual electricity' and fatal charm, and who wrote 'I would rather lose with him than gain with his opposites',[23] has come down in history for ever branded as the evil secretary incarnate.

The government's handling of Cuffe and its determination to rewrite history according to its own preconceptions, giving to evil a scholar's face, was an unqualified success. Its efforts, however, to portray Essex's sedition as the product of long-term, calculated plotting has persuaded no one. Neither Bacon's artistry nor the

---

*In the state papers there is an entirely different version of Cuffe's last words whereby Cuffe makes it devastatingly clear that he knew full well the bitter role he, the low-born scholar, had been forced to play. 'I am here adjudged to die for plotting a plot never acted, for an act never plotted. Justice will have her course. Accusors must be heard. Greatness will have the victory. Scholars and martialists (though learning and valour should have the preeminence yet) in England must die like dogs and be hanged. To mislike this were folly; to dispute of it but time lost; to alter it impossible, but to endure it manly and to scorn it magnanimity. The Queen is displeased, the lawyers injurious, and death terrible; but I crave pardon of the Queen, forgive the lawyers and the world, and desire to be forgiven, and welcome death.' (*C.S.P. Domestic, 1601-1603 with Addenda 1547-1865*, p. 15.) It would be nice to believe Cuffe spoke these words, but the speech smatters too much of hindsight.

carefully worked out official fiction of premeditated villainy has been able to convince historians that the Earl's treason was not in fact one of the most inept, ill-planned, befuddled, and addle-headed examples of sedition ever to have emerged from those sirens of Tudor politics — wishful thinking, paranoia, and desperation. The Crown's carefully woven fabrication unravelled because it lacked three essential threads of the story. It totally ignored the role of the Queen in Essex's tragedy; it pushed aside the Earl's mounting desperation in the face of his mistress's wrath; and it sought to impose upon Devereux's final hysterical plottings a rationality that never existed except in terms of the dark logic and 'corrupt' reasoning of a melancholic who was always in fear and was convinced that enemies lay 'in wait for him, and that some do purpose to slay him'.[24]

What originally produced Elizabeth's fury is not clear. Possibly in barging in upon her unannounced and catching her at ten of the morning *sans* wig, *sans* rouge pot, *sans* the theatrical costuming of royalty, Essex committed the ultimate crime: he stumbled upon the wizened, wrinkled and misshapen reality that hid behind the facade of majesty.[25] Elizabeth was deeply, irrevocably hurt in her womanhood, and as Nicholas Breton said, there was no weapon quite as sharp as 'the tongue of a scolding queen'.[26] Equally possible, the Queen was just as injured in her pride, for she informed the French Ambassador after the Earl's execution that she had warned Essex he should be 'careful not to touch my sceptre'.[27] No one knew so well as Gloriana 'how to humble the haughty spirit', and Elizabeth, once she learned the full extent of Essex's conversation with Tyrone, was convinced, as Henry Wotton suggested, that her one-time favourite had overreached himself and 'had a mind not to be satisfied but upon his [own] conditions'.[28] Essex had agreed at that fatal interview to present the Queen with twenty-two articles which the Irishman regarded as being essential to a lasting settlement. The first six dealt with matters of religion, 'the knot', which Devereux felt 'had to be loosed' before any final peace could be negotiated. The remaining terms had to do with Irish civil disabilities which Tyrone was also determined to remedy. What incensed the Queen, however, was not so much Essex's impudent reasonableness in the face of decades of Protestant English preju-

dice towards Catholic Irishmen as the personal basis on which he
and Tyrone had come to their understanding; it smacked of a rival
and masculine divinity. Tyrone, Elizabeth learned to her outrage,
had informed Essex that his affection for the Earl was such that
he would accept Devereux's word of honour as the basis for a truce
whereas he would not have done so 'for any other'. Gloriana's royal
jealousy was transparent when she ordered the Secretary for Ireland to inform Tyrone that if he 'would forbear to draw his sword
against our Lieutenant rather than against us, we shall take ourself
thereby [to be] much dishonoured...'[29]

Whatever the cause, the Queen's fury was monumental and prolonged, 'some sparks of indignation' remaining, as Henry Wotton
later said, 'unquenched even with his blood'.[30] Her initial reaction
to Essex's appearance in her closet gave little warning of the wrath
to follow, and at first she listened to his complaints and explanations with apparent sympathy, but shortly thereafter, when Sir John
Harington, who had accompanied the Earl on his return from Ireland, entered her chamber, 'she frowned and said, "What, did the
fool bring you too?...By God's Son I am no Queen, that *man*
is above me."'[31] The Queen's emotions steadily moved from concern and understanding to chilly questioning as to why he had
returned, and finally to open anger. He was ordered first to explain
his behaviour to a rump council — all that could be mustered at
such short notice — then told to wait upon her Majesty's pleasure
in his rooms, and finally, after a full-scale three-hour interrogation
by the entire Council, he was informed that he must leave the court
and be confined in Lord Keeper Egerton's charge at York House.

Essex's reaction to the dismal failure of his flamboyant appearance
in the Queen's boudoir and the total ruin of his political career
ran true to form. He suffered nervous collapse aggravated by
dysentery brought back with him from Ireland; he indulged his
delight in writing lamenting letters; and he blamed Cecil for having poisoned his mistress's mind and misrepresented his actions.[32]
Sir Robert Cecil, however, was manifestly not the villain; Elizabeth
herself was determined to punish her Lord Lieutenant and abate
'his greatness by degrees'.[33] And there commenced a nine-month
stand-off between the Queen and her Council on how to handle

the arrant Essex, Gloriana demanding a public trial in Star Chamber, her advisers urging moderation and clearly regarding any punishment for military errors to be a dangerous and deplorable development.

From York House during October and November poured forth reports that Essex was dying, these being interspersed with the usual quota of fawning letters from the ailing Earl: 'Receive, I humbly beseech your Majesty, the unfeigned submission of the saddest soul on earth. I have offended in presumption, for which my humble soul doth sigh, sorrow, languish and wish to die.'[34] Neither the state of Essex's health nor the thought of his proud soul wishing to die could move the unforgiving sovereign. On November 29th she obtained in Star Chamber a public pronouncement of the reasons for her displeasure, and throughout January she pestered her legal officers to collect evidence for a formal trial, avowing the whole time that his sickness was a sham. Virtually at the eleventh hour Essex's trial was averted by Cecil, who first persuaded Devereux to write one of his more obsequious letters confessing his manifest faults, and then convinced the Queen to accept his repentance at face value.[35] By mid-March Essex had fallen into a state of religious melancholia and self-pity in which he sought an explanation for his troubles in having violated God's laws by failing to observe every hour of the Sabbath. When Dr John Overall, his old tutor, advised him not to be so mechanistically literal in his interpretation of God's Word and that a certain amount of restrained recreation was permissible on Sundays, Essex replied: 'It may be so, yet it is safer to forbear: and hereafter I will forbear.'[36] In his desperation there was obvious satisfaction in placing the responsibility for failure on God, not Essex.

At last on March 20th, Essex was released from York House, only to be held prisoner in his own home where Sir Richard Berkley was installed as his jailor. As the weeks slipped slowly into months, Devereux moved from the sick soul's ecstasy in its 'marriage feast' with God[37] into a more secular, if not more healthy-minded, concern for his political welfare. The old shibboleths returned to haunt him. He picked up rumours that his own words were being printed and used against him, and in a frenzy he wrote to the Queen that he had long suffered the weight of her indignation but now he was subject to 'the malicious insinuations' of enemies who 'first envied me for my happiness in your favour, and now hate me out of custom; but, as if I were thrown into a corner like a dead carcase, I am gnawed on and torn by the vilest and basest creatures upon earth. The prating tavern haunter speaks of me what he lists; the frantic libeller writes of me what he lists; already they print me and make me speak to the world, and shortly they will play me in what forms they list upon the stage.'[38] The Earl's appetite for complaining about his enemies was insatiable, but embedded in his letter was another, even more disturbing, fear: his mistress might not renew his farm of sweet wines which terminated on September 29th and which was the economic foundation of his political existence. Without it he would go bankrupt; no wonder he offered fervently to kiss her 'fair correcting hand' and hoped that his Queen 'meant to correct and not to ruin' him.[39]

Elizabeth's correcting hand continued to use the rod. Essex's re-education in better manners was not finished nor the humbling of his pride complete. If Gloriana could not persuade her Council to test the Earl's loyalty before a court of law, she could at least insist on a public censure of his mismanagement of her armies in Ireland, and on June 5th he was ordered to attend upon eighteen councillors and judges, sitting at York House, to hear his official reprimand and punishment. From eight in the morning until nine at night no misdeed was left unnoted or uncondemned: he had disobeyed his sovereign's order in returning home, he had written threatening letters to the Council, he had ignored the original military plans for the suppression of the Irish rebellion, he had created a multitude of idle knights, he had made the Earl of Southampton General of the Horse, and he had far exceeded his authority in negotiating with the traitor Tyrone. Nor were those earlier words — 'Cannot princes err? Cannot subjects receive wrong?' — forgotten, and Francis Bacon presented the official line when he bluntly informed the Earl 'this I must truly say, that by the common law of England a prince can do no wrong'.[40] The final, but clearly unhappy, sentence — the lords were still uneasy at the notion of a general being punished for his failures in the field — was that the Earl was to refrain from exercising the authority of his various offices, and 'return to the place whence he came, under such restraint as before, until her Majesty's pleasure should be further known'.[41]

Never known for her hasty decisions, Elizabeth delayed revealing her pleasure until August 26th when Essex was ordered to York House and told he was free to go where he chose, except that he was in no way 'freed of her Majesty's indignation', and he was instructed never to 'presume to approach the court or her person'.[42] Gloriana was indulging in her usual infuriating and dangerous half measures. What she gave in one hand — his liberty — she took away with the other — any chance to speak to her or rebuild his political career. Nevertheless, he informed his mistress that he 'kissed her royal hand and that rod which had corrected him, not ruined him; but he could never be possessed of his wonted joy till he beheld again those benign looks of her which had been his star to direct and guide him'.[43]

Essex had cause to get down upon the knees of his heart, for he was dying financially. His credit was withering away as he approached September 29th and the Queen's decision to renew or cancel his farm of sweet wines. Until, as one cynical observer remarked, 'I see his licence for sweet wines renewed...or some other substantial favour answerable to it, I shall esteem words but as wind and holy water of [the] court'.[44] If Elizabeth was determined her Essex should grovel, she got her wish, for throughout the autumn of 1600 she received an onslaught of letters from 'shaming, languishing, despairing' Essex, all smothered in humble pie. He revealed to her his desperation in plain language: the farm was his only 'means of satisfying a great number of hungry and annoying creditors, which suffer me in my retired life to have no rest'.[45] As the date of expiration passed, Essex grew more frantic:

If your Majesty grant this suit, you are most gracious, whatsoever else you deny or take away. If this cannot be obtained, I must doubt whether that the means to preserve life, and the granted liberty, have been favours or punishments; for till I may appear in your gracious presence, and kiss your Majesty's fair correcting hand, time itself is a perpetual night, and the whole world but a sepulchre unto your Majesty's humblest vassal.[46]

On October 30th, Gloriana made her decision: she would keep the profits of the farm for herself. Eighteen days later, Devereux made one final effort. On November 17th, Elizabeth's Ascension Day, he opened full the flood valves of his humiliation and offered his 'dread sovereign' his manhood, pride, and abject contrition.

Only miserable Essex, full of pain, full of sickness, full of sorrow, languishing in repentance for his offences past, hateful to himself that he is yet alive, and importunate on death, if your sentence be irrevocable, he joys only for your Majesty's great happiness and happy greatness; and were the rest of his days never so many...he would lose them all to have this happy seventeenth day many and many times renewed with glory to your Majesty, and comfort of all your faithful subjects, of whom none is accursed but your Majesty's humblest vassal.[47]

Alas, the deluge of saccharine words had lost their sweet. Gloriana was pleased but acidly commented that 'all is not gold that glistereth', adding 'that an unruly horse must be abated of his provender, that he may be the easier and better managed'.[48] The Queen's decision to deny Essex his farm of sweet wines may only have been another turn of the rack upon which she sought to punish her Earl by slow degrees, and possibly, when the torture was complete, she intended to return the farm to a broken Essex. Equally probable, the Queen, frustrated in her determination to destroy him by legal means in Star Chamber, had contrived her revenge by creating the machinery of his self-destruction. Whichever it was, deliberate or inadvertent, Gloriana herself set Essex upon the path of treason. As Bacon later said, clearly with Essex and Elizabeth in mind, 'roughness...is a needless cause of discontent: severity breedeth fear, but roughness breedeth hate'.[49]

Devereux was desperate. The old graces — his magnetic personality, endearing ingenuousness, and dulcet phrases — on which he had so long relied to control his mistress were now useless or unavailing. More and more it seemed as if he were living in a 'looking-glass' political world in which he was being asked to play the role of the king's messenger: 'He's in prison now, being punished: and the trial doesn't even begin till next Wednesday: and of course the crime comes last of all.' The Earl was being condemned without cause, and as contemporaries prophesied his discontent bred 'adventurous imaginations', for 'he that hopeth no good, feareth no evil'.[50] Of evil there was abundant evidence, for Essex knew himself to be encompassed and smothered by the lies of his enemies: how else could he explain the Queen's adamant and ruthless behaviour? Her roughness had indeed warranted his hatred, but it was not permissible to hate God's vice-regent on earth. It was neither politically nor psychologically possible, and all of Essex's pent-up fury and depression erupted upon that spider Cecil and his associates in evil, Raleigh, Cobham, and the Earl of Nottingham, who spun their nefarious webs of hatred, deliberately misrepresenting the Earl's behaviour and entrapping the Queen's mind. Essex and all the melancholy malcontents, bankrupt aristocrats and outcasts of court politics who rallied to his colours were victims of a vast conspiracy that was not only aimed at keeping the Earl away from the Queen and ultimately envisioned his assassination but was also directed at Gloriana herself, the Protestant faith and the entire kingdom.

Isolated from the realities of court and surrounded by malcontents, most of whom mixed stupidity, greed and laziness in proportions disastrous to their own careers and to the Earl they admired and followed, Essex allowed his imagination and paranoia free rein. Conjoining scraps of plausible evidence drawn out of context to a host of false inferences, and displaying Tudor susceptibility for patterns of similarities and correspondences, he wove a fantastic, albeit perversely logical, tapestry of treason in which the Cecil gang plotted to turn England over to the Catholics, and on Elizabeth's death to place the Infanta of Spain upon a throne that rightly belonged to James of Scotland. Throughout the realm, pro-Spanish creatures of Robert Cecil had been strategically placed in anticipation of the Queen's demise and a Spanish bid for her crown. Raleigh had recently been appointed Governor of Jersey, an obvious design to weaken the western defences in case of a Spanish move. Cecil's brother-in-law Lord Cobham was in another militarily sensitive post as Lord Warden of the Cinque Ports. Who managed the navy, 'the walls of this realm', but Lord Admiral Nottingham, another Cecil ally, and who had been made Lord President of the North but Sir Robert's own half-brother? In Ireland Sir George Carew, the Cecil minion whom years before Essex had sought to remove from court by appointing him Lord Lieutenant of Ireland, was now Governor of Munster, the 'province which of all others is fittest for the Spaniards' designs'.[51]

There was further sinister evidence that Cecil was planning a Spanish coup: it could not be sheer coincidence that the government had suddenly relaxed its campaign against Jesuits and English Catholics, and most ominous of all, Cecil himself was reported to have said 'the Infanta's title comparatively was as good in succession as any other's'.[52] Any doubt that Essex and his companions might have had about Cecil's true intentions and the existence of treason close to the Queen was swept away in early January 1601 when on the 9th the Earl of Southampton was brutally attacked and nearly killed by Lord Grey, a known friend and political supporter of Cecil. The episode was in reality a violent and childish explosion between two peers who detested one another and, if anything, was nothing more than disturbing evidence of the growing instability within Tudor politics as the Queen neared death. But Essex knew better. To his frantic mind, it was proof that his enemies were on the move; they had ceased merely to deprive him of access to the Queen; they were now planning to murder him as well as his friend Southampton. Now was the time to prepare for the worst.[53]

The government's description of those final weeks before Essex stumbled into open treason is deceptive, for it pictures furtive conspirators meeting at Drury-house, plotting a political coup with care and precision. In fact, had the Crown known or elected to utilize the full extent of Essex's imaginative schemings, it could have made an even more damning case, for Essex returned several times to his original notion of a military takeover by the army in Ireland in tandem with a Scottish invasion led by James VI. How much the Queen knew about the pressure Devereux placed upon his one-time political ally, Lord Mountjoy, who had taken command in Ireland, to send troops to England, liberate the Earl from house arrest, seize the court and stage a reconciliation between Essex and his monarch, or his equally dangerous suggestion to James to station an army on the English border and demand that Elizabeth declare the Stuart king her legal heir is shrouded in confusion.[54] What is most probable is that the government deemed it impolitic to mention James at all and inexpedient to destroy Mountjoy who was busily proving his loyalty by doing in Ireland what Essex had originally set out to do — defeat the rebel Tyrone. Therefore, the decision was made to concentrate on Drury-house and that band of hellhounds who met there to discuss the various means to their nefarious ends.

On the surface the government's interpretation was exactly what happened. What, however, the Crown failed to mention was the endless talk, hopeless disagreement, and clear unwillingness on the part of the conspirators to assume responsibility for specific decisions and actions. It was one thing to talk wildly and imaginatively about treason; quite another to enact it.[55] There seems to have been initial agreement that a two-pronged attack on court and Tower was desirable but impractical — the rebels had insufficient military force. Hours therefore were spent on dividing the good guys from the bad, debating how many of the 120 names supplied to them by Essex and said to be his supporters could be relied upon, and discussing, in case of an attack upon the court, where to strike, whom to arrest, and who could be trusted. The first meeting broke up in indecision and confusion. Next morning, February 3rd, when the group reconvened, Sir John Davies offered a concrete proposal: infiltrate the court at Whitehall with men of lesser rank who would arouse the least suspicion, introducing them piecemeal throughout the various sections of the household during the course of the day; then at a predetermined signal overpower the royal guards, seize the Great Court Gate so that no government reinforcements could enter, and wait for Essex and his noble entourage to make their grand entrance before the Queen. Raleigh, Cecil and a handful of others would be arrested; heralds would proclaim the event to the city; and Essex would instruct the Queen to call a Parliament to remedy the woes of the kingdom and undo 'the mischievous malice of such men as be desirous to break the public unity'.

By the standards of Tudor treason Davies's scheme was perfectly sensible. Where it fell to pieces was in the assigning of roles; everyone turned out to be spineless revolutionaries when it came to specific commitments, Ferdinando Gorges announcing he 'utterly misliked that course, as besides the horror I felt at it, I saw it was impossible to be accomplished'. Southampton, quick-tempered and never strong on constructive thinking, retorted in exasperation: 'Then we shall resolve upon nothing, and it is now three months or more since we first undertook this.' That talk had been going on for three months — probably the Irish-Scottish invasion scheme — was news to Gorges, and he suggested that it would be best to discuss matters further with Essex's allies in the city; but this was 'so evilly liked'. he said, 'that we broke up, resolved upon nothing, and referred all to the Earl of Essex himself'.[56] Both means and ends were clearly floundering in a sea of atavistic fears that invariably beset Tudor traitors whenever they began to ponder on the sinister implications of holding a divine-right monarch by force of arms.

For the next four days the conspirators continued to do nothing, fulfilling Raleigh's dictum that 'dangerous enterprises, the more they be thought upon, the less hope they give of good success'. Then on February 7th the government decided to act. Essex in exile had become too dangerous to ignore. He had failed to heed the most rudimentary formula for any successful conspiracy: 'Silence and Discretion should be linked together like dog and bitch, for of these is gendered Security.'[57] The government was fully aware that the Earl had thrown open his doors 'to all comers' and was entertaining 'sword-men, bold confident fellows, men of broken fortunes, discontented persons and such as saucily use their tongues in railing against all men'.[58] Essex had become the magnet which attracted the sweepings and leftovers of Tudor politics — impecunious aristocrats unable to tap the Queen's bounty, impoverished gentlemen who had lost both 'blade and limbs' in the military service of an ungrateful country, melancholic and over-educated peers who sought to serve their sovereign but were denied office, out-of-work soldiers bent on 'mutinies at home',[59] and religious idealists and pragmatists — Puritan and Catholic — who viewed the approaching change in dynasty with both hope and alarm and sensed in Devereux a saviour and a solace to their persecuted faiths. In short, he collected all the flotsam and jetsam floating dangerously upon the political waters of a society that could not approach economic and political grievances except in terms of individual pride, perversity and wickedness. Essex had become all things to all forms of malcontent, and when a society was unable to cure the source of social and economic disease by transforming and reforming itself, then, in order to survive, it had to destroy the magnet that gathered discontent together in politically dangerous quantities.

Late on Saturday evening, February 7th, an alarmed Privy Council sent Mr Secretary Herbert to request Essex's presence in order to explain all the commotion at his London residence. The Earl stalled, first protesting ill health and then excusing himself on the grounds that he did not dare appear before the Council because he had reports of plans to murder him. Until the arrival of Herbert, sedition had been verbal, a combination of those wagging tongues, bragging threats and wishful thinking so characteristic of Tudor treason; but now boasts would have to be tested and the comfortable deferring until tomorrow would have to end. Having failed to exercise the slightest degree of secrecy, and certainly knowing that the government was keeping a close eye on his household,[60] Essex should not have been surprised that the Privy Council was concerned by the tempo of life at Essex House. Nevertheless, he and his colleagues in treason panicked, jumping to the conclusion that Cecil had penetrated the Drury-house discussions and as a consequence the court was heavily guarded, making any possibility of a surprise attack or secret infiltration impossible. Only two options seemed to remain for Essex: gather together his forces and flee, or gamble that his friends in the city would rally to his defence. Flight was ignominious; and so without checking with his London allies and relying solely upon the unsubstantiated authority of a mysterious and imprecise report that his friends[61] — particularly Sheriff Thomas Smith who was said to have 1,000 men at his call — were waiting upon his instructions, Essex marched forth on Sunday morning, February 8th, to rebellion without concern for planning, attention to detail, or previous discussion with Sheriff Smith. He trusted solely to hearsay and luck, thereby adding evidence to the verdict that 'the average Tudor traitor was quite incapable of taking action at the right moment'. Indeed, the entire tragedy followed grimly Raleigh's dictum that certain disasters 'proceed not of disorder, nor human imperfection, but from a certain fatal fury, which neither counsel nor constancy of men can withstand'.[62]

To the very last moment there was uncertainty which way Essex, accompanied by the Earls of Southampton and Rutland and a handful of other lords plus 200 armed swordsmen, would turn — east to the city or west to what was in fact the still defenceless court, for not a councillor could bring himself to believe that Essex would use armed force against his Queen. But Devereux, following his star and living in an age that still believed in miracles, chose London and Sheriff Smith's non-existent soldiers. True to his convictions, as he clattered down the Strand towards Ludgate, he shouted to the gaggling crowds: 'For the Queen! For the Queen! A plot is laid for my life.'[63] The plan, such as it was, was to have made an early start in order to meet up with the throngs of Londoners gathered at Paul's Cross for the Sunday sermon, but the encounter with and imprisonment of the four councillors sent to question him about his actions had delayed the start, and the vast congregation had dispersed. The populace he met on the way stood amazed by the spectacle of the popular Earl shouting to them to arm themselves and join him on his march to Whitehall. The credulous stood and cheered, thinking the Earl and the Queen were reconciled; the incredulous slipped quietly away and shuttered down the windows of their houses; and, as the government reported in its version of the rebellion, not a single citizen from the chiefest to the meanest joined the crusade. Ashen-faced and badly shaken, Essex headed for Fenchurch Street and the home of Sheriff Smith, only to have that elusive official duck out the back door and scamper away to the protection of the Lord Mayor. Without foresight, planning, or proper military equipment, the enterprise was doomed, and Essex froze, incapable of any concerted action or constructive thinking. For three invaluable hours, he and his companions made free with the Sheriff's food and drink, talking wildly and determining nothing. He even made the Cecilian plot to betray the country to the Infanta of Spain seem ridiculous when, with 'a napkin still tucked around his neck', he rushed out into the street crying that 'England is bought and sold to the Spaniard!'[64]

The carefully constructed fictions of Essex's conspiracy world dissolved into the tragic but pathetic bravado of a leader who had lost faith in his own cause. He could not accept himself as a proclaimed traitor, and he dismissed the news that heralds throughout the city were declaring him a public enemy as the work of Robert Cecil: 'Pish! the Queen knoweth not of it.'[65] But many of his friends thought otherwise, and they began to slip away, each man looking after his own safety. There was no other choice but to retreat or surrender to the Lord Mayor of London, and Devereux decided to turn homeward to Essex House in the hope that he could use his hostages, as Camden said, while 'there was room for and hope of pardon, no blood having been yet spilt, the Queen remaining doubtful of the success and the citizens' minds still uncertain'.[66] The fates that determine the perversity of events, however, had no intention of allowing Essex an escape. His hostages would, without his knowledge, shortly go free, his way back to Essex House via Ludgate was barred by the Queen's forces, and without orders his swordsmen, frustrated by having done little but wait upon their leader to wine and dine for three hours at Sheriff Smith's, fell upon the Crown's troops. Most galling and frustrating of all, the Earl's swaggering gallants who had set out four hours earlier with such confidence were resoundingly defeated by Sir John Leveson and a company of the Bishop of London's men. Blood had now been shed and all expectation of pardon was gone. There was nothing else left but every man for himself, and Essex with a handful of dispirited and frightened fugitives fled towards the river, hired boats, and made their way back to Essex House by water, having accomplished in eight hours absolutely nothing. Sir John Leveson supplied the only possible epitaph to a disaster that mystified contemporaries and has baffled historians ever since: 'I answered [Essex] that it was above my capacity to understand the designs of his Lordship.'[67]

The truth of the matter, of course, was that there was no design, only paranoid fantasizing, and even that was destroyed during Essex's trial which along with Southampton's took place on February 19th, 1601 at Westminster Hall. His defence was twofold: his motives, he said, were pure — he had not designed treason, only an interview with the Queen — and he had done what he did on the basis of the Law of Nature, 'driven of necessity to his own defence, since he had understood, not by uncertain rumours or conjectures but by most assured and credible messages, that he was destined to be slain...by his enemies'.[68] He had, he maintained, only been 'drawn into this hazard' by those who had the Queen's ear and had abused it. His sole purpose was simply to come with eight or nine honourable persons and prostrate himself at 'her Majesty's feet', to put himself 'unto her mercy' and to beg that she would dismiss from her service those 'who, by reason of their potency with her, abused her Majesty's ears with false information'.[69] The government made short shrift of the Earl's innocent and loyal conscience, for when Southampton unwisely asked the Attorney General what he thought he and Essex would have done to the Queen had they succeeded in their purpose, Coke answered: 'the same which Henry of Lancaster did against Richard the Second. He went to the King and fell on his knees, pretending only to beg the removing of his evil counsellors, but having once gotten the King in his power, he deprived him both of his crown and life.'[70]

History for the Tudors was the window through which to read and understand contemporary events, and from the start Essex had been associated in the public mind with Henry IV. As far back as February 1599, when John Hayward published and dedicated his *Life and Raigne of Henry IIII* to the Earl, Devereux had been linked with the overmighty Bolingbroke who had defied the divinity that 'doth hedge a king' and had set himself up as Henry IV.[71] Certainly Elizabeth was convinced of the relationship. When, during the Earl's house arrest, the Queen was casting about for credible evidence of disloyalty, she pounced upon the *Life and Raigne of Henry IIII*, referred to herself as Richard II, and exposed the book to that paranoid scrutiny with which Elizabethans were wont to approach their literature. She even suggested to Francis Bacon that the unfortunate author be put on the rack in order to discover the true purpose of his scholarship.[72] The action of Essex's more militant followers on the evening before the rebellion, when they bribed the Lord Chamberlain's players to put on Shakespeare's *Richard II* at the Globe Theatre, could only have confirmed the Queen and her government in the conviction that the Earl was in fact modelling himself on Henry Bolingbroke and was set upon becoming 'Robert the Last' of his earldom and 'Robert the First' of the kingdom.[73]

As for those 'most assured and credible messages' proving the existence of enemies set upon slaying Essex, the Crown set out to prove that they were the deliberate fabrications and figments of the Earl's seditious imagination. Bacon, speaking on behalf of the government, pointed out that Cobham, Cecil, and Raleigh were far too well off to hazard their estates and political careers by committing 'so foul a deed', and that Essex's fictional plots against his life not only fell to the ground 'by reason of their various inconsistencies' but also were nothing but a camouflage, 'a usual thing with traitors to strike at princes, not directly, but through the sides of their ministers'.[74]

It was easy enough for Essex to brush aside the state's evidence that his life was never in danger from Cobham and Raleigh, and he scornfully asked his peers who would ever believe the word of that lying 'fox' Raleigh. As for Cobham, Devereux dismissed him as 'such a backbiter and informer I would have removed [him] from the Queen though it had cost me the loss of my right hand'.[75] Cecil, however, was another matter, and Essex staked his reputation on publicly proving the Secretary a traitor. 'I can', he claimed, 'prove this much from Sir Robert Cecil's own mouth; that he, speaking to one of his fellow counsellors, should say that none in the world but the Infanta of Spain had right to the crown of England.'[76] Instantly, Cecil stepped out from the curtain behind which he had been listening to the trial and called Essex's bluff. 'I challenge you to name the councillor to whom I should speak these words. Name him if you dare. If you do not name him, it must be believed to be a fiction.'[77] Essex refused, appealing to

Southampton for confirmation. Then Southampton named the Earl's own uncle, Sir William Knollys, the Controller of the Queen's Household. Immediately Cecil was down upon his knees before Lord Buckhurst, the Lord High Steward of the Court, begging that a gentleman of the chamber be sent to the Queen with a request to command Knollys to attend upon the court. This the Lord Steward did, and Cecil added a parting admonition that the messenger 'not acquaint Mr Controller with the cause why you come for him'.[78] It was the climax of the trial — in a sense the climax of the long duel between Essex and Cecil — for the Earl's life and the Secretary's career hung upon the answer Sir William gave. When asked what Cecil had said to him, Knollys replied that he could not recall the Secretary speaking anything seditious; Cecil had simply been commenting upon a highly provocative book by the Jesuit Robert Parsons, alias Doleman, on the problem of the succession to the throne, and had said 'is it not a strange impudence in that Doleman to give a equal right in the succession of the Crown to the Infanta of Spain as any other'.[79] In a single sentence the conspiracy theory on which Essex had staked his rebellion collapsed, and all he could do was to mutter lamely that the words had been 'reported to me in another sense'.[80]

Plodding Cecil, the tortoise, had triumphed largely because he followed the rules of political success: never put anything incriminating into writing, wrap your true meaning in dissimulation, never wear your heart upon your brow, and always remember that political fictions, necessary to the smooth operation of Tudor politics, should never be confused with reality. And he pressed his advantage, candidly admitting that 'councillors of state have many conferences; I confess I have said that the King of Spain is a competitor of the Crown of England, and that the King of Scots is a competitor; and my Lord of Essex, I have said, is a competitor, for he would depose the Queen and call a Parliament, and so be very King himself.'[81] By the time the Secretary finished the gilded Earl stood naked, a political pariah and outcast, a proven incompetent and dreamer who had sought to usurp the throne and had ignominiously failed.

Essex had nothing left except his pride and sense of theatrics, and to the bitter, demoralizing conclusion, he maintained the charade. Let his enemies vilify him and shower him with untruths, he still knew his conscience to be pure, himself to be a loyal subject, and by the 'God which knowest the secrets of all hearts', he denied ever having 'sought the crown of England' or ever having 'wished to be of higher degree than a subject'.[82] To the terrible and inevitable sentence — 'to be hanged, bowelled and quartered' which only the Queen's mercy could commute into a more honourable death on the block — he boldly answered: 'I am not a whit dismayed... I think it fitting that my poor quarters, which have done her Majesty true service in divers parts of the world, should now at the last be sacrificed and disposed of at her Majesty's pleasure.'[83]

In the theatre of life such words, at least to modern ears, have a certain appeal — the lonely, martyred hero standing in defiance of tyrannical authority. But to Tudor sentiments, Essex was compounding his sins. He had committed treason, and his failure in sedition was clear proof that his crime was directed not only against the Queen but also against God Himself. Instead of expressing proper remorse, 'his chief care was to leave a good opinion in the people's minds now at parting'.[84] Treason began in the heart and only public confession and repentance could save the rebel's soul, and when his chaplain and friend, the Reverend Abdy Ashton, came to visit him in his cell, the Earl encountered not comfort and sympathy but harsh denunciation and a crash course on how to die well.[85] Ashton accused his Lord of hypocrisy: Essex's underlying aim, he said, had really been 'an ambitious seeking of the crown'. To the Earl's ardent denials, he warned: 'You must remember you are going out of the world, you know what it is to receive Sentence of Death here, but yet you know not what it is to stand before God's Judgment seat, and to receive the Sentence of Eternal Condemnation.'[86] His Lordship had to be made to see the truth — his treason was not simply a crime against humanity, it was a sin against God's universe, and only full confession of his faults could save his soul from everlasting damnation.

It only took a day for the Earl's defences to crumble before the assault of years of religious and political conditioning. He suddenly, devastatingly, saw himself for what society held him to be: a proud, ambitious, self-deluded traitor who had cast away salvation for a fantasy spawned by Satan himself. In his misery Essex called his enemies to him and confessed that he was 'the greatest, the most vilest, and most unthankful traitor that ever has been in the land.... Yesterday, at the bar, like a most sinful wretch, with countenance and words, I imagined all falsehood.'[87] He had, he confessed, plotted to seize the Tower of London, hold the Queen hostage, and rule through a puppet sovereign, forcing her to call a Parliament to revenge himself upon his enemies. He bore no malice towards Cobham or Raleigh, and he apologized profusely to Cecil for his outbreak of hatred during the trial. In four closely penned pages he poured forth his own sins and those of his associates who, he maintained, had betrayed his soul to the devil: Cuffe, Blount, Southampton, and even his sister Penelope, 'who did continually urge me on with telling me how all my friends and followers thought me a coward, and that I had lost all my valour; she must be looked to, for she hath a proud spirit'.[88] Once started, the floodgates of repentance opened wide. It was now 'his duty to God and the Realm to clear' his conscience, and he admitted 'he knew that her Majesty could not be safe while he lived'.[89]

Devereux had broken, but the collapse was not yet complete. Before he could die well, one further step was necessary: the Earl had not yet confessed himself to be at fault. Throughout his life the enemy had been to blame; after the calamity of his rebellion, his friends and relatives were forced to share the responsibility for his failure. Before Essex could become, as he desired, 'another man',[90] he had to confess that the source of the evil lay within him and that only he was responsible for the tragedy and villainy of his life. And at the moment of death he did, as society required, die a 'new' man. On Wednesday, February 25th, he stood bareheaded before the execution block determined that the world would see 'a strong God in a weak man'.[91] In a very private ceremony within the Tower, hidden away from public view, he confessed himself to be 'a most wretched sinner', his sins 'more in number than the hairs' of his head. His youth had been spent in 'pride, lust, uncleanness, vainglory and divers other sins'. He was 'puffed up with pride, vanity and love of this world's pleasures', and

> Not withstanding divers good motions inspired into me from
> the spirit of God, the good, which I would, I have not done;
> and the evil, which I would not, that have I done. For all which
> I humbly beseech my saviour Christ to be a mediator to the eternal
> Majesty for my pardon; especially for this my last sin, this great,
> this bloody, this crying, this infectious sin, whereby so many
> have for love of me been drawn to offend God, to offend their
> sovereign, to offend the world.[92]

Then, putting off his gown and ruff, he knelt before the block in
prayer, imploring God's 'blessed angels' to convey his soul 'to the
joys in Heaven'. Finally, removing his doublet and displaying the
usual scarlet waistcoat so symbolic of the occasion, he lay on his
stomach in the straw and fitted his head to the concave of the block.
It took three strokes of the axe to sever his head.

No man, according to the sixteenth-century formula, died 'more
Christianly' than Essex.[93] Although the devil had been victorious
in corrupting and enticing the Earl into treason, his achievement
had been incomplete, for in the ultimate scheme of things, God
had triumphed: Devereux had died repentant. The sixteenth century knew that, despite his crime, his soul had escaped damnation,
and John Davies, observing that, exactly a decade after the Earl's
death, pews had been placed over the spot in the Tower Chapel
where he had been buried, caught the flavour of his generation's
troubled but essentially optimistic response to the Essex tragedy
when in 1611 he wrote:

> So, he's a foot-stool made for them that pray,
> And men preyed on him too while he had breath;
> So men pray on him both in life and death;
>   But noble Essex, now thy lov's so free,
>   That thou dost pray for them that pray on thee.[94]

Tudor and early Stuart England could handle Essex as a victim of evil men, but society could only sense darkly the subterranean geneses of those phobias, fantasies, and melancholic paralyses that had tormented the Earl and trapped him into senseless, ineffectual treason. Devereux had been the prey of culturally and educationally induced paranoia which, even as he stood on the scaffold in that first year of a new century, was beginning to lose its hold on politics. As the seventeenth century waxed, the young were exposed less and less to Sirach's cynical warnings to be on the look-out for the hidden motives of the 'enemy', for Ecclesiasticus was high on the Puritan list as a spurious specimen of human frailty and deviousness, not God's authentic word. During the last half of the sixteenth century it was relegated along with other apocryphal pieces of Scripture to a separate and inferior place at the end of the Old Testament. Before 1600 the Geneva Bible had dropped the books of the Apocrypha entirely, and by 1629 there was mounting Puritan demand that the King James Bible should also be issued without them.[95]

Parental advice literature, although it retained its popularity well into the eighteenth century, became more a collection of literary *bons mots* wrapped in Poloniusque pomposity about the human condition than a compilation of practical admonitions directed to success in political life. Francis Osborne's *Advice to a Son* (1656) pictured a world equally as satanic as anything imagined by Northumberland, Raleigh, and Wentworth, but Osborne was clearly more interested in the well-turned phrase and quotable shock value of his observations — 'He that seeks perfection on earth leaves nothing new for the saints to find in heaven' — than in the political and daily usefulness of his aphorisms.[96] Moreover, his 'enemy' was no longer the sinister Iago of earlier decades but a generic and universal type akin to Hobbes's brutish man in a state of nature. By the century's end, society for Lord Halifax in his 'Advice to a Daughter' and later for Lord Chesterfield in his *Letters to his Son* still warranted cynical caution, but the evil of mankind had been largely displaced by its folly and extravagance, and the 'enemy' was no longer a villain but a knave whose rascality was inherent in human nature: 'It is the fools and knaves that make the Wheels of the World turn. *They* are *the World;* those few who have Sense of Honesty sneak up and down single, but never go in Herds.'[97] The world might indeed be quite mad, but it most certainly was no longer evil.

Satan, so vital and cunning in his handling of Essex, was losing his grip both on society and the universe. His disciples, dangerous enough to be executed as public enemies during the Lancaster witch trials of 1612, had by the eighteenth century been transformed in the popular mind into comic figures — players of practical jokes, known for 'their many sports and pastimes'.[98] And his black ama- nuensis, 'the enemy', found it increasingly difficult to operate effec- tively in a world that no longer accepted the philosophical doctrine of correspondences but sought instead the distinctions, not the similarities, between all things. Iago was losing his venom in an intellectual and social milieu which preferred to explain and handle villainy in terms of the evils of society and its organizational fail- ings and not on the basis of the sins of the individual. Merchant Mr Thomas Mun in his advice to his son (1664) was concerned primarily with duty, money, and the true nature of national wealth and not with demonic personalities bent on destroying God's design or on cheating honest artisans.[99] A world overflowing with plots and conspiracies and constantly exposed to the warfare between good and evil was poorly suited to the new cosmos governed by Newton- ian laws and inhabited by a dispassionate deity who conducted himself more according to John Locke's notions of good breeding than to the dictates of an interfering and wrathful god who was constantly at odds with Lucifer. The conspiracy theory of politics and history, of course, never totally disappeared and 'dangerous plots' to impose either Romanism or tyranny or a combination of both upon God's Englishmen remained the orthodox interpretation of history as the kingdom plunged into regicide and its final experience with that rare political experiment — successful treason. Nevertheless, political and historical analysis was on the verge of a revolution as vast as the Civil War itself when Sir William Petty sought to apply 'political arithmetic' and 'the art of reasoning by figures' to economics and history and to express himself 'in terms of number, weight, or measure'.[100]

Even those pillars that had held up the educational edifice in which Essex had been trained — rhetoric, with its combative and agonistic

approach to knowledge, and decorum, with its carefully rehearsed
role-playing — would eventually crumble before the Rousseauian
romantic ideal of the self-fulfilled, fully developed, free individual
who was capable of realizing his own, not society's full potential,
and who possessed the choice of serving either mankind or
himself.[101] Essex, whose virtues were so obviously his vices in
disguise and whose tragedy was as much an indictment of his society
as a study in mental illness, was never given such a choice. Nor
were all the other traitors whose bungling ineptitude brought them
to the block, for every Tudor gentleman knew that he had not been
'born for self alone but for country and for kindred', a claim that
left 'but a small part of him for himself'. As much as Essex and
his breed might wriggle and squirm and cry out in anguish, they
could never free themselves from the script that society demanded
they recite or from the misconceptions, fears, and 'black poison
of suspect' which religious and social training had indelibly
implanted upon their minds. Each enacted a destiny, beset by
paranoid delusions, which was peculiar to himself; but each traitor's
maladjusted response to the normal rhythm of politics was shaped
and delineated by a concatenation of cultural, educational, economic,
and political impulses that gave to Tudor England its distinctive
signature and that set the fatal tempo of his life, guaranteeing that
treason would never prosper.

NOTES

Part references only are given in the notes. For complete titles, names of editors, and dates of editions, see the bibliography. Spelling and punctuation of most quotations have been modernized.

I 'TREASON DOTH NEVER PROSPER'

1 *Original Letters*, I, no. 200, p. 211. G.R. Elton, by and large successfully, demonstrates that the Reformation and break with Rome produced a dangerous rash of plots. 'The policy of the 1530's encountered sufficient, if often sporadic opposition; many men disliked what was going on, and said so, and a number tried to take positive action. Therefore, there *was* a problem.' In all some 308 traitors died during the period 1532–40. (*Policy and Police*, pp. 4 and 387ff.) Loades, *The Reign of Mary Tudor*, notes that Mary 'was not noticeably reluctant to execute traitors' and gives the count for her reign, exclusive of Guildford Dudley and Lady Jane Grey, both of whom were left over from Northumberland's plot, as 132 (p. 282). The

number most often quoted for Elizabeth's reign is 183 (Hughes, *Reformation in England,* III, p. 338).

2 Perlin, *Description,* p. 27.

3 'An Exhortation Concerning Obedience' (1574), p. 113. After the collapse of the Wyatt rebellion against Mary in 1554, John Christopherson in his *Exhortation to all menne to take hede and beware of rebellion* (1554) drew an obvious conclusion: if the Queen 'had been an adversary of His truth and of His holy word', God 'would never have so aided her'. (sig. Q iiii.)

4 The Wisdom of Solomon, *The Apocrypha,* p. 179.

5 The version quoted is from 'An Exhortation Concerning Obedience' (see note 3). Ecclesiastes 10:20 reads slightly differently in the King James Version (1611) and has a more economic flavour.

> Curse not the king, no not in thy thought;
> And curse not the rich in thy bedchamber:
> For a bird of the air shall carry thy voice,
> And that which hath wings shall tell the matter.

6 Taverner, *Proverbes . . . of Erasmus* (1545), fols iiii-v.

7 Raleigh, 'The Cabinet-council', p. 61. There is no need to debate the issue whether Raleigh actually wrote 'The Cabinet-council' and 'Maxims of State', whether he stole the ideas as was so common in the sixteenth century, or whether they are simply attributed to him. See Pierre Lefranc, *Sir Walter Ralegh Ecrivain, l'oeuvre et les idées,* Paris, 1968, pp. 64, 67–70.

8 Bacon, 'Of Sedition and Troubles', *Essays,* p. 411; Raleigh, 'The Cabinet-council', p. 84. See also 'An Homily against Wilful Rebellion', p. 574.

9 Cecil, *Execution of Justice* (1583), p. 5.

10 *Lisle Letters* VI, p. 75.

11 Hume, *Treason and Plot,* p. 88.

12 Edwards, *Marvellous Chance,* esp. p. 106; Loades, *Mary Tudor,* pp. 365–68.

13 Walpole, *The Discoverie and Confutation of a tragical fiction* (1599), pp. 8–14.

14 *Lisle Letters* IV, pp. 83–85; VI, pp. 53–134, 213. The full story is told in all of its rich improbability and detail by Muriel St Clare Byrne in the lavishly edited *Lisle Letters.* My account is heavily dependent on her careful reconstruction.

15 Gottfried, *Epidemic Disease in Fifteenth Century England,* pp. 187–222.

16 For a general discussion of the economic state of the aristocracy, see Stone, *Crisis of the Aristocracy,* esp. pp. 184–85.

17 Foxe, *Actes and Monuments,* V, p. 514.

18 *Lisle Letters* V, p. 89.

19 Raleigh, 'The Cabinet-council', p. 89.

20 The story and various quotations are taken from Holinshed's *Chronicles* (as written by John Stow), 'A True and Plaine Declaration of the Horrible

Treason Practised by William Parrie ...' IV, pp. 561–87.

21 *Ibid.*, p. 578; Clapham, *Elizabeth of England*, p. 22 has a slightly different version of this story.

22 Strype, *Annals* III (1) p. 363; see also pp. 337–39.

23 *Ibid.*, pp. 364–67; Pollard, 'William Parry', *D.N.B.*; Mathew, *Celtic Peoples*, pp. 237–38; and Jardine, *Criminal Trials*, I, pp. 245–51.

24 *C.S.P. Foreign 1583-84*, p. 658.

25 *C.S.P. Scottish 1584-85*, p. 585.

26 Strype, *Annals* III (1) pp. 364–75 has a detailed account of Parry, much of which can be checked in *C.S.P. Foreign 1583-84*, nos 77, 91, 94, 168, and pp. 657 and 658; *C.S.P. Foreign 1583 and Addenda* no. 301; *C.S.P. Dom. 1581-90*, pp. 33, 160; *C.S.P. Dom. Addenda 1580-1625*, pp. 6–7, 10, 100, 101, 113.

27 Holinshed, *Chronicles*, IV, p. 568.

28 *C.S.P. Dom. 1581-90*, no. 86, p. 33; Strype, *Annals* III (1) p. 375.

29 *C.S.P. Dom. Addenda 1580-1625*, no. 27, p. 10; *C.S.P. Dom. 1581-90*, no. 23, p. 160; *C.S.P. Foreign 1583 and Addenda*, no. 394; *C.S.P. Foreign 1583-84*, no. 168; Strype, *Annals* III (1), p. 371.

30 Hicks, *An Elizabethan Problem*, p. 65; Holinshed, *Chronicles*, IV, p. 562; *D.N.B.*, 'Parry'.

31 Neale, *Elizabeth I and her Parliaments 1584-1601*, pp. 36–43; 44–51.

32 Holinshed, *Chronicles*, IV, p. 571.

33 Hughes, *The Reformation in England*, III, pp. 298, 376, basing his argument mostly on the works of J.H. Pollen, 'Plots and Sham Plots', *The Month*, and 'Dr Parry', *Ibid.*, April 1902, June 1902, p. 614 holds the most extreme view about the government's guilt in destroying Parry. The best account is in Hicks, *The Strange Case of Dr William Parry*, in *Studies*, pp. 343–62 of which a shorter version can be found in *An Elizabethan Problem*, pp. 61–70. See also Hume, *The Great Lord Burghley*, pp. 390–93.

34 Read, *Lord Burghley and Queen Elizabeth*, pp. 300–301.

35 Froude, *History of England*, XI, pp. 657–61; XII, pp. 80–85.

36 *D.N.B.*, 'Edmund Neville'.

37 See, for instance, A.F. Pollard, 'William Parry', *D.N.B.*; Williams, *Elizabeth*, pp. 267–68; and Neale, *Elizabeth I and her Parliaments 1584-1601*, p. 40.

38 The full story of Seymour's treason has yet to be written, especially his efforts to build up a semi-military presence in Gloucestershire. Many of the documents have been printed in Haynes, *State Papers* and Nichols, *Literary Remains of King Edward VI*. The best secondary account of Seymour is in Jordan, *Edward VI: The Young King*, pp. 368–85. Seymour, *Ordeal by Ambition* is a family history of the Seymours and is less well researched or thought-out than Jordan's work on the reign of Edward. See also three older accounts: Froude, *History of England*, V, pp. 145–53; Maclean, *Life of Sir Thomas Seymour;* and Pollard, *Protector Somerset*, pp. 177–99; and Strype, *Ecclesiastical*

Memorials, II, pt i, pp. 191–200.

39 P.R.O., S.P. 10, vol. I, fol. 55.

40 Cobbett, *State Trials,* I, quoting Bishop Hugh Latimer, pp. 506–508; Haynes, *State Papers,* p. 69.

41 Seymour, *Ordeal by Ambition,* pp. 211, 237; Pollard, *Protector Somerset,* p. 198; Maclean, *Life of Sir Thomas Seymour,* p. 58.

42 Clapham, *Elizabeth of England,* pp. 51–52. See also Haynes, *State Papers,* p. 69.

43 Haynes, *State Papers,* pp. 90–91; H.M.C. *Salisbury Mss,* I, no. 303; Seymour, *Ordeal by Ambition,* p. 222.

44 Tytler, *England under the Reigns of Edward VI and Mary,* I, pp. 148–49; Bush, *Government Policy of Protector Somerset,* p. 136; Haynes, *State Papers,* p. 76.

45 Jordan, *Edward VI: The Young King,* p. 371.

46 Haynes, *State Papers,* pp. 61–2, 73; P.R.O., S.P. Domestic, Edward VI, iv, 14, quoted in Jordan, *Edward VI: The Young King,* p. 371.

47 Haynes, *State Papers,* pp. 79, 80–81, 90–91.

48 *Ibid.,* pp. 81, 106.

49 *Ibid.,* p. 82.

50 Tytler, *England under the Reigns of Edward VI and Mary,* I, pp. 143–46.

51 Seymour, *Ordeal by Ambition,* p. 230; See also Tytler, *England under the Reigns of Edward VI and Mary,* I, pp. 146–48, 154.

52 H.M.C. *Salisbury Mss,* I, no. 303; *A.P.C.,* II, pp. 259–60; Seymour, *Ordeal by Ambition,* p. 230. To make matters worse, Richard Page was Somerset's 'father-in-law', having married the dowager Lady Stanhope, the mother of the Duchess of Somerset (Nichols, *Literary Remains,* p. xxxi).

53 P.R.O., S.P. 10, IV no. 26, ff. 53–54, Earl of Warwick to William Cecil, July 1548.

54 B.L., Harl. 249, fol. 26. Printed in Nichols, *Literary Remains,* pp. cxv-cxix.

55 Haynes, *State Papers,* p. 75; Jordan, *Edward VI: The Young King,* p. 376.

56 Haynes, *State Papers,* p. 74.

57 *A.P.C.,* II, pp. 259–60.

58 Tytler, *England under the Reigns of Edward VI and Mary,* I, p. 139; H.M.C. *Salisbury Mss,* I, no. 300; Haynes, *State Papers,* pp. 76–79.

59 Haynes, *State Papers,* p. 81.

60 *Ibid.,* pp. 75–77, 79–80, 81–82.

61 *Ibid.,* pp. 105–106.

62 *Ibid.,* p. 106.

63 Strype, *Ecclesiastical Memorials,* II (1) p. 192; *A.P.C.,* II, pp. 250–51; Seymour, *Ordeal by Ambition,* p. 236.

64 *C.S.P. Spanish 1547-1549,* pp. 339, 343, 345.

65 Jordan, *Edward VI: The Young King,* pp. 382–85; H.M.C. *Salisbury Mss,* I, no. 283; Strype, *Ecclesiastical Memorials,* II (ii), no. z, pp. 397–98; Haynes, *State Papers,* pp. 104–105.

66 Jordan, *Edward VI: The Young King,* pp. 382–85.

67 Haynes, *State Papers*, p. 81.

68 *Ibid.*, p. 107.

69 *Ibid.*, pp. 84–85.

70 *C.S.P. Spanish, 1547-1549*, pp. 332–34, 340, 349–50.

71 *Ibid.*, pp. 336, 347; Haynes, *State Papers*, pp. 107–108.

72 Haynes, *State Papers*, pp. 88, 106.

73 Cobbett, *State Trials*, I, p. 506, quoting Bishop Hugh Latimer.

74 *Ibid.*, p. 506.

75 Elizabeth, *Letters*, p. 20.

76 Treason under Henry VII was chronic but most of the traitors are two-dimensional paper figures in history. In all likelihood the Pilgrimage of Grace (1536–37) should be associated with the 1538 executions of the Courtney-Pole families since, as Elton argues, only incompetence prevented their linking up with Lord Darcy and Robert Ashe during the earlier rebellion. The Earls of Northumberland and Westmorland should be tied with the Norfolk débâcle of 1570. Then, of course, there are the endless plots — largely religiously motivated — to restore Catholicism or replace the Tudors. Sir Thomas Wyatt's and his colleagues' ill-timed and worse organized treason against Mary should also be included on the list. See Elton, *Reform and Reformation;* Fletcher, *Tudor Rebellions;* Loades, *Two Tudor Conspiracies;* Hume, *Treason and Plot;* and Edwards, *Marvellous Chance.*

77 Scarisbrick, *Henry VIII*, pp. 121–22.

78 Elton, *Reform and Reformation*, p. 281.

79 *Lisle Letters*, VI, p. 98.

80 Jordan, *Edward VI: The Young King*, p. 49; Chapman, *Two Tudor Portraits*, pp. 107, 126.

81 Jordan, *Edward VI: The Young King*, p. 381.

82 Williams, *Elizabeth*, p. 268; Neale, *Elizabeth I and her Parliaments 1584-1601*, p. 41; Pollard, 'William Parry', *D.N.B.*

83 Beer, 'Northumberland: The Myth of the Wicked Duke', p. 12.

84 Williams, *Thomas Howard*, p. 256.

85 Lacey, *Essex*, pp. 261–62.

86 Jordan, *Edward VI: The Young King*, p. 373.

87 Craig, *The Enchanted Glass*, p. 205 (the italics are mine). Craig's view should be compared to other similar statements. 'In the country as a whole there were innumerable opportunities for dispute and violence.' (Joseph, *Shakespeare's Eden*, pp. 91–92.) 'In Tudor times the mass violence which had marked the preceding ages was succeeded by an age in which violence became confined to the individual. The state had been regulated and laws had been written on the books, but personal character, with its inheritance of fierceness and independence, had not changed.' (Bowers, *Elizabethan Revenge Tragedy*, pp. 15–16.) 'It is hardly necessary to add that there is with this excess of imagination also a superabundance of passion, and that this

violent imagination is dependent upon the excess of passion.' (Bundy, 'Shakespeare and Elizabethan Psychology', p. 538.) There is also Elton's more restrained comment that 'Henry VIII's England was not an easy country to govern... Men had weapons about them and were readily enough moved to use them. Arguments quickly became quarrels, and there were always daggers handy to draw blood. The records are full of such violence because too many men (and women) believed in taking the law into their own hands. This was a rough, superstitious, excitable and volatile society which the King's government had to rule...' (*Policy and Police*, pp. 4–5.)

88 Einstein, *Tudor Ideals*, p. 122; Marlowe, *Tamburlaine*, I, ii, 174; V, ii, 405.
89 Adams, *The Divells Blanket*, (1614), pp. 77–78.
90 Nashe, *Pierce Penilesse His Supplication to the Divell*, pp. 52, 54; Barclay, *A Discourse of the Felicitie of Man*, (1603), pp. 132–33.
91 Segar, *The Booke of Honor and Armes*, (1590), p. 20.
92 Smith, *The Common-welth of England*, (1589), p. 123.
93 Stone, *Crisis of the Aristocracy*, p. 223.
94 In an unpublished manuscript Susan Maclean Kybett presents the thesis that much of Tudor England suffered from chronic vitamin C deficiency which produced, especially among the ruling elements, many of the characteristics noted by Lawrence Stone. Besides irritability, fatigue, aches, pains and sores, scurvy produces 'erratic moods' and eventually it attacks 'the nervous system producing paranoia and extreme melancholy'. (Chapter one, 'The Last Decade of Henry Tudor', p. 13, and chapter two, 'Scurvy in the Eighteenth Century', p. 29.) See also Greaves, *Society and Religion*, p. 477.
95 Lasch, *The Culture of Narcissism*, p. 87.
96 Erikson, 'Living in a World without Stable Points of Reference', p. 14.
97 Lyons, *Voices of Melancholy*, p. 23.
98 Jonson, *Every Man in His Humour*, II, iii, 55–67 (the italics are mine).

II 'THE BLACK POISON OF SUSPECT'

1 Hofstadter, *Paranoid Style*; Shapiro, *Neurotic Styles*, esp. chapter 3, 'Paranoid Style', pp. 54–107 upon which the following definition is largely based.
2 I am indebted to my colleague Ivor Wilks for this story.
3 A.A. Milne, *Winnie-the-Pooh*, p. 47.
4 Abbé Barreul, *Memoires pour servir à l'histoire du Jacobinisme* (Hamburg, 1803), quoted in Hofstadter, *Paranoid Style*, p. 12.
5 Hofstadter, *Paranoid Style*, p. 7.
6 Shils, *The Torment of Secrecy*, p. 30.
7 Quoted in Krauthammer, 'The Humanist Phantom', p. 21.
8 Raleigh, 'Maxims of State', p. 124. See chapter 1, footnote 7.
9 North, 'Dedication', *Dial of Princes* (1582), fol. Aiii.

10 Advice came in all shapes and forms: directions, memorials, instructions
   and precepts of various kinds directed to the young; books of maxims,
   aphorisms and pithy sayings of contemporaries but more often lifted from
   the Bible and the classics, known collectively as commonplace books and
   appearing under a multitude of different titles; lessons from history; warnings and lamentations about court and city life; treatises on how to succeed
   in life, especially at court or in a particular office; how-to-do-it books on
   such subjects as how to select a friend or how to use an enemy; essays of
   all varieties; letters both private and public and designed for popular consumption; autobiographies; works of educators; courtesy books; and, of
   course, sermons (although these last I have not used extensively since I wished
   to concentrate on secular works dealing with political and social life). The
   standard work on the subject is John Mason, *Gentlefolk in the Making.* Louis
   B. Wright has a useful introduction to his *Advice to a Son: Precepts of Lord
   Burghley, Sir Walter Raleigh and Frances Osborne.* W. Lee Ustick, 'Advice
   to a Son: a Type of Seventeenth-Century Conduct Book', *Studies in Philology,*
   XXIX (1932) pp. 409–41; Jacob Zeitlin, 'Commonplaces in Elizabethan
   Life and Letters', *Journal of English and Germanic Philology,* XIX (1920),
   pp. 47– 65; and Siegmund Betz, 'Francis Osborn's Advice to a Son', *Seventeenth Century Studies,* ed. Robert Shafer, are good brief studies. James Craigie
   has a long discussion of instructions to princes in the second volume of
   his edition of James VI's *The Basilicon Doron.* Napoleone Orsini, '"Policy"
   or the Language of Elizabethan Machiavellianism', *Journal of the Warburg
   and Courtauld Institute,* vol. 9 (1946), pp. 122–34 is useful, and much can
   be learned from Ruth Kelso, *The Doctrine of the English Gentleman in the
   Sixteenth Century;* Stone, *The Crisis of the Aristocracy* and *The Family, Sex
   and Marriage in England 1500-1800;* Mervyn James, 'English Politics and
   the Concept of Honour 1485–1642'; Richard Greaves, *Society and Religion
   in Elizabethan England;* Louis B. Wright, *Middle-class Culture in Elizabethan
   England,* esp. chapter V; and H.S. Bennet's three volume *English Books and
   Readers.*
11 Greene, 'Greenes Vision' in *Works,* XII, p. 216.
12 Baldwin, *Morall Philosophie,* p. v; Wright, *Advice to a Son,* pp. xix-xx, and
   Middle-class Culture, p. 150; and Rossetti, *Early Italian and German Books
   of Courtesy,* E.E.T.S., extra series, vol. 8.
13 Rowlands, *The Courte of Civill Courtesie* (1582).
14 James VI, *Basilicon Doron,* I, p. 11.
15 Cecil, *A Memorial for Thomas Cecil* (1561), p. 5.
16 Read, *Mr Secretary Cecil and Queen Elizabeth,* p. 216.
17 These nuggets in order of appearance come from: *Good Advice to a Governour,* p. 72; Breton, *The Court and Country* (1618), in *Works,* II, p. 10; 'Essex
   to the Earl of Rutland' in Devereux, *Earls of Essex,* I, p. 325; Breton, *Wits
   Private Wealth* (1639) p. 10; Breton, *A Packet of Mad Letters* (London, 1637),

p. 15 no. 33; George Herbert, *The Temple* (1633) p. 61; Patrik Scot, *A Fathers Advice* (1620), p. 28; 'Sir Henry Sidney to his son' in Bourne, *A Memoir of Sir Philip Sidney*, p. 21; Devereux, *Earls of Essex*, I, p. 330; Breton, *A Packet of Mad Letters*, p. 15; Wentworth, 'Advice to his Son' (1604), p. 9; Breton, *The Court and Country*, p. 9; Richard Vaughan, 2nd Earl of Carbery, 'Advice to his Son' (1651), p. 89; Cecil, *A Memorial for Thomas Cecil* (1561), p. 5.

18 Breton, *The Court and Country*, p. 9.

19 Ames, *A Fresh Suit Against Humane Ceremonies*, (1633), 9th page of unpaginated preface.

20 Wentworth, 'Advice to his Son', p. 14.

21 Marston, *The Malcontent*, I, i, 80 (p. 16).

22 Bacon, *Advancement of Learning*, p. 240; 'Of Suspicion', *Essays*, p. 454; 'Of Envy', *Ibid.*, p. 393; 'Of Simulation and Dissimulation', *Ibid.*, p. 388.

23 Jonson, *Every Man out of His Humour*, (1600), III, iv, 92.

24 Baldwin, *Morall Philosophie*, fols 52 (p. 119), 156 (p. 327), 168 (p. 350), 173 (p. 360).

25 Ling, *Politeuphuia, Wits Commonwealth*, (1597), pp. 65, 256, 467.

26 *Warnings and Counsels for Noblemen*, (1577), p. 74.

27 Cecil, *Certain Precepts* (1584), p. 13.

28 Hoby, *Diary*, p. 50.

29 Du Maurier, *Golden Lads*, pp. 73, 93.

30 Birch, *Memoirs of Elizabeth*, I, p. 13.

31 Ling, *Politeuphuia, Wits Commonwealth*, p. 65.

32 Baldwin, *Mirror for Magistrates*, II, pp. 349–59.

33 Edwards, *Marvellous Chance*, p. 29.

34 B.L., Sloane Mss. (1523) 'Maxims and Sayings' fol. 35.

35 Elyot, *The Book named the Governor*, p. 154.

36 Higford, *The Institution of a Gentleman*, (1660), p. 594.

37 Wentworth, 'Advice to his Son', p. 14.

38 *Ibid.*, pp. 9, 18.

39 Raleigh, *Instructions to His Son*, (1632), p. 26. The Earl of Carbery cautioned his son that 'letters pass not away as words do; they remain upon record, are still under the examination of the eye and [when] tortur'd sometimes they are to confess that of which they were never guilty', 'Advice to his Son', p. 86.

40 Percy, *Advice to His Son*, (1609), pp. 75, 85, 114.

41 Raleigh, 'The Cabinet-council', pp. 89, 90, 94, 103, 110, 114.

42 Wentworth, 'Advice to his Son', pp. 12, 22.

43 *Ibid.*, p. 23.

44 *Ibid.* Northumberland agreed and he warned of tradesmen and tenants, 'the one minds to betray you, the other intends to make you pay for their courtesy' and 'the oath of a mechanical man is not to be trusted', *Advice*

to His Son, p. 53.

45 Raleigh, *Instructions to His Son*, pp. 19, 24. The distinction between flattery and friendship was a constant theme in Tudor and Stuart England. 'Flattery from friendship is hard to be dissevered: for as much as in every motion and effect of the mind they be naturally mingled together.' (Baldwin, *Morall Philosophie*, fol. 128.) 'Flatterie is hardly discerned from friendship . . .' (Vaughan, *The Golden Grove*, I, 'of flatterie', p. 132.)

46 Taverner, *Proverbes. . . of Erasmus*, 1545, fol. xxxii.

47 Wentworth, 'Advice to his Son', p. 18 (margin).

48 There is no adequate treatment of the concept and role of the friend in the sixteenth century. Lawrence Stone, *Family, Sex and Marriage*, p. 97, mentions the friend, and so does Mervyn James, *English Politics and the Concept of Honour*, pp. 20, 21, 31. No one can read Elton's *Policy and Police* (see for instance p. 21) without sensing how important the friend was for surviving in Tudor England. On the other hand, how dangerous a friend could be is obvious from the careers of Dr William Parry and Sir Gregory Botolf. See Laurens J. Mills, *One Soul in Bodies Twain*, for a literary treatment of friendship.

49 Breme, *The Mirrour of Friendship*, (1584); Edwards, *Damon and Pithias*; Raleigh, *Instructions to His Son*, p. 19.

50 Charles Titchburne, one of the members of the Babington Plot, confessed at his execution that friendship had brought him hither: 'Let me be a warning to all young gentlemen. . .I had a friend, and a dear friend of whom I made no small account, whose friendship hath brought me to this. He told me the whole matter, I cannot deny. . . I always thought it impious and denied to be dealer in it; but the regard of my friend caused me to be a man in whom the old proverb was verified. "I was silent and so consented".' (Cobbett, *State Trials*, I, p. 1157.) The reader should recall Dr Parry's lament about his 'friend' Edward Neville.

51 B.L., Sloane Mss. (1523), fol. 37.

52 Cecil, *Certain Precepts*, p. 12.

53 Peacham, *The Truth of Our Times*, p. 204.

54 Ling, *Politeuphuia, Wits Commonwealth*, p. 115.

55 Breme, *The Mirrour of Friendship*, (1584), fol. Bv.

56 *Ibid*; Ling, *Politeuphuia, Wits Commonwealth*, p. 118.

57 Edwards, *Damon and Pithias*, pp. 68, 83.

58 Breme, *The Mirrour of Friendship*, preface. Compare Paice, *The Maner to chose and cherysshe a frende* (1533?).

59 Percy, *Advice to His Son*, pp. 74–75.

60 Cornwallis, *Essayes*, (1597), p. 22. Breton, *The Mothers Blessing* (1603), p. 9.

61 Ling, *Politeuphuia, Wits Commonwealth*, p. 116.

62 Baldwin, *Morall Philosophie*, fols. 81 (p. 176), 128 (p. 270), 178 (p. 371).

63 Peacham, *The Truth of Our Times*, p. 205.

64 Martyn, *Youths Instruction,* (1612), p. 49.

65 Paice, *Howe one may take profit of his Enemyes,* (1533?), fols 4, 8; Richard Vaughan, Earl of Carbery's advice to his son in the next century was much the same: 'Though I wish you no enemies, yet I may tell you what good may be got from them. They will not flatter you, and they will exercise your virtues.' 'Advice to his Son', p. 97.

66 Baldwin, *Morall Philosophie,* fol. 81 (p. 177).

67 Bacon, *Advancement of Learning,* p. 272. Variants of this quotation can be found in Taverner, *The Flowers of Sencies,* (1547), and his *Proverbes of Erasmus,* (1545). The original sentiment was taken by Erasmus from Cicero's *De Amicitia* (Cicero, *Friendship,* pp. 39–40).

68 Baldwin, *Morall Philosophie,* fol. 116 (p. 347).

69 Breton, *A Murmurer,* (1607), p. 9.

70 Winchester, *The Lord Marques idlenes,* p. 30.

71 Kinsman, '"The Proverbes of Salmon Do Playnly Declare". . . ascribed to Sir Frances Bryan', p. 288.

72 Baldwin, *Morall Philosophie,* fol. 180 (p. 375).

73 Paranoid fathers such as Raleigh, Percy, and Wentworth were not the only ones to sense the enemy. They were joined by a host of others. William Higford spoke to his grandson of 'your enemies' who will laugh you to scorn (*The Institution of a Gentleman,* p. 587) and Thomas Elyot in *The Education or Bringinge up of children,* (1533), counselled his reader: 'Reconcile thee not too soon to thine enemy without good advisement' (p. 43). William Tipping's, *The Father's Counsell* warned that 'where the enemy comes he commonly sweeps clean and leaves men almost as naked to the world as nature brought them into it' (p. 193); and William Vaughan classified under 'the name of Enemy. . . six sorts of people' (*The Golden Grove,* p. 75). Nicholas Udall in *Apophthegnes,* (1542), listed in his index-table of contents: 'Enemies, how a man should be avenged on his enemies' (p. 72) and 'Enemies, how they are to be overcome' (p. 155). Lord Herbert of Cherbury in his *Life* (1642) used the word when speaking of fencing lessons and young men learning to 'make a thrust against their enemy' (pp. 31–32).

74 Whitney, *Choice of Emblemes.*

75 *Lisle Letters,* I, p. 435.

76 *Ibid.,* II, no. 152, p. 92; V, no. 1112, p. 50; no. 1153, p. 115; no. 1154, p. 116; no. 1445, p. 528.

77 Breton, *The Court and Country,* p. 16.

78 Hoby, *The Book of the Courtier,* (1561); North, *Dial of Princes,* originally published 1557, but the 4th book by Guevara, dealing with the courtier, was not included until 1568. Guevara starts his advice with ten rules for successful behaviour of which one (no. 3) cautions that 'although every man offer his service to you and seem to be at your commandment when you shall need him: yet I tell you (sir) I would not wish you had either

need of them or of me: for many of those fine and curious courtiers which are the first that offer themselves to draw on your side, and to stand by you if need be, are commonly (at the very pinch) the first and readiest to throw stones at our faces.' (fol. 358.)

79 Ducci, *Ars avlica or the courtiers arte,* pp. 108, 278.

80 *Traité de la Court ou Instruction des Courtisans* was first published in Holland in 1616 and thereafter went through countless pirated editions. John Reynolds and Edward Walsingham translated the work independently of one another, but Walsingham, deservedly, received the greater credit, and his translation can be read in Gordon Tullock's edition: *A Practical Guide for Ambitious Politicians.*

81 Walsingham, *A Practical Guide,* pp. 15, 26, 132.

82 *Ibid.,* pp. 6–7, 53–56.

83 Elyot, *The Book named the Governor,* pp. 234–36; Percy, *Advice to His Son,* p. 110.

84 Bryan, *A Dispraise of the Life of a Courtier,* fols dvi, kviii, li. Bryan had as his model Aeneas Sylvius Piccolomini's letter *Miseriae Curialium,* translated and turned into poetry by Alexander Barclay. Bryan's words about 'heads off by the shoulders' bear striking resemblance to Barclay's: 'To men of power some often stoop and beck,/ Which gladly would see their heads from their neck.' (*The Miseryes of Courtiers and Courtes,* p. 38.)

85 *The Court of James the first,* fol. F2.

86 Cecil, *Certain Precepts,* p. 12; Percy, *Advice to His Son,* pp. 107, 108.

87 James VI, *Basilicon Doron,* I, pp. 71–72, 107.

88 Bacon, 'The Self-politician or the art of rising in life' in *Advancement of Learning,* pp. 258–75. For the quotations, see pp. 260, 261, 266, 271.

89 Robert Beale, 'A Treatise of the office of a Councellor and Principall Secretarie to her Majestie' (1592). Beale was Sir Francis Walsingham's brother-in-law and personal secretary and was also clerk of the Privy Council and filled in as Principal Secretary when Walsingham was out of town.

90 *Ibid.,* p. 425; Cecil, *Master Secretarie's Answer to the Earle of Bedford,* (1642), pp. 16–17. By 1642 the two Cecils, father and son, had been confused. The treatise, however, is by William, not Robert.

91 Beale, 'A Treatise', pp. 427, 428, 437–38, 441, 443.

92 Lasch, *The Culture of Narcissism,* pp. 106 passim.

93 Jennings, *Routes to the Executive Suite,* p. 7.

94 Ringer, *Winning Through Intimidation,* pp. 16, 39–41.

95 Hofstadter, *Paranoid Style,* p. 31.

96 Vaughan, 'Advice to his Son,' p. 102; Percy, *Advice to His Son,* p. 52; Baldwin, *Morall Philosophie,* fol. 65 (p. 144).

97 Breton, *Wits Private Wealth.* p. 10.

98 Cleland, *Institution,* p. 110; Vaughan, *The Golden Grove,* I, p. 140.

99 Higford, *Institution of a Gentleman,* p. 592.

100 Breton, *A Murmurer,* (1607), p. 13.

101 More, *Utopia.* 'When I consider and turn over in my mind the state of all commonwealths flourishing anywhere today, so help me God, I can see nothing else than a kind of conspiracy of the rich, who are aiming at their own interests under the name and title of the commonwealth.' (p. 241.)

102 More, *Apology* (1533), p. 156.

103 Elton, *Reform and Reformation,* p. 66.

104 More, *Apology,* p. 157.

105 Gardiner, *A Declaration,* (1546), fols. 151–53.

106 More, *Apology,* pp. 158–59.

107 Tyndale, *The Parable of the Wicked Mammon* (1527), p. 42. Stephen Greenblatt, *Renaissance Self-fashioning,* chapter two, has a fascinating discussion of Tyndale's view of historical change and authority.

108 Tyndale, *Obedience of a Christian Man,* p. 191.

109 Gardiner, *Letters,* p. 206.

110 *Ibid.,* pp. 319–20.

111 Henry VIII, *Letters,* p. 224.

112 Loades, *The Reign of Mary Tudor,* pp. 434–35.

113 *Statutes of the Realm,* IV, pt I, I Mary St. 2.c.1. p. 200.

114 Strype, *Ecclesiastical Memorials,* III, pt 2, p. 347.

115 James VI, *Basilicon Doron,* I, p. 79.

116 MacCaffrey, *Queen Elizabeth and the Making of Policy 1572-1588,* p. 131, quoting from D'Ewes *Journal,* pp. 285–87.

117 This quotation and those that follow come from Cecil, *Execution of Justice,* (1583), pp. 4, 7, 9, 14, 36–37.

118 Allen, *Defence of English Catholics* (1588); the quotations that follow can be found on pp. 79, 140, 223, 230.

119 Many of the ideas that follow come from Spivack, *Shakespeare and the Allegory of Evil,* (see esp. pp. 13–16, 27–56, 152–57, 209–214, 373–75, 423–25), and from West, *Shakespeare and the Outer Mystery,* (esp. pp. 102–107).

120 Dekker, 'The Bel-man of London', p. 116.

121 Shakespeare, *Measure for Measure,* V, i, 56 ff.

122 Udall, *Respublica,* I, i. 69–86.

123 Gardiner, *Letters,* pp. 480–92, esp. 492.

124 Foxe, *Actes and Monuments,* V, p. 230.

125 Shakespeare, *Othello,* I, i, 65; Cyril Tourneur, *The revengers tragaedie,* II, i, 101–102.

126 Bevington, *Tudor Drama and Politics,* pp. 204–205.

127 Skelton, *Magnificence,* pp. 196–97.

128 Shakespeare, *Henry VIII,* V, i, 124–40.

129 Philip, *pacient and meeke Grissill,* fol. E ii, lines 932–35.

130 Spivack, *The Allegory of Evil,* pp. 27–56.

131 *L.P.* XVIII (2) no. 235 (2).

132 *Ibid.*, XV, no. 954.

133 Rye, *England as seen by foreigners*, p. 24.

III 'THE AGREEMENT OF ITS MINDS'

1 Vaughan, *The Golden Grove*, II, p. 103. Simon, *Education and Society* and Charlton, *Education in Renaissance England* are both good surveys. Strauss, 'The State of Pedagogical Theory c. 1530', pp. 70–93, although directed to the Continent, is the best treatment of Tudor education available.

2 Starkey, *Dialogue*, p. 144. With more obvious Protestant bias, Thomas Becon expressed much the same idea a generation later: 'If the youth were godly and virtuously brought up, and in the fear of God trained from their young years and were taught diligently the word of God from time to time, not only all contention of doctrine but also all corruption of life should soon fall away and all godliness and virtue succeed in the places thereof.' *The Catechism* (1559), pp. 377–82.

3 B.L. Harleian Mss. 4894, 'Robert Rypon Sermonum Liber', fol. 182.

4 Watson, *Vives: On Education*, pp. 266–67.

5 More, *Epigrams*, no. 94, p. 172; Starkey, *Dialogue*, p. 51.

6 Cleland, *Institution*, p. 127.

7 Shakespeare, *Richard II*, II, iii, 83–84; Cleland, *Institution*, p. 26.

8 Jonson, *Timber or Discoveries*, p. 54.

9 Mulcaster, *Positions*, p. 105.

10 Ascham, *The Schoolmaster*, pp. 70, 110–11.

11 Wilson, *Arte of Rhetorique*, (1553), p. 229 (fol. 109). The seventeenth-century version of this is slightly different — 'of sloth cometh pleasure, of pleasure cometh riot, of riot comes whoring, of whoring comes spending, of spending comes want, of want comes theft, of theft comes hanging'. Ben Jonson, *et. al.*, *Eastward Ho*, IV, iii, 286–89.

12 Ascham, *The Schoolmaster*, p. 84.

13 Gardiner, *Letters*, no. 72, pp. 136–37.

14 Elyot, *The Education or Bringinge up of children* (1533), pp. 5–6.

15 Ascham, *The Schoolmaster*, p. 34: 'For the pure clean wit of a sweet young babe is, like the newest wax, most able to receive the best and fairest printing.' Vaughan, *The Golden Grove*, II, p. 106: 'Waxe, as long as it is soft and clammy, receiveth any impression or seal, but being hardened, it receiveth none.' Ling, *Politeuphuia, Wits Commonwealth*, p. 354: 'As wax is ready and pliant to receive any kind of figure or print, so is a young child apt to receive any kind of learning.' For the vessel quote, see Kempe, *The Education of Children* (1588), p. 219.

16 For a perceptive discussion of the optimistic and pessimistic views of sixteenth-century education, see Strauss, 'The State of Pedagogical Theory c. 1530', pp. 72–77.

17 Taverner, *Proverbes of Erasmus* (1529), fol. xix; James VI, *Basilicon Doron*, I, p. 109; Elyot, *The Book named the Governor*, pp. 15–16; Vives, *Instruction of a Christian Woman*, fol. 2; Byman, 'Childraising and Melancholia', p. 71. The theory is developed at length in Boaistuau's *Theatre of the World*, p. 55: Children 'forced to suck the milk of a strange woman, yea, and many times of such a one, as may be found best cheap, what corruption or deformity so ever she have, the which many times is so contagious unto children, that it were better for them to be nourished of some brute beast in the wilderness than to be put into the mercy of such nurses, for not only the body remaineth infected and marred...but...[also] the print and mark in the souls of this vicious nursing...'

18 Kempe, *The Education of Children* (1588), p. 218.

19 Erasmus, *De pueris instituendis*, in *Opera Omnia Desiderii Erasmi*, I (Amsterdam 1971), p. 50, quoted in Strauss, 'Pedagogical Theory', p. 75.

20 Quoted in Baldwin, *Petty School*, pp. 117–18 from Erasmus, *Opera Omnia* (1703), vol. I, p. 1033.

21 Kempe, *The Education of Children in Learning*, p. 222.

22 *Ibid.*, p. 221.

23 Proverbs 30:17.

24 Gouge, *Works*, I, p. 10.

25 Elyot, *The Book named the Governor*, p. 103. Roger Ascham also emphasized the home as the well-spring of personal virtue and social order. 'The remedy of this [disorder] doth not stand only in making good common laws for the whole realm, but also (and perchance chiefly) in observing private discipline every man carefully in his own house...' (*The Schoolmaster*, p. 45.)

26 Mulcaster, *The Elementarie*, p. 24.

27 Rhodes, *The boke of Nurture*, pp. 71–81.

28 P.R.O., S.P. I, vol. 82, fol. 158 (*L.P.*, VII, 153).

29 Smyth, *Lives of the Berkeleys*, II, p. 386.

30 Mulcaster, *The Elementarie*, p. 61.

31 Both quotations come from Strauss, 'The State of Pedagogical Theory c. 1530', pp. 82, 83.

32 Recorde, *The Grounde of Artes* (first printed 1542), (1561), fol. xi.

33 Wilson, *Arte of Rhetorique* (1553), pp. 177–78 (fols 83–84).

34 *Ibid.*, pp. 188–89 (fol. 89).

35 Charles Hoole, *Sententia*, fol. A2 from Plimpton, *The Education of Shakespeare*, p. 91.

36 Maturinus Corderius, *Dialogues*; Colloquy no. LXVIII is printed in Plimpton, *The Education of Shakespeare*, pp. 93–96. Corderius was eighty-five when he published his *Dialogues* in 1564.

37 Whittinton, *Vulgaria* (1520), p. 69. Whittinton's grammar failed to receive the blessings of humanistic educators because his examples were home-spun and were not drawn from Cicero and other approved classical authors. Never-

theless, his text was still regarded by some schoolmasters as being useful as late as 1638 (Baldwin, *Small Latine*, II, pp. 690, 697–98).

38 Elyot, *The Book named the Governor*, p. 29.

39 Erasmus, *Christian Prince*, p. 146–47.

40 Brinsley, *Ludus Literarius* (1627), pp. 174–75, quoted in Baldwin, *Small Latine*, I, p. 294.

41 Elyot, *The Book named the Governor*, pp. 36 and 231; Baldwin, *Morall Philosophie*, p. 368 (fol. 177).

42 North, *[Plutarch's] Lives* (1579), 'Amiot to the Reader', fols. iiii-vii; Baldwin, *Morall Philosophie*, p. 368 (fol. 177).

43 Watson, *Vives: On Education*, p. 233; Peacham, *The Complete Gentleman*, p. 64; Fiston, 'Preface', to Caxton, *History of Troy*, pp. A3r-A3v.

44 'An Homily against...Wilful Rebellion', p. 551.

45 Baldwin, *Morall Philosophie*, fol. 53 (p. 121); Mulcaster, *Positions* (1581), p. 133.

46 Quoted in Rickert, *The Babee's Book*, pp. xvii-xviii.

47 Dod and Cleaver, *A Plaine and Familiar Exposition*, (1606), pp. 203–210.

48 *Practical Wisdom*, p. 57. William Baldwin in his *Morall Philosophie* agreed with Sidney: 'None ought to rule, except he first have learned to obey' (fol. 54, p. 122). Christopher Sutton voiced a similar attitude when he wrote: 'Order is ye mother and preserver of things: for sure it is that the society of man consisteth in ruling and obeying; obedience is the virtue that teacheth all their duty to God and man.' (*Disce vivere* (1604), p. 323.)

49 Gouge, *Works*, II, p. 331.

50 Percy, *Advice to His Son*, p. 60.

51 See Cruttwell, 'Physiology and Psychology in Shakespeare's Age', pp. 75–89; Bundy, 'Shakespeare and Elizabethan Psychology', p. 519; and Babb, *The Elizabethan Malady*, pp. 17–20. The best door into sixteenth-century psychology is through Godwin, *Robert Fludd, Hermatic Philosopher.*

52 Vaughan, 'Advice to his Son' (1651), p. 94.

53 Baldwin, *Morall Philosophie*, fol. 54 (p. 122); Raleigh, 'Maxims of State', p. 1.

54 Percy, *Advice to His Son*, p. 72. For the importance of 'moderation', see Elyot, *The Book named the Governor*, p. 210, and Peacham, *The Complete Gentleman*, p. 144.

55 Elyot, *The Education or Bringinge up of children*, p. 10; Ascham, *The Schoolmaster*, p. 96.

56 Puttenham, *Arte of Poesie* has an entire chapter on decorum (ch. xxiii). The best modern treatment is McAlindon, *Shakespeare and Decorum*, esp. ch. I.

57 McAlindon, *Shakespeare and Decorum*, p. 8.

58 Colet, *A ryght frutefull monycion*, (1534), unpaginated (pp. 9–10).

59 Jonson, *Timber or Discoveries*, p. 42. George Puttenham voiced much the same concern when writing about important people: 'In speaking or writing of a Prince's affairs and fortunes there is a certain *Decorum*, that we may not use the same terms in their business as we might very well do in a

meaner person's... As for example, if an historiographer shall write of
an Emperor or King, how [on] such a day he joined battle with his enemy
and being over-laid ran out of the field and took [to] his heels,...the terms
be not decent; but of a mean soldier or captain, it were not undecently
spoken.' *Arte of English Poesie*, p. 273. Kings, thought Puttenham, should
speak like kings and require 'words, phrases, sentences and figures' that
were 'high, lofty, eloquent and magnificent in proportion'. *Ibid.*, p. 152.

60 Nashe, *The Anatomie of Absurditie*, p. 46.

61 Watson, *Vives: On Education*, p. 182.

62 Vaughan, 'Advice to his Son', p. 101.

63 B.L., Sloane Mss. 1523, fol. 27.

64 Ascham, *The Schoolmaster*, p. 86; Cleland, *Institution*, p. 64; Elyot, *The Book named the Governor*, p. 99.

65 Lathrop, 'Translations', p. 45.

66 Barclay, *the myrrour of good maners* (1520), fol. Fii; see also fol. Bii. Margaret Hoby in her *Diary* speaks of a perfectly educated young lady about whom Dr Donne made the compliment 'that she knew well how to discourse of all things, from Predestination to Slea Silk!' (p. 60.)

67 Sennett, *Fall of Public Man*, pp. 45–106, esp. p. 82.

68 Ascham, *The Schoolmaster*, p. 68. See also xxii and p. 13.

69 *Ibid.*, p. 115.

70 Taylor, *The English Mind*, p. 264; Esler, *The Aspiring Mind*, pp. 114–15; Puttenham, *The Arte of English Poesie*, p. 283.

71 Puttenham, *Ibid.*, p. 181.

72 Cleland, *Institution*, p. 170.

73 P.R.O., S.P. 10, vol. 8, fol. 4.

74 Percy, *Advice to His Son*, p. 119.

75 There is a thoughtful and provocative discussion of this metaphor and sixteenth-century role-playing in Greenblatt, *Renaissance Self-fashioning*, pp. 26–31, 160–64. See also Ong, *Rhetoric, Romance and Technology*, p. 109.

76 James VI, *Basilicon Doron*, I, p. 163. Earlier in the book James says: 'For kings being public persons, by reason of their office and authority, are as it were set...upon a public stage in the sight of all the people; where all the beholders eyes are attentively bent, to look and pry in the least circumstance of their secretest drifts.' (p. 12.)

77 Ascham, *The Schoolmaster*, xxiv.

78 See for example, Cleland, *Institution*, p. 95; Elyot, *The Book named the Governor*, p. 15; Peacham, *The Complete Gentleman*, p. 12; Harington, *Nugae Antiquae*, I, pp. 131–35. See also Stone, *Crisis of the Aristocracy*, p. 674.

79 Cherbury, *Life*, pp. 28–29.

80 Rowlands, *The Courte of Civill Courtesie*, pp. 2–3.

81 Bacon, *Advancement of Learning*, p. 260.

82 Greenblatt, *Renaissance Self-fashioning*, p. 162. He continues: 'These books

are closely related to the rhetorical handbooks that were also in vogue — both essentially compilations of verbal strategies and both based upon the principle of imitation.' See also pp. 164, 228.

83 *Ibid.,* pp. 1–4.

84 Taverner, *Garden of Wisdom* (1539), fol. c.

85 Peacham, *The Complete Gentleman,* p. 144.

86 Rowlands, *The Court of Civill Courtesie* (1582), p. 4. See also Stone, *Crisis of the Aristocracy,* p. 42.

87 Elyot, *The Book named the Governor,* p. 98.

88 Peacham, *The Complete Gentleman,* pp. 23–24.

89 For a general discussion of talent versus training, see Strauss, 'Pedagogical Theory', pp. 77–78. Tudor education was unbelievably optimistic about what it could achieve and the receptiveness of children to learning: 'Learning teacheth more in one year', said Roger Ascham, 'than experience in twenty...' *The Schoolmaster,* p. 50.

90 Elyot, *The Book named the Governor,* p. 17.

91 Mulcaster, *Elementarie,* pp. 261–62.

92 Puttenham, *Arte of English Poesie,* pp. 42–43.

93 'A gentleman', wrote Isaac Barrow, 'hath more talents committed to him, and consequently more employment required of him: if a rustic labourer, or a mechanic artisan, hath one talent, a gentleman hath ten;...he hath accomplishment and refinement of parts by liberal education; he hath the succours of parentage, alliance, and friendship; he hath wealth, he hath honour, he hath power and authority, he hath command of time and leisure; he hath so many precious and useful talents intrusted to him, not to be wrapped up in a napkin, or hidden under ground; not to be squandered away in private satisfactions; but for negotiation, to be put out to use, to be improved in the most advantageous way to God's service.' ('Of Industry in our Particular Calling, as Gentlemen', pp. 218–19.) Clement Ellis, later in the seventeenth century, said that 'this must needs be the greatest obligation [that] can be laid upon the gentleman to labour *harder,* and do better than other men, because he is beforehand, not only furnished with good tools, by an ingenuous education to work withal, but hath...received so great a part of his reward already...' (*The Gentle Sinner,* p. 161.) Richard Mulcaster in his *Positions* (1581) agreed: there was less excuse for the sons of gentlemen to fail than those of humbler folk. (p. 199ff.)

94 Starkey, *Dialogue,* p. 191.

95 *The Institucion of a Gentleman* (1568) fol. Giii ('To reade Hystories and avoyde Idleness').

96 Much of the material that follows is a distillation of T.W. Baldwin's impressive study of Tudor education: *William Shakespere's Petty School* and *William Shakespere's Small Latine and Lesse Greeke.* Also useful are Foster Watson, *The Old Grammar Schools;* Arthur F. Leach, *English Schools At The*

Reformation 1546-8; David Cressy, *Education in Tudor and Stuart England;* John Lawson and Harold Silver, *A Social History of Education in England;* William Harrison Woodward, *Desiderius Erasmus Concerning the Aim and Method of Education,* especially his translation of Erasmus's *De Pueris statim ac Liberalites instituendis libellus* (1529); and George A. Plimpton, *The Education of Shakespeare.*

97 Watson, *The Old Grammar Schools,* p. 81; Simon, *Education and Society,* p. 99; Cressy, *Education in Tudor and Stuart England,* document no. 24, p. 30. The only household schooling about which we have detailed evidence is Edward VI's palace school where Edward and his classmates seem to have closely followed a normal grammar school curriculum. (Baldwin, *Small Latine,* I, p. 217. See also *Ibid.,* chapters X and XI.)

98 Quoted in Baldwin, *Petty School,* p. 33 from William Marshall's *Primer* (1535).

99 Plimpton, *The Education of Shakespeare,* pp. 47–53.

100 *Ibid.,* p. 67.

101 Burton, *Three Primers,* p. 458.

102 Joseph, *Shakespeare's Eden,* p. 109.

103 Baldwin, *Small Latine,* I, pp. 139, 164–66; Watson, *The Old Grammar Schools,* p. 110; DeMolen, 'Richard Mulcaster: An Elizabethan Savant', p. 31. The age of student attendance at school is a question of considerable dispute. Baldwin says children entered petty school between the ages of four to eight and went on to grammar school between eight and nine. (*Petty School,* p. 29.) DeMolen argues a much later date of matriculation: seven to eight for primary school and eleven to twelve for grammar school and seventeen for the university ('Ages of Admission to Educational Institutions in Tudor and Stuart England', pp. 207–19). Lawrence Stone simply says there was no standard age. ('The Educational Revolution in England 1560–1640', p. 57.)

104 Thompson, 'Erasmian Humanism', p. 22; Simon, *Education and Society,* p. 123.

105 Wilson, *The Arte of Rhetorique,* fol. 1 (p. 13).

106 Francis R. Johnson's introduction to Richard Rainolde, *The Foundacion of Rhetorike* is by far the best short discussion of rhetoric. Howell, *Logic and Rhetoric in England, 1500-1700* is excellent but somewhat contrived, and Richard McKeon, 'Rhetoric in the Middle Ages', pp. 1–32 presents a splendid analysis of the medieval background. See also Seigel, *Rhetoric and Philosophy in Renaissance Humanism.* There are endless works connecting rhetoric to sixteenth-century literature; possibly the best is Altman, *The Tudor Play of Mind.* The most provocative of all works on rhetoric and the one to which the concluding pages of this chapter are indebted is Ong, *Rhetoric, Romance and Technology.*

107 Ciceronian rhetoric was traditionally divided into five parts: *dispositio, inventio,*

elocutio, memoria, and *pronuntiatio* but the last two tended to be played down or omitted in most sixteenth-century manuals.

108 Quintilian's *Institutio Oratoria* was a close runner-up.

109 Watson, *Vives: On Education,* p. 108; Ascham, *The Schoolmaster,* p. 107. The best general discussion of *copia* and commonplace books can be found in Ong, *Rhetoric, Romance and Technology,* pp. 29–43, 70–79. See also Jacob Zeitlin, 'Commonplaces in Elizabethan Life and Letters', pp. 47–65.

110 Erasmus's *Adagia* (1500) which eventually reached over 400 entries; his *Parabolae, sive Similia* (1513) and the eight books of his *Apophthegmatum* (1531). A similar compilation to Erasmus's volumes but better organized was Nannus Mirabellius's *Polyanthea* which Henry VIII used as a small boy. (Bower's introduction to Baldwin, *Morall Philosophie,* p. xii.)

111 *The Welspring of wittie Conceites,* (1584), 'A briefe tale', plus pp. 32–33.

112 Richard Sherry's *A Treatise of Schemes and Tropes* (1550) was standard. So also was Henry Peacham's ambitiously titled *The garden of eloquence conteyning the figures of grammer and rhetoric from whence maye bee gathered all manner of flowers, coulors, ornaments, exortations, formes and fashions of speech . . .* (1577).

113 Erasmus, *Modus conscribendi Epistolas* in *Opera* (1703), I, pp. 353–54, quoted in Baldwin, *Small Latine,* II, p. 241.

114 *Ibid.* Thomas Wilson was equally optimistic: 'There is no one tale among all the poets but under the same is comprehended some thing that pertaineth either to the amendment of manners, to the knowledge of truth, to the setting forth of Nature's work or else of the understanding of some notable thing done . . .' *Arte of Rhetorique,* fol. 104 (p. 219).

115 Puttenham, *Arte of Poesie,* p. lxxiv.

116 Shapiro, *Neurotic Styles,* p. 31.

117 Elizabeth was a master of spontaneity and often delivered her speeches to Parliament as if they were *ad lib* productions when, in fact, they were carefully rehearsed and repeatedly rewritten performances. Smith, *Elizabeth Tudor,* pp. 82–83.

118 Sidney, *Apology,* p. 122.

119 Baldwin, *Small Latine,* I, pp. 207, 217, 682, 685–87; Ascham, *The Schoolmaster,* p. 37; Elyot, *The Book named the Governor,* p. 39; Noble, *Shakespeare's Biblical Knowledge,* p. 43; Plimpton, *The Education of Shakespeare,* p. 57. The connection between Ecclesiasticus and advice literature is mentioned briefly by Betz, 'Francis Osborn's Advice to a Son', pp. 57–62. Osborne's advice was in fact in his day (1658) dismissed by one critic as 'a diseased piece of an *Apocripha*' (*Ibid.,* p. 60, n15).

120 Ecclesiasticus, (1537 translation). The passages are from 1:1, 3:1–2, 3:12, 6:7–13, 8:12–18, 9:13, 11:29–34, 12:1, 12:10–12, 12:16.

121 Chase, 'The Distichs of Cato', pp. 21, 23, 29, 31, 39, 43.

122 Lathrop, *Translations,* pp. 45–46.

123 Baldwin, *Morall Philosophie,* fol. 172 (p. 359). See also p. vi.

124 *Ibid.,* fol. 52 (p. 118).

125 Ling, *Politeuphuia, Wits Commonwealth* (1597), pp. 432, 467–68.

126 *The Welspring of wittie Conceites* (1584), pp. 32–33.

127 Taverner, *Proverbes of Erasmus* (1545), pp. xxx, xxxi.

128 Rainolde, *The Foundacion of Rhetorike,* fols v-x.

129 Seybolt, *Renaissance Student Life,* pp. 44–45; see for a discussion of the 'privy spy', Brown, *Elizabethan Schooldays,* pp. 118–119.

130 Ong, 'Agonistic Structures in Academia: Past to Present', pp. 1–11; *Rhetoric, Romance and Technology,* pp. 2–7, 47, 63–66.

131 Watson, *Vives: On Education,* pp. lix-lx, 177.

132 Wilson, *The Arte of Rhetorique,* fol. 5 (p. 21), fol. 55 (p. 121), fol. 57 (pp. 124–25).

133 Erasmus, *Modus conscribendi Epistolas* in *Opera* (1703), I, pp. 363–64, quoted in Baldwin, *Small Latine,* II, pp. 248–49.

134 Baldwin, *Small Latine,* I, p. 90.

135 Translated in Plimpton, *The Education of Shakespeare,* pp. 113–14. See also Baldwin, *Small Latine,* II, pp. 367–69.

136 Baldwin, *Small Latine,* II, p. 367. How many grammar school students went on to Oxford and Cambridge and the Inns of Court and whether they were serious students once they got there is a debatable issue. See Charlton, *Education in Renaissance England,* pp. 137–39.

137 William Hayne, *Certaine Epistles of Tully* (1611), B4v, quoted in Baldwin, *Small Latine,* II, p. 371.

138 Ong, 'Agonistic Structures in Academia: Past to Present', pp. 2–4; *Rhetoric, Romance and Technology,* p. 28.

139 Altman, *Tudor Play of Mind,* pp. 3, 43–44; Ong, *Rhetoric, Romance and Technology,* p. 66.

140 Competition was not only built into the rhetorical structure of education but also into the theory of a gentleman: 'To attain unto virtue, all gentlemen ought earnestly to labour and to strive among themselves which of them may excel [the] other therein... That gentleman therefore which loveth uprightness in all his doings, which seeketh to excell others in valiancy of arms, in knowledge and dexterity in all honest things doth not only deserve the name, but also the estimation of an honourable gentleman.' From *Institucion of a Gentleman* (1568), fol. Gi ('Of honour and worship').

141 Ong, *Rhetoric, Romance and Technology,* pp. 63–66, 130–33; Craig, *The Enchanted Glass,* p. 206, says: 'One would recall...the argumentative quality of Elizabethan discourse and point out that a custom of that sort carries with it a habit, not only of seeing two sides of every question, but of searching them out and exploiting them. One would merely claim that the practice of conceptual thinking and over-hasty action was strongly characteristic of ordinary Renaissance minds...' See Bowers, *Elizabethan*

Revenge Tragedy, pp. 31–33, and Stone, *Crisis of the Aristocracy*, pp. 223–34, for growing violence in late Elizabethan and Jacobean society.

142 Ong, *Rhetoric, Romance and Technology*, pp. 63–64.

143 Puttenham, *Arte of English Poesie*, p. 154.

144 Thompson, *Translations of Lucian*, p. 33.

145 Puttenham, *Arte of English Poesie*, p. 186.

146 *Ibid.*, p. 154.

147 Bevington, *Tudor Drama and Politics*, pp. 8–9.

148 *C.S.P. Spanish* (1558–1567), no. 286, p. 404; see also no. 256, pp. 367–68.

149 Cunliffe, 'The Queenes Majesties Entertainment at Woodstocke', p. 93.

150 Nashe, *A Countercuffe to Martin Junior*, (1589), p. 182.

151 *Willobie His Avisa* (1594), p. 230.

152 *Ibid.*, p. 187.

153 Watson, *Vives: On Education*, p. 120.

IV   TUDOR COSMOLOGY AND COMMONALITY

1 Lovejoy, *The Great Chain of Being*, p. 15.

2 See *Ibid.*, pp. 102–104 for an interesting discussion of this point.

3 By far the best discussion of medieval and early modern cosmology and its philosophical, psychological and social implications is Lovejoy, *The Great Chain of Being*. Brief and more directed to literature is Tillyard, *The Elizabethan World Picture*. Lewis, *The Discarded Image* is a brilliant analysis of the early modern mind and how to understand it. Excellent also are Craig, *The Enchanted Glass* and Joseph, *Shakespeare's Eden*, esp. chapter 6.

4 Peacham, *The Complete Gentleman*, p.11; Elyot, *The Book named the Governor*, pp. 3–4.

5 Craig, *The Enchanted Glass*, p. 202. For the doctrine of correspondences, see *Ibid.*, pp. 8–11 and Tillyard, *The Elizabethan World Picture*, chapters 6 and 7. Bacon's quotations come from *the Advancement of Learning*, p. 258.

6 Radding, 'Superstition to Science', pp. 952–55 (the quotation is on p. 954). Basing his ideas on Piaget's *The Child's Conception of the World*, Radding has a fascinating discussion of the medieval and early modern mind and its inability, by modern standards, to cluster material into rational categories or generalizations.

7 Translated in Wilson, *The Arte of Rhetorique*, (1553), pp. 54–80.

8 Sadler, *The State Papers and Letters*, I, p. 7.

9 *L.P.* XV, no. 498 (59).

10 Baldwin, *Morall Philosophie*, fol. 179 (p. 373).

11 Geertz, 'Centers, King and Charisma: Reflections on the Symbolics of Power', p. 156. Smith, 'Christ, What a Fright', pp. 124–26.

12 Carpenter, *Architophel* (1638), fol. D8.

13 Ecclesiasticus (1537 translation), 30:14; Leviticus 26: 14–21; see also Thomas,

Religion and the Decline of Magic, p. 80.

14 Radding, 'Superstition to Science', p. 953.

15 Cranmer, *Miscellaneous Writings and Letters,* p. 235.

16 Vaughan, *The Golden Grove,* II, pp. 145–49.

17 Hall, *Heaven upon earth,* pp. 107–108.

18 Greene, *Groats-worth of Witte* (1592), p. 38; see also Thomas, *Religion and the Decline of Magic,* p. 324.

19 Hoby, *Diary,* p. 70.

20 Elyot, *Of The Knowledge Which Maketh A Wise Man,* p. 170.

21 Thomas, *Religion and the Decline of Magic,* p. 638.

22 Fenner, *The Artes of Logike and Rethorike* (1584), p. 163.

23 Baldwin, *Morall Philosophie,* fol. 93 (p. 201).

24 Tomaschek, 'Great Earthquakes and Uranus', *Nature,* vol. 184, pp. 177–78. See also his defence, vol. 186, pp. 236–38.

25 Jahoda, *The Psychology of Superstition,* pp. 108–26.

26 Baldwin, *Morall Philosophie,* fol. 157, (p. 329).

27 Hoby, *Diary,* p. 193.

28 Lewis, *The Discarded Image,* p. 218.

29 Caxton, *Mirrour of the world,* pp. 48, 59–60, 171–72, 174–77; Maimonides, *The Guide of the Perplexed,* quoted in Lovejoy, *The Great Chain of Being,* p. 100.

30 Laurentius, *A Discourse of...Melancholike Diseases,* pp. 14–15.

31 Boaistuau, *The theatre or rule of the world,* (1581), p. 271; Montaigne, 'Apology for Raimond Sebond', *Essays,* II, p. 110.

32 Quoted in Tillyard, *The Elizabethan World Picture,* p. 66 from Photius's *Life of Pythagoras;* see also Tillyard, p. 73.

33 Bacon, 'Of the Wisdom of the Ancients,' p. 747.

34 Sebon, *La Theologie Naturelle,* (1566), fol. 156.

35 The Wisdom of Solomon, *The Apocrypha,* p. 187. For descriptions of hell, see Burton, *Anatomy of Melancholy,* pp. 163–64, and Owst, *Literature and Pulpit,* pp. 294, 551; Patch, *The other world,* p. 321; and Petrey, *Christian Eschatology and Social Thought,* pp. 112–13, 316, 347.

36 P.R.O., S.P. I, vol. 195, ff. 213–214 (*L.P.* XIX (2), no. 726).

37 Geertz, 'Centers, Kings and Charisma: Reflections on the Symbolics of Power', p. 153.

38 P.R.O., S.P. I, vol. 133, fols 51–53 (*L.P.* XIII (1), no. 1199 (2)).

39 Ling, *Politeuphuia, Wits Commonwealth,* p. 510. Feng, 'Devil's Letters', p. 104; Vatter, *The Devil in English Literature,* pp. 11–26, 69–116. For one of the longer and most readable Tudor discourses on the devil, see Nashe, *Pierce Penilesse, His Supplication to the Divell* (1592), pp. 99–119.

40 Thomas, *Religion and the Decline of Magic,* p. 472, quoting from G. Gifford, *A Discourse of the Subtill Practices of Devilles* ... (1587), sig. D3ᵛ.

41 Cyprian, *Writings,* I, p. 455; Hoby, *Diary,* p. 198.

42 Patrik Scot, *A Fathers Advice or Last Will to his Sonne* (1620), ch. I, sect.

30. See also Spivack, *The Allegory of Evil*, pp. 76–79.

43 Milton, *Paradise Lost*, IV, 677–78.

44 Thomas, *Religion and the Decline of Magic*, pp. 472, 476; see also pp. 469, 475.

45 Baldwin, *Morall Philosophie*, p. 114.

46 Thomas, *Religion and the Decline of Magic*, pp. 92, 477.

47 *Ibid.*, pp. 502, 507, 508, 513, 625.

48 Ponet, *A Shorte Treatise of politike power*, fol. kiiii-kv.

49 Vaughan, *The Golden Grove*, II, p. 54.

50 *Ibid*; Morison, *An Exhortation to Styrre all Englyshe men* (1539), fol. B (p. 15); Baldwin, *Morall Philosophie*, p. 164.

51 Elyot, *The Book named the Governor*, p. 1. For a general discussion of the metaphor see Hale, *The Body Politic*, pp. 41, 67, 70.

52 Raleigh, 'Maxims of State', p. 144; *Ibid.*; 'A Collection of Political Observations', p. 102.

53 Peacham, *The Complete Gentleman*, p. 28.

54 Hooker, *Of the Laws of Ecclesiastical Polity*, I, p. 93.

55 *Ibid.*

56 Raleigh, 'A Collection of Political Observations', p. 95.

57 Breton, *A Murmurer*, p. 12.

58 Gardiner, *Letters*, p. 274.

59 Pierce, *Introduction to the Marprelate Tracts*, p. 182; Parker, *Correspondence*, p. 437.

60 Vaughan, *The Golden Grove*, II, p. 162.

61 Breton, *A Murmurer*, p. 9.

62 Elton, *Policy and Police*, pp. 46–47, 74–82.

63 Baldwin, *Morall Philosophie*, fol. 120, (p. 255).

64 *Lisle Letters*, V, no. 1429, p. 502.

65 B.L., Additional Ms. 48047, fol. 64 (the full charge is ff. 61–79).

66 Bacon, 'Of Seditions and Troubles', *Essays*, p. 407.

67 Stow, *Survey of London*, p. 131.

68 *C.S.P. Foreign 1553-1588*, p. 119.

69 B.L., Cotton Mss, Titus B II f. 174 [182]. The examination does not end with Margary Miles but continues for five more pages (fols 174 [182]–177 [185]).

70 Manning, 'The Origins of the Doctrine of Sedition', passim.

71 Baldwin, *Morall Philosophie*, fol. 45 (p. 104).

72 Vaughan, *The Golden Grove*, II, p. 39. See also Hale, *The Body Politic*, p. 58.

73 Breton, *A Dialogue...upon the Dignitie or Indignitie of man* (1603), p. 15.

74 Richard Greenham, *Grave Counsels and Godlie Observations*, p. 4.

75 Breton, *A Murmurer*, p. 7.

76 Arendt, *Eichmann in Jerusalem*, pp. 287–90.

77 Gardiner, 'Gardiner's answer to Bucer' in *Obedience in church and state*, p. 183; Breton, *A Murmurer*, p. 11; Corrie, *Certain Sermons*, p. 67.

78 Spivack, *The Allegory of Evil*, pp. 45–50.

79 Machin, *The Dumb Knight* (1608), p. 133.

80 MacCaffrey, *Queen Elizabeth and the Making of Policy*, p. 137. Roger Manning in 'The Origins of the Doctrine of Sedition', p. 103 has much the same thing to say about other Tudor statesmen.

81 Vatter, *The Devil in English Literature*, p. 194.

82 Puttenham, *The Arte of English Poesie* (1589) p. 299.

V 'THE WORLD IS QUEASY'

1 *Lisle Letters*, III, pt I, p. 54.

2 Shapiro, *Neurotic Styles*, p. 3.

3 H.M.C. *Salisbury Mss.*, II, no. 132. p. 52.

4 Carré, 'Francis Bacon the "Peremptory Royalist",' p. 373.

5 Puttenham, *Arte of English Poesie*, pp. 298–99.

6 *Lisle Letters*, IV, p. 152; H.M.C. *Hastings Mss.*, IV, p. 333. Attacks on the evils and miseries of the court were standard fare, Alexander Barclay setting the pace with his lengthy poetic adaptation (circa 1515) of Aeneas Sylvius Piccolomini's (1405–1464) short Latin satire, *Miseriae Curialium*. In Barclay's version two simple shepherds discuss the horrors of the court and the plight of the courtier who must endure not only:

> On every side enviers him await,
> Devising means to bring him from his state.
> A man of power which many men may deare [harm?
>   challenge? annoy?]
> Hath ever ill will, thus may he many fear.

but also a host of repulsive discomforts. He dined on table cloths black with grease, and

> ... in court I tell thee by my soul
> For most part thou must drink of a common bowl,
> And where greasy lips and slimy beard
> Hath late been dipped to make some mad [maggot]
>   afeard,
> On that side must thou thy lips wash also,
> Or else without drink from dinner must thou go.

Food at court was unappetizing at best: meat 'lean, tough and old, or it come to board unsavoury and cold', and cheese:

> All full of maggots and like to the rainbow,
> Of divers colours as red, green and yellow,
> On each side gnawn with mice or with rats
> Or with vile worms, with dogs or with cats.

As for the communal sleeping accommodation, Barclay leaves nothing to the imagination:

> But if it be fortune thou lie within some town
> In bed of feathers, or else of easy down.
> Then make thee ready for flies and for gnats,
> For lice, for fleas, punaises [bugs], mice and rats.
> . . .
> Thy sheets shall be unclean, ragged and rent,
> Loathly unto sight, but loathlier to scent.
> In which some other departed late before
> Of the pestilence, or of some other sore.
> Such a bedfellow men shall to thee assign,
> That it was better to sleep among the swine.
> So foul and scabbed, of hard pimples so thin,
> That a man might grate hard crusts on his skin.
> . . .
> One cougheth so fast, anothers breath doth stink,
> That during the night scant mayest thou get a wink.
> . . .
> And sometime these courtiers them more to incumber,
> Sleep all in one chamber nere twenty in number.
> Then it is great sorrow for to abide their shout,
> Some fart, some flingeth, and others snort and rout.
> Some boke [push or butt], and some babble, some cometh
>   drunk to bed,
> Some brawl and some jangle when they be beastly fed.
> Some laugh, and some cry, each man will have his will,
> Some spue, and some piss, not one of them is still.

In sum

> The wretched lazar [leper] with clinking of his bell
> Hath life which doth the courtiers life excell.

(*The Miseryes of Courtiers and Courtes*, pp. 37, 76, 79–80, 83, 109–110.)

7 Newdigate-Newdegate, *Gossip from A Muniment Room*, p. 9.
8 Quoted in Read, *Mr Secretary Cecil*, p. 332.
9 Webster, *The White Devil*, V, vi, 261; North, *Philosopher of the Court*, p. 113; Harington, *Nugae Antiquae*, I, p. 343.

10 Cornwallis, *Essayes* (1597), p. 203. For Sir Francis Walsingham the 'fittest seat' for honesty was 'the country where there will be little need of any greater ability, and it will be least subject to corruption'. ('Anatomizing of Honesty, Ambition, and Fortitude' (1590), *Somers tracts,* I, pp. 499–502.)

11 Geertz, 'Centers, Kings, and Charisma: Reflections on the Symbolics of Power', p. 169.

12 Elton, 'Tudor Government... The Court', p. 217.

13 Peacham, *The Complete Gentleman,* p. 12; see also Houghton, 'The English Virtuoso in the Seventeenth Century', pt. I, pp. 51–73.

14 Smith, *The Elizabethan World,* p. 89.

15 Stone, *The Crisis of the Aristocracy,* pp. 465–66, 470, 474–75; MacCaffrey, 'Place and Patronage', pp. 99, 106–108; Elton, 'Tudor Government... The Court', p. 214; *Ibid.,* 'The Council', p. 208.

16 *Lisle Letters,* vol. VI, no. 861, p. 83; P.R.O., S.P. 10, vol. I, fol. 25; Sargent, *Sir Edward Dyer,* pp. 18–19.

17 Stone, *The Crisis of the Aristocracy,* pp. 211–13; MacCaffrey, *Queen Elizabeth and the Making of Policy,* ch. 16; *Ibid.,* 'Place and Patronage'.

18 Quoted in MacCaffrey, 'Place and Patronage', p. 108.

19 Einstein, *Tudor Ideals,* p. 119. The *Lisle Letters* are a gold mine of information on the operation of patronage and the importance of the gift in practical politics.

20 *Lisle Letters,* III, pp. 82, 367, 426–27, 446, 450; V, pp. 311, 686; VI, p. 42; Elton, 'Tudor Government... The Court', pp. 216, 218.

21 *Lisle Letters,* III, no. 693, p. 359.

22 *Ibid.,* V, no. 1233, p. 229.

23 *Ibid.,* III, no. 694, p. 359.

24 Walsingham, *A Practical Guide,* p. 5; how to attract the prince's attention is discussed by Thomas Fuller in 'The Favourite', *The Holy State,* p. 192.

25 B.L. Sloane Mss. 1523, 'Maxims and Sayings', fol. 26.

26 Raleigh, 'A Collection of Political Observations', p. 113.

27 Quoted in Stone, *The Crisis of the Aristocracy,* p. 402; Fuller, 'The Favourite', *The Holy State,* p. 196.

28 The *Lisle Letters* are filled with examples of the cost entailed by the system and the endless delays involved in waiting upon someone else's pleasure — 'his grace saith the matter requireth no great haste'; 'My Lord Privy Seal made answer the matter required no haste.' (III, no. 745, p. 452; V, p. 436).

29 Nott, *Wyatt,* II, p. 89. Wyatt's complaints were in no way original and were drawn from an already well established tradition:

What he [the prince] commandeth, that needs do
  thou must,
Be it good or ill, rightwise or unjust.

> Laugh when he laugheth, all if thine heart be sad,
> Weep when he weepeth, be thou never so glad.
> Laud when he laudeth, though it be not laudable,
> Blame what he blameth, though it be commendable.
> And shortly to speak, thou must all thing[s] fulfill
> As is his pleasure, and nothing at thy will.
> (Barclay, *The Miseryes of Courtiers and Courtes*, p. 43.)

30 *Lisle Letters*, VI, p. 3.
31 Sargent, *Sir Edward Dyer*, p. 83.
32 Nashe, *Christ's Tears over Jerusalem*, I, p. 102.
33 Peacham, *The Truth of Our Times*, p. 205.
34 Lasch, *The Culture of Narcissism*, p. 119, in part quoting Thomas Szasz, *The Myth of Mental Illness*, N.Y., 1961, pp. 275–76.
35 Walsingham, *A Practical Guide*, p. 124. See also Fuller, 'The Favourite', *The Holy State*, pp. 195–96 and Ducci, *Ars avlica*, pp. 216–17.
36 Raleigh, 'A Collection of Political Observations', p. 97.
37 Bacon, *Advancement of Learning*, pp. 248–49.
38 Haynes, *State Papers*, p. 442.
39 Percy, *Advice to His Son*, p. 125.
40 Walsingham, *A Practical Guide*, p. 43.
41 Whythorne, *Autobiography*, p. 47; Percy, *Advice to His Son*, p. 119. For a picture of the servant and his ability to manipulate his master, see H.M.C., *Middleton Mss.*, pp. 504–85.
42 Walsingham, *A Practical Guide*, p. 121.
43 Quoted in Williams, *Elizabeth the first*, p. 330.
44 Raleigh, 'A Collection of Political Observations', p. 96.
45 Francis Bacon in his well-known letter of political advice to young Essex recommended the pretence of 'some journeys' as 'to see your living and estates in Wales' which could easily be cancelled at the Queen's request. Bacon, 'Letters', pp. 228–29.
46 *C.S.P. Spanish 1558-1567*, no. 268, p. 382.
47 Clapham, *Elizabeth of England*, pp. 75–76.
48 Devereux, *The Earls of Essex*, I, p. 395.
49 Stone, *The Crisis of the Aristocracy* is the gospel for studying the economic habits, financial plight, and dependence upon the royal bounty of the aristocracy. See esp. pp. 139–43, 429–33, 456–59, 469, 479–80, 564.
50 Williams, *Thomas Howard*, p. 241, where the Duke's letter is printed in full.
51 Stone, *The Crisis of the Aristocracy*, pp. 416, 423.
52 *Lisle Letters*, I, p. 23.
53 Sargent, *Edward Dyer*, pp. 18–36, 76, 132–37, 140.
54 Lyly, *Campaspe* (1584), IV, iv, 27–30.
55 The story of Anthony Cooke's sad career is told in McIntosh, 'The Fall

of a Tudor Gentle Family', pp. 279–97.

56 *Ibid.,* pp. 289–90.

57 Walsingham, *A Practical Guide,* p. 43.

58 *Lisle Letters,* V, p. 97.

59 Fuller, 'The Favourite', in *The Holy State,* p. 195.

60 Rieff, *Freud, The Mind of the Moralist,* p. 239 in part quoting Freud, *Totem and Taboo,* SE XIII, pp. 49–50.

61 Read, *Lord Burghley and Queen Elizabeth,* p. 291.

62 Vaughan, *The Golden Grove,* II, p. 99.

63 B.L., Sloane Mss. 1523, 'Maxims and Sayings', fol. 33; *Lisle Letters,* III, no. 792, p. 534.

64 C.H. Williams, *The Making of Tudor Despotism,* London, 1928, revised 1935.

65 Elton, *Policy and Police,* pp. 327–33, 350–54, 370–75, 380.

66 P.R.O., S.P. I, vol. 76, fol. 74 (*L.P.* VI, 503).

67 Philip Julius, 'Diary', p. 65.

68 Stone, *The Crisis of the Aristocracy,* p. 98.

69 Thomas, *Religion and the Decline of Magic,* p. 527.

70 Loades, *Mary Tudor,* pp. 283–84.

71 Raleigh, 'Maxims of State', p. 10.

72 du Maurier, *Golden Lads,* p. 153.

73 *Lisle Letters,* III, p. 566.

74 *Ibid.,* no. 522, p. 61.

75 See chapter III, pp. 108–109.

76 Allen, *Admonition to the Nobility and People of England,* (1588), p. xv.

77 Bacon, 'Of Followers and Friends', *Essays,* p. 494.

78 Wilson, *The State of England,* pp. 42–43. He gave as his example the Tower 'where the Lieutenant and Steward, Master of the Ordinance and Lieutenant of the same have been ever in my remembrance vowed enemies'.

79 Vaughan, *The Golden Grove,* I, p. 135.

80 Vaughan, 'Advice to his Son', p. 104.

81 Webster, *The Duchess of Malfi,* pp. 44–45; *Lisle Letters,* IV, p. 61. See also the detailed story of Lord Lisle's encounter with Lord Daubeney in which he clearly maintained an informant in Daubeney's household, V, pp. 167–69, 188–89, 194–95, 304–305, 450.

82 Shils, *The Torment of Society,* pp. 21–24.

83 Percy, *Advice to His Son,* p. 111.

84 Whythorne, *Autobiography,* p. 47.

85 *L.P., Addenda,* I, pt 2, no. 1363.

86 Elton, *Policy and Police,* pp. 329, 331. There are a number of examples of Cromwell receiving information from contacts either located at Calais or passing through. See *Lisle Letters,* I, p. 653 and V, pp. 692–93.

87 Francis Bacon, 'Of Great Place', *Essays,* p. 401.

88 *L.P.* XIII (1), no. 1241.

89　Nashe, *Pierce Penilesse,* p. 32.

90　Walsingham, *A Practical Guide,* pp. 92–93; Edwards, *Damon and Pithias,* p. 9.

91　Bacon, *Advancement of Learning,* p. 243. Baldwin, *Morall Philosophie,* p. 134 (fol. 60) had much the same opinion: 'A small fault in a prince seemeth worse than a greater in a private person.'

92　More, *Richard III,* p. 81.

93　Elton, *Reform and Reformation,* p. 262. Powell's *Tom of all Trades* (1631) gives a vivid picture of the competition for the spoils of office, especially those of fallen ministers. The lapse of a benefice, he said, 'for not presenting in due time' is as 'rare to find out as a faithful fiduciarie or a fast friend' (p. 154). See also *Lisle Letters,* V, no. 1436, p. 512.

94　P.R.O., S.P. I, vol. 124, fol. 193 (*L.P.* XII (2), no. 655).

95　Perlin, *Description,* p. 27.

96　Breton, *I would and would not,* (1614), p. 5.

97　Walsingham, *A Practical Guide,* p. 60.

98　Smith, *Henry VIII,* p. 59 and Ellis, *Original Letters,* 2nd ser., II, p. 255. Scripture supported royalty on this point: 'Where the word of a king is, there is power: and who may say unto him, What doest thou?' (Eccles. 8: 4).

99　P.R.O., S.P. I, vol. 77, ff. 175–76b (*L.P.* VI (1), 755).

100　Shakespeare, *Henry V,* II, ii, 20–24. Shakespeare had more to say on the subject in *Henry VIII*: 'I presume', Henry says to Cardinal Wolsey,

> That as my hand has open'd bounty to you,
> My heart dropp'd love, my power rain'd honour, more
> On you than any; so your hand and heart,
> Your brain, and every function of your power,
> Should, notwithstanding that your bond of duty,
> As 'twere in love's particular, be more
> To me, your friend, than any.
>
> (III, ii, 185–91).

101　Elton, 'Tudor Government...Parliament', p. 187; 'Tudor Government...The Crown', pp. 218–21.

102　Cokayne, *Complete Peerage,* I, p. 31, note g. This quotation was brought to my attention in Terence Murphy's unpublished doctoral dissertation, 'The Maintenance of Order in Early Tudor Kent 1509–1559', p. 280.

103　MacCaffrey, *The Shaping of the Elizabethan Regime,* p. 365.

104　Read, *Lord Burghley and Queen Elizabeth,* pp. 372–73.

105　*Ibid.,* pp. 373–74.

106　Walsingham, *A Practical Guide,* p. 96.

107　See Elton, 'Tudor Government...The Court', p. 226, and James, *English Politics and the Concept of Honour,* p. 1.

108　Nott, *Wyatt,* II, p. 279.

109 *C.S.P. Spanish*, V, no. 76, p. 203.
110 Loades, *Mary Tudor*, pp. 77, 84–85.
111 *L.P.* VIII, no. 1096, pp. 429–30.
112 Osborne, *Advice to a Son* (1656), p. 85.
113 Stapleton, *Sir Thomas More*, p. 192.
114 Tytler, *England under Edward and Mary*, I, p. 229.
115 Quoted in Read, *Mr Secretary Cecil and Queen Elizabeth*, p. 78.
116 Walsingham, *A Practical Guide*, p. 137.
117 Birch, *Memoirs of Queen Elizabeth*, II, p. 176.
118 Clapham, *Elizabeth of England*, p. 77.
119 John, 'Roger Manning, Elizabethan Courtier', p. 63.
120 *State Papers Henry VIII*, II, no. cvi, pp. 280–81.
121 Raleigh, 'The Cabinet-council', p. 114.
122 Bacon, *Advancement of Learning*, p. 247.
123 Murdin, *State Papers*, pp. 153, 166–67, 168–70.
124 Smith, *Elizabeth Tudor*, p. 139.
125 Cecil, *The State and Dignitie of a Secretarie of Estates Place*, p. 3. By the seventeenth century Robert Cecil and his father Lord Burghley had been confused. The tract is by William Cecil.
126 *L.P.* IV, no. 1318, p. 580.
127 Hall, *Union of Two Noble Famelies*, fols cxxxix, cxlii. Elton, *Policy and Police*, p. 183.
128 Read, *Lord Burghley and Queen Elizabeth*, pp. 328–29.
129 Devereux, *Earls of Essex*, I, pp. 186–88.
130 Gardiner, *Letters*, no. 125, p. 321.
131 Osborne, *Advice to a Son*, p. 47.
132 Quoted in Smith, *Elizabeth Tudor*, p. 64.
133 Bacon, 'Of Seditions and Troubles', *Essays*, p. 411. See also *Advancement of Learning*, p. 248.
134 Clapham, *Elizabeth of England*, p. 86. George Puttenham made almost the same observation: 'In a noble Prince nothing is more decent and welbeseeming his greatness, than to...let none humble suitors depart out of their presence (as near as may be) miscontented. Wherein her Majesty hath of all others a most regal gift ...' *Arte of English Poesie*, p. 297.
135 Shakespeare, *Richard II*, III, i, 8–10. As early as November 1531 Stephen Vaughan was writing: 'If any are flatterers of their prince, whose image in earth signifies the image and power of God, God shall utterly destroy them. If it is a sin to be an evil counsellor to one man, how much more to a prince who governs a realm.' *L.P.*, V, no. 533.
136 By the eighteenth century the theory was so much a part of the British Constitution that it was used to persuade the colonists to remain loyal. 'When the truth of things', wrote John Zubly in 1775, 'once reaches his [George III's] notice, a generous pity will force his heart' and 'will com-

mand redress...that all our present distress is owing to evil
counsellors...that the wicked being removed from before the King, his
throne may be established in righteousness.' (*The Law of Liberty*, fol. 23.)

137 Bacon, 'Of Envy', *Essays*, p. 396.
138 Vaughan, 'Advice to his Son', p. 99.
139 Strype, *Annals*, III, pt 2, no. LVIII, pp. 382–83.
140 Raleigh, 'Maxims of State', p. 15.
141 Walsingham, *A Practical Guide*, p. 90.
142 Read, *Lord Burghley and Queen Elizabeth*, p. 437. Sir John Harington must
    have overheard Lord Burghley's complaints, for he wrote: 'When the busi-
    ness did turn to better advantage, she did most cunningly commit the good
    issue to her own honour and understanding; but when ought fell out con-
    trary to her will and intent, the council were in great strait to defend their
    own acting and not blemish the Queen's good judgment. Herein...the
    Lord Treasurer would oft shed a plenty of tears...' (*Nugae Antiquae*, I,
    pp. 357–58.)
143 Digges, *Compleat Ambassador*, p. 203.
144 Burton, *Anatomy of Melancholy*, pp. 332–34. Stephen Greenblatt wrote of
    Tudor politics that it was 'fundamentally insane, its practitioners in the
    grip of "frenzies." And it is not only political life, in the narrow sense,
    that is so judged, but the great body of man's social relations.' (*Renaissance
    Self-fashioning*, p. 15.) It should also be noted that both Thomas Norfolk,
    the 4th Duke of Norfolk, and Robert Devereux, the 2nd Earl of Essex,
    suffered from migraine headaches and various other nervous afflictions when-
    ever the political tension increased.

VI A 'WONDER TO BEHOLD'

1 Allen, *Defence of Catholics*, (1588), p. 236.
2 Hofstadter, *Paranoid Style*, p. 39.
3 The two most provocative treatments in recent years of this immense subject are Jean Delumeau, *La peur en Occident, xive-xviiie siècles* and Bouwsma,
  'Anxiety and the Formation of Early Modern Culture'.
4 Erasmus, *Epistles*, I, p. 82.
5 Ecclesiasticus, (1537 translation), 30:18.
6 Cranmer, *Letters*, p. 15. Renewed Protestant emphasis on human depravity,
  God's sovereignty, and the duality of good and evil has been commented
  on by many scholars. See esp. Hoopes, *Right Reason*, p. 98; Thomas, *Religion
  and the Decline of Magic*, pp. 79, 110; Greaves, *Society and Religion*, pp. 7–9;
  Tillyard, *Elizabethan World Picture*, pp. 75–76.
7 Bradford, *Writings*, p. 38.
8 Foxe, *Actes and Monuments*, IV, p. 699.
9 Elton, 'Tudor Government...The Court', pp. 226–27, and *Policy and Police*,

pp. 44–45.

10 *L.P.* IV, pt 3, no. 6179.

11 P.R.O., S.P. 10, vol. 8, fol. 4; Foxe, *Actes and Monuments,* VIII, p. 110.

12 Thomas, *Religion and the Decline of Magic,* pp. 542–43.

13 *C.S.P. Spanish,* I (1558–1567), no. 244, pp. 351–52.

14 Allen, *Defence of Catholics* (1588), p. 237.

15 Cleland, *Institution of a Young Noble Man,* p. 109.

16 Tyndale, *Obedience of a Christian Man,* p. 324.

17 Cleland, *Institution of a Young Noble Man,* p. 109.

18 P.R.O., S.P. I, vol. 241, fol. 3 (*L.P.* Add. Ms. no. 1209); Foxe, *Actes and Monuments,* IV, p. 688; Sanders, 'Report to Cardinal Morini', p. 38.

19 Tyndale, *Obedience of a Christian Man,* p. 185.

20 P.R.O., S.P. I, vol. 77, fols 175–176b (*L.P.* VI, no. 775). For a discussion of absolute truth see Hoopes, *Right Reason,* p. 4.

21 Vatter, *The Devil in English Literature,* pp. 24, 114. For the association of Antichrist with the Pope, see Emmerson, *Antichrist in the Middle Ages* and Hill, *Antichrist in Seventeenth-Century England.* Mary Douglas treats the social and psychological conditions necessary for belief in evil in *Natural Symbols,* esp. chs 7 and 8.

22 Spivack, *The Allegory of Evil,* pp. 373–75, 423–25.

23 Vatter, *The Devil in English Literature,* pp. 106–108; Thomas, *Religion and the Decline of Magic,* pp. 470, 477.

24 Watson, *Vives: On Education,* p. 84.

25 Thomas, *Religion and the Decline of Magic,* pp. 454–55, 462, 483, 498.

26 *Ibid.,* pp. 111, 535–36, 540, 542–43, 566.

27 See chapter II, pp. 54–57.

28 Erikson, 'Living in a World without Stable Points of Reference', p. 14.

29 Kaulek, *Correspondance de Castillon et de Marillac,* no. 242, p. 211.

30 B.L. Harleian Mss., 4990, fol. 1 (*L.P.* XVII, App. A, 1). See also Starkey, 'Representation through Intimacy', pp. 221–22.

31 Cavendish, *Life and Death of Wolsey,* p. 160; Roper, *Life of More,* p. 200.

32 Quoted in Ridley, *Thomas Cranmer,* p. 83, which is a liberal translation from Richard Sampson's treatise on the supremacy. Printed in Strype, *Ecclesiastical Memorials,* I, pt ii, pp. 162–75.

33 Deuteronomy, 13:6–9.

34 'An Exhortation concerning Obedience', and 'An Homily against Wilful Rebellion', pp. 104–17. 551–99; Cobbett, *State Trials,* I, p. 1045.

35 Greene, *James the Fourth,* p. 211.

36 Elton, 'Tudor Government...The Court', p. 212.

37 Smith, *De Republica Anglorum,* pp. 62–63. For a discussion of the growing rigidity and competition at court under Elizabeth, see Elton, 'Tudor Government...The Court', pp. 209, 211.

38 Lyons, *Voices of Melancholy,* pp. 17–18; 20–21; Laurentius, *A Discourse...of*

Melancholike diseases, (1599), pp. 72–140; Bright, *A Treatise of Melancholie,* (1586), pp. 101–110; 123–25.

39 Laurentius, *A Discourse . . . of Melancholike diseases,* (1599), p. 100; Lyons, *Voices of Melancholy,* pp. 34–35.

40 Burton, *Anatomy of Melancholy,* pp. 332–33.

41 Evans, *The Psychiatry of Robert Burton,* p. 48.

VII 'WIN THE QUEEN'

1 Camden, *Elizabeth,* p. 621.

2 For a complete discussion of Essex's date of birth, see Harrison, *Essex,* pp. 329–30. If Henry Wotton is correct, Essex could have been born in 1565, *Reliquiae Wottonianae,* pp. 19, 40. See also note 3 below.

3 Venn and Venn, *Book of Matriculations,* p. 236; Ball and Venn, *Admissions to Trinity College,* p. 125. Venn and Venn say (p. x) a child under fourteen could not take the oath required to matriculate. Essex matriculated in 1579; this would then place his birth in 1565. Children could informally enter a university several years before they actually matriculated. See also Harrison, *Essex,* pp. 4–5; Devereux, *Earls of Essex,* I, pp. 165–69.

4 DeMolen gives the following statistics for admission into Oxford and Cambridge during the sixteenth century:

Oxford — no. of males	Age	Cambridge — no. of males
0	9	1
6	10	1
10	11	6
17	12	11
36	13	5
62	14	34
144	15	84
147	16	203
171	17	268
154	18	278
89	19	68
68	20	25
22	21	5
14	22	4
-	-	-
0	38	1
-	-	-
1	48	0

'Ages of Admission', p. 217. See also Ong, *Rhetoric, Romance and Technology,* p. 149.

5 Wotton, *Reliquiae Wottonianae,* p. 19. *D.N.B.,* 'Henry Wotton'.

6 The standard biographies of Essex are Walter Devereux, *Lives and Letters of the Devereux, Earls of Essex*, 2 vols (1853); G.B. Harrison, *Life and Death of Robert Devereux, Earl of Essex* (1937); and Robert Lacey, *Robert Earl of Essex, An Elizabethan Icarus* (1971).

7 Devereux, *Earls of Essex*, I, p. 90.

8 Sidney, *Letters*, I, p. 141.

9 Devereux, *Earls of Essex*, II, p. 491.

10 *Ibid.*, I, pp. 323–24.

11 Birch, *Memoirs of Elizabeth*, I, p. 488.

12 Wotton, *Reliquiae Wottonianae*, p. 2. The spelling of Essex's estate varies from author to author; Devereux, *Earls of Essex*, I, p. 171 = Lanfey; Lacey, *Essex*, p. 22 = Lamphy; Harrison, *Essex*, p. 5 = Llandfydd; Wotton, 'Of Robert Devereux', p. 2 = Lampsie.

13 Wotton, *Reliquiae Wottonianae*, pp. 23, 41.

14 Camden, *Elizabeth*, p. 624.

15 Breton, *Court and Country*, p. 16.

16 Watson, *Vives: On Education*, p. 2.

17 *Practical Guide for Ambitious Politicians*, p. 137.

18 Ben Jonson accused Elizabeth of wagering only on loaded dice; C.H. Herford and P. Simpson, *Ben Jonson*, vol. I (Oxford, 1925), p. 142, quoted in Stone, *The Crisis of the Aristocracy*, p. 569.

19 Bacon, 'Letters', p. 256.

20 *Ibid.*, p. 226; also Devereux, *Earls of Essex*, I, p. 395.

21 Wotton, *Reliquiae Wottonianae*, pp. 11–12.

22 Harington, *Nugae Antiquae*, I, p. 166.

23 Quoted in Stone, *The Crisis of the Aristocracy*, p. 489.

24 Wotton, *Reliquiae Wottonianae*, p. 52.

25 Lacey, *Essex*, p. 31.

26 Puttenham, *Arte of Poesie*, p. 300.

27 Harrison, *Essex*, p. 28; Wotton, *Reliquiae Wottonianae*, p. 18.

28 Smythe-Palmer, *The Ideal of a Gentleman*, p. 75; Camden, *Elizabeth*, pp. 623–24.

29 Devereux, *Earls of Essex*, I, p. 186.

30 *Ibid.*, p. 185.

31 *Ibid.*, p. 184.

32 *Ibid.*, pp. 186–89.

33 *Ibid.*, pp. 204–205.

34 *Ibid.*, pp. 222–23.

35 *Ibid.*, p. 234.

36 *Ibid.*

37 *Ibid.*, pp. 249–50.

38 Birch, *Memoirs of Elizabeth*, II, p. 264.

39 *Ibid.*, I, p. 155.

40 Bacon, 'Letters', pp. 226–31.
41 Smith, *Elizabeth*, p. 206.
42 Birch, *Memoirs of Elizabeth*, II, p. 220.
43 Quoted in du Maurier, *Golden Lads* p. 149; Birch, *Memoirs of Elizabeth*, I, p. 290.
44 Birch, *Memoirs of Elizabeth*, I, p. 289.
45 H.M.C. *Salisbury Mss*, VII, p. 10.
46 Birch, *Memoirs of Elizabeth*, I, p. 152.
47 *Ibid.*, p. 150.
48 *Ibid.*, p. 152.
49 *Ibid.*, p. 185.
50 Camden, *Elizabeth*, p. 524.
51 Birch, *Memoirs of Elizabeth*, I, p. 153.
52 *Ibid.*, pp. 121, 123, 167.
53 *Ibid.*, pp. 166–67.
54 *Ibid.*, p. 172.
55 *Ibid.*, p. 150.
56 Bacon, 'Apology', p. 211.
57 Birch, *Memoirs of Elizabeth*, I, p. 181.
58 *Ibid.*, p. 483.
59 Birch, *Memoirs of Elizabeth*, II, p. 131.
60 *Ibid.*, p. 61.
61 *Ibid.*, p. 141.
62 *Ibid.*, p. 289.
63 Sidney, *Letters*, pp. 22–24.
64 Birch, *Memoirs of Elizabeth*, II, p. 296.
65 Cadwallader, *Career of Essex*, p. 22.
66 Handover, *Second Cecil*, p. 182; Wotton, *Reliquiae Wottonianae* p. 8; Lacey, *Essex*, p. 201; Birch, *Memoirs of Elizabeth*, I, p. 491.
67 Lacey, *Essex*, p. 201.
68 Burton, *Anatomy of Melancholy*, p. 333.
69 Shapiro, *Neurotic Styles*, p. 91.

VIII 'IF YOU HAVE ANY ENEMIES'

1 Cadwallader, *Career of Essex*, p. 22.
2 *C.S.P. Domestic 1595-1597*, p. 533; Devereux, *Earls of Essex*, I, pp. 468–69.
3 Maisse, *Journal*, pp. 67–68.
4 *Ibid.*, p. 49.
5 Birch, *Memoirs of Elizabeth*, II, p. 384; Camden, *Elizabeth*, p. 556.
6 Birch, *Memoirs of Elizabeth*, II, pp. 384–86. The italics are mine.
7 *Ibid.*, p. 389.
8 *Ibid.*, p. 388.

9 *Ibid.*, pp. 386–88.

10 *Ibid.*, p. 387.

11 Chamberlain, *Letters,* p. 15; Devereux, *Earls of Essex,* I, p. 493.

12 H.M.C., *Salisbury Mss.* VIII, pp. 318–19.

13 Jardine, *Criminal Trials,* I, p. 297.

14 Birch, *Memoirs of Elizabeth,* II, p. 391.

15 Hurstfield, *The Queen's Wards,* pp. 262–64, 268, 279–81, 343.

16 *Ibid.*, pp. 288–89, 297; H.M.C. *Salisbury Mss.* VIII, p. 415.

17 Chamberlain, *Letters,* p. 23.

18 H.M.C. *Salisbury Mss.* VIII, pp. 416–17.

19 Hurstfield, *The Queen's Wards,* pp. 293–96.

20 Chamberlain, *Letters,* p. 28.

21 Birch, *Memoirs of Elizabeth,* II, p. 415.

22 Camden, *Elizabeth,* pp. 567–68.

23 Bacon, 'Letters', pp. 246–50.

24 H.M.C., *Salisbury Mss.* IX, pp. 10–11.

25 Camden, *Elizabeth,* p. 568.

26 Harington, *Nugae Antiquae,* I, pp. 241–42.

27 Camden, *Elizabeth,* p. 568.

28 Chamberlain, *Letters,* pp. 44, 46; Harrison, *Essex,* p. 216.

29 Cadwallader, *Career of Essex,* pp. 31–33; Devereux, *Earls of Essex,* II, pp. 13–15; Birch, *Memoirs of Elizabeth,* II, p. 396.

30 Devereux, *Earls of Essex,* II, pp. 17, 21, 22; *C.S.P. Irish, 1599-1600,* p. 6.

31 Devereux, *Earls of Essex,* II, p. 28.

32 Cadwallader, *Career of Essex,* p. 38.

33 Quoted in Lacey, *Essex,* p. 222.

34 Devereux, *Earls of Essex,* II, p. 44.

35 *Ibid.*, p. 43.

36 *Ibid.*, pp. 44–45.

37 *Ibid.*, p. 45.

38 Sir Robert Cecil was appointed Master of the Wards on May 21st, 1599.

39 Birch, *Memoirs of Elizabeth,* II, pp. 417–18.

40 *Ibid.*, p. 420.

41 *C.S.P. Irish 1599-1600,* pp. 95–96.

42 *Ibid.*, pp. 98–100.

43 *Ibid.*, pp. 105–106.

44 Birch, *Memoirs of Elizabeth,* II, p. 424.

45 *Ibid.*, p. 426.

46 John Chamberlain reported on August 23rd, 1599 that Essex had created fifty-nine knights. 'It is much marvelled that this humour should so possess him.' (Chamberlain, *Letters,* p. 63.) By the time he left Ireland on September 24th he had bestowed knighthoods on a total of eighty-one of his followers and captains.

47 Harington, *Nugae Antiquae*, I, p. 178.

48 Madox, *An Elizabethan in 1582*, p. 186.

49 Cadwallader, *Career of Essex*, p. 48; Mathew, *Celtic Peoples*, pp. 371, 381.

50 The best account, although biased in Essex's favour, of what actually happened at Ballaclinche Ford and the terms decided on can be found in Cadwallader, *Career of Essex*, pp. 52–55.

51 Cadwallader, *Career of Essex*, p. 53.

52 H.M.C., *Salisbury Mss.* XI, p. 73.

53 Devereux, *Earls of Essex*, II, pp. 61–65.

54 *Ibid.*, p. 68.

55 *Ibid.*, pp. 73–75.

56 Camden, *Elizabeth*, pp. 572–73.

57 Harrison, *Essex*, pp. 246–47; Lacey, *Essex*, p. 238.

58 H.M.C., *Salisbury Mss.* XI, p. 72; cf. pp. 47–49.

59 *Ibid.*

60 *Ibid.*

61 Matter, *My Lords and Lady of Essex*, p. 14. Bacon, 'Declaration of Treasons', p. 146.

IX 'GIVE LOSERS LEAVE TO TALK'

1 Nashe, *Pierce Penilesse*, p. 9.

2 Carpenter, *Architophel*, fol. B9.

3 Bacon, 'Declaration of Treasons'. All quotations fall between pp. 136–65.

4 Harington, *Nugae Antiquae*, I, p. 180.

5 Naunton, *Fragmenta Regalia*, p. 123.

6 Fuller, *Worthies*, I, p. 452.

7 Cobbett, *State Trials*, I, p. 1437.

8 H.M.C., *Salisbury Mss.*, X, p. 286. For Sir Gilly Meyrick, see also Mathew, *Celtic Peoples*, pp. 340–55.

9 *D.N.B.*, art. Henry Cuffe; see also Mathew, *Celtic Peoples*, pp. 405–407.

10 H.M.C., *Salisbury Mss.*, VII, pp. 234, 423, 524.

11 Cecil, *Letters to Carew*, p. 74.

12 Bacon, 'Declaration of Treasons', pp. 150–51.

13 Lacey, *Essex*, p. 109.

14 Wotton, *Reliquiae Wottonianae*, pp. 31–32.

15 *Ibid.*, pp. 32–34; see also Cobbett, *State Trials*, I, p. 1442.

16 Cobbett, *State Trials*, I, p. 1414.

17 *Ibid.*, p. 1439.

18 *Ibid.*, p. 1443; see also Camden, *Elizabeth*, p. 626.

19 Cobbett, *State Trials*, I, pp. 1443–44.

20 Bacon, 'Declaration of Treasons', p. 180.

21 *Ibid.*, pp. 175, 206.

22 Cobbett, *State Trials*, I, p. 1413. For a variation of this speech see *C.S.P. Dom. 1601-1603 with Addenda 1547-1565*, p. 15.

23 H.M.C., *Salisbury Mss.*, IX, p. 270.

24 Laurentius, *A Discourse of...Melancholike diseases*, (1599), p. 93.

25 Sidney, *Letters*, II, p. 127.

26 Breton, *The Figure of Foure*, p. 5, no. 101.

27 Chamberlin, *Elizabeth*, p. 278.

28 Wotton, *Reliquiae Wottonianae*, p. 49.

29 Cadwallader, *Career of Essex*, p. 62.

30 Wotton, *Reliquiae Wottonianae*, p. 53.

31 Harington, *Nugae Antiquae*, I, pp. 341, 356.

32 Most of what follows can be found in Birch, *Memoirs of Elizabeth*, II, pp. 437ff and Camden, *Elizabeth*, pp. 597-622.

33 Raleigh, *Maxims of State*, p. 14.

34 Devereux, *Earls of Essex*, II, p. 83.

35 Sidney, *Letters*, II, p. 167.

36 Harrison, *Essex*, p. 255.

37 Essex to Southampton, *Somers tracts*, I, p. 504.

38 Devereux, *Earls of Essex*, II, pp. 98-99.

39 *Ibid.*

40 Birch, *Memoirs of Elizabeth*, I, p. 450.

41 Cadwallader, *Career of Essex*, p. 70, from *C.S.P. Dom., Addenda 1580-1625*, p. 399; see also Devereux, *Earls of Essex*, I, pp. 100-106.

42 Cecil, *Letters to Carew*, p. 23.

43 Camden, *Elizabeth*, p. 602.

44 Chamberlain, *Letters*, p. 89.

45 Devereux, *Earls of Essex*, II, p. 126.

46 *Ibid.*, p. 127.

47 *Ibid.*, p. 128.

48 Camden, *Elizabeth*, pp. 602-603.

49 Bacon, 'Of Great Place', *Essays*, p. 400.

50 Raleigh, 'A Collection of Political Observations', p. 89.

51 James VI, *Correspondence*, pp. 82-83.

52 Harrison, *Essex*, p. 307. Cf. Cobbett, *State Trials*, I, p. 1351.

53 Lacey, *Essex*, pp. 262-67.

54 Most of the evidence, such as it is, comes from Henry Cuffe, Charles Danvers, Southampton and Christopher Blount. See James VI, *Correspondence*, pp. 81-110; the statements given by Bacon in his 'Declaration of Treasons', pp. 166-206; and *C.S.P. Dom. 1598-1601*, pp. 544-99.

55 Most of what follows can be found in two versions of Sir Ferdinando Gorges's examinations, H.M.C., *Salisbury Mss.*, XI, p. 69 and *C.S.P. Dom. 1598-1601*, pp. 577-78.

56 *C.S.P. Dom. 1598-1601*, pp. 577-78.

57 Harington, *Nugae Antiquae*, I, p. 394.
58 Camden, *Elizabeth*, p. 603; the most thorough examination into the economic basis of the rebellion and the political degeneration of the leaders is in Stone, *The Crisis of the Aristocracy*, pp. 400–402, 458, 484–85, 778.
59 Nashe, *Pierce Penilesse*, p. 85.
60 There is considerable evidence of a network of spies in Essex's household. Birch refers to intelligence given to Cecil 'by a young man of good family who was a domestic of the Earl, and had been educated with him from his childhood, and was so much trusted by him, that his Lordship made no scruple to discourse in his hearing with friends concerning their most secret designs'. (*Memoirs of Elizabeth*, II, p. 464.) Moreover, one of Essex's complaints against Cecil, Cobham, and Raleigh was that they 'laid his own servants spies to entrap him'. (H.M.C., *Salisbury Mss.*, XI, p. 70.)
61 The existence of a messenger or message from the city remains one of the most mysterious aspects of this strange affair. Camden says that while Essex and his captains were arguing over 'the love and affection of the Londoners and the uncertain disposition of the vulgar, behold one came in of set purpose, who, as if he had been sent from the citizens, made large promises of assistance from them against all his adversaries'. (*Elizabeth*, p. 607.) Camden is clearly suggesting chicanery — the report was false — but the only documented contact Essex had with the city was when he sent Mr Temple (probably the same man as his secretary) to London the evening before the rebellion. (Cobbett, *State Trials*, I, p. 1336; see also *C.S.P. Dom. 1601-1603 with Addenda*, pp. 8–9, 61.) Lacey deduces from this that Temple was the agent who reported that Sheriff Smith could raise 1,000 men in support of the Earl. (*Essex*, p. 284.)
62 Raleigh, 'A Collection of Political Observations', p. 118.
63 Camden, *Elizabeth*, p. 609.
64 Harrison, *Essex*, p. 288; Cobbett, *State Trials*, I, p. 1353; Camden, *Elizabeth*, p. 610.
65 H.M.C., *Salisbury Mss.*, XI, p. 68.
66 Camden, *Elizabeth*, p. 610.
67 H.M.C., *Salisbury Mss.*, XI, p. 61.
68 Camden, *Elizabeth*, pp. 613–24; Cobbett, *State Trials*, I, pp. 1348–50.
69 Cobbett, *State Trials*, I, p. 1349.
70 Camden, *Elizabeth*, p. 616.
71 Sidney, *Letters*, I, pp. 359–60. Much has been written about John Hayward, Essex, Henry IV, and Richard II: Evelyn Albright, 'Shakespeare's Richard II and the Essex Conspiracy', *P.M.L.A.*, XLII, pp. 686–720; Ray Heffner, 'Shakespeare, Hayward, and Essex', *P.M.L.A.*, XLV, pp. 754–80; Evelyn Albright, 'Shakespeare, Hayward, and Essex Again', *P.M.L.A.*, XLVII, pp. 698–901; Margaret Dowling, 'Sir John Hayward's Troubles over his Life of Henry IV', *The Library*, 4th series, XI (1930–31), pp. 212–24.

72 Bacon, 'Apology', p. 218.

73 Cobbett, *State Trials*, I, p. 1339.

74 Camden, *Elizabeth*, p. 616.

75 *Ibid.*

76 Cobbett, *State Trials*, I, pp. 1351-52.

77 Harrison, *Essex*, p. 308. Harrison has the best account of the entire trial and the verbal duel between Essex and Cecil.

78 Cobbett, *State Trials*, I, p. 1352; Harrison, *Essex*, p. 308.

79 Harrison, *Essex*, p. 309.

80 Camden, *Elizabeth*, p. 617.

81 Harrison, *Essex*, p. 310.

82 *Ibid.*

83 Cobbett, *State Trials*, I, p. 1358.

84 Chamberlain, *Letters*, p. 105.

85 The best analysis of Essex's spiritual conversion and Ashton's role is in Beach Langston, 'Essex and the Art of Dying', *The Huntington Library Quarterly*, no. 2, Feb. 1950, pp. 109-29. See also Birch, *Memoirs of Elizabeth*, II, pp. 475-76. Harrison, *Essex* (pp. 315-16) and others tend to view Ashton as a base instrument of the Crown, and part of a government scheme to 'break' the Earl.

86 Langston, 'Essex and the Art of Dying', p. 124; Birch, *Memoirs of Elizabeth*, II, p. 476.

87 Langston, p. 125; Harrison, *Essex*, p. 318; Winwood, *Memorials*, I, p. 301.

88 Harrison, *Essex*, p. 319; Lacey, *Essex*, p. 313.

89 Bacon, 'Declaration of Treasons', p. 175; see also Birch, *Memoirs of Elizabeth*, II, p. 478.

90 Langston, 'Essex and the Art of Dying', p. 126; Bacon, 'Declaration of Treasons', p. 176.

91 *C.S.P. Dom. 1598-1601*, p. 592.

92 Harrison, *Essex*, p. 323; Devereux, *Earls of Essex*, II, pp. 187-88.

93 *Letters of Robert Cecil to George Carew*, p. 72.

94 Davies, *Scourge of Folly*, p. 57.

95 *The Apocrypha*, p. vii.

96 Osborne, *Advice to a Son*, p. 93. See also Betz, 'Francis Osborn's Advice to a Son', pp. 3-67.

97 Halifax, 'Moral Thoughts and Reflections', p. 231.

98 Swanson, *Popular Literature*, p. 134.

99 Mun, *England's Treasure*, p. 1.

100 Petty, *Tracts*, p. 207.

101 Much has been written on this subject, but for a start read Ong's final chapter 'Romantic Difference and the Poetics of Technology', in *Rhetoric, Romance and Technology*.

BIBLIOGRAPHY

of books and articles cited in footnotes

Acts of the Privy Council of England, ed. J.R. Dasent, 32 vols, London, 1890–1907.

Adams, Thomas, *The Divells Blanket*, London, 1614.

Allen, William Cardinal, *An Admonition to the Nobility and People of England and Ireland concerning the Present Warres made for the Execution of His Holines Sentence, by the highe and mightie Kinge Catholike of Spaine*, Antwerp, 1588.

—— *A True, Sincere, and Modest Defence of English Catholics* (1588), ed. Robert M. Kingdom, Ithaca, New York, 1965.

Altman, Joel B., *The Tudor Play of Mind: Rhetorical Inquiry and the Development of Elizabethan Drama*, Berkeley, 1978.

Ames, William, *A fresh Suit against Humane Ceremonies in Gods Worship* . . . Rotterdam(?), 1633.

The Apocrypha: An American Translation, trans. Edward J. Goodspeed, New York, 1957.

Arendt, Hannah, *Eichmann in Jerusalem: A Report on the Banality of Evil,* New York, 1963.

Ascham, Roger. *The Schoolmaster (1570),* ed. Lawrence V. Ryan, Ithaca, New York, 1967.

Babb, Lawrence, *The Elizabethan Malady: A Study of Melancholia in English Literature from 1580 to 1642,* East Lansing, Michigan, 1951.

Bacon, Francis, *Advancement of Learning and Novum Organum,* ed. James E. Creighton, New York, 1899.

—— 'A Declaration of the Practices and Treasons attempted and committed by Robert Late Earl of Essex . . .' in *Works,* new edition in 10 vols, vol. III, London, 1826.

—— 'Essayes or Counsels, Civill and Morall', in *Works,* ed. James Spedding, et. al., vol. VI, London, 1890.

—— 'Letters', in *Works,* new edition in 10 vols, vol. III, London, 1826.

—— 'Of the Wisdom of the Ancients', *Works,* ed. James Spedding, vol. VI, London, 1890.

Baldwin, T.W., *William Shakespere's Petty School,* Urbana, Ill, 1943.

—— *William Shakespere's Small Latine & Lesse Greeke,* 2 vols, Urbana, Ill, 1944.

Baldwin, William, *Mirror of Magistrates,* 2 vols, ed. Joseph Haslewood,

London, 1815.

—— *A Treatise of Morall Philosophie: Wherein is Contained the Worthy Sayings of Philosophers, Emperours, Kings, and Orators: Their Lives and Answers* (1547), ed. Robert H. Bowers, Gainesville, Florida, 1967.

Ball, W.W. R. and, Venn, J.A., *Admissions to Trinity College, Cambridge,* vol. II (1546–1700), London, 1913.

Barclay [Bercley], Alexander, *Here begynneth a ryght frutefull treatyse intituled the myrrour of good maners, coteynyng the iiii vertues called cardynall compyled in latyn by Domynike Mancyn. And translate into englysshe . . . by Alexander Bercley priest and monke of Ely.* London: 1520.

Barclay [Bercley], Richard, *A Discourse of the Felicitie of Man or His Summum bonum,* London, 1603.

—— *The Miseryes of Courtiers and Courtes in the Eclogues of Alexander Barclay,* ed. Beatrice White, E.E.T.S., London, 1928.

Barrow, Isaac, 'Of Industry in our Particular Calling, as Gentlemen', in *The Theological Works* in 8 vols, vol. III, Oxford, England, 1830.

Beale, Robert, 'A Treatise of the office of a Councellor and Principall Secretarie to her Majestie', printed in Conyers Read, *Mr Secretary Walsingham and the Policy of Queen Elizabeth,* vol. I, appendix pp. 423–43, Oxford, England, 1925.

Becon, Thomas, *The Catechism* (1559), ed. J. Ayre, Cambridge, England, 1844.

Beer, Barrett L., 'Northumberland: The Myth of the Wicked Duke and the Historical John Dudley', *Albion,* spring 1979.

Bennet, H.S., *English Books and Readers,* vol. I 1475–1557, vol. II 1558–1603, vol. III 1603–1640, Cambridge, England, 1952–70.

Betz, Siegmund, 'Francis Osborn's Advice to a Son', *Seventeenth Century Studies,* ed. Robert Shafer, Princeton, 1933.

Bevington, David, *Tudor Drama and Politics: A Critical Approach to Topical Meaning,* Cambridge, Mass., 1968.

Birch, Thomas, *Memoirs of the Reign of Queen Elizabeth from the Year 1581 till her Death,* 2 vols, London, 1754.

Boaistuau, Peter, *Theatrum Mundi, The theatre or rule of the world, wherein may be seene the running race and course of every mans life . . .* trans. John Alday, London, 158l.

Bourne, H.R. Fox, *A Memoir of Sir Philip Sidney,* London, 1862.

Bouwsma, William J., 'Anxiety and the Formation of Early Modern Culture', in *After the Reformation: Essays in Honor of J.H. Hexter,* ed. Barbara C. Malament, Phila., 1980.

Bowers, Fredson Thayer, *Elizabethan Revenge Tragedy 1587-1642,* Princeton, 1940.

Bradford, William, *Writings, containing Sermons, Meditations, Examinations, etc.,* ed. Aubrey Townsend, Cambridge, England, 1848.

Breme, Thomas, *The Mirrour of Friendship: both how to Knowe a Perfect friend, and to choose him,* London, 1584.

Breton, Nicholas, *The Court and Country, or A Briefe Discourse betweine the*

Courtier and Country-man (1618) in *The Works in Verse and Prose of Nicholas Breton*, vol. II of 2 vols, ed. Alexander B. Grosart, Edinburgh, 1879.

—— *A Dialogue... upon The Dignitie or Indignitie of man* (1603) in *Works*, vol. II.

—— *The Figure of Foure: Wherein are sweet flowers gathered...* (London, 1636) in *Works*, vol. II.

—— *I would and would not* (1614) in *Works*, vol. I.

—— *The Mothers Blessing* (1602) in *Works*, vol. II.

—— *A Murmurer* (1607) in *Works*, vol. II.

—— *A Poste with a Packet of Mad Letters* (1637) in *Works*, vol. II.

—— *Wits Private Wealth* (1609) in *Works*, vol. II.

Bright, Timothy, *Treatise of Melancholie containing the causes thereof, and reasons of the strange effects it worketh in our minds and bodies...* London, 1586.

Brown, J. Howard, *Elizabethan Schooldays*, Oxford, England, 1933.

Bryan, Francis (Briant, Frauncis), *A Dispraise of the Life of a Courtier, and a commendacion of the life of the labourying man*, London, 1548.

Bundy, Murray W., 'Shakespeare and Elizabethan Psychology', *The Journal of English and Germanic Philology*, October 1924.

Burton, Edward, ed. *Three Primers put forth in the Reign of Henry VIII*, Oxford, England, 1834.

Burton, Robert, *The Anatomy of Melancholy*, ed. Floyd Dell and Paul Jordan-Smith, New York, 1938.

Bush, M.L., *The Government Policy of Protector Somerset*, London, 1975.

Byman, Seymour. 'Childraising and Melancholia', *Journal of Psychohistory*, vol. 6, no. 1, 1978.

Cadwallader, Laura H., *The Career of the Earl of Essex from the Island Voyage in 1597 to his Execution in 1601*, Philadelphia, 1923.

Calendar of State Papers, Domestic, ed. M.A.E. Green, London, 1856–72.

Calendar of State Papers, Foreign, Edward VI and Mary, 1547-53, ed. W.B. Turnbull, London, 1861; *Elizabeth*, ed. Joseph Stevenson, *et. al.*, London, 1863–1950.

Calendar of State Papers, relating to Ireland of the Reign of Elizabeth, ed. Ernest George Atkinson, London, 1899.

Calendar of State Papers Relating to Scotland, ed. Joseph Bain, *et. al.*, Edinburgh, 1898–1952.

Calendar of State Papers, Spanish, ed. M.A.S. Hume and Royall Tyler, London, 1862–1954.

Camden, William, *The historie of the most renowned and virtuous Princess Elizabeth, late queen of England*, London, 1630.

Carbery, Earl of: see Vaughan, Richard.

Carpenter, Nathanael, *Architophel, or The picture of a wicked politician*, London, 1638.

Carré, Mayrick H., 'Francis Bacon the "Peremptory Royalist,"' *History Today*, June 1959.

Carroll, Lewis, *Through the Looking-Glass and What Alice found there*, London, 1962.

Cavendish, George, *The Life and Death of Cardinal Wolsey*, in *Two Early Tudor*

Lives, ed. Richard S. Sylvester and Davis P. Harding, New Haven, 1962.

Caxton, William, *Caxton's Mirrour of the world* (1481?), ed. Oliver H. Prior, E.E.T.S., Extra Series vol. 110, London, 1913.

Cecil, Robert, *Letters. . . to Sir George Carew,* ed. John Maclean, Camden Soc., London, 1844.

Cecil, William, *Certain Precepts for the Well Ordering of a Man's Life* (1584) in L.B. Wright, *Advice to a Son,* Ithaca, New York, 1962.

—— *Execution of Justice in England* (1583), ed. Robert M. Kingdom, Ithaca, 1965.

—— *Master Secretarie's Answer to the Earle of Bedford,* London, 1642.

—— *A Memorial for Thomas Cecil* (1561) in L.B. Wright, *Advice to a Son,* Ithaca, New York, 1962.

—— *The State and Dignitie of a Secretarie of Estates Place, with the care and perill thereof,* London, 1642. Also printed in *Harleian Miscellany,* vol. 9 (1809), pp. 282–95.

Chamberlain, John, *Letters. . . during the Reign of Elizabeth,* ed. Sarah Williams, Camden Soc., vol. 9, London, 1861.

Chamberlin, Frederick, *The Sayings of Queen Elizabeth,* London, 1923.

Chapman, Hester W., *Two Tudor Portraits: Henry Howard, Earl of Surrey and Lady Katherine Grey,* London, 1960.

Charlton, Kenneth, *Education in Renaissance England,* London, 1965.

Chase, Wayland J., trans., 'The Distichs of Cato: A famous Medieval Textbook', *University of Wisconsin Studies in the Social Sciences and History,* no. 7, Madison, 1922.

Cherbury, Herbert Lord, *Life of Edward First Lord Herbert of Cherbury,* ed. J.M. Shuttleworth, Oxford, England, 1976.

Chesterfield, Earl of [Philip Dormer Stanhope], *Letters to his Son. . . on the fine art of becoming a man of the world. . .* Washington and London, 1901.

Christopherson, John, *Exhortation to all menne to take hede and beware of rebellion,* London, 1554.

Cicero, Marcus Tullius, (also Francis Bacon & Ralph Waldo Emerson), *Friendship,* Chicago, 1891.

Clapham, John, *Elizabeth of England,* ed. E.P. & C. Read, Philadelphia, 1951.

Cleland, James, *The Institution Of A Young Noble Man,* London, 1607, ed. Max Molyneux, New York, 1948.

Cobbett's Complete Collection of State Trials, vol. I, ed. T.B. Howell, London, 1809.

Cokayne, G.E. *Complete Peerage of England, Scotland, Ireland, etc. . .* vol. I of 13 vols, London, 1910–49.

Colet, John, *A ryght frutefull monycion, cŏcernyng the ordre of a good chrysten mannes lyfe, very profytable for all maner of estates. . .* London, 1534.

Cornwallis, William, *Essayes,* ed. Don Cameron Allen, Baltimore, 1946.

The Court of the most illustrious and most Magnificent James, the first. . . With divers rules, most pure precepts and selected definitions lively delineated, London, 1617.

Craig, Hardin, *The Enchanted Glass: The Elizabethan Mind in Literature,* Oxford,

England, 1950.

Cranmer, Thomas, *Miscellaneous Writings and Letters,* ed. J.E. Cox, Cambridge, England, 1846.

Cressy, David, *Education in Tudor and Stuart England,* London, 1975.

Cruttwell, Patrick, 'Physiology and Psychology in Shakespeare's Age', *Journal of the History of Ideas,* XII, January 1951.

Cunliffe, J.W., 'The Queenes Majesties Entertainment at Woodstocke', *Publications of the Modern Language Association of America,* vol. 26, no. 1, March 1911.

Cyprian, St, *Writings,* vol. II, trans. S. Thelwall, *et al.,* Edinburgh, 1869-70.

Davies, John, *Scourge of Folly* (1611) in *Complete Works,* vol. II, ed. Alexander Grosart, Edinburgh, 1878.

Dekker, Thomas, 'The Bel-man of London', in *Non-Dramatic Works of Thomas Dekker,* 5 vols, ed. Alexander Grosart, vol. 3, London, 1884-86.

Delumeau, Jean, *La peur en Occident, xive-xviiie siècles: une cité assiégée,* Paris, 1978.

DeMolen, Richard L., 'Ages of Admission to Educational Institutions in Tudor and Stuart England', *History of Education,* 1976, vol. 5, no. 3.

—— 'Richard Mulcaster: An Elizabethan Savant', Shakespeare Studies, VIII (1976).

Devereux, Walter B., *Lives and Letters of the Devereux, Earls of Essex in the reigns of Elizabeth, James I, and Charles I, 1540-1646,* 2 vols, London, 1853.

Digges, Dudley, *The Compleat Ambassador: or Two Treaties of the intended marriage of Qu: Elizabeth,* London, 1655.

Dod, John and Cleaver, Robert, *A Plaine and Familiar Exposition of the Ten Commandments* ... London, 1606.

Douglas, Mary, *Natural Symbols: Explorations in Cosmology,* London, 1970.

Ducci, Lorenzo, *Ars avlica or the courtiers arte,* ed. Blount, trans., London, 1607.

du Maurier, Daphne, *Golden Lads: Sir Francis Bacon, Anthony Bacon and Their Friends,* New York, 1975 (London, 1975).

Ecclesiasticus, or The Wisdom of Sirach, in the Bible, trans. Thomas Matthew, London, 1537.

Edwards, Francis, *The Marvellous Chance: Thomas Howard, Fourth Duke of Norfolk and the Ridolphi Plot 1570-72,* London, 1968.

Edwards, Richard, *Damon and Pithias* in *The Dramatic Writings of Richard Edwards, Thomas Norton and Thomas Sackville,* ed. John S. Farmer, New York, 1966.

Einstein, Lewis, *Tudor Ideals,* New York, 1921.

Elizabeth I, *The Letters of Queen Elizabeth,* ed. G.B. Harrison, London, 1935 (1968).

Ellis, Clement, *The Gentle Sinner, or England's Brave Gentleman characterized in a letter to a friend...* Oxford, England, 1660.

Ellis, Henry, *Original letters, illustrative of English history,* 2nd ser., 4 vols, London, 1827.

Elton, G.R., *Policy and Police: Enforcement of the Reformation in the Age of Cromwell,* London, 1972.

—— *Reform and Reformation, England 1509-1558,* Cambridge, Mass., 1977

(London, 1977).

—— 'Tudor Government: The Points of Contact', *Transactions of the Royal Historical Society,* 5th series, 'I Parliament' vol. 24 (1974); 'II The Council' vol. 25 (1975); 'III The Court' vol. 26. (1976).

Elyot, Thomas, *The Book named the Governor,* ed. S.E. Lehmberg, New York, 1962.

—— *The Education or Bringinge up of children* (1533) in Robert D. Pepper, *Four Tudor Books on Education,* Gainesville, Florida, 1966.

—— *Of The Knowledge Which Maketh A Wise Man,* ed. Edwin J. Howard, Oxford, Ohio, 1946.

Emmerson, Richard K., *Antichrist in the Middle Ages,* Seattle, 1981 (Manchester, 1981).

Erasmus, Desiderius, *The Education of a Christian Prince,* trans. Lester K. Born, New York, 1936.

—— *The Epistles of,* trans. F.M. Nicholas, 3 vols, London 1901–18.

Erikson, Kai, 'Living in a World without Stable Points of Reference', *World Issues,* December 1976–January 1977, vol. 1, no. 2.

Esler, Anthony, *The Aspiring Mind of the Elizabethan Younger Generation,* Durham, N.C., 1966.

Evans, Bergen, *The Psychiatry of Robert Burton,* New York, 1944.

'An Exhortation Concerning Good order, and Obedience to Rulers and Magistrates' (1574), in *Certain Sermons Appointed by the Queen's Majesty . . .* ed. George E. Corrie, Cambridge, England, 1850.

Feng, Helen C., 'Devil's Letters: Their History and Significance in Church and Society 1100–1500'. Unpublished doctoral dissertation, Northwestern University, August 1982.

Fenner, Dudley, *The Artes of Logike and Rethorike, plainelie set foorth in the Englishe tounge, easie to be learned and practised:. . .* (1584) in Robert D. Pepper, *Four Tudor Books on Education,* Gainesville, Florida, 1966.

Fiston, Thomas, 'Preface' to William Caxton, *The Ancient History of the Destruction of Troy,* London, 1596.

Foxe, John, *Actes and Monuments,* ed. George Townsend, 8 vols, London, 1843–49.

Froude, James A., *History of England from the fall of Wolsey to the Defeat of the Spanish Armada,* 12 vols, New York, 1877.

Fuller, Thomas, 'The Favourite', in *The Holy State and the Profane State,* London, 1840.

—— *The History of the Worthies of England,* 2 vols, London, 1811.

Gardiner, Stephen, *A Declaration of suche true Articles as George Joye hath gone about to confute as false,* London, 1546.

—— *The Letters of Stephen Gardiner,* ed. James A. Muller, Cambridge, England, 1933.

—— *Obedience in church and state,* ed. P. Janelle, Cambridge, England, 1930.

Geertz, Clifford, 'Centers, Kings, and Charisma: Reflections on the Symbolics of Power', in *Culture and Its Creators; Essays in honor of Edward Shile,* ed. Joseph

Ben-David and Terry Nichols Clark, Chicago, 1977.

Giovanni, della Casa, *Galateo or the Book of Manners,* trans. R.S. Pinne-Coffin, London, 1958.

Godwin, Joscelyn, *Robert Fludd, Hermetic Philosopher and Surveyor of Two Worlds,* Boulder, Colorado, 1979 (London, 1979).

Good Advice to a Governour, in *Queen Elizabethe's Achademy* . . . ed. F.J. Furnivall, E.E.T.S., Extra Series VIII (1869).

Gottfried, Robert S., *Epidemic Disease in Fifteenth Century England: the Medieval Response and the Demographic Consequences,* New Brunswick, New Jersey, 1978 (Leicester, 1978).

Gouge, William, *The Works of William Gouge,* 2 vols, London, 1627.

Greaves, Richard L., *Society and Religion in Elizabethan England,* Minneapolis, 1981.

Greenblatt, Stephen, *Renaissance Self-fashioning: From More to Shakespeare,* Chicago, 1980.

Greene, Robert, *Groats-worth of Witte, bought with a million of Repentance,* (1592), ed. G.B. Harrison, London, 1923.

—— *James the Fourth,* in *The Dramatic and Poetical Works of Robert Greene and George Peel,* ed. Alexandre Dyce, London, 1883.

—— *The Life and Complete Works in Prose and Verse of Robert Greene,* in 12 vols, ed. Alexander B. Grosart, London, 1881–83.

Greenham, Richard, *Grave counsels, and Godlie Observations. . .* in *The Works,* London, 1601.

Hale, David G., *The Body Politic: A Political Metaphor in Renaissance English Literature,* The Hague, 1971.

Halifax, George Savile, Marquess of, 'Advice to a Daughter', in *The Complete Works,* ed. Walter Raleigh, Oxford, England, 1912.

Hall, Edward, *The Union of the Two Noble and illustre famelies of Lancastre & Yorke,* London, 1548.

Hall, Joseph, *Heaven upon earth, and Characters of vertues and vices,* ed. Rudolf Kirk, New Brunswick, N.J., 1948.

Handover, P.M., *The Second Cecil, The Rise to Power 1563-1604 of Sir Robert Cecil, later first Earl of Salisbury,* London, 1959.

Harington, John, *The Epigrams of Sir John Harington,* ed. Norman E. McClure, Philadelphia, 1926.

—— *Nugae Antiquae: being a Miscellaneous Collection of Original Papers* . . . in 2 vols, ed. Thomas Park, London, 1804.

Harrison, G.B., *The Life and Death of Robert Devereux,* London, 1937.

Haynes, Samuel and Murdin, William, *A Collection of State Papers relating to Affairs in the Reigns of King Henry VIII, King Edward VI, Queen Mary and Queen Elizabeth from the years 1542-1570. . . left by William Cecill Lord Burghley,* London, 1740.

Henry VIII, *The Letters of King Henry VIII,* ed. Muriel St Clare Byrne, London, 1968.

Herbert, George, *The Temple* (1633) in *Works,* ed. G.H. Palmer, Boston, 1905.

Hicks, L., *An Elizabethan Problem, Some Aspects of the Careers of Two Exile-Adventurers,* New York, 1964.

—— *The Strange Case of Dr William Parry, The Career of an Agent-Provocateur, Studies,* 1948.

Higford, William, *The Institution of a Gentleman, or Advice to His Grandson,* London, 1660.

Hill, Christopher, *Antichrist in Seventeenth-Century England,* London, 1971.

Hill, Thomas, *The Moste pleasaunte Arte of the Interpretacion of Dreames, whereunto is annexed sundry Problemes with apte aunsweares...* London, 1576.

Historical Manuscript Commission. *Calendar of the Manuscripts of the Marquis of Salisbury preserved at Hatfield House, Hertfordshire,* parts 1–24, London, 1883–1976.

—— *Report on the Manuscripts of Lord Middleton Preserved at Wollaton Hall, Nottinghamshire,* London, 1911.

Hoby, Margaret, *Diary of Lady Margaret Hoby 1599-1605,* ed. Dorothy M. Meads, London, 1930.

Hoby, Thomas, trans., *The Book of the Courtier* (1561), ed. Drayton Henderson, New York, 1948.

Hofstadter, Richard, *The Paranoid Style in American Politics and Other Essays,* New York, 1952 (Vintage Book, 1962).

Holinshed, Raphael, *Hollinshed's Chronicles of England, Scotland and Ireland,* in 6 vols, London, 1807–1808.

'An Homily against Disobedience and Wilful Rebellion' (1574) in *Certain Sermons Appointed by the Queen's Majesty...,* ed. George E. Corrie, Cambridge, England, 1850.

Hooker, Richard, *Of The Laws of Ecclesiastical Polity,* in *The Works of Richard Hooker,* 4 vols, ed. W. Speed Hill, Cambridge, Mass., 1977.

Hoopes, Robert, *Right Reason in the English Renaissance,* Cambridge, Mass., 1962.

Houghton, Walter E., 'The English Virtuoso in the Seventeenth Century', Part I, *The Journal of the History of Ideas,* III (Jan. 1942).

Howell, Wilbur S., *Logic and Rhetoric in England, 1500-1700,* New York, 1961.

Hughes, Philip, *The Reformation in England,* 3 vols, London, 1954.

Hume, Martin, *The Great Lord Burghley; a study in Elizabethan Statecraft,* New York, 1968.

—— *Treason and Plot: Struggles for Catholic Supremacy in the Last Years of Queen Elizabeth,* London, 1901.

Hurstfield, Joel, *The Queen's Wards: Wardship and Marriage Under Elizabeth I,* Cambridge, Mass., 1958 (London, 1973).

The Institucion of a Gentleman, London, 1568.

Jahoda, Gustav, *The Psychology of Superstition,* London, 1969.

James I, *Correspondence... with Sir Robert Cecil and others... with an Appendix containing papers illustrative of translations between King James and Robert Earl of Essex,* ed. John Bruce, Camden Soc., London, 1861.

James VI, *The Basilicon Doron,* ed. James Craigie, 2 vols, London, 1944.

James, Mervyn, 'English Politics and the Concept of Honour 1485–1642', *Past and Present Supplements,* no. 3, 1978.

Jardine, David, *Criminal Trials,* 2 vols, London, 1832.

Jennings, Eugene E, *Routes to the Executive Suite,* New York, 1971.

John, Lisle C., 'Roger Manning, Elizabethan Courtier', *Huntington Library Quarterly,* vol. 12, November 1948.

Jonson, Ben, *Eastward Ho,* in *The Complete Plays,* vol. II, ed. G.A. Wilkes, Oxford, England, 1981.

—— *Every Man in His Humour,* in *The Complete Plays.* vol. I.

—— *Every Man out of His Humour,* (1600), in *The Complete Plays,* vol. I.

—— *Timber or Discoveries,* ed. Ralph S. Walker, Syracuse, New York, 1953 (London, 1976).

Jordan, W.K., *Edward VI: The Young King, the Protectorship of the Duke of Somerset,* Cambridge, Mass., 1968.

Joseph, B.L., *Shakespeare's Eden: The Commonwealth of England 1558-1629,* London, 1971.

Julius, Philip, 'Diary of the Journey of Philip Julius, duke of Stettin-Pomerania, through England in the Year 1602', *Transactions of the Royal Historical Society,* New Series, VI (1892).

Kaulek, Jean, *Correspondance Politique de MM de Castillon et de Marillac,* (1527–1542), Paris, 1885.

Kelso, Ruth, *The Doctrine of the English Gentleman in the Sixteenth Century,* Urbana, Ill, 1929.

Kempe, William, *The Education of Children in Learning,* (1588), in Robert D. Pepper, *Four Tudor Books on Education,* Gainesville, Florida, 1966.

Kinsman, Robert S., '"The Proverbes of Salmon Do Playnly Declare": a Sententious Poem on Wisdom and Governance, ascribed to Sir Francis Bryan', *Huntington Library Quarterly,* autumn 1979.

Krauthammer, Charles, 'The Humanist Phantom', *The New Republic,* July 25, 1981.

Lacey, Robert, *Robert Earl of Essex, An Elizabethan Icarus,* London, 1971.

Langston, Beach, 'Essex and the Art of Dying', *The Huntington Library Quarterly,* no. 2, February 1950.

Lasch, Christopher, *The Culture of Narcissism,* New York, 1979 (London, 1980).

Lathrop, Henry B., 'Translations from the Classics into English from Caxton to Chapman 1477–1620', *University of Wisconsin Studies,* no. 35, Madison, 1933.

Laurentius, M. Andreas, *A Discourse of the Preservation of the Sight: of Melancholike diseases; of Rheumes, and of Old age,* trans. Richard Surphlet, London, 1599.

Lawson, John and Silver, Harold, *A Social History of Education in England,* London, 1973.

Leach, Arthur F., *English Schools At The Reformation 1546-8,* Westminster, 1896.

Letters and Papers, Foreign and Domestic, of the Reign of Henry VIII, 21 vols, ed.

J. Gairdner and R.H. Brodie, London, 1862–1910.

Lewis, C.S., *The Discarded Image, An Introduction to Medieval and Renaissance Literature,* Cambridge, England, 1964.

Ling, Nicholas, *Politeuphuia, Wits Commonwealth,* London, 1597.

Lisle Letters, 6 vols, ed. Muriel St Clare Byrne, Chicago, 1981 (London, 1983).

Loades, D.M., *The Reign of Mary Tudor: Politics, government, and religion in England, 1553-1558,* New York, 1979 (London, 1979).

—— *Two Tudor Conspiracies,* Berkeley, 1965.

Lovejoy, Arthur O., *The Great Chain of Being: A Study of the History of an Idea,* Cambridge, Mass., 1936.

Lyly, John, *Campaspe,* (1584), in A.K. McIlwraith, *Five Elizabethan Comedies,* Oxford, England, 1934.

Lyons, Bridget G., *Voices of Melancholy: Studies in literary treatments of melancholy in Renaissance England,* London, 1971.

McAlindon, T., *Shakespeare and Decorum,* New York, 1973.

MacCaffrey, Wallace T., 'Place and Patronage in Elizabethan Politics' in *Elizabethan Government and Society,* ed. S.T. Bindoff, London, 1961.

—— *Queen Elizabeth and the Making of Policy 1572-1588,* Princeton, 1981.

—— *The Shaping of the Elizabethan Regime,* Princeton, 1972.

Machin, Lewis [and Markham, Gervase], *The Dumb Knight* (1608) in *A Select Collection of Old English Plays, originally published by Robert Dodsley in the year 1744,* vol. 5, ed. W. Carew Haslitt, New York, 1874–1876 (1964).

McIntosh, Marjorie K., 'The Fall of a Tudor Gentle Family: The Cookes of Gidea Hall, Essex, 1579-1629', *Huntington Library Quarterly,* vols 41–42 (1977–79).

McKeon, Richard, 'Rhetoric in the Middle Ages', *Speculum,* XVII (1942).

Maclean, John, *Life of Sir Thomas Seymour,* London, 1900.

Madox, Richard, *An Elizabethan in 1582: The Diary of Richard Madox, Fellow of All Souls,* ed. Elizabeth S. Donno, Hakluyt Soc., 2nd series, vol. 147, London, 1976.

Maisse, André Hurault, Sieur de, *Journal,* (1597), trans. G.B. Harrison and R.A. Jones, London, 1931.

Manning, Roger B., 'The Origins of the Doctrine of Sedition', *Albion,* vol. 12, summer 1980.

Marlowe, Christopher, *Tamburlaine the Great,* ed. U.M. Ellis-Fermor, New York, 1930 (1966).

Marston, John, *The Malcontent,* (1604), ed. G.B. Harrison, London, 1933.

Martyn, William, *Youths Instruction,* London, 1612.

Mason, John E., *Gentlefolk in the Making: Studies in the History of English Courtesy Literature and Related Topics from 1531-1774,* Philadelphia, 1935.

Mathew, David, *The Celtic Peoples and Renaissance Europe: A Study in the Celtic and Spanish Influences on Elizabethan History,* New York, 1974.

Matter, Joseph Allen, *My Lords and Lady of Essex: Their State Trials,* Chicago, 1969.

Mills, Laurens J., *One Soul in Bodies Twain: Friendship in Tudor Literature and Stuart Drama*, Bloomington, Indiana, 1937.

Milne, A.A., *Winnie-the-Pooh*, New York, 1961 (London, 1926).

Milton, John, *Paradise Lost*, (1667) in *English Masterpieces*, ed. Maynard Mack, New York, 1950.

Montaigne, Michel de, *The Essays of* . . . vol. II of 3 vols, trans. and ed. Jacob Zeitlin, New York, 1934.

More, Thomas, *The Apology*, (1583) in *The Complete Works of St Thomas More*, vol. 9, ed. J.B. Trapp, New Haven, 1979.

—— *The History of King Richard III*, in *The Complete Works of St Thomas More*, vol. 2, ed. Richard S. Sylvester, New Haven, 1963.

—— *Latin Epigrams*, ed. Leicester Bradner & Charles Lynch, Chicago, 1953.

—— *Utopia*, in *The Complete Works of St Thomas More*, vol. 4, ed. Edward Surtz and J.A. Hexter, New Haven, 1965.

Morysine [Morison], Richarde, *An Exhortation to styrre all Englyshe men to the defence of theyr countreye*, London, 1539.

Mulcaster, Richard, *The first Part of the Elementarie which entreateth chefelie of the right writing of our English Tung* (1582), ed. E.T. Campagnac, Oxford, England, 1925.

—— *Positions wherein those primitive circumstances be examined which are necessarie for the training up of children* . . . (1581), ed. Richard DeMolen, New York, 1971.

Muller, James A., *Stephen Gardiner and The Tudor Reaction*, London, 1926.

Mun, Thomas, *England's Treasure by Forraign Trade*, New York, 1895.

Murdin, William — see Haynes and Murdin.

Murphy, Terence R., 'The Maintenance of Order in Early Tudor Kent 1509–1559'. Unpublished doctoral dissertation, Northwestern University, June 1975.

Nashe, Thomas, *The Anatomie of Absurditie* (1589), vol. I of 5 vols in *The Works of Thomas Nashe*, ed. Ronald B. McKerrow, London, 1910.

—— *Christ's Tears over Jerusalem*, vol. II in *The Works*.

—— *A Countercuffe to Martin Junior* (1589), vol. II in *The Works*.

—— *Pierce Penilesse, His Supplication to the Divell*, (1592), ed. G.B. Harrison, London, 1924.

Naunton, Robert, *Fragmenta Regalia: Memoirs of Elizabeth, her Court and Favourites*, London, 1824.

Neale, John, *Elizabeth I and her Parliaments 1584-1601*, London, 1957.

Newdigate-Newdegate, Lady, *Gossip from A Muniment Room, being passages in the lives of Anne and Mary Fytton 1574-1618*, London, 1897.

Nichols, J.G., *Literary Remains of King Edward VI*, 2 vols, Roxburghe Club, 1857.

Noble, Richmond, *Shakespeare's Biblical Knowledge*, London, 1935 (1969).

North, George, trans., *The Philosopher of the Court, written by Philbert of Vienne in Champaigne*, London, 1575.

North, Thomas, trans., *The Dial of Princes compiled by the reverend father in God, Don Antony of Guevara* . . . London, 1582.

—— trans., *The Lives of the Noble Grecians and Romanes compared together by that grave learned Philosopher and Historiographer, Plutarke of Chaeronea*, London, 1579.

Northumberland, Earl of — see Percy, Henry.

Nott, G.F., *The Works of Henry Howard Earl of Surrey and of Sir Thomas Wyatt the Elder*, vol. II of 2 vols, London, 1815–16.

Ong, Walter J., 'Agonistic Structures in Academia: Past to Present', *Interchange*, vol. 5, no. 4, 1974; Ontario Institute for Studies in Education.

—— *Rhetoric, Romance, and Technology: Studies in the Interaction of Expression and Culture*, Ithaca, New York, 1971.

Original Letters Relative to the English Reformation 1531-58, 2 vols, ed. Hastings Robinson, London, 1846–47.

Orsini, Napoleone, '"Policy" or the Language of Elizabethan Machiavellianism', *Journal of the Warburg and Courtauld Institute*, vol. 9 (1946).

Osborne, Francis, *Advice to a Son* in L.B. Wright, *Advice to a Son*, Ithaca, New York, 1962.

Paice, Richard, *Howe one may take profit of his Enemyes*, London, 1533 (?).

—— *To chose: The Maner to chose and cherysshe a frende*, London, 1533(?).

Parker, Geoffrey, *Philip II*, Boston, 1978.

Parker, Matthew, *Correspondence*, ed. John Bruce and Thomas T. Perowne, Cambridge, England, 1853.

Patch, H.R., *The other World According to Descriptions in Medieval Literature*, Cambridge, Mass., 1950.

Peacham, Henry, *The Complete Gentleman* . . . ed. Virgil B. Heltzel, Ithaca, New York, 1962.

—— *The garden of eloquence conteyning the figures of grammer and rhetoric from whence maye bee gathered all manner of flowers, coulors, ornaments, exortations, formes and fashions of speech* . . . London, 1577.

—— *The Truth of Our Time: Revealed out of One Man's Experience by Way of Essay*, (1638), ed. Virgil B. Heltzel, Ithaca, New York, 1962.

Pepper, Robert D., ed., *Four Tudor Books on Education*, Gainesville, Florida, 1966.

Percy, Henry, *Advice to His Son*, ed. G.B. Harrison, London, 1930.

Perlin, Étienne, *Description des royaulmes d'Angleterre et d'Escosse . . . par 1558*, London, 1775. A slightly different version under the name of Stephen Perlin can be found in *The Antiquarian Repertory*, vol. IV, London, 1809.

Petrey, R.C., *Christian Eschatology and Social Thought*, New York, 1956.

Petty, William, *Tracts chiefly relating to Ireland*, Dublin, 1769.

Philip, John, *The Commodye of pacient and meeke Grissill*, ed. R.B. McKerrow, Malone Society Reprints, London, 1909.

Pierce, William, *An Historical Introduction to the Marprelate Tracts*, New York, 1909.

Plimpton, George A., *The Education of Shakespeare: Illustrated from the Schoolbooks in Use in his Time*, London, 1933.

Pollard, A.F., *England under Protector Somerset*, London, 1900.

Ponet, John, *A Shorte Treatise of politike power, and of the true Obedience, which subiectes owe to kynges and other Governours* ... Strasburg, 1556.

Powell, Thomas, *Tom of all Trades; or, the Plaine-way to Preferment,* London, 1631.

Practical Wisdom or the Manual of life, the Counsels of Eminent Men to their children, London, 1824.

Puttenham, George, *The Arte of English Poesie,* (1589), ed. Gladys D. Willcock and Alice Walker, Cambridge, England, 1936.

Radding, Charles, 'Superstition to Science: Nature, Fortune and the Passing of the Medieval Ordeal', *American Historical Review,* vol. 84, October 1978.

Rainolde [Reynolds], Richard, *The Foundacion of Rhetorike,* ed. Francis R. Johnson, New York, 1945.

Raleigh, Walter, 'The Cabinet-council', in *The Works,* vol. VIII, (Burt Franklin Reprints), New York, n. d.

—— *Instructions to His Son and to Posterity,* (1632), in L.B. Wright, *Advice to a Son,* Ithaca, New York, 1962.

—— 'Maxims of State', in *The Works,* vol. VIII.

Read, Conyers, *Lord Burghley and Queen Elizabeth,* London, 1960.

—— *Mr Secretary Cecil and Queen Elizabeth,* London, 1955.

Recorde, Robert, *The Ground of Artes: Teaching the worke and practice of Arithmetike, both in whole numbres and Fractions,* London, 1561.

Rhodes, Hugh, *The boke of Nurture and schoole of good maners for men, servants, and children* in *Babees Book,* ed. F.J. Furnivall, E.E.T.S. XXXII, London, 1868.

Rickert, Edith, *The Babee's Book: Medieval Manners for the Young: Done into modern English from Dr Furnivall's Text,* New York, 1908.

Ridley, Jasper, *Thomas Cranmer,* Oxford, England, 1962.

Rieff, Philip, *Freud, The Mind of the Moralist,* Chicago, 1959, 1961, 1979.

Ringer, Robert J., *Winning Through Intimidation,* Los Angeles, 1973.

Roper, William, *The Life of Sir Thomas More,* in *Two Early Tudor Lives,* ed. Richard S. Sylvester & Davis P. Harding, New Haven, 1962.

Rossetti, William, *Early Italian and German Books of Courtesy* in *Queene Elizabethes Achademy* ... ed. F.J. Furnivall, E.E.T.S. Extra Series, VIII, London, 1869.

Rowlands, Samuel, *A New Yeeres Gift, The Courte of Civill Courtesie: Fitly furnished with a plesant porte of stately phrases and pithie precepts: assembled in the behalfe of all younge gentlemen...* London, 1582.

Rye, William B., *England as seen by foreigners in the days of Elizabeth and James the first,* London, 1865.

Sadler, Ralph, *The State Papers and Letters,* 2 vols, ed. A. Clifford, Edinburgh, 1809.

Sanders, Nicholas, 'Report to Cardinal Morini on the change of religion in 1558–59', ed. F.A. Gasquet, *Catholic Record Society,* I, 1904–1905.

Sargent, Ralph M., *The Life and Lyrics of Sir Edward Dyer,* Oxford, England, 1968.

Scarisbrick, J.J., *Henry VIII,* Berkeley, 1968 (London, 1968).

Scot, Patrik, *A Fathers Advice or Last Will to his Sonne,* London, 1620.

Sebon, Raymon [Raymundus de Sabunde], *La Theologie Naturelle,* trans. into French by Ian Martin, Paris, 1566. (Original Latin edition, 1480.)

Segar, William, *The Booke of Honor and Armes. Wherein is discoursed the causes of Quarrell, and the nature of Iniuries, with their repulses*, London, 1590.

Seigel, Jerrold E., *Rhetoric and Philosophy in Renaissance Humanism* ... Princeton, 1968.

Sennett, Richard, *Fall of Public Man*, New York, 1974.

Seybolt, Robert F., trans., *Renaissance Student Life: the Paedologia of Petrus Mosellanus*, Champaigne, Ill, 1927.

Seymour, William, *Ordeal by Ambition, An English family in the shadow of the Tudors*, New York, 1973.

Shakespeare, William, *Henry V*.

—— *Henry VIII*.

—— *Richard II*.

Shapiro, David, *Neurotic Styles*, The Austin Riggs Center Monograph Series no. 5, New York, 1965.

Sherry, Richard, *A Treatise of Schemes and Tropes*, London, 1550.

Shils, Edward A., *The Torment of Secrecy: The Background and Consequences of American Security Policies*, Glencoe, Ill, 1956.

Sidney, Henry, *Letters and Memorials of State . . . written and collected by Sir Henry Sydney, Sir Philip Sidney, Sir Robert Sydney, Robert, 2nd Earl of Leicester and Philip Lord Viscount Lisle . . . from the original at Penshurst Place in Kent*, 2 vols, ed. Arthur Collins, London, 1746.

Sidney, Philip, *An apology for poetry; or, the defence of poesy*, ed. Geoffrey Shepherd, London, 1965.

Simon, Joan, *Education and Society in Tudor England*, Cambridge, England, 1966.

Skelton, John, *Magnificence*, in *The Complete Poems of John Skelton*, ed. Philip Henderson, London, 1931.

Smith, Lacey Baldwin, 'Christ, What a Fright; the Tudor Portrait as an Icon', *Journal of Interdisciplinary History*, vol. IV (1), summer 1973.

—— *Elizabeth Tudor: Portrait of a Queen*, London, 1976.

—— *The Elizabethan World*, Boston, 1972 (published as *The Elizabethan Epic*, London, 1966).

—— *Henry VIII: The Mask of Royalty*, Boston, 1973 (London, 1971).

Smith, Thomas, *The Common-welth of England, and maner of Government Thereof*, London, 1589.

Smyth, John, *Lives of the Berkeleys 1066-1618*, 3 vols, ed. John Maclean, Gloucester, 1883.

Somers tracts, A collection of scarce and valuable Tracts . . . particularly of . . . the late Lord Somers, ed. Walter Scott, 13 vols, London, 1809–15.

Spivack, Bernard, *Shakespeare and the Allegory of Evil: The History of a Metaphor in Relation to his Major Villains*, New York, 1958.

Stapleton, Thomas, *The Life and Illustrious Martyrdom of Sir Thomas More*, trans. P.E. Hallet, London, 1928.

Starkey, David, 'Representation Through Intimacy', in *Symbols and Sentiments:*

Cross-cultural Studies in Symbolism, ed. Joan Lewis, London, 1977.

Starkey, Thomas, *A Dialogue Between Reginald Pole and Thomas Lupset*, ed. Kathleen M. Burton, London, 1948.

State Papers during the Reign of Henry VIII, vol. II of XI vols, London, 1830–52.

The Statutes of the Realm, XI vols, London, 1819 (1963).

Stone, Lawrence, *The Crisis of the Aristocracy 1558-1641*, Oxford, England, 1965.

—— 'The Educational Revolution in England 1560–1640', *Past and Present*, no. 28, July 1964.

—— *The Family, Sex and Marriage in England 1500-1800*, New York, 1977 (London, 1977).

Storr, Anthony, 'The Man', in *Churchill Revised: A Cultural Assessment*, New York, 1969.

Stow, John, *The Survey of London* (1603), Everyman's Library, London, n. d.

Strauss, Gerald, 'The State of Pedagogical Theory c. 1530: What Protestant Reformers Knew about Education', in *Schooling and Society: Studies in the History of Education*, ed. Lawrence Stone, Baltimore, 1976.

Strype, John, *Annals of the Reformation and Establishment of Religion in the Church of England during Queen Elizabeth's Happy Reign*, 3 vols in 6 parts, Oxford, England, 1824.

—— *Ecclesiastical Memorials*, 3 vols in 6 parts, Oxford, England, 1822.

Sutton, Christopher, *Disce vivere. Learne to live; a briefe forme of learning to live, wherein is shewed that the life of Christ is the most perfect patterne of direction to the life of a Christian...* London, 1604.

Swanson, Phyllis M., 'Popular Literature in the Eighteenth Century: the Dicey Chapbooks'. Unpublished Northwestern University doctoral dissertation, June 1985.

Taverner, Richard, *Flores Aliquot Sententiarum ex varies: the flowers of Sencies gathered out of sundry writers by Erasmus in Latine*, London, 1547.

—— *The Garden of Wisdom wherein ye maye gather moste pleasant flowres, that is to say, proper wytty and quycke sayenges of princes, philosophers, and dyvers other sortes of men*, London, 1539.

—— *Proverbes or Adagies gathered of the Chiliades of Erasmus*, London, 1545.

Taylor, Henry Osborn, *The English Mind: Thought and Expression in the Sixteenth Century*, New York, 1962.

Thomas, Keith, *Religion and the Decline of Magic*, New York, 1971 (London, 1971).

Thompson, Craig R., 'Erasmian Humanism', in *Society and History in the Renaissance*, Washington, 1960.

—— *The Translations of Lucian by Erasmus and St Thomas More*, Ithaca, New York, 1940.

Tillyard, E.M.W., *The Elizabethan World Picture*, New York, 1960 (London, 1972).

Tipping, W., *The Father's Counsell; or Certain Useful Directions, for all Young Persons... whose portion it is... to be left in a fatherless or friendlesse condition*, (London, 1643) Harl. Misc., IX (1812).

Tomaschek, R., 'Great Earthquakes and the Astronomical Position of Uranus', *Nature, A Weekly Journal of Science,* vols 184 pp. 177–78 and 186 pp. 236–38.

Tourneur, Cyril, *The revengers tragaedie,* in *The Works of Cyril Tourneur,* ed. Allardyce Nicholl, London, 1930.

Tyndale, William, *Obedience of a Christian Man,* in *Doctrinal Treatise and Introductions to Different Portions of the Holy Scripture,* ed. Henry Walter, Parker Society, Cambridge, England, 1848.

—— *The Parable of the Wicked Mammon,* (1527) in *Doctrinal Treatise.*

Tytler, Patrick F., *England under the Reigns of Edward VI and Mary. . . A Series of Original letters,* 2 vols, London, 1839.

Udall, Nicolas, *Apophthegmes, that is to saye, prompte, quicke, wittie and sentencious saiynges of certain Emperors, Kinges, Captaines, Philosophiers and Oratours. . . gathered and compiled in Latine by. . . Erasmus,* London, 1542.

—— *Respublica, an Interlude for Christmas 1553,* ed. W.W. Greg, E.E.T.S. Original Series no. 226, London, 1952.

Ustick, W. Lee, 'Advice to a son: A Type of Seventeenth-Century Conduct Book', *Studies in Philology,* XXIX, no. 3, July 1932.

Vatter, Hannes, *The Devil in English Literature,* Bern, Switzerland, 1978.

Vaughan, Richard, 2nd Earl of Carbery, 'Advice to his Son [Francke]',(1651), ed. Virgil B. Heltzel, *Huntington Library Bulletin,* no. 11, April 1937.

Vaughan, William, *The Golden Grove,* in William F. Marquardt, 'The Golden Grove, by Sir William Vaughan: A Critical Edition.' Unpublished doctoral dissertation, Northwestern University, February 1949.

Venn, John and Venn, J.A., *The Book of Matriculations and Degrees: a Catalogue of those who have been matriculated or been admitted to any degree in the University of Cambridge from 1544-1659,* Cambridge, England, 1912.

Vives, Juan L., *A Very Fruitful and Pleasant Boke called the Instruction of a Christian Woman,* London, 1547.

Walpole, Richard, (?) *The Discoverie and Confutation of a tragical fiction, devysed and played by Edward Squyer. . . ,* March 1, 1599.

Walsingham, Edward, *A Practical Guide for Ambitious Politicians,* ed. Gordon Tullock, Columbia, S.C., 1961.

Walsingham, Francis, 'Anatomizing of Honesty, Ambition and Fortitude', (1590), in *Somers Tracts,* vol. I, pp. 499–502.

Warnings and Counsels for Noblemen (1577) in *Queene Elizabethes Achademy . . .* ed. F.J. Furnivall, E.E.T.S. Extra Series, VIII, London, 1869.

Watson, Foster, *The Old Grammar Schools,* Cambridge, England, 1916.

—— *Vives: On Education. A Translation of the De Tradendis Disciplinis of Juan Luis Vives,* Cambridge, 1913.

Webster, John, *The Duchess of Malfi,* in *The Complete Works,* in 4 vols, ed. F.L. Lucas, vol. II, London, 1927.

—— *The White Devil,* in *The Complete Works,* vol. I.

The Welspring of wittie Conceites. . . by W. Phist, student, London, 1584.

Wentworth, William, 'Advice to his Son', *Wentworth Papers 1597-1629,* ed. J.P. Cooper, Camden Society, 4th series, vol. 12, London, 1973.

West, Robert H., *Shakespeare & the Outer Mystery,* Lexington, Kentucky, 1968.

Whitney, Geoffrey, *A Choice of Emblemes,* ed. Henry Green, London, 1866.

Whittinton, Robert, *Vulgaria: Grammaticulorum institutio,* (London, 1520), ed. Beatrice White, E.E.T.S. Original Series, 3187, London, 1932.

Whythorne, Thomas, *The Autobiography of Thomas Whythorne,* ed. James M. Osborn, Oxford, England, 1961.

Williams, C.H., *The Making of Tudor Despotism,* rev. ed., London, 1935.

Williams, Neville, *Elizabeth the first Queen of England,* New York, 1968.

—— *Thomas Howard fourth Duke of Norfolk,* London, 1964.

Willobie His Avisa (1594), ed. G.B. Harrison, London, 1926.

Wilson, Thomas, *The Arte of Rhetorique,* (1553), ed. Robert H. Bowers, Gaineville, Florida, 1962.

Wilson, Thomas, *The State of England,* ed. F.J. Fisher, Camden Society, series 3, vol. LII, London, 1936.

Winchester, Lord William Marquess of, *The Lord Marques Idlenes: Conteining manifold matters of acceptable devise; as sage sentences. . . No lesse pleasant to peruse, than profitable to practise,* London, 1586.

Winwood, Ralph, *Memorials of Affairs of State in the Reigns of Q. Elizabeth and K. James I,* 3 vols, London, 1727.

Woodward, William Harrison, *Desiderius Erasmus Concerning the Aim and Method of Education,* New York, 1964.

Wotton, Henry, *Reliquiae Wottonianae or A Collection of Lives, Letters, Poems . . .* London, 1651.

Wright, Louis B, *Advice to a Son: Precepts of Lord Burghley, Sir Walter Raleigh and Frances Osborne,* Ithaca, New York, 1962.

—— *Middle-class Culture in Elizabethan England,* Chapel Hill, N.C., 1935.

Zeitlin, Jacob, 'Commonplaces in Elizabethan Life and Letters', *Journal of English and Germanic Philology,* XIX, (1920).

Zubly, John, *The Law of Liberty,* Philadelphia, 1775.

INDEX

advice literature, 40–58, 115, 274–75, 283 n. 10, 286 n. 65, n. 73

Allen, Cardinal William, 63, 189; and English paranoia, 178; on spying, 161–62; and the succession, 183; *A True, Sincere and Modest Defence of English Catholics*, 65–66

Altman, Joel, 112

anabaptists, 62

Antichrist:see Satan

Aphthonius: *Progymnasmata*, 99, 107–108

Arendt, Hannah, 138

Ascham, Roger, 75, 87, 88, 89, 91n., 102; *The Schoolmaster*, 289 n. 15, 290 n. 25, 293 n. 89

Ashton, Rev. Abdy, 247, 271

Audley, Thomas, 150

Azores expedition, 215–16

Bacon, Anne, 43, 214

Bacon, Anthony, 43, 161; and Essex, 207–209, 209, 214

Bacon, Francis, 269; account of the Essex rebellion, 240–47; and cosmology, 120, 128; on the court, 152; and Essex, 207–209, 211, 211–12, 215, 226, 258, 260, 303 n. 45; on evil ministers, 175; on kingship, 174–75; and paranoia, 43, 48; on political success, 54, 152–53, 154–55, 198; on retirement from court, 170–71; on rhetoric, 111; on role playing, 90; on rumours, 136; on spying, 162

Baldwin, William, 125; *Mirror of Magistrates*, 44, 124; and paranoia, 43, 48, 121; *Treatise of Morall Philosophie*, 40, 57, 83, 85, 106, 131, 285 n. 45, 291 n. 48, 305 n. 91

Barclay, Alexander: *The Miseryes of Courtiers and Courtes*, 287 n. 84, 300–301 n. 6

Barreul, Abbé, 38

Barrow, Isaac: 'Of Industry in our Particular Calling, as Gentlemen', 293 n. 93

Basset, Jane, 161

Beale, Robert, 186, 287 n. 89; 'A Treatise of the office of a Councellor and Principall Secretarie', 54–56

Becon, Thomas: *The Catechism*, 289 n. 2

Bedford, (Edward Russell) Earl of, 54

Berkley, Richard, 257

Blount, Christopher, 228, 237–38, 242, 243, 244, 249, 272

Boaistuau, Peter: *Theatre of the World*, 290 n. 17

Bodley, Thomas, 211

Bonde, John, 143

Bonner, Bishop Edmund, 182

Botolf [Buttoliff], Gregory, 5–11, 16, 19, 30, 32, 146, 147, 161, 250, 285 n. 48; background, 5–6, 94; conspiracy of, 4, 7–11, 13

Bradford, John, 63

Breme, Thomas: *Mirrour of Friendship*, 47

Breton, Nicholas, 47–48, 49, 57, 59, 134, 135, 138, 143, 165, 197, 255

Brinsley, John, 82, 111

Brooke, Henry Lord Cobham, 215, 217, 230, 245, 261, 262, 269, 272

Brown, Oliver, 7, 8

Browne, John, 10, 11

Bryan, Francis: *A Dispraise of the Life of a Courtier,* 49, 53

Buckingham, Dukes of: see Stafford

Burton, Robert, 190, 217

Bury, John, 87

Byrne, Muriel St Clare, 31

Cadiz expedition, 210, 213–15

Calais, 4, 6–10, 13

Camden, William, 197, 268, 315 n. 61

Campion, Edmund, 64

Carbery, Earl of: see Vaughan, Richard

Carew, George, 262

Carey, Robert, 167

Castiglione, Baldassare: *The Courtier,* 51, 91

Catholicism, 4; and conspiracy theory of history, 61–63, 65–66; fear of, 17, 61–66, 68, 182–84; medieval, 185–86; see also Jesuits

Cato: distichs of, 96, 105

Cecil, Robert, 43, 145, 147, 209; and Anthony Cooke, 157; competition with Essex, 206–207, 211–12, 214, 215, 217, 218–20, 230, 232, 256, 261–62; and Essex rebellion, 257, 261–64, 265, 267, 269; made Principal Secretary, 214; and trial of Essex, 269–70, 272; and trial of Henry Cuffe, 252

Cecil, Thomas, 41

Cecil, William Lord Burghley, Lord Treasurer, 14, 16, 17, 18, 19, 54–55, 63, 156, 172, 194, 206–207; and conspiracy theory of history, 60–66, 68; on the court, 145; death of, 223–24; and doctrine of evil minister, 175–76; *The Execution of Justice in England,* 64–66, 141; and execution of Mary Stuart, 167–68; and friendship, 46; *Memorial,* 41; on need to be at court, 155; and office of Principal Secretary, 171; and paranoia, 43, 159, 167–68; on retirement from court, 170; on success at court, 53–54, 151; on treason, 3, 141

Chamberlain, John: *Letters,* 312 n. 46

Chapuys, Eustace, Imperial Ambassador, 168

Cheke, John, 102

Cherbury, Lord Herbert of: see Herbert, Edward

Chesterfield, Lord: *Letters to his Son,* 274

Christopherson, John, 278 n. 3

Cicero, Marcus Tullius, 75, 87, 97–98, 195; *Amicitia,* 46

Clapham, John, 175

Cleaver, Robert, 84

Cleland, James, 57, 87, 88, 184

Coke, Edward, Attorney General, 252–53, 268

Colet, John, 86

commonplace books: see advice literature

Cooke, Anthony: career of, 157

Corbett, Edward, 5, 6, 7, 8, 9, 10, 11, 147

Corderius, Maturinus: *Dialogues,* 80–81

Cornwallis, William, 47, 145

cosmos [Tudor], 118–32; and anthropomorphism, 128–30; and coincidence, 125; dimensions of, 126–27; doctrine of correspondence, 120–22; doctrine of primacy, 119–20; God's role in, 122–26, 130–31; man's role in, 126–28; nature of, 119, 123; and Neoplatonism, 121–22; and paranoia, 132; role of Satan in, 119–20, 129–31

Counter-Reformation: see Catholicism, fear of

court [English]: attraction of, 145, 154–55; boredom at, 146, 158, 190; bribery at, 25; competition at, 147; description of, 144–45, 151, 300–301 n. 6, 302–303 n. 29; doctrine of evil minister, 171–76; Elizabethan, 198–99; expenses of, 16, 150, 157; opposition politics, 166–69; and paranoia, 51–58, 144–46, 152–77; and patronage, 146–52; position of sovereign, 150, 152–55, 168–69, 174–76; Renaissance, 189–90; retirement from, 169–71

Court of Wards, 194, 223, 224, 236
Courtney, Henry Marquis of Exeter, 30, 31
Cox, Richard, 129
Cranmer, Thomas, Archbishop of Canterbury, 68, 123
Cromwell, Thomas, 78, 149, 150, 154, 163, 168, 174, 304 n. 86
Cuffe, Henry: on Essex's personality, 192, 197; and the Essex rebellion, 244, 249–55, 272; execution of, 254, 254n.; trial of, 252–54

Danvers, Charles, 243, 249
Davies, John, 243, 249, 252, 263–64, 273
Davison, William, Secretary, 167, 202, 210, 211; his son, 210
Devereux, Robert, Earl of Essex, 30, 31, 123, 161; and Azores expedition, 215–16; and the Bacon brothers, 207–209, 211–12, 240; birth, 193; and Cadiz expedition, 213–15; campaign in France, 204–206; his chaplain, 247, 271; childhood, 194–95; competition with Robert Cecil, 206–207, 211–12, 214, 215, 218–20, 230, 232, 256, 261–62; confession of, 271–73; and the Court of Wards, 223–24, 230, 236; created Earl Marshal, 219; created Master of the Horse, 201; and Cuffe, 244, 249–55; his debts, 259; and decorum, 196–97, 247; described, 197; and divinity of kings, 219, 221–22; and doctrine of evil ministers, 173–74, 203; early career at court, 195, 200–204; education, 193, 194–95; and Elizabeth I, 167, 171, 173–74, 199–200, 202–203, 210–12, 213, 215, 220–23, 223, 224–25, 227–28, 231–33, 234–36, 242, 255–61; execution of, 272–73; family, 193–94, 248; his father Walter, 193–94; in Ireland, 226–38; and Lopez, 209–210, 216; as Lord Lieutenant of Ireland, 226–27; and the military mind, 233; and monopoly of sweet wines, 204, 258,

259–60; his mother Lettice, 194, 199, 202, 221, 248; and paranoia, 197–98, 208–210, 216–17, 218–19, 221–22, 230–31, 236–38, 255, 256, 257–58, 261–62, 268, 274–76; and patronage, 211–13, 215; personality, 192, 196, 196–97, 199–200, 201–203, 216–17, 237–38, 307 n. 144; and Portugal voyage, 203–204; poverty, 194, 200; his rebellion: 239–68, 315 n. 61, official version, 240–55, responsibility for, 260–61; and secretary Davison, 202; his sister Dorothy Perrot, 173, 202; his sister Penelope Rich, 272; and Southampton, 229, 242, 243, 258, 262, 266; and syphilis, 216; and treason, 236–38, 264–65; his trial, 268–71; and Tyrone, 228–29, 233–34, 235–36, 240–41, 255–56, 258
Devereux, Walter, 1st Earl of Essex, 193–94; his debts, 156, 194
Devil: see Satan
Dod, John, 84
Dorset, (Henry Grey) Marquis of, 26, 78
Dorset, (Margaret) Dowager Marchioness of, 78
Ducci, Lorenzo: Ars avlica, 51
Dudley, John, Earl of Warwick, Duke of Northumberland, 21, 30, 31, 277 n. 1
Dudley, Robert, Earl of Leicester, 14, 148, 150, 156, 167–68; death of, 204; and Essex, 198; expedition to the Lowlands, 172, 200–201
Dyer, Edward, 148, 150, 151, 156–57, 173, 203

Ecclesiasticus, 101–105, 274
education [Tudor]: age of students, 294 n. 103; aims of, 72–101, 95, 116–17; and commonplace books, 82–83, 98–100; and courtesy books, 77, 90–91; curriculum, 95–101; dangers of, 93–94; and decorum, 86–93, 144, 275–76; difficulty of, 76–79; environment vs heredity, 75–76, 290

n. 17; grammar school, 96–101; holistic nature of, 79–83; and individualism, 86, 91–93; and nature of evil, 74–76; and obedience, 73–76, 83–84; and paranoia, 101–117; petty school, 95–96; and rhetoric, 80–83, 86–87, 97–101, 109–115, 144, 275–76, 296–97 n. 141; and self-control, 85–86; and the social élite, 93, 94; and *sprezzatura*, 100; theory of a gentleman, 296 n. 140; and treason, 74; universities, 296 n. 136, 309 n. 3, n. 4

Edward VI, 20, 23, 102, 129; education, 102, 294 n. 97; and Thomas Seymour, 24–26, 29

Edwards, Richard: *Damon and Pithias*, 47

Egerton, Thomas, Lord Keeper, 195, 220, 221–22, 242, 245–46, 256

Elizabeth I, 4, 11, 12–13, 13–14, 15, 16, 65, 170, 189; and Catholicism, 183; and death of Burghley, 223–24; and doctrine of evil minister, 173–74, 174–76, 307 n. 142; and Dorothy Perrot, 173, 202; and Edward Dyer, 156–57; and Essex: 167, 171, 173–74, 200–207, 211–13, 213, 215, 219–23, 223, 224–25, 227–28, 231–33, 234–36, 242, 255–61, and Essex rebellion, 255–68, responsibility for Essex rebellion, 260–61; and execution of Mary Stuart, 167–68, 201–202; how to control her, 207–208; and Leicester, 172; and *Life and Raigne of Henry IIII*, 268–69; and melancholia, 190; and paranoia, 114; and the Parry plot, 12–18; personality, 198–99; and political success, 175; portraits of, 122; and Seymour, 24, 29, 30; speeches of, 89n., 114, 295 n. 117

Ellis, Clement: *The Gentle Sinner*, 293 n. 93

Elton, G.R., 31, 145–46; on friendship, 285 n. 48; on Reformation, 182; and treason, 277 n. 1, 281 n. 76; and Tudor despotism, 160, 163; on

violence, 282 n. 87

Elyot, Thomas, 44, 77, 82, 87, 102, 286 n. 73; *The Book named the Governor*, 93; *Bringinge up of children*, 75

Erasmus, Desiderius: Aesop's *Fables*, 96, 97; and anxiety, 180; and commonplace books, 98; *De Copia*, 99; on education, 76, 82, 100; on kings, 2; on marriage, 121; *Proverbes*, 45; and the Reformation, 182; and rhetoric, 110, 113

Erikson, Kai, 35, 176–77

espionage: at court, 25, 145; domestic, 28, 116, 154–55, 162–63; and Essex, 315 n. 60; foreign, 17, 18; and government spies, 159–65; at school, 108–109; warnings about, 43

Essex: see Devereux, Robert

Fowler, John, 25–26

Foxe, John: description of Calais, 7

French Ambassador: see Maisse, André Hurault or Marillac, Charles de

friendship, 45–50

Fuller, Thomas, 169; *Worthies*, 249

Gardiner, Stephen, Bishop of Winchester, 61–62, 62, 63, 174; and conspiracy theory of history, 67; on education, 75; and nature of change, 134–35

Geertz, Clifford, 71, 129

Giovanni, della Casa: *Book of Manners*, 91

Gorges, Ferdinando, 243, 246–47, 252, 264

Gouge, William, 84

Greenblatt, Stephen: *Renaissance Self-fashioning*, 292–93 n. 82, 307 n. 144

Greene, Robert, 40, 188

Grey, Jane, 22, 26, 91n., 277 n. 1

Guevara, Don Antony: see North, Thomas

Hales, John, 187

Halifax, Lord: 'Advice to a Daughter', 274

Harington, John, 145; and Elizabeth,
  307 n. 142; on Elizabeth's court,
  199; and Essex, 226-27, 247-48,
  256; on treason, 1
Harrison, G.B., 114
Hatton, Christopher, 15, 156, 167, 206;
  success at court, 150
Hayne, William, 112
Hayward, John: *Life and Raigne of
  Henry IIII,* 268-69
Henry VII, 13
Henry VIII, 7, 20, 22, 121, 123, 129,
  149, 167, 170, 174; and conspiracy
  theory of history, 62, 67, 69; his
  court, 189-90; described, 70-71,
  172; and divinity of kings, 166, 187;
  education of, 295 n. 110; primer of,
  95; and Reformation, 182, 183, 184;
  will of, 24
Herbert, Edward Lord Cherbury, 89-
  90, 286 n. 73
Herbert, John, Secretary, 244, 265
Hertford, (Edward Seymour) Earl of, 135
Higford, William, 44, 57, 286 n. 73
Hill, Thomas: *The Moste pleasaunte Arte
  of the Interpretacion of Dreames,* 132n.
history, conspiracy theory of: see
  paranoia
Hoby, Margaret, 43, 91n., 124, 125-26,
  130, 292 n. 66
Hoby, Thomas, 51
Hofstadter, Richard, 36, 179, 218
Hooker, Archbishop Richard, 133-34
Howard, Admiral Charles, Earl of
  Nottingham, 123, 219, 220, 230,
  261, 262; and Cadiz expedition, 213-
  15; made Earl of Nottingham, 218
Howard, Henry Earl of Surrey, 30, 31
Howard, Katherine, 78, 146
Howard, Thomas, 3rd Duke of
  Norfolk, 159
Howard, Thomas, 4th Duke of
  Norfolk, 4, 30, 31, 32, 153, 155,
  156, 170, 171, 307 n. 144
Hungerford, Walter, Lord, 121
Husee, John, 51, 148, 149-50, 156, 158;
  on the court, 144, 159, 161

Iago, 67, 69, 70, 140, 249, 253, 275
Imperial Ambassador: see Chapuys,
  Eustace or Van der Delft, François
Ireland, 225-26; defeat at Yellow Ford,
  222-23, 225; Essex in, 226-38
Isocrates: *Orations,* 87, 106, 194

James VI of Scotland and I of England,
  41, 54, 63, 76, 89, 135, 202, 262,
  263, 292 n. 76
Jesuits, 4, 17; fear of, 63-66, 68
Jonson, Ben, 35, 43, 74
Jordan, W.K., 31, 32

Kempe, William, 76
kingship: nature of, 24; see also court:
  position of sovereign
Knollys family: see Devereux
Knollys, Lettice (also Devereux,
  Leicester, Blount), 194, 199, 202,
  221, 248
Knollys, William, Controller of the
  Queen's Household, 144-45, 219-
  21, 223-24, 245, 270

Lacock Abbey, 27, 28
Lambert, John, 67
Leicester, Earl of: see Dudley, Robert
Leveson, John, 267-68
Ling, Nicholas, 43, 48; *Politeuphuia,
  Wits Commonwealth,* 40-41, 106-107,
  289 n. 15
Lisle letters, 9, 156
Lisle, Lord: see Plantagenet
Littleton, John, 243, 252
Lopez, Roderigo, 4, 209-210, 216, 217
Louvain: University of, 8, 10
Lucifer: see Satan
Luther, Martin, 180, 181, 184-85
Lyly, John, 149

McCaffrey, Wallace, 141
McCarthy, Senator Joseph, 38-39, 69
Maisse, André Hurault, Sieur de, French
  Ambassador, 219, 255
Manning, Roger, 170
Marillac, Charles de, French
  Ambassador, 70

Marlowe, Christopher: *The Massacre at Paris*, 68
Martyn, William: *Youths Instruction*, 48
Mary I, 24, 29, 30, 62, 73, 136–37, 161, 167, 169, 174; and treason, 277 n. 1, 278 n. 3, 281 n. 76
Mary Queen of Scots: see Stuart, Mary
Mason, John, 10, 136
May Day: riots of 1517, 59–60
Meyrick, Gilly, 249
Mildmay, Walter, 167
Milne, A.A., 38
More, Thomas, 164, 169, 170; and conspiracy theory of history, 59–61, 288 n. 101; and rhetoric, 113; and treason, 139
Mosellanus, Petrus: *Paedologia*, 108–109
Mountjoy, Charles Blount, Lord, 263
Mulcaster, Richard, 83; *Positions*, 293 n. 93
Mun, Thomas, 275

Nashe, Thomas, 86, 114, 152, 164
Naunton, Robert: *Observations on the Late Queen Elizabeth*, 248–49
Neville, Edward, 13, 14, 15, 18, 18–19, 28, 163
Neville, George Lord Abergavenny, 167
Neville, Henry, 252
Neville, Thomas, 164–65
Norfolk, Dukes of: see Howard, Thomas
North, George, 145
North, Thomas: *Dial of Princes*, 51, 286–87 n. 78
Northumberland, Duke of: see Dudley, Robert
Northumberland, Earl of: see Percy, Henry
Nottingham, Earl of: see Howard, Charles

O'Neil, Hugh, Earl of Tyrone, 223, 225, 228–29, 233–34, 236, 240–41, 255–56, 258
Ong, Walter, 109, 112
Osborne, Francis: *Advice to a Son*, 174, 274
Overall, John, 257

Page, Richard, 24, 26, 280 n. 52
Paget, William, 88, 148, 182
Paice, Richard: *Howe one may take profit of his Enemyes*, 48
paranoia [cultural], 34–35, 36–40; and advice literature, 40–58, 115–16, 286 n. 65, n. 73; compared to twentieth century, 55–57; conspiracy theory of history, 37–40, 59–66, 130–31, 189; and cosmos, 131; and the court, 144–45, 158–77; decline of, 274–76; and diet, 282 n. 94; and divinity of kings, 186–90; and Ecclesiasticus, 101–105; and education, 101–117; and the enemy, 48–50, 55–57, 59–60, 107, 115–16, 131–32, 286 n. 65, n. 73; and the evil minister, 171–76; and foreign observers, 70–71; and friendship, 46–50, 105–106, 285 n. 45, n. 48, n. 50; and melancholy, 190; and the Moral Majority, 39, 65; and political survival, 51–58, 143–77; and Protestantism, 62–65, 180–86; and rhetoric, 109–115; and sixteenth-century anxiety, 179–80; and society, 135–41: and the spy, 160–65; and the stage, 66–70
Parker, Archbishop Matthew, 135
Parr, Queen Catherine, 21–22, 25
Parry, William, 4, 11–19, 28, 29, 30, 31, 32, 67, 147, 157, 163, 249, 250; background, 11–12, 16–18, 94; causes of treason, 18–19; conspiracy to kill Elizabeth, 12–19; denial of treason, 15
Parsons, Robert (Doleman), 270
patronage, 5, 146–52, 302 n. 19, n. 28, 305 n. 93; and Essex, 210–13; and the 'friend', 148–49; and lordship, 148–49
Peacham, Henry, 92, 93, 133, 146, 152; *The Truth of Our Time*, 48
Percy, Henry, 9th Earl of Northumberland, 53, 85, 101, 154, 163; advice to son, 45, 47, 53–54, 57, 88–89, 274, 284–85 n. 44; on patronage, 153
Perlin, Étienne, 1, 165

Perrot, Dorothy, 173, 202

Petty, William, 275

Philip II of Spain, 63, 200, 203, 204, 215; and Counter-Reformation, 183; and promotion at court, 164n.

Philip, John: *Pacient and meeke Grissill,* 68

Philpot, Clement, 5, 6, 7, 8–9, 10–11, 19, 30, 147, 148

Philpot, Peter, 6, 11, 148

Plantagenet, Arthur, Lord Lisle, 5, 6, 8, 10, 51, 146, 148, 158; debts of, 156; Honor, 5, 10, 161; and patronage, 149–50

Pole, Henry Lord Montague, 30, 31

Pole, Reginald, Cardinal, 7–8, 62

Popham, John, Lord Chief Justice, 245

Protestantism: conspiracy theory of history, 60–61, 62–65; doctrine, 181, 185–86; and paranoia, 62–63, 180–86; and predestination, 186; Reformation, 60; and sin, 181, 185

Puttenham, George: *Arte of English Poesie,* 88, 94, 114, 291–92 n. 59, 306 n. 134; view of courtier, 142, 144, 168, 200

Rainolde, Richard: adaptation of Aphthonius's manual, 107–108; *Foundation of Rhetorike,* 105

Raleigh, Walter, 133, 245, 261; advice to his son, 41, 44–45, 45, 46, 274; 'Cabinet-council', 45; and Cadiz expedition, 213–14; competition with Essex, 173–74, 201, 202–203, 216–17, 230; on the court, 152; disgraced, 206; and doctrine of evil minister, 176; and Essex rebellion, 261, 264, 269, 272; as evil minister, 173–74; on human nature, 150–51, 266; *Maxims of State,* 85; on need to be at court, 155; and paranoia, 41, 44–45, 101, 114; on retirement from court, 170; on spying, 161; and style, 88; on treason, 3, 9, 264

Recorde, Robert, 79–80

Reformation: see Protestantism

Refuge, Eustache du, 52–53; on

doctrine of evil minister, 176; *A Practical Guide for Ambitious Politicians,* 68, 154, 165–66, 168, 170, 207; see also: Walsingham, Edward

Reynolds (Devereux's secretary), 209

Rhodes, Hugh: *Boke of Nurture and schoole of good manners,* 77

Richard III, 29

Ridolfi plot, 4

Rieff, Philip, 158

Ringer, Robert, 59; *Winning Through Intimidation,* 56–57

Rowlands, Samuel: *Courte of Civill Courtesie,* 90, 92–93

Russell, John, 149, 150, 154

Rutland, (Henry Manners) Earl of, 23, 26, 28, 162

Rutland, (Roger Manners) Earl of, 195

Satan [Antichrist, Devil, Lucifer], 36–37, 38, 59, 61, 65; decline of, 275; and the nature of evil, 66–69, 74–76, 117, 118–19, 121–22, 134, 135, 138–39, 140–41, 185; and paranoia, 119; revival of, 184–86; role in cosmos, 129–31; in society, 133, 135, 138–39; and treason, 239, 247–48, 250–51, 273

Seymour, Edward, Duke of Somerset, Lord Protector, 4, 19–20, 20, 21, 88, 169; relations with brother, 21, 21–22, 23, 26, 28, 29; wife: see Stanhope, Anne

Seymour, Thomas, Baron Sudley, Lord Admiral, 4, 19–30, 31, 32, 162, 247; background, 20; execution of, 29–30; and friendship, 46; as Lord Admiral, 27; personality of, 21, 22–23; treason, 23–30; wife of, 21; see also Parr, Catherine

Shakespeare, William: and evil, 69–70, 140; and the evil minister, 175; *Henry V,* 166; *Henry VIII,* 68, 305 n. 100; *King Lear,* 69; *Measure for Measure,* 67; *Othello,* 69–70, 254, see also Iago; 'Rape of Lucrece', 114–15; *Richard II*: 175, and Essex rebellion,

269; *Richard III*, 69, 140; *Titus Andronicus*, 69
Shapiro, David, 36
Sharington, William, 26–27, 27–28
Sidney, Philip, 84, 101, 200, 203, 215
Sidney, Robert, 215
Skelton, John: *Magnificence*, 68
Smith, Sheriff Thomas, 246, 266–67, 315 n. 61
Smith, Thomas, 34, 169
Smyth, John, 78, 146
society, 132–41; divine nature of, 132–33; nature of change, 133–35, 137–38; and paranoia, 135–41; and political rumours, 135–37; role of Satan in, 133, 135, 138–39; size of ruling élite, 147; structure of, 133–34, 188–89
Somerset, Duke of: see Seymour, Edward
Southampton, Earl of: see Wriothesley, Henry
Spenser, Edmund, 151, 159
Stafford, Edward, 3rd Duke of Buckingham, 30, 31
Stafford, Henry, 2nd Duke of Buckingham, 44
Stafford, Thomas, 4
Stanhope, Anne, Duchess of Somerset, 21, 280 n. 52
Stanhope, Michael, 24, 26
Starkey, Thomas, 73
Stettin-Pomerania, Duke of, 160
Stockwood, John, 110–11
Stone, Lawrence, 34, 160, 282 n. 94
Stow, John, 11
Stuart, Mary Queen of Scots, 4, 12, 13, 167, 201–202
Sutton, Christopher: *Disce vivere*, 291 n. 48

Taverner, Richard, 45; *The Garden of Wisdom*, 92
Thomas, Keith, 124, 130, 161; and witchcraft, 185, 186
Throckmorton plot, 17
Tipping, William: *The Father's Counsell*, 286 n. 74
Titchburne, Charles, 285 n. 50

Towler, Margaret, 164–65
treason: amount of, 277–78 n. 1, 281 n. 76; Botolf conspiracy, 5–11; causes of, 3, 137–41, 247–48, 264–65; definition of, 1; and doctrine of correspondences, 121; and education, 74; Essex rebellion, 239–68; fictitious, 3–4; God and, 2; ineptitude of, 2, 3, 4, 9, 13, 30–35, 265, 267, 276; and opposition politics, 166–69; and paranoia, 34–35, 36–40; Parry plot, 11–19; and political rumours, 135–37; prevalence of, 1; prevention of, 3, 139; punishment of, 2–3, 15, 141; responsibility for, 138–41; self-defeating nature of, 1, 3, 4, 32–35; Seymour's palace revolution, 19–30; and society, 138–41; society's attitude towards, 2, 21–22, 32–35, 138–41, 239; violence and, 281–82 n. 87
Trevisano, Andrea, 71
Turner, William, 67
Tyndale, William, 61, 161, 184
Tyrone, Earl of: see O'Neil, Hugh

Udall, Nicholas: *Apophthegmes*, 286 n. 73; *Respublica*, 67

Van der Delft, François, Imperial Ambassador, 29
Vaughan, Richard Earl of Carbery, 57, 162, 175; advice to son, 284 n. 39, 286 n. 65
Vaughan, Stephen, 306 n. 135
Vaughan, William, 123, 132, 148, 159, 162; *The Golden Grove*, 57, 285 n. 45, 286 n. 73, 289 n. 15
Vives, Juan, 73, 109–110, 112, 250

Walsingham, Edward, 287 n. 80; *A Practical Guide for Ambitious Politicians*, 51–52; see also Refuge, Eustache du
Walsingham, Francis, 16, 17, 18, 168, 172, 206, 287 n. 89, 302 n. 10; and paranoia, 43–44

Webster, John, 145
Welspring of wittie Conceites, 98–99, 107
Wentworth, William, 221; advice to
    his son, 274; and paranoia, 42, 44,
    101
Whittinton, Robert: *Vulgaria*, 81–82,
    290–91 n. 37
Whythorne, Thomas, 154, 163
William of Orange, 17
Williams, William, 164
Wilson, Thomas, 86–87; *Arte of
    Rhetorique*, 80, 110, 295 n. 114
Wilson, Thomas: *The State of England*,
    162, 304 n. 78
Winchester, (William Paulet) Marquis
    of: 'Evill and Wicked Men', 49
Wine, Pastor Leo, 39, 65
Wolsey, Cardinal Thomas, 172, 174

Worcester, (Edward Somerset) Earl of,
    245
Wotton, Henry, 193; on Elizabeth, 198;
    on Essex's personality, 197, 256; and
    Essex rebellion, 251
Wriothesley, Henry, Earl of
    Southampton: attack on, 262; and
    Essex rebellion, 243, 249, 251–52,
    264, 266; in Ireland, 229, 237–38,
    242, 258; trial of, 268; and trial of
    Essex, 270, 272
Wyatt, Thomas, 53, 87, 151, 159, 168,
    278 n. 3, 281 n. 76, 302–303 n. 29

Yellow Ford, 222–23, 225

Zubly, John: and the evil minister, 306–
    307 n. 136